I AM AN EXCELLENT PROPERTY MANAGER

Your Personal Mentor and Practical On-the-Job Road Map
to Enhance Your Skills and Help You Become a Highly Effective
Hands-On, Results-Oriented Residential Property Manager

SIMONE STACIA ANN GRANT

ISBN: 978-1-4834-9169-1 (sc)
ISBN: 978-1-7168-5212-1 (hc)
ISBN: 978-1-4834-9170-7 (e)

Library of Congress Control Number: 2018911956

Lulu Publishing Services rev. date: 03/09/2020

This book is dedicated to honest, hardworking property managers who strive to do their very best every day on the job. Remember—when life throws you a curveball, whether large or small, do not quit! Instead, take the GPS approach. When you are driving to a destination and you make a wrong turn, your GPS does not say, "End of trip!" Your GPS will say, "Recalculating," meaning, it is processing your current location to put you back on track and finding the next-best route to get you to your destination. Embrace your current location, and allow your GPS to take you to your desired destination.

Endorsements

I Am an Excellent Property Manager is an invaluable reference filled with experienced-based case studies. Each chapter is thorough and informative. An excellent resource for anyone in this field. I would consider this the "go-to" guide book for anyone wanting to further advance their skills.

- **Tamila Darsalia**
  Senior Property Manager and former colleague

Your guiding principles from friends and family that resulted in some positive and amazing results in your job were inspiring to me. *Requirements and Job description of a Property Manager* frames the job well as the qualities of an excellent property manager. This is particularly interesting as what you described can be applied universally to many professions. *Staffing* –This chapter was very interesting to me. I liked, "Treat your staff as your best tools and assets because they are. Polish your staff and they will shine for you."

Tenant Complaints and Concerns- I appreciated your advice on solving complaints with listening, owning up to a mistake, following through and sharing the story with your staff to prevent repeats.

Professional and Personal Development- Just an awesome chapter sharing life wisdom and motivational points of views.

Simone, I was impressed how thorough and comprehensive your book is. Your language and your style of writing was clear concise and very well organized. All in all, a very comprehensive book manual regarding property management.

- **Dr. Roberta Koch**
  Chiropractor

Contents

List of Illustrations

Introduction

The mistaken and limited view many have of a residential property manager is that such a person rents apartments, collects rent and fixes leaky toilets. Residential property management is a much more complex profession than what the average person may think. The responsibilities of a residential property manager require an integrated approach to management. Not only do residential property managers collect rent, but also they help to set new rents and make adjustments to the rent. They get rid of leaky toilets and replace them with energy-efficient toilets. From my personal experience, residential property management involves overseeing, and co-ordinating with balance, the interrelated functions of residential building systems, equipment, landscaping, tenants, staff, contractors, budget and government agencies to enhance the useful life of the income property in order to produce profits.

To efficiently function in your role as a residential property manager, you must understand the provincial laws or your local laws as they relate to the Residential Tenancies Act (RTA). The laws quoted in *I Am an Excellent Property Manager* are from the Ontario RTA. In addition to the RTA, property managers must know the bylaws of the various cities where they manage properties. Property managers must also be abreast of market conditions and how to position their units, and by extension their properties, to constantly attract the right tenants and retain them.

After I decided to make the transition from hospitality management to property management, I started out as a trainee manager and eventually became a property manager. The trainee opportunity allowed me to see what some property managers were doing. While it was a great observation role, it did not tell me how to get things done. In my observation role, I saw only the middle steps of certain tasks; I did not see how things got started and how they progressed to completion. When I received my portfolio, I had no mentor and had to learn as I went along. My boss at the time had an amazing coaching approach to management. I benefitted a lot from that management style but still felt lost and did not want to impose on anybody's time by asking too many questions. Thankfully, one colleague took an interest in me. That colleague would step into my office and ask from time to time, "Why aren't your incoming trays moving? Do you have [this]? Do you have [that]? You are going to need [this] for the operations meeting." These simple but genuine questions and comments from that colleague helped me to figure out what I needed to do and gave me an idea of the time frame associated with getting some of those things done. I also relied on transferable skills and experiences learned in the hotel industry, and also those from when I worked as a teacher and a tutor, to navigate my way through the complex duties and responsibilities of my job as a residential property manager.

The challenges that came with the role were numerous, especially in my first year, but those challenges were not greater than my deep hunger for new knowledge. I was in a new country with a plethora of opportunities, and I intended to soak them up like a sponge. Coupled with this was the fact that I had prayed for this job. No, I'd made a list, and I had gotten exactly what I'd prayed for on that list. Because of this answered prayer, I viewed each day at work, along with the *natural* challenges that came with the job, as a gratitude day or gratitude moment. My job was a divine gift.

After meditating, I would jump out of bed each morning with great zest and a sense of purpose for the day. I would show up for work one hour before the required start time every day. I had tremendous joy and passion for my job. I viewed my portfolio as a business within the company. I was an intrapreneur. I took a personal interest in every aspect of my properties. Applying what I had learned in my hospitality management and tourism management courses was helping me to get positive results on the financial statements. For that reason, I loved my job even more. I told myself I would be the best and convinced myself of it. Every morning before leaving for work, I would tell myself, "I am an excellent property manager."

Just before I started my job as a property manager, a friend told me to just allow myself to be taught, even if I already knew what was being taught. When I was working in the hotel industry, my brother who is in senior management gave me some advice. He said, "You do not manage people. You manage behaviour. It is easier to manage behaviour than people. Treat people how you want them to behave. Before you make a decision, ask yourself, *What kind of behaviour do I want to evoke or promote in my staff?*" Another piece of advice I took to heart came from my late aunt who was a retired operating room nurse in Jamaica. She said, "Listen to the people who report to you. They have more power than you think. They know and understand the terrain of the job more than you do. Help them to be better than how you found them, and they will move mountains for you." Finally, a close friend of mine advised me once, "Find the difficult or hard-to-please staff or ringleader. Get to know that person, and bring him or her on board. Once you have that person on board, the others will fall into place." These bits of advice were my guiding principles that I used to get some positive and amazing results on the job.

On orientation day for my master's degree at New York University (NYU), I and the rest of my graduating class were shown a video of an NYU graduation day. As we watched the graduation video, we were told to start with the end goal in mind and never give up, regardless of what happened along the way. That illustration has stuck with me in both my professional life and my personal life. With that illustration in mind, at the end of every financial year, I would meet with my staff at their respective locations to celebrate the accomplishments of the year that had just ended, and we'd remind ourselves of the previous goals that we'd set for the new financial year. Included on that list of goals was how we would celebrate the next set of accomplished goals.

I knew that the financial statements told a story. I made it my duty to plan with my staff the story I wanted to be told, and I worked fervently toward bringing that planned story to fruition. This resulted in many impressive net operating incomes (NOIs). It was always exciting to relate the strategies used to achieve the results, or the factors that contributed to any decrease in numbers. Financial review meetings were always fun; I looked forward to them. As the numbers trended in the right direction, and as the properties gradually turned around for the better, my knowledge, passion and confidence kept growing.

I remember being off work for an extended time because I had been in a motor vehicle accident. When I returned to work, the staff at my largest location presented me with cheesecake and a colourful bouquet of flowers, along with a card that read, "Welcome back to a great property manager. We love you and we missed you." The card was signed by all my staff. Their kind gesture warmed my heart and reaffirmed what I told myself every morning before leaving for work: "I am an excellent property manager." That statement coming from my staff was my seal of approval—hence the title of this book.

I Am an Excellent Property Manager taps into the various duties and responsibilities you will encounter in your role as a residential property manager. Though the book is written from a Canadian standpoint—specifically Ontario—most of the challenges in residential property management mentioned herein extend beyond the boundaries of Ontario. These challenges span the globe and apply to wherever a residential rental property is found. The chapter titles in the book are derived from the typical job description of a residential property manager. I contacted experts from various organizations within Canada, United Kingdom and the United States of America, and I researched articles and books to support the information in each chapter. The chapters all complement each other, with some repetition for emphasis, demonstrating that residential property management requires an integrated management approach. By studying and observing this integrated approach, you can build your awareness of residential property management and form a clearer financial picture of your properties.

I Am an Excellent Property Manager is the book I should have read when I started out in residential property management. I would have definitely used it as my reference book. Like a mentor and detailed road map, it would have helped me to navigate the challenges much better. I hope by reading this book, you will gain a hands-on understanding of and develop a deeper appreciation and love for your job in high-rise multifamily residential property management.

Acknowledgments

Thank you to the companies, authors and owners of Web sites who gave me permission to cite their work. Your prompt response made me feel alive and helped to fuel the desire to complete *I Am an Excellent Property Manager*.

A special thank-you to Rat Lab Exterminators and Apex Pest Control Inc., representatives of which I was able to interview. And Apex representatives reviewed my chapter on pest control and offered their invaluable feedback.

A deep thank-you to Tamila Darsalia, my former colleague and current friend who believed in me, understood my challenges and read my manuscript to ensure the content reflected the needs of the industry. Thank you also for being the one who stuck your head in my office and inquired about my trays. Your endorsement of *I Am an Excellent Property Manager* consoled me and serves as a confirmation that the content is logical and practical for the industry.

Thanks to Dr. Roberta Koch, my chiropractor, whose astute care and interest in my well-being was a breath of fresh air. You are a true champion and a gift to your profession. Thank you for taking the time to read my manuscript and offer your sincere endorsement.

Thank you to Theresa Bradley-Banta, author of *Invest in Apartment Buildings: Profit Without the Pitfalls*. Theresa, I feel privileged to have received your support. Thank you for taking time out from your busy schedule to read my manuscript and offer your heartfelt endorsement.

Thanks to my recovery team for their continued care to my physical and psychological health. Despite the circumstances under which you came into my life, I am grateful for the contributions you have made.

Thanks to my spiritual family in Jamaica, the USA and Canada for their love and emotional support.

Thank you to Markion Stanbury, my teaching mentor and close friend from Jamaica, who continues to support me and who provided me with timely encouragement and reassurance along the writing journey that I had it within me to complete the book. I am glad not only that our paths crossed in teaching but also that we remain friends, staying in touch and supporting each other.

Tricia Murray, my classmate and friend since the days of University of Technology, Jamaica (UTech), thank you for being my sounding board. You were practical and unbiased with your feedback, not just for this publication but also for my career and professional life.

Most importantly, my profound and immense gratitude to my loving God Jehovah and his Son Jesus for answering my prayers, blessing me with an amazing career in residential property management and inspiring me to write this book with pure gratitude and passion to share my knowledge despite the mountains of challenges I have endured.

Requirements and the Job Description of a Residential Property Manager

Job descriptions will vary from company to company and according to geographic location. The job description of a residential property manager will typically look like the following:

Marketing

- Ensure vacant apartments are rented on a timely basis.
- Be able to set rents and adjust rents according to market conditions.
- Be able to conduct market surveys and act on them.
- Be able to review vacancy report and recommend promotions.

Staffing

- Be able to manage and lead a diverse team.
- Demonstrate ability to train and mentor staff within the portfolio.
- Be able to recruit based on needs of the property or the property of colleagues.
- Be able to work in a team and on own initiative.
- Demonstrate ability to work collaboratively with the departments of legal administration, accounts receivable and payable, HVAC, central rental, life safety, human resources, in-house maintenance, and property standards to achieve desired results.
- Provide strategic leadership skills to supervise staff within the assigned portfolio.
- Be able to keep accurate records and Notes to File when discussing performance or giving staff feedback.
- Keep team informed of pertinent policy and procedure changes.
- Be able to hold regular and meaningful staff meetings.

Administration

- Ensure leases/tenancy agreements convey accurate information before signing.
- Demonstrate excellent oral and written communication skills, including presentation and public speaking skills.

- Be able to write letters and notices.
- Ensure that proper file management for tenants are maintained.

Relationship Management

- Have strong cultural sensitivity awareness to effectively address all tenants, staff, coworkers and others.
- Be able to anticipate and address tenants' concerns, including service requests.
- Be able to work with various government organizations, including police, fire department, immigration, city or municipal health department, city or municipal building inspection department and various regulatory bodies.
- Have experience in dealing with multiple contractors and trades in the following areas: painting, drywall, tiling (ceramic, vinyl composition and luxury vinyl plank), carpet installation, plumbing, electrical, landscaping, snow removal, asphalt, door and window installation, pest control, welding, and fire and flood restoration.

Financial

- Be able to review and process accounts receivable and accounts payable documents and information.
- Be able to review and process invoices submitted by contractors.
- Demonstrate excellent project management skills to manage multiple capital improvement projects and minimize their impacts on tenants or residents.
- Assess monthly, quarterly and annual financial and operational performance of each building within portfolio.
- Work with the acquisition team during acquisitions, dispositions and refinancing of properties at various locations within the company.
- Participate in the due diligence process as required.
- Review tenant chargeback reports and follow up on any overdue payments with site staff and legal and accounting departments.
- Prepare detailed "tender packages"; review and negotiate quotes/bids; negotiate contracts and award contracts.
- Be able to work within a budget.
- Be able to prepare and provide pertinent explanations of financial audits or reviews.
- Communicate with accounting staff and vendors/suppliers/contractors as needed.
- Communicate with accounting department on tenant issues, and notify branch or area manager if charges are over the norm.
- Ensure proper parking and locker or storage audits are done and are accurate.

Maintenance

- Be able to conduct inspections—interior and exterior of building, occupied apartments, vacant apartments and annual in-suite inspections—and then delegate relevant tasks and follow up on findings.
- Be able to manage a portfolio of multiple residential high-rise buildings in different cities with varied amenities such as laundry room, indoor or outdoor pool, social or party room, cinema room/centre, guest suite, on-site storage, game room and/or exercise room.
- Have a thorough knowledge of occupational health and safety rules and regulations.
- Ensure maintenance of all equipment is completed.

Key Competencies

- Demonstrate excellent time management and goal-setting skills.
- Know and understand the Residential Tenancies Act and keep abreast of any updates.
- Be able to manage different emergencies such as major flood or fire and catastrophic situations.
- Be able to analyze and resolve problems while exercising good judgement.
- Be able to work well under pressure and multitask within any given period of time.
- Be able to think globally and work collaboratively.
- Be flexible and be willing to work demanding hours when necessary.
- Be able to work with constant interruptions and maintain calm and professional demeanour.
- Be policy- and procedure-driven with demonstrated experience in firmly and tactfully projecting the strong policy-driven culture of the company.
- Have strong computer skills and the ability to work with the company software system.

2

Assigned Buildings in Portfolio

Unit count	Number of floors	Floor breakdown	Units per floor	Address	Amenities	Abbrev.	City
Stand-alone or single							
128	16 P1 + ODP	Floors 2–12 have units. There is no #13 apartment.	8	29 TLC Ave.	ODP/ UGP, P	29 TLC	A
Community of four buildings							
110	14	Floors 2–16 have units. There is no #13. Top floor has only six units.	8 (+6)	910 Motivation St.	L, UGP, PSR, E/G, SLR	910M	B
110	14	Floors 2–16 have units. There is no #13. Top floor has only six units.	8 (+6)	920 Motivation St.	L, UGP, PSR, E/G, SLR	920M	
110	14	Floors 2–16 has units. There is no #13. Top floor has only six units.	8 (+6)	930 Motivation St.	L, UGP, PSR, E/G, SLR	930M	
110	14	Floors 2–16 have units. There is no #13. Top floor has only six units.	8 (+6)	940 Motivation St.	L, UGP, PSR, E/G, SLR	940M	
Stand-alone or single							
116	15 (P1)	Floors 1–16 have units. Top floor has only four units. There is no #13.	8 (+4)	428 Inspirational Dr.	L, UPG, PSR	428I	B

Unit count	Number of floors	Floor breakdown	Units per floor	Address	Amenities	Abbrev.	City
		Community of two buildings					
192	24 + P1 and P2	First floor has no units. Floors 2–26 have units.	8	528 Action Rd.	L, E/G, CR, LR, PSR, P, ODP, UGP, SLR	528A	C
192	24 + P1 and P2	First floor has no units. Floors 2–26 have units.	8	534 Action Rd.	L, E/G, CR, LR, PSR, P, ODP, UGP, SLR, GS	534A	
		Stand-alone or single					
130	15 + P1 and P2	Floors 2–15 have units.	10	999 Elite and Spoiled Cir.	L, CR, UGP, LSR, GS, P, PSR	999 ES	C
1198 total units		Total of 9 buildings					

There is no 13th floor and no unit #13. Units begin on the second floor, except for 428 Inspirational Drive (428I). This location has units at the lobby level. These buildings are hypothetical. However, they reflect similar situations and circumstances that I experienced within my portfolio that spanned various cities.

Amenities Key

CR – Cinema room
L – Laundry
E/G – Exercise room/gym

SLR – Storage locker room
GS – Guest suite
ODP – Outdoor parking
UGP – Underground parking

P – Pool
PSR – Party/social room

A. Explanation of Tenant Base

29 TLC Avenue: This location has one-, two- and three-bedroom units. Residents are a mix of working-class families with school-age children. This location has high tenant traffic, especially in the afternoon because of the many families. Your challenges at this location are bedbugs and cockroaches. Your vacancy tends to arise from these issues. Your tenants are a little rough on the building and each other. You will need to spend a lot of time here and give this location a lot of time and logical care (TLC).

910, 920, 930 and 940 Motivational Street: This location is a very diverse community with a mix of families with school-age children and pets (dogs and/or cats).

<u>428 Inspirational Drive</u>: This location has a very diverse tenant base with a high immigrant or newcomer population. There is a mix of singles and families with children. Sometimes vacancies are the result of deportations or job changes. The location is great, which means that vacant units get rented fast.

<u>528 and 534 Action Drive</u>: The tenants at this community are like those of the Elite and Spoiled group, except these tenants are a little more content. They are mostly retired, with children and grandchildren visiting them. They have pets and are attached to them. A few have children still living with them. The buildings are quiet and the location is ideal, with spectacular views all around regardless of where your apartment is located. These tenants have disposable income and are not afraid to spend the money.

<u>999 Elite and Spoiled Circle</u>: This location has a mix of professionals, mature students and retired professionals who have sold their houses and want the benefit of living in a high-end apartment. The rent is very high, above market value, and the tenants feel their needs should be anticipated. They maintain their apartments well. They do not like to hear the word *no*. That word *no* gets them mad. They like to have their own way. Every tenant drives and will drive you crazy if they do not get what they want.

Qualities of an Excellent Residential Property Manager

We have indicated in our introduction that residential property management involves overseeing, and co-ordinating with balance, the interrelated functions of residential building systems, equipment, landscaping, tenants, staff, contractors and government agencies to enhance the useful life of the property to produce a profit. Most established property management companies have systems in place to maintain and protect their investments. These systems on their own are useless; they require skilled human resources to put them into action to make the properties effective and profitable. The human resources at the locations of these apartment buildings are crucial to the success of these properties because they act as the blood that keeps the building(s) functioning. This is because without competent site staff, you cannot properly do the following things:

- care for the concerns of tenants
- have clean buildings
- rent the apartments
- collect the rents
- maintain the equipment at the buildings

Biology teaches us that oxygenated blood must be pumped around the body by a healthy heart. That healthy heart is you, the excellent residential property manager of the portfolio. Just like a healthy heart, your excellent approach to residential property management will motivate your site staff to work and help to keep the investments alive or pumping and profitable.

To be an excellent property manager, excellence and the ability to lead must be in your DNA. The *Oxford Dictionary* defines *DNA* (deoxyribonucleic acid) as "a self-replicating material present in nearly all living organisms as the main constituent of chromosomes. It is the carrier of genetic information." In other words, DNA is something that is in your genes, blood or makeup. This is not only biological; social, environmental and psychological factors also influence your DNA. You must have in your DNA certain characteristics that will enable you to reach your full potential as an excellent property manager.

A. The DNA of an Excellent Residential Property Manager

An excellent residential property manager is a top performer who is results-oriented and focused on the bigger picture or the main objectives of the job. Excellent property managers are "hands-on," which means they get involved in a practical way. It has been said that a top performer is someone who consistently surpasses all others in results. The performance of a top performer is based purely on talent and habit, which act as a catalyst allowing the individual to take hold of opportunities when they present themselves. You must visualize success in your mind's eye and be willing to navigate the rough path of life to get there. Top-performing property managers understand that success does not come overnight. According to the late motivational speaker Jim Rohn, "You should be the person you want to be. Success is something you attract by being attractive." Attracting success will require you to develop distinct sets of traits or qualities that others have used to achieve their goals. Some of these traits are as follows: discipline, organization, being a go-getter, being a continuous learner, self-confidence and goal-setting skills.

Let us see how each of these traits or characteristics can help to mould a person into being an excellent property manager. These characteristics will also be the building blocks of becoming an excellent property manager. Align them and practise them well and you will withstand the storms and tornadoes that will come without warning on the job.

Discipline

As an excellent property manager, you will need to have discipline, which will keep you grounded, and go against the natural inclination to relax and take whatever comes. Discipline will be your fuel that will drive you as an excellent property manager to becoming a top performer. It is an unshakeable habit you must develop to control your time, zero in on goals and adapt to unexpected changes. This habit helps top performers to follow a plan and stick with it. If you lack discipline, you will be an average property manager who has no focus and who manages by instilling fear in your staff to hide your own incompetence.

Organization

As an excellent property manager, you will need to be governed by a system of order to get things done and achieve your goals. Being organized will allow you to stay focused and utilize resources to maximize results. Being organized helps excellent property managers to have clarity of thought and avoid chaos. Average property managers are faced with situations of hit-or-miss. They wing everything. They take a back seat and leave everything to the staff to do. This manifests itself in the excessive power they give their staff and in the fact that they themselves have no clue about what is happening at their buildings. This power must not be confused with empowerment, the latter of which is a guided form of authority. Lack of organization makes average property managers great athletes in that they keep chasing dreams instead of being guided to their dreams.

Being a go-getter

Excellent property managers have a deep desire and drive to work hard and reach their dreams or vision set by the company, their team and themselves. They are not afraid to fight or push through the odds to succeed. They are not satisfied with mediocrity. Top-performing property managers get things done right by their own internal standards, which are usually set higher than the accepted norm. Top-performing property managers differ from average-performing property managers in that they do not complain. Instead, they discuss matters and aspire to make things better. They spend time with others who will improve and inspire them. Therefore, you will need to choose carefully the people with whom you associate and whom you call your friends.

Being a continuous learner

To be an excellent property manager, you must develop an appetite and desire to add to your knowledge and improve technical skills that are directly related to the job. Continuous learning should also improve soft skills or social skills. Continuous or professional development is discussed in detail in the chapter Professional and Personal Development.

Self-confidence

Self-confidence entails self-awareness. It involves feeling good about who you are and what you are about. It is a strong conviction of your purpose. Self-confidence helps to build your image and how people perceive you. This trait should come effortlessly to you so that it enters your mind without your having to think about it. This is referred to as unconscious competence: you cannot explain how you are doing the things that are correct in order to get the results.

Goal-setting skills

Goals can be short-term, medium-term or long-term, spanning years into the future. Goals that you set are strategies or rungs on a ladder connecting you to your dreams or desires. Once you commit your goals to paper, this becomes what others call a vision board. Goal setting is also an achievement plan or map. These plans should be measurable and include time lines. Bradley Foster in his "10 Steps to Successful Goal Setting" states the following about setting goals:

1. Belief. The first step to goal setting is to have absolute belief and faith in the process. If you don't believe you can absolutely transform your life and get what you want, then you might as well forget about goal setting and do something else. If you are in doubt, look around you. Everything you can see began as a thought. Make your thoughts turn into reality.

2. Visualize what you want. Think of what you deeply desire in your life or where you want your company to be a year from now. What changes have to take place? What do you need to know or learn? What spiritual, emotional, personal, financial, social or physical properties

need to be addressed? The clearer you are with each of these dimensions will bring your vision into sharp focus. The clearer you are, the easier it will be to focus on making it happen.

3. Get it down! Writing down your goals is key to success. By writing down your goals, you become a creator. Failure to write down your goals often means you will forget them or won't focus on them. Have them written down where you can see them every day.

4. Purpose. Knowing why you want to achieve your goals is powerful. Identifying the purpose of your goal helps you instantly recognize why you want that particular goal and whether it's worth working toward. Knowing why you want something furnishes powerful motivation to see it through to the finish. After all, if the purpose of earning a million dollars is to put it in the bank for a rainy day, you probably won't be as motivated as you will if you need it to pay for your child's cancer treatment.

5. Commit. This might sound obvious to you but it's a step that has disastrous consequences when it's taken lightly. Write a few pages about why and how you are committing to each goal; why it's important to you, what it means to you, why the outcome is necessary and what are you going to do to make it happen. Without strong commitment you aren't likely to follow through.

6. Stay focused. By focusing on your goals, you manifest. You may not know how you'll reach your goals, but when you make a daily practice of focus, they become easier to reach. Having your goals written down somewhere where you will see them each day is a good idea. Your mind will notice that there is a discrepancy between where you are now and where you want to be which will create pressure to change. If you lose focus you can always bring it back. Without a regular practice of focusing on your goals you may be distracted by something.

7. Plan of action. Being really clear about what you want, knowing your purpose, writing your goals down, committing to them, and staying focused gives you the power of clarity to write down a list of action steps. You may not know all the steps ahead of time but you will know the next steps that take you in that direction. Having goals without a plan of action is like trying to complete a complex project without a project plan. There is too much going on, it's too disorganized, you miss deadlines and you don't have priorities. Eventually you get frustrated and the project/goal fails or collapses under its own weight.

8. No Time Like the Present. To show how committed you are to your goals, think of something you can do right now that will get you moving toward fulfilling your goals. Even if it's just making a phone call, do it now. You will be surprised how this simple step reinforces all the previous steps and gets you motivated and moving toward what you desire. If you are not motivated to do something right now, how are you going to get motivated tomorrow?

9. Accountability. To push through when things get tough, you have to hold yourself accountable unless you bring in outside help like a coach who provides it for you. It makes sense

to have someone beside yourself who can provide valuable feedback at critical junctures, like a friend or a mentor. Telling your friends and family about your goals may give you the accountability your need.

10. Review. Make it part of your day to review your goals and take action. This keeps your goals alive and top of mind. It's a good time to convert the overall plan into discrete action steps that you can take throughout the week. It will also help you be aware if one goal feels stuck and you are overcompensating on another goal.

By following these steps and practicing your goals each day, you have all the elements you need to succeed and achieve your goals. It isn't always easy to push through. Some days will be easier than others but if you keep focused on your goals you will be amazed at the progress you will make. Remember, almost everything begins as a thought. You can be what you imagine if you follow these simple steps.

Source: Bradley Foster, "10 Steps to Successful Goal Setting," https://www.huffingtonpost.com/ bradley-foster/how-to-set-goals_b_3226083.html, May 7, 2013, updated July 7, 2013. Reproduced with the permission of Bradley Foster, November 6, 2017.

In short, goal setting helps to put things into perspective. It becomes your target or desired destination. Setting goals also helps to enhance your core values and build who you become.

B. Core Values of an Excellent Property Manager

Top-performing property managers are governed by internal core values that are both personal and professional. Core values help to shape who top-performing property managers are and how they get things done. Core values are your deep inner qualities. They define who you truly are and what you are made of. They are your mental immune system and internal compass. When things are not going the way they should, or when you have major decisions to make, where inside of yourself do you go for recovery and for answers? Here are some core values you could tap into:

Passion

The process of attaining your goal gives you great excitement that nothing can replace or remove. Even when the chips are down, the excitement never dims. Indeed, it grows more intense. As a top-performing property manager, you will find that sometimes this is all you have when life throws you a curveball. Your passion will find a way to keep you moving forward.

Emotional intelligence

Being able to discern and manage your own emotions as well as the emotions of those around you is a great skill to have as an excellent property manager. With emotional intelligence, you become mindful or conscious of what is happening around you, including what is going on with the people in your work world. Emotional intelligence makes you better able to approach staff, tenants and those with whom you work and allows you to be effective regardless of their state of mind. Managing with compassion and empathy is to display emotional intelligence. It enables a top-performing property manager to relate and connect with others in their sorrow, anxiety, pain or joy. Emotional intelligence allows you to put yourself in the other person's shoes, giving you the ability to feel and see things from their standpoint. How would you want to be treated? Learn to emotionally connect with the heart of others and respect their dignity. Emotional intelligence will be further discussed in the chapter titled Staffing.

Honesty

To be honest means being truthful no matter the cost. It is about being upright and moral. Honesty helps you to maintain your integrity, inner core values and conscience (that is as long as your conscience is properly trained and not numb). Being honest means, you do not alter the truth to suit your desires. There is no selfishness in honesty. Honesty helps you to see the good in other people. Honesty is being open and clear about your intentions and how you communicate.

Humility

Arrogance, pride and behaving as though you know it all is not befitting of an excellent property manager. These characteristics are synonymous with underachievers and will only work against you. Humility keeps top-performing property managers grounded and open-minded. An excellent property manager knows that humility adds resilience and is a key ingredient in being a successful manager. Knowing your limitations as an excellent property manager does not mean you are weak; it shows you have good judgement. Having humility will allow you to ask for help and input from the team, your branch manager or your colleagues when necessary.

Respect

Respect is deep feeling of admiration for people based on their achievements or how they conduct themselves. It involves proper acceptance of and courtesy toward others. To receive respect, you must be able to give respect. Never underestimate the knowledge of your staff, your tenants or the people you interact with each day. They are human beings like you and deserve to be treated as such. You never know whom they are connected to. Certain connections could be your downfall if you treat such people with any less respect than they are entitled to.

Teamwork and team building

Teamwork is being able to work co-operatively by embracing the skills of others to get things done well.

Good judgement

Having good judgement involves the ability to collect and sort information and ask others pertinent questions to arrive at a proper conclusion. Good judgement may not be a life-or-death characteristic, but it could mean the difference between a few hundred dollars or even thousands of dollars. Therefore, when faced with any decision-making situation, ask yourself, *What behaviours will this decision evoke, and how much will it cost in terms of time, money and emotional energy in the long run?* This will give you an idea of the ripple effect your decision will have and how these effects might align with the company goals.

Tolerance

You will require this trait to endure interactions with difficult tenants, unwilling staff, other unreasonable people and competitive colleagues. Having an open mind will help you to put up with and accept certain situations that are out of your control or outside your area of authority.

Trust

Trust allows you to form relationships with others. As a property manager, you will find that your staff, tenants, branch manager, senior managers and contractors, along with various outside organizations, will rely on your professional skills. They will want to feel comfortable relating a degree of confidential information to you. When you make others feel comfortable when in your presence, it makes it possible for them to trust. When others trust you, they will volunteer valuable information to you effortlessly without your even asking or mentioning anything about the topic in question. Trust requires unwavering reliability and your commitment to deliver.

Professionalism

You possess a certain skill set acquired through standardized training and practice to bring about a particular result. Each profession has expected behaviour and conduct that must be demonstrated. Your management skills and conduct must show that you know what you are doing. This must also be demonstrated in your deportment, both when you are relaxed and under pressure.

Leadership skills

As an excellent property manager, you must have, above all other skills, the ability to lead or influence others. In your role as a property manager, you are going to have different people reporting to you and looking for direction. The more immediate of these people are tenants, building managers and superintendents, other staff and contractors. According to John Maxwell, author of *The 21 Irrefutable Laws of Leadership*, "Leadership is the ability to influence, nothing more or nothing less." Maxwell says, "It's the leader that will make the position." Hence, the strength of your leadership skill will determine your effectiveness as a property manager. If you do nothing else, build on this skill. Then your results will seem effortless. You will add tremendous value to your portfolio, regardless of how often your portfolio is changed, and by extension to the company.

Excellent communication skills

How you give and receive information, whether oral, written or non-verbal, says a lot about who you are as a property manager. The information must be clear to whoever is receiving it. An excellent property manager must know how to impart information and how to determine the correct time to give that information. When information is delivered at the right time, the recipient is able to absorb and process what was said. Communication skills also involve assessing the other party or parties and oneself. What is the body language? Is it an unspoken need, anger, hurt or joy? This may be done through proper use of questioning and listening. Learn to master the art of communication; it is a very important skill of an excellent property manager.

Cultivating the above-listed characteristics and core values of an excellent property manager will allow you to do a proper self-assessment and self-examination. See what you need to improve on in order to execute your responsibilities with grace and calculated risk. Remember—because you are the heart that keeps the staff (that is, the blood) at the properties going/pumping, you need to be healthy. The next chapter will help you to look a little closer at yourself so that you may make the needed adjustments.

Personal Appearance and Grooming

A. Building Your Image

Your job as a property manager makes you a professional, and given that you are a professional, the people you work with, work for and manage will have their own perceptions of who you are and what you are about. You can influence how others view you based on the image you project. Your hygiene, your clothing, how you speak and the manner in which you conduct yourself all help to build your image and create the impression people will have of you. This will ultimately become your own brand or what you represent. As an excellent property manager, you must have a reputation that differentiates you from other property managers. Visualize who you want to be and build on that visualization with great determination. Your professional image gives an impression of confidence, competence and intelligence. People will take you seriously and view you as someone to be respected.

Business attire varies according to location and culture. The most significant part of your image is formed by the clothing you wear. Some office dress codes may be business casual, smart casual, formal or not clearly stated. Whatever you wear, do not be Mr. Sloppy or Ms. Sloppy, or have the attitude that anything goes. Regardless of what you wear, whether it is your own clothing or a company uniform, wear fresh, clean clothes to work every day that fit your body type. Your clothing also includes underwear, socks, hosiery, ties and petticoats.

B. Hygiene and Grooming

Clean clothes and clean shoes that fit will make you feel good about yourself, which will eventually reflect in your countenance and boost your confidence. No one should be able to tell what colour undergarments you are wearing. If they can see the colour of your underwear or see the underwear itself, then you are not properly dressed. (This excludes marinas or tee shirts worn by men under their shirts to absorb moisture or perspiration.) If your dress, skirt or pants are thin to the point that others can see through the garment, you are improperly dressed and have become a distraction, and in some cases an embarrassment. Blouses or shirts should not be low cut. Whatever clothing you wear, it should not expose your armpits if you reach up or your underwear if you bend down.

Shirts, blouses, pants and any garment that requires ironing/pressing should be clean, crisp and wrinkle-free. As an intern at a five-star hotel in New York City, I was taught to wear jackets closed. A closed jacket, I was told, "makes you look professional and sharp." Neckties, if worn, should be free of soil, without fraying or bulging caused from damaged lining. On the matter of footwear, every property manager must invest in comfortable shoes. The job includes a lot of walking and lengthy periods of standing during building inspections and site visits. I find that the Naturalizer brand has very comfortable women's shoes that will allow you to carry out this aspect of the job with comfort and ease. If you search the Internet, you will find other brands that offer a selection of comfortable shoes to fit everyone regardless of gender.

Shower every morning before you leave for work. Failing to shower defeats the purpose of wearing clean clothes, as you will have a dirty body. While soap and water are the basic ingredients to having a clean body, be sure to use antiperspirant, body splash, after-shave splash, lotion, body butter or skin moisturizer to complete the process. Some offices insist on a fragrance-free environment. Keep this in mind when purchasing toiletries; you do not want to irritate or offend anyone. If you do not have such an environment, milder fragrances are always best. Remember your job involves not only your colleagues in the office but also the tenants, your staff, contractors and many others. Bear in mind that as the weather changes, it may affect your body chemistry. In warmer weather, you will be outside a lot more and doing more inspections, which may cause you to sweat. It is always good to know your toiletries are working for you, rather than against you. Be conscious of your body chemistry and change your toiletries according to the weather if you must.

Facial hair should be clean and neatly maintained. The hair on your head should be clean, combed or brushed, and styled each day. Do not neglect your oral health. If your company offers health benefits, make use of any dental coverage. Have cleanings and checkups done at least twice each year, or as often as your health benefits allow. Any glasses worn should be in very good condition. They should not have any broken arms or any cracked lenses, or look warped when you wear them. Every time you put your glasses on, make sure they are clean and sit well on your face. Taking pride in yourself is a way of managing and maintaining your image. If you don't take yourself seriously, no one else will.

Fingernails may seem insignificant, but they should be clean and neatly shaped at all times. Clean and neat fingernails and toenails say a lot about you. Maintaining your nails is something you should not ignore. A nail clipper and nail buffer are great inexpensive tools to have. They require no professional skill to use; hence, you can use them yourself. Having hands and feet professionally done can be a real treat and a real boost to your self-esteem and image. While your toes and feet may not always get seen at work, a pedicure can do wonders, lifting your spirit and making you feel clean and light. While a student at the University of Technology, Jamaica, I operated a nail salon on campus. Recipients of this service always commented on how much lighter and how special they felt after they'd gotten either a manicure or a pedicure.

Your grooming and overall image should reflect the person you wish to represent. Before you leave your home in the mornings, always ask yourself, *What image or message am I sending?* It should always be the image of an excellent professional-looking residential property manager.

Another area that should not be neglected is the vehicle that you drive. Your job as a property manager requires travelling; therefore, you must have access to a reliable motor vehicle. I find the Hyundai Santa Fe Sport to be an elegant-looking, reliable, comfortable, fuel-efficient vehicle. Another thing I love about this vehicle is that it provides great support for my back, which has been injured, and allows me to get in and out of the seat with ease. Whether you believe it or not, the vehicle you drive is also part of your image. Your vehicle sends a message of who you are. According to Antonio Centeno of Real Men Real Style (RMRS), "Not all of us have the option to drive an expensive car. However, you still can drive something that specifically fits your lifestyle. It doesn't take much effort to keep your vehicle clean but it could provide big payoffs in terms of what opinions people form of you. Your car should be a reflection of your own unique character and the sort of life you are living." While the particular article I've quoted is geared toward men, anyone can benefit from the information. Whatever you drive, keep it clean both inside and outside. Papers should not be all over your vehicle. Use small storage containers to keep things in place and organized.

Like it or not, remember by your image you are judged. Therefore, you must take every step necessary to always project an image of professionalism.

Starting Your Day

A. Have a Routine and Structure to Your Day

Start tomorrow's workday today. When I was a child growing up and going to school, my dad always encouraged me and my siblings to press/iron all our uniforms or, for those who were working, their work clothes for the week. He was concerned about his hydro bill or electricity bill, and that was his way of controlling the usage and, hence, his bill. Therefore, all uniforms were ironed or pressed on a Sunday afternoon or evening. The only thing I understood back then was that we all had one less thing to do in the mornings to start our day. I merely complied then, but when I became an adult, I discovered that I'd learned something from that exercise. That practice helped me to have a long-range view of things for the week. I follow that practice to this day. I never have to worry about what I am going to wear any morning before I go off to work. That is always taken care of on a Sunday after laundry is done. Hence, I would recommend arranging your work clothing on a Sunday before the start of the workweek. If you are not able to do so, get or pay someone to do it for you. It will eliminate much wasted time each morning.

If you have children, teach them this concept as well. Regardless of their age, if you start them early, this will make it part of their daily or weekly routine and set them up for greater things in life. Back in Jamaica, when I worked in the hotel industry, some housekeepers would show up to work late every day. They always blamed their tardiness on their children and or a lack of transportation. To help the housekeepers arrive on time to work, a manager and I charted a simple and doable plan for them. In departmental training, we encouraged the housekeepers with younger children to have their kids clean their own shoes when they got home from school and to pack their bags for school the day before. If the housekeepers had babies and/or toddlers to take to daycare or to the babysitter, we encouraged them to pack the baby's or toddler's bag the day before and to do whatever else they could do the day before. Sometimes those overnight or day-before preparations took only five or ten minutes to do. That five or ten minutes meant not missing the bus or taxi the next day and arriving on time for work. Many expressed their appreciation for the simple solution.

This practice of preparing for the week is very common. It is employed in different aspects of our lives. When you go on business trips or family vacations, you know well ahead of time what you will wear each day, to whatever meetings or restaurants you are going to attend and to the homes of whatever friend(s) you are going to visit. You plan the details of your vacation or trip day by day. If you do not have certain items, you go out and purchase them before the trip. Some of us even examine the clothes we will wear to see if they still fit and if they require dry cleaning, and if our shoes, accessories, socks or hosiery goes well with our planned choice of garments to wear. Preparation both in personal and professional life helps with the flow of how things should go or how you want them to go. Once your preparation is completed, you are more relaxed and capable of handling whatever the day throws at you.

During the summer months along the Hamilton, Ontario, Waterfront Trail, you will find a variety of waterbirds. If you walk the trail in the early morning, you will notice that the birds, regardless of their kind, have a morning routine. Before their days get busy, they gather together and begin a grooming process. Sometimes you will see one bird, depending on its type, grooming another bird of its kind, after which the favour is returned. In this social grooming process, the birds, I presume, serve as each other's mirror. This is a great example of teamwork—and a great grooming technique. I've noticed that shortly after the grooming process is completed, the birds will huddle together as if they are having a conversation about what each will be doing for the day. Should you visit the trail later in the morning, you will find that the majority of the birds have already gone off to carry out the day's activities. If these birds have such a structured routine for how to start their day, then we humans have no excuse.

Show up for work professionally dressed each day. Always start each day doing what was left over from the day before. Carry forward any task(s) on your to-do list you did not complete. Think ahead and add the tasks you will complete the next day to your list. Your daily to-do list is your road map for the day. It will help you gauge how much mental, emotional and physical energy you will need for the day to complete your tasks. Begin your actual day by arriving to work at least one hour early. Hardly anyone will be present to engage you in idle talk and waste your time. This will allow you to get settled both mentally and emotionally. It will also set the pace and tone for the day. Whatever beverage you use to start your day with, grab it as soon as you set your bag/case down, and then head back to your office. Greet any colleague you see with your best smile and a cheerful attitude, and then continue to your office and close the door. This will send a message that you are busy and do not wish to be interrupted.

B. Keep Your Paperwork Flowing/Moving

Use this precious one-hour block of time as if your job and life depended on it. At this time of the day, before the rush begins, your thoughts are more likely to flow. You will have fewer interruptions or distractions. During this quality time, you can address any of the following:

- sensitive letters to tenants or to prepare for any upcoming court hearing
- letters to staff or Notes to File
- any employee performance evaluation

- any special project or the like
- the signing of leases/tenancy agreements

You may use the first 15 minutes to clear or sort your incoming trays. As you do this, sign and quickly take any documents to other departments for processing or the file room to be filed. If you receive faxed documents from your buildings that require following up, set these aside in the respective building folder for follow-up either when you call or when you visit the building.

C. Lease/Tenancy Agreement Signing

As of April 30, 2018, a standard lease for Ontario came into effect. Most individual residential property owners and property management companies, are now required to use this standard lease also known as the Residential Tenancy Agreement. As you sign off on the tenancy agreement or the lease applicable to your company or region, check the lease/tenancy agreement to ensure the following:

- correct spelling of tenants'/residents' names, including the names of any guarantors or cosigners
- correct number of tenants/residents listed
- correct address including apartment number, postal/zip code (you may have more than one building on the same street with different postal or zip codes)
- correct start and end date of the lease
- correct charge for parking and correct number of parking spots. If you have different types of parking, such as indoor and outdoor, this should be specified. Be sure to check or indicate the type of parking if you charge for parking.
- correct charge for storage facility.
- correct amount of base rent per month, including any prorated amount
- check the total to ensure the lawful rent is correct (base rent plus any amenities).
- no errors about who will be paying for certain services, such as heating, hydro, water, sewage, air conditioning (AC) and cable
- any amenities included in the apartment/unit, such as fridge, stove, microwave, dishwasher, washing machine and dryer. These services or amenities will vary from building to building depending on your tenant base/type. Ensure the tenants are getting the amenities they are paying for.

In addition to the above, ensure the lease has all the attached pages of rules and regulations or additional terms that are unique to your properties or company. Once you have signed the leases along with their other applicable pages, place them in the respective outgoing tray or slot designated for your buildings. Keep in mind that the lease may specify the days you visit the buildings, as tenants/residents may want to sign the lease ahead of time. It is also great if leases are delivered to the buildings ahead of time so your on-site rental office staff can organize the move-in of new tenants/residents and ensure it goes smoothly.

The next 15 minutes could be used to clear voice mails or answer e-mails requiring follow-up. For greater efficiency, you may record your greeting daily. This message will tell callers you clear your voice mail each day and will get back to them in a timely manner (for example: *You have reached the voice mail of [your name]. Today is Monday, August 10. I will be in the office until [state the time]. Please leave me a detailed message at the tone, and I will return your call at my earliest convenience. Have a great day*). If you wish, you may omit the date and simply leave the other part of the greeting. As you clear your voice mail, you may wish to adjust your to-do list, as you will most likely have to return calls during operating hours or regular business hours. Try to return calls closer to the beginning of the workday. For tenants who you know will consume most of your time, call them back closer to lunch or toward the end of the day, or after you have completed the most time-sensitive tasks on your to-do list. Ensure you have a message book designated to record messages you clear. Be specific when you make notes. Some tenants can be so angry that they do not leave any unit or apartment number, and sometimes not even their name or telephone number. Make a note of that as well, for example, Tenant called August 10. No name, telephone number or address. Angry message is, "Shower tap cannot turn off! Rental office will not answer when I call them or respond to my messages. Asking that they call me back now or else!" This will be something to investigate when you contact your buildings later in the morning. Taking detailed notes will protect you when the tenant calls back to say you did not return his or her call. You can then acknowledge you did receive the message, say that you regret the maintenance issue the tenant is experiencing, and inform the tenant that he or she left no contact information for you to return the call.

D. Morning Briefings

If your building staffs start each workday at 8:00 a.m. or whatever time, allow them to conduct their five-minute morning briefings and get settled. I learned the value of morning briefings, or "lineup," while an intern at a five-star hotel in New York City. This quick five-minute meeting gave an overview of what would be happening in the hotel for the day.

One community I was assigned to had issues with staff showing up for work late every day despite the fact that they lived on the property. I reiterated the start time for work and instructed them all to do a morning briefing. Morning briefings solved the problem. It forced everyone to be on time, and it set the tone for the day. The briefing acted as the to-do list for the property, giving an overview of the goals the team had to achieve each day. Morning briefings should give a quick overview of the day, as follows:

- ✓ You should also include any out of the ordinary notes from overnight security, contract cleaner(s), night staff and or after hours answering services that may have forwarded reports or log of calls that require your attention, or the attention of your site staff.
- ✓ List any contractor(s) who will be on-site for the day and what they will be doing for the day. Mention who will be with the contractor. The purpose of the visit may include water shutdown or shut-off to do plumbing repairs. Mention any pest control treatments and who will accompany the technician.
- ✓ Discuss any work orders for tenants'/residents' apartments. State the amount of work orders that will be done for the day. Name any difficult tenant whose apartment maybe among the work orders. If there are no work orders, mention who will be ordering supplies.

- ✓ Mention the names of the apartments that are moving in (move-ins) and or apartments that are moving out (move-outs).
- ✓ Mention the names of the vacant apartments that will require cleaning and who will clean them.
- ✓ Mention if there will be any visitors from the branch office or headquarters (HQ), or any visits from city inspectors.
- ✓ Make note of any inspection that will be conducted by the property manager (PM) and who will accompany the PM.
- ✓ Mention the next staff meeting and its location. This is to allow staff to reserve the date and time to accommodate the staff meeting.
- ✓ Indicate any staff who are away on training, out sick or away on holiday.
- ✓ Mention who will be covering for any staff not present.

Post this format inside the rental office or in the back office (if you have a back office) at each building within your portfolio. It will condition the staff to follow the outline and not stray. If you have a stand-alone building, the briefing should be conducted inside the rental office and never inside an employee's apartment. Even if the rental office is attached to the personal apartment of the employee, the briefing should be conducted in the designated office area. If the building has a single building manager, call that building first and do the briefing with that manager. The scheduled activities at the building will let you know what time of day is best for you to visit (and when it is best not to visit) that building.

You may want to start calling your building managers at or around 8:15 a.m. If the building managers are not on duty, then speak with the team who covered the building overnight. Keep your conversations brief and professional. Your conversation can go something like this: "Good morning. How are you?" If they say "good" or "well," tell them, "Nice to hear." Ask if they had a good night or weekend, and if the latter, whether they worked or were off for the weekend. This will give you insight into any out-of-the-ordinary activities at the building that your staff may not have reported to you throughout the night. This brief conversation will provide useful information about your team members' home lives and their overall frame of mind. Make brief notes as you speak. Your notes do not have to be fancy; just stick to the facts.

Confirm any appointments you made with staff the day before or inform them of any changes, as well as of any 24-Hour Notice of Entry that needs to be served for the following day. If you are going to be in an all-day meeting, let them know. Advise them to call only if there is an emergency. You can also use this opportunity to relate the message you cleared earlier from the angry tenant who left no telephone number. Your staff may say something like, "It was Mrs. Brown, but we will get back to her." Be sure to get the tenant's contact number immediately and have your staff member call you within an hour to confirm he or she has addressed the tenant's concerns. Find out why the tenant's call was not returned, and ensure it never happens again. Note this on the "follow-up" side of your to-do list. By doing this, you will train your staff to complete the task as requested. They will know that you will definitely follow up. Inform your staff also that you will be calling Mrs. Brown to let her know you have spoken to the staff who will be addressing the issue within the hour. Before you end the call, ask your staff if they need anything from you and tell them that they should feel free to call you if you they do need anything. Call your other buildings and use the same approach. As soon as you get the chance, call the tenant Mrs. Brown. Validate her concerns by apologizing for the delay and for any inconveniences caused, and thank her for her call. Tell her you would have called earlier if she had not forgotten to leave her number, requiring that you get it from your staff. Remind her to leave her number the next time she calls. Leave the lines of communication open by thanking her and telling her that she should call you if she has any further issues.

E. Powering Through Your To-Do List

The following is the suggested sequence for completing the items on your to-do list:

1. Complete your morning routine as we have stated above
2. Check in with your area manager (AM).
   a. Once you have called all the rental offices or properties that are part of your portfolio, you may check in with your branch or area manager for any project he or she may have for you or to find out if an update is needed on any project he or she has assigned to you.
   b. If you have nothing for your AM to sign or your AM does not require your attention, proceed with the other tasks on your to-do list.
3. Check with your administrative assistant or receptionist for any document(s) that require(s) your attention.
4. Continue to check your e-mails and respond completely to anyone needing information.
5. Where possible, return tenant calls.
6. Return calls or follow up with contractors. Request quotes or follow up on quotes for work to be completed.
7. Follow up with other departments for pertinent information or as required
8. Have a break.
9. Continue with any task that requires urgent attention.
10. Have your lunch.
11. Visit your buildings as scheduled.

Whatever task you have on your to-do list, work with great speed until it is completed. As you busily work your day away, remember to take a mid-morning break. Having a small bowl with apples or pears on a table in your office can serve as your snack area. Be sure not to put out too much, as fruits are highly perishable. Every day is a journey. Your to-do list is your guide. Just as you would fill up your vehicle with gas to continue your journey, you must top up your body's energy, in the form of lunch, to serve as fuel to complete the day's journey. Never skip your lunch.

After lunch, if you have no in-office meetings, use the afternoon to visit your buildings. Your building visits must be purposeful and methodical. Following a system will allow you to achieve maximum productivity and satisfaction every time you visit a building. It will keep you in the know and help you to better understand and control your budget. You do not have to visit all the buildings in one day. You can do concentrated visits so each building gets the attention it needs.

Property/Site Visits

Sometimes it is better to start your day in the branch office to keep the paperwork flowing. Following the system outlined in the previous chapter will assist you in creating a smoother flow to your paperwork that will make you feel fulfilled and energized. Use the other half of the day to do your field visit, site visit or property visit, whatever you call it.

A. Importance of Physically Visiting the Properties

These visits are necessary. There is no substitute for visiting the properties. Use these visits to connect the following: the flow of paperwork, tenant complaints and your budget in action. When you leave the office and physically go out to the buildings, you will learn, see and hear a lot more. Use the visits to inspect the following core operational areas:

1. building structure and exterior curb appeal
2. landscaping and grounds
3. Systems and routines—cleaning, renting, rent collection, all safety logs
4. special or capex projects
5. mechanical/utility rooms—HVAC, fire systems, elevators, boiler room, electrical system, workshops/maintenance, workstations
6. vacant and ready apartments, occupied apartments and apartments being renovated or repaired
7. tenants' requests and concerns, such as work orders that may require your approval
8. common areas, including amenities

You can also meet with contractors, tenants and staff. *Your visits must always be purposeful and methodical.* Following a system will allow you to achieve maximum productivity and satisfaction every time you visit your building(s).

13. If there is training scheduled for you and any of your staff, that must also be included on the calendar.

14. If you have a day designated for signing invoices, start your invoice signing in the morning as the process can sometimes be lengthy. Invoice signing will be addressed under the chapter titled Accounts Payable.

Always have a visual overview of what your day, week and month should be. This goes back to goal setting. A visual overview helps you to be more organized and focused and remain in control of your day and time. Everything may not go according to plan, but it can go close to plan. A personal schedule helps to create a flow and rhythm that programs you to set and achieve goals. If you think this is silly, study the achievements of top athletes and you will see they all have schedules and progressive routines that they stick to as closely as possible. Without that kind of structure or arrangement, they cannot achieve greatness. Do not keep your schedule in your head. By putting it on paper where you can see it, you will be more committed to comply with and embrace your plan of action as a reality to achieve results.

C. Building Inspections

Site visits start as soon as you can see the building(s) from the road. Look at the curb appeal of the building(s) objectively. Proceed with caution and scan the building(s) as far as your eyes can see, including the roof and rooftop equipment or antennas. Cell towers and antennas should be straight, not tilted or falling apart. If they do not meet these standards, contact the respective company asap to address the defect. Do not overlook the balconies. If you know the apartment layout and your risers, it will help you to accurately determine and assess the issues or concerns at each building and let you know which tenant should be contacted to address any problem. You may see a hanging plant on a balcony on the 20th floor. However, because you know your risers, you can confidently say apartment 2004 has hanging plants. The tenant must be notified to remove the plant asap, before it gets swept away by the wind and falls below, hitting someone or someone's property. This knowledge and swift action can avert any accident and save the company from any liability. As you get closer to the building(s), find a safe place to stop in the parking lot or on the roadside and make notes of things that are not in harmony with the décor, aesthetics or rules of the building(s). If you have a building inspection form, either hard copy or electronic, you can make note of these types of deficiencies. You might even drive or walk around the property to get a better view of things. Some items and activities to be on the lookout for as you get closer are indicated below:

D. Exterior Building Inspection

i. Building Structure and Curb Appeal

- Most elevator room or other type of mechanical room (usually boiler room) sits at the very top of the building. It can sometimes look like the top tier of a cake. If this is the case for any of your buildings, how does the wall of your elevator room look from afar? Does it require painting? Is the paint colour consistent with the colour scheme of the building? Can any repainting be done from the regular budget, or is this an item to include on your next capital expenditure (capex) wish list? If the building has metal siding, ensure it is in excellent condition.

- Laundry or clothesline on balcony, or floor rugs on balcony railings, tells potential tenants/residents that anything goes, that your tenants are in control of the building and not you, and that tenants/residents are free to do as they wish. It also says you have no or limited laundry facilities. Laundry and falling cigarettes are perfect companions to start fires. End this practice of laundry on the balcony by sending a notice to all tenants if the practice is widespread. If you see only one apartment doing this, then a letter to the tenant explaining that he or she is in violation of the lease/tenancy agreement is good enough. Since people normally hang laundry out to dry in warmer weather, sending a notice or newsletter before the warmer weather begins is a good way to prevent this behaviour. Do not tolerate any form of laundry on the balcony. It makes your building look cheap and kills curb appeal.

- Any mattress on a balcony could be a sign that the tenant has a bedbug problem. Depending on your geographic location, a mattress on the balcony could indicate a case of bedwetting. However, since we are talking about North America, specifically Ontario, I would lean more toward the case of bedbugs, simply because diapers are available for any age, children or adults. In most cases a mattress on the balcony is a sign you have a major bedbug problem. If a building does have bedbugs, then the residents of that particular apartment are not following procedures for the treatment of such pests. Even if your building does not have bedbugs, remember that mattresses and falling cigarettes are also perfect companions to start fires. Stop this practice by first getting the unit inspected by the pest control technician and then advising the tenant to remove the mattress. You could also send the tenant a letter demanding that he or she remove the mattress from the balcony. The matter of getting tenants to co-operate with pest treatments is addressed in the chapter titled Pest Control.

- Some of your tenants may think it is cool to hang bicycles over the balcony. As the property manager, you need to know that this practice is dangerous. A bicycle hanging on the balcony is another sign that your tenants, not you or your staff, are in control of the building, that you have no rules and that tenants/residents can do as they wish. Falling bicycles can result in serious and untold damages to property and life, either pet or human. If you have glass railing balconies, hanging bicycles can fall and break these glass panels. Then you would have a bicycle and heavy broken glass crashing from above to cause more damage, injury or death below. This must be dealt with urgently. You do not want that kind of publicity or heartache. I had one falling bicycle case that resulted in broken glass. Thankfully there were no injuries to anyone or any damages resulting from the broken glass. The glass was replaced, and the tenant was charged back and warned.

- Hanging plants on the ceiling of the balcony, the wall of the balcony or the outward ledge of the balcony can fall and cause serious damage, injury or death. Treat this as a health and safety hazard and address it with urgency. Yes, hanging plants may look very nice, but they are not safe. Also, hanging plants encourage tenants to make holes in the building structure.

- Satellite dishes attached to the wall or balcony railings can cause structural damage. Satellite dishes can safely be placed on tripod stands. Make sure those tripod stands are not bolted to the ground.

- Mop heads hanging over balcony to dry are unsightly and kill your curb appeal. They are also unsafe for the tenants below when the water drips from the mop. Stop this practice immediately.

- Be on the lookout for missing bricks, mortar missing between bricks and/or major cracks in the wall. These should be reported to your property standards department, with zoomed-in pictures in an urgent e-mail, and followed up until the matter is settled. If not addressed properly, any of these structural problems can cause water to penetrate the building and snowball into major problems.

- Downspouts should be properly attached and not falling off the building. Each tip should have a backsplash to channel water away from the building. Sometimes downspouts fall apart in the winter because water freezes in them.

- There should be no missing or lifting of metal flashing. On a windy day, listen out for any flashing that is flapping in the wind.

- Look for any refrigerators on the balcony. Does your lease/tenancy agreement exclude large appliances other than what you provide? Is a refrigerator classified as regular balcony furniture? If not, have the tenant remove the appliance. What does your lease including any rules and regulations attached to the lease say? Enforce what your lease/tenancy agreement says.

- Look for cluttered balconies used as storage. Tenants/residents who are using their balconies for storage should be notified that they are to cease doing so, and follow-up visits or inspections should be done to enforce compliance. Do not allow storage sheds, small or large, on balconies. A storage shed is not a form of balcony furniture. Again, what does your lease say?

- Closet doors that have fallen off their tracks or that have been removed by the tenants to alter the apartment to their liking are sometimes left on the balcony. The closet door is not designed to go on the balcony and should be returned to its proper place.

- Look for flags on the balconies. One flag up is an invitation for all flags. What does your lease/tenancy agreement say about flags? Displaying flags can turn potential tenants away, as some may not want to rent at the building if they know that people of certain nationalities live there. If it is clearly stated in the lease including the rules that no flags are to be displayed, be firm and make sure to enforce the rule. Keep the property neutral. Some tenants may challenge you and display the flag on the inside like a curtain. You may not be able to do anything about the display of the flag unless your lease/tenancy agreement says curtains or window treatments should have white backing. Some properties will place a flag pole at the front of the building and display the country's flag there.

- Look for motor vehicle tires on the balconies. You may want to promote your storage facility if you have one, or install one and charge monthly for its use. What does your lease say about motor vehicle tires on the balconies? If you do not have any storage facilities where tenant can store tires, you can collect brochures from reputable tire storage facilities in the area and leave them in the laundry room. Another option you could include in any letters you send to tenants about removing tires is that they investigate tire storage facilities in the area or at their car dealership.

- Umbrellas on balconies pose a safety problem if they are blown away by the wind. An umbrella can also be a landing place for a lit cigarette, or a diverter, sending the cigarette onto something combustible and starting a balcony or apartment fire. Are umbrellas considered balcony furniture?

- Nets or nettings including curtains look ugly as well as sloppy, make your building look cheap and tell potential renters you have a pigeon problem. They also kill curb appeal. If you have a pigeon problem, work with your pest control contractor to get rid of the nuisance.

- Some tenants may install lattice around glass balconies or metal balconies with spindles for privacy. This kills curb appeal and should not be allowed.

- Look for tin foil and other reflective materials on windows. Sometimes this is a sign of a marijuana/cannabis grow operation (grow op). Some tenants/residents may say they work nights and sleep in the days, and thus they use the foil to keep out the sun. Sympathize with the tenant and offer alternative suggestions, such as curtains with backing. Do not encourage the use of foil or other reflective materials to cover the windows. State in writing the date for inspection, at which point you expect the tin foil to be removed. *Marijuana/ Cannabis Grow Operation* will be discussed in details under the chapter titled Emergencies.

- Air conditioning (AC) should be properly installed. Do not allow tenants who are installing window AC units to use plyboard to substitute for the window around the AC units. This is another curb appeal killer. Decide ahead of time and inform your tenants about what will be safe and aesthetically acceptable to install around the window AC units to keep them in place.

- If the tenants/residents of your building(s) pay separately for AC, your staff can randomly check windows for AC units installed during a slower part of the month (during the summer) to see if those apartments did in fact pay the extra fee for the AC use. If they did not, then that AC may be illegally installed. Also remember that some ACs are standing/portable units that can be left inside the apartment instead of being installed as window units. Your staff should still be on the look out for window brackets or panels that are used to vent the AC hose through windows. If the vent hose cannot be detected from the outside, these may be discovered when your staff are completing work orders tenants have submitted. Your staff should find out from the tenant/resident and confirm if the form was completed but got lost, if the form was never handed in, or if the tenant/resident simply forgot. If the tenant refuses to comply, then the legal department should be contacted, or you can use compassion—whichever is more beneficial in the long run. It is important to note that, a vent hose in the window may not necessarily be from a standing or portable AC unit, it could be the vent from a grow box used to grow marijuana/cannabis. *Marijuana/Cannabis Grow Operation* will be discussed in details under the chapter titled Emergencies.

- Check for consistency in balcony paint. Some tenants/residents may feel that the custom colour they have painted inside their apartment must be extended to the balcony. If this is done, inform the tenants/residents in writing that they are in violation of the lease. Clearly state they will be billed/invoiced for the repainting of the wall to the original colour. The painting should be done without delay, weather permitting. Remember you and your staff are in control of the property; the tenants/residents comply as per the lease and with the Residential Tenancies Act (RTA) or local tenant laws. Get tenant(s) or resident(s) to comply by using a professional, tactful, polite and firm approach. I remember looking from one building over at another building and spotting the floor of a balcony painted in a very obvious colour. I had a letter sent to that tenant to remove the paint and restore the balcony to its original condition. Thankfully the tenant complied. Whenever you are in a vacant apartment, use the opportunity to look around outside, especially if the apartment is high above others. This will give you a bird's-eye view of the property. If you are in a community setting, look over at the other buildings to ensure tenants are complying with the terms of the lease.

- Be on the lookout for discoloured balcony slabs that may have algae along the sides or stripping of paint. If you see one balcony slab looking like this, schedule an inspection of that apartment and determine if the algae is the result of tenants watering plants or of pets relieving themselves on the balcony. Several balconies with algae could be a sign that they all require painting. This is an item you could add to your capex wish list. Before you add the painting of the balcony to your wish list, speak with your property standards department. What you perceive as algae could be underlying conditions associated with balcony slab deterioration. Cooking on a balcony can also result in discolouration of the ceiling of the slab.

- The fire code is not clear on having a barbecue on the balcony. However, what does your lease/tenancy agreement say? Does the lease allow for having barbecues on the balcony? If so, it should be specific. If the lease does not allow for barbecues on the balcony, your company may want to consider putting No Barbecue stickers on all balcony doors or balconies for all to see. I have had a few balcony fires that were the result of barbecuing. For one of the fires, I cannot remember if the propane exploded, but I remember replacing the balcony glass, cleaning the brick of the balcony and testing the structure of the floor slab and the ceiling slab to see if the heat from the fire compromised it. Also, the balcony ceiling was repainted. You can have a designated area on the property with barbecue pits where tenants can barbecue using their own charcoal.

- Metal balcony panels that are rusting and require painting should be painted. Do not forget that rust could mean you have a bigger issue. Therefore, before you paint any balcony panels that are rusting, have your property standards department check them out. The metal panels may not be strong enough or require changing out, which may mean a major capital expense. Once property standards department gives you the go ahead to paint, if only a small number of the panels, whether metal or concrete, require painting, you could paint a few each month, weather permitting. If the number in need of painting is going to put a strain on your repair and maintenance (R&M) budget, add this to your capex wish list. If your tenants make a practice of putting laundry, including rugs, on the balcony panels to dry, this could cause stripping of the paint. Implement measures to stop this practice.

- Missing window screen(s) should be installed. Window screens keep out bugs and insects. Window screen should not be confused with window restrictor, the latter of which is designed to limit the opening of openable windows and prevent children from falling through from height. If you happen to see any wide-opened window, investigate if the window has a restrictor. If a child should fall through the window, your company could be held liable. Treat this as urgent and ensure it gets addressed. It may be necessary to call your building manager or superintendent and show him or her the potential danger. Follow up with your staff until the matter is resolved.

- Are there missing windows? Instruct your staff to enter any unit with proper notice and find the cause of the missing window. Replace the window regardless of who is at fault. You can charge the tenant and go through the legal process afterward. Comply with safety first and complain after.

- Do any balconies look like a forest or a farm with large plants and vegetable gardens? This is a sign that the tenant/resident has been allowed to do this for some time. There is a strong possibility that you are going to have resistance from this tenant. You may commend the tenant for his or her interest in plants but say that the way the balcony looks is in violation of the lease. If you have space on the property, you can accommodate a vegetable garden and ask the tenant for his or her input on how to set it up. This approach validates the tenant's desire to plant or have a garden and allows you to tactfully indicate that the balcony is not the location for such a hobby of that magnitude. If the tenant refuses to comply, then submitting an N5 is your next best option. Remember too that during some emergencies the balcony is a means of egress (departure or exit) and ingress (access or entry).

- Look around for decorations or holiday lights. These are more personal and a demonstration of a person's faith. If your company allows tenants to use outdoor decorations or lights, they should be removed as soon as the holiday season is over. If you allow for one, you must allow for all; otherwise, you could be hit with a discrimination application to the LTB or Human Rights Tribunal.

- Any door leading to the building or to utility rooms from the outside should be in good to excellent condition, not requiring painting or changing out. Make sure these doors have correct signage and are accessible.

- If the name of the property is affixed to the building, ensure no letters are missing. Replace missing, damaged or faded letters immediately, as it enhances the building's curb appeal and marketability. Also, it is part of the building's address, which is important for emergency vehicles when trying to locate the building. In addition, the walls where the building's name is affixed should be in good condition.

- Wires such as cables along the side of the building should be encased in conduits similar in colour to the building's colours so they blend in and not stand out.

- Conduits for electrical wires should not be rusting. If they are, they should be painted or replaced with plastic as long as the use of plastic is not a violation of any electrical code. Also, plastic conduits should be in good condition and not be broken.

- Foyers and cantilevers should be in good to excellent condition, free from algae and with uniform paint in good condition. They should not have any nests of birds, wasps/hornets or any form of pests. Ensure cantilevers and foyers are free from cobwebs, which tend to collect bugs. Any light or light shade must be in good condition with the proper wattage bulb. Lights should be on a timer. Also, when you get to a part of the building where you are high enough and can look around on the outside, check the top of the foyer or cantilever to make sure it is not accumulating garbage. If vehicular traffic can access under the foyer or cantilever, for safety reasons, be sure to install boldly written MAXIMUM CLEARANCE signs and additional signs such as, NO BUSES ALLOWED, or NO TRUCKS ALLOWED for all to see. This is to alert motorists and others of the height restrictions to prevent serious damage to vehicles, building structure and or lighting.

- Replace missing caps or coverings of standpipe/Siamese connections or Fire Department Connections [FDCs], to meet fire code. These Siamese connections or Fire Department Connections [FDCs], are normally located on the exterior walls of the buildings. Some properties depending on their age and location, may have freestanding or sidewalk standpipe/Siamese connections or Fire Department Connections [FDCs]. Regardless of what you have and what they are called, make sure they have caps or coverings. There is a strong possibility, the fire department can order you to flush the system, to ensure it is not clogged with debris, if you have missing caps or coverings. This is to ensure your standpipe system performs at optimum during a fire emergency. If local code allows, in some cases, it may be best to use plastic caps or coverings instead of metal caps. This is because vandals will remove metal coverings and sell them as scrap metal. Also, ensure proper signs with correct verbiage as per fire code, are displayed within the areas where they are located. Make sure standpipes/ Siamese connections or Fire Department Connections [FDCs] (and any fire hydrants located on your properties), are painted in the required red colour and any other additional colour(s) if necessary. At all times, they MUST be fully visible, recognizable and accessible to the fire department. Therefore, landscaping, fence, wall, bush, shrubbery or trees must not pose any obstruction.

- Ensure any exposed gas pipes are painted in applicable code colour.

- The building should be free from graffiti. If you fail to remove any graffiti, it will only attract more.

Word of caution

If you are assigned a building with multiple issues or concerns similar to those listed above or below, display tact regarding any widespread violations. Do not go in and do a massive clean sweep in order to get everyone to comply. It will backfire on you by angering your tenants and causing a rebellion or uproar. Your first approach may be to start a quarterly or monthly newsletter, depending on your tenant base and the severity of the violations. In your newsletter, you may address anticipated seasonal behaviours. Any tenant who disregards the warnings in the newsletter should be sent letters, and then the appropriate legal actions can follow. You can focus on one violation at a time.

I remember a large community I was assigned to where every building had widespread violations. To calm the majority of the tenants, I started by sending a general notice indicating some upcoming capex projects planned for the location that were to improve the curb appeal of the community. I then noted some violations that were widespread and asked for the co-operation of all to enhance the community. When those projects were finished, another notice was sent out to thank the tenants. In addition to the notices, I arranged an annual barbecue to show appreciation for the tenants. The tenants saw that it was not an attack on them, or a case of them being targeted, but instead an effort to improve the community. There were a few instances of resistance, but eventually the tenants came around and even provided information about other tenants they knew who were violating some aspect of the lease.

ii. Landscaping and Grounds

- Addresses / street numbers must be clearly visible from the road for all to see, both during the day and at night, especially for emergency response vehicles, which must quickly locate the address and access the property when the need arises. There should be no obstruction from bushes, trees or anything else. If the building address sign is not illuminated and has floodlights that are projected onto the sign at night, make sure the correct wattage bulbs are in place and working.

- If you mulch, use sod or put rocks around lawn building signs, it can help to reduce dirt spatter when it rains. It also enhances curb appeal and marketability.

- Check and ensure that any sandwich board signs, such as Open House or Vacancy signs, are properly anchored. Loose signs have been swept up by the wind, causing damage to vehicles. Sadly, I had to deal with one such incident. Do your best to secure sandwich board signs. Ropes and pegs can safely anchor these signs. For safety reasons, make sure your staff know what runs below the ground, such as electrical wiring or gas lines. To ensure safety, you can call the relevant authorities to locate any utility lines before you dig or drive anything into the ground.

- All other signs throughout the property must be visible to all. Faded signs are ineffective in that they cannot convey the intended message.

- How does your landscaping look? Is it striking and better than that of the competition? If it is summer, your lawns must be low cut, free of weeds and nicely maintained, and the edges neatly trimmed. Tree roots should not be exposed. They should be mulched in the appropriate colour to enhance the colour scheme of the property. For safety reasons, remove all dead trees and dead branches. This will prevent trees and branches from falling and injuring anyone. No tree should be touching the building or obscuring lights, security video cameras or walkways. Your landscaping should be more appealing than the competition's.

- Flower gardens should be neatly manicured and inviting with tastefully appointed flowers to accentuate the curb appeal and marketability of the property. Ensure there is no trash or cigarette butts in gardens.

- There should be no litter or trash scattered over any other area of the property.

- Garbage bins, especially large bins, must have lids to prevent garbage from blowing all over the property. Lids also help to keep out rodents, raccoons, stray dogs and other animals. Ensure bins remain on your property at all times. Especially after garbage pickups, bins should not be lingering on the sidewalk or the road. This is dangerous and opens the company up to all kinds of liability issues.

- Any lawn benches should be in good to excellent condition, as should the areas where the lawn benches are located.

- Do you have a lawn sprinkler system for the warm weather? If you do, make sure it is working and sprinkling the areas that need watering. If your lawn sprinkler is on a timer, adjust the setting or suspend the sprinkling during the rainy season to conserve water.

- Perimeter fences and retaining walls should be in excellent condition, not bracing over or damaged by trees. Address any cracks in walls or damage to chain link fences before they get worse, weather permitting. Any wooden fences should be upright and in good to excellent condition.

- For trees that are removed, ensure roots are grinded down to the ground. The area should not present a tripping hazard.

- Remove and replace any broken curbstones. If you remove the curbstones, be sure to replace them with new stones immediately. This is to avoid exposing the steel spikes used to hold the stones in place. When these spikes are exposed, they pose a serious safety hazard.

- Make note of uneven walkways, driveways or sections of parking lots, and correct any by spray painting the hazard with yellow until the area can be fixed. Another quick temporary fix is asphalt patch. This does not last forever. Bear in mind that while it is a quick fix, it can look very unsightly if not properly done, or become a hazard if it is bumpy. You can take pictures of the parking lot and add it to your capex wish list in hopes of repaving the parking lot if you have multiple potholes, large cracks and uneven areas. Make sure there are no weeds growing in between cracks or tree roots extending in the parking lot that are causing the cracks.

- Catch basins and drains must have properly fitting covers that will not become loose during snow plowing.

- Ponding in the parking lot caused by rain could be a sign that you have clogged drains. Or you may have to create a trench or slope the area to eliminate the problem.

- Keep Off the Grass signs should be posted to minimize traffic on the grass. Note carefully, not all tenants will obey such signs. What the sign does is to help reduce the number of people who walk on the grass and damage it. It also reduces the number of pet owners who allow their dogs to pee on the grass, thus preventing or minimizing brown spots on the grass.

- Pet Waste sign with waste bags should not be on the grass. Remember you want to keep tenants off the grass. Post the sign and provide the bags at the curb.

- Where possible, reseed balled and missing grass spots. In some areas, it may be necessary to lay new sod.

- All light poles or posts should be straight, not rotted and painted where necessary. No wires should be exposed. Missing bulbs should be replaced, and bulbs should be encased in globes or appropriate shades/cages. For additional safety, all light posts erected in the parking lot or close to the curb of the parking lot onto concrete columns, should be painted yellow, to increase their visibility, especially during poor weather conditions and at nights. Another safety note to consider is, once steel in the concrete post is exposed, you should first try and get the column assessed by the relevant department or contractor to determine if the column can be repaired, reinforced or replaced. If you must replace a column, determine ahead of time how this will impact the tenants or the property in general.

- Perimeter fences that have lights erected on columns should be in good to excellent condition. They must also have uniform globes. Any missing globes or lights should be replaced. If you are not able to replace the globes because the style is no longer available on the market, think about changing them all out either through the regular budget or by making it a capex project. Be sure to get a few extras if you change out all the globes or lights. That way you will have replacements if one or more gets broken.

- No lights should be on during the day. If lights are on, ensure timers are working and adjusted to the correct time for lights to go off according to each season. If you happen to visit the property at night or you are leaving the property at dusk, check to see if lights have the same colour bulbs. Be consistent with the light colours.

- Bulk garbage should be in a designated area or removed from the property before other tenants take it back inside the building. Swift removal helps to minimize the spread and infestation of bedbugs and other insects or pests. Having enclosed areas for bulk garbage enhances the curb appeal and marketability of the property.

- Go across the street or walk around the block and look at the property objectively to see if anything jumps out at you. How well does your building measure up to the competition? Examine the sidewalks as you carry out your inspections. Are there any trip hazards on the sidewalks? Ensure major cracks and broken sidewalks are repaired. If the city can address the damage that is great, if not you may have to address the damage through your building's budget.

- For any construction project being done on the property, make sure workers are wearing their personal protective equipment (PPE) and practising safety. Personal protective equipment may include but is not limited to protective gear worn on the head, foot, hand or eye; any gear that protects hearing or respiration; and items like a safety vest and fall protection gear or other applicable protection. The last thing you want is a tenant calling the Ministry of Labour to shut down the work site. Also, if you see any of your staff, whether inside or outside, not wearing their PPE, point this out immediately and ensure they use it.

- If you have an outdoor pool, visit your municipal Web site and ensure your pool conforms to the standards and regulations of the city's health department. The same goes for indoor pools. Also, whether you have outsourced the care of your pool or your staff have that responsibility, a log should be kept of daily tests, weekly tests and chemicals added, as well as maintenance done such as vacuuming or backwashing. Be sure to initial the log every time you check it. Learn how to test for chemicals in the water. Once in a while, get the pool testing kit and check the water yourself in the presence of your staff or the pool attendant / lifeguard assigned by the company you have contracted to care for the pool. Your staff or the contracted staff will know that you will not tolerate any cutting of corners. Failure to maintain the pool could result in its closure by the health department.

iii. Outside Parking

- Post the recommended speed limit for the property to reduce speeding. Another option you can try is to install speed humps/bumps at various spots throughout the property to reduce speeding.

- Speed humps/bumps should be painted in the proper yellow colour or other designated colour to indicate Caution or Hump/Bump, and a sign should be posted at each speed bump. This alerts pedestrians and motorists, as well as snow removal contractors, to the presence of the speed bump.

- Curbstones should be painted. If they are not painted, they should have reflectors, which give a better outline of the roadway, especially in the dark.

- If you have a large property or community, where possible use one-way signs to control vehicular traffic flow, and post stop signs at intersections.

- Tenant parking spots must be properly numbered. Consider repainting faded parking lines and spot numbers. Spot numbers allow for better control, aid in assigning parking spots to tenants and make auditing easier.

- Be sure to address vehicles that are leaking oil. This oil can be tracked into the building and pose a challenge to keeping the building clean. Also, prolonged oil leakage can eat away and damage the pavement, resulting in potholes, which are trip hazards.

- All vehicles in the tenant parking areas must have visibly posted property parking stickers displayed, indicating they are paying for their spots and are authorized to park on the property.

- All vehicles must have a valid registration sticker. No inoperable vehicle should be on the property. The property is not a junkyard. Inoperable vehicles are places for homeless individuals to hide and take up residence. A valid registration sticker is an indication the vehicle is insured. You want to ensure that if there are accidents or damage stemming from any vehicle on property, the vehicle insurance can absorb the cost. I had two separate incidents where tenants vehicles damaged the perimeter fence. Both fences were replaced through the tenants car insurance.

- Ensure there are proper and adequate approved city/bylaw signs or other signs that are visible and strategically posted indicating the following:

  o   Fire Access Route / Emergency Access Route

- o   Tenant Parking
- o   Visitor Parking
- o   Garbage Route – No Parking
- o   Service and Contractor Vehicle Parking
- o   Employee/Staff Parking
- o   Handicapped/Disabled Parking
- o   No Trucks Allowed
- o   Stop signs and directional/one-way signs where applicable
- o   Paid Parking signs and parking meters (which must have clear instructions posted)

- There should be proper directional signs leading to the rental office if one is on the property.

- If you have a large outside parking area serving more than one building, one way to clearly separate the sections designated for each building is to use different colours to number the parking spots. All lines could be yellow or white and the spot numbering could be done in green for one building, red for another building, blue for another building, etc.—or whatever local code allows

- Use traffic mirrors in tight and narrow parking lanes or areas to increase visibility and promote safety.

- If you have steps leading from the outside parking to the underground parking, ensure those areas are clean and well lit. Any handrails should be firm, not shaking, rusting or rotting at the base or foot of the rail. Change or reinforce where necessary. There should be no flaking of paint. Hard flaking paint can cut the hand like a splinter. For health and safety reasons, flaking paint should be stripped/scraped off and the handrail repainted.

iv. Cold Weather

- Before the cold season starts, make sure your lawn sprinkler, if you have one, is winterized, meaning that all water is blown out of the lines to prevent freezing, which could ultimately damage the lines. The timer should be off and other applicable parts should be removed. This is a task you could ensure gets addressed by your landscaping contractor, if it is mentioned in the contract that they are responsible for the winterization. Staff should only winterize the sprinkler system if they are trained and local laws allow for it.

- If the temperature outside is cold and several apartments have windows opened, it could mean the heat is on too high in the building. The matter should be reported to HVAC for investigation.

- Check to see if parking lot and walkways are plowed or cleared of snow and salted. Make sure your snow removal contractor is vigilant about snow removal. After a snowfall, you should call the building to confirm that your snow removal contractor has plowed or is plowing the snow. If you are at the property, check the neighbouring/competition properties to see if they are cleared. If you have a difficult contractor who will give you any excuse for his or her failure to clear the snow at your building, you should be able to say that the contractor for the property next door was able to clear that property. But if you have to resort to this tactic, it is time to look around for a new contractor—before the next cold season. If your snow removal contractor clears only the parking lot and driveway, you should have a plan for clearing the other areas he or she is not contracted to do. Are the other areas cleared by your site staff? If so, make sure your site staff have appropriate and functioning tools and equipment, especially motorized equipment or vehicular equipment with plow, to clear snow from narrow walkways on the property. Do not neglect to clear sidewalks around the property; otherwise, you will get fined by the city. Some bylaws require snow to be cleared from sidewalks and entrances, within 24 hours after the snowfall. Ensure sidewalks and other areas are cleared within the stipulated bylaw for your region. Worse yet, you could have a slip-and-fall accident and open yourself up to a lawsuit. Clearing the snow is also practising health and safety. Make sure your staff and contractor log each time they clear the snow. This is proof you have done your due diligence and will serve as evidence should a claim be brought against you.

- If you are walking the property, look out for any black ice and have those spots salted (or use a combination of sand and salt or a mixture of de-icing materials, if the temperature is too low for the salt to melt the ice).

- Because it is impossible for the snow removal contractor to clear the snow between parked vehicles, if not included in the snow removal contract, your site staff should not forget to salt between parked vehicles or parking spots. Salting between parked vehicles help to prevent vehicle occupants from slipping when they exit their vehicles.

- Are snowbanks blocking pathway access or impeding vehicular traffic? If so, have these removed. Ensure snowbanks do not block fire hydrants on your property. Also, snow banks should not cover catch basins and drains. This allows melted snow to runoff and prevent ponding.

- No children should be playing in any snowbank, snow pile or snow mound, large or small. One precaution you can take is to post a notice or send a newsletter at the start of the colder season advising tenants not to allow their children to play in snowbanks, saying that it can be dangerous to do so. You can post a reminder in the common areas after any heavy snowfall. (*See sample Snow Safety Notice.*)

- What if you run out of spaces to put the snow? In extreme cases where you have several high mounds or high piles of snow accumulated from increased snowfall or a major blizzard, there is a strong possibility you may have to haul snow off the property. Your snow removal contractor can load the accumulated snow to a dump truck and haul the snow to a designated snow dump site. Removing mounds or piles of accumulated snow from the property can free up parking spaces, especially if tenants are paying for those parking spots. It will definitely help with curb appeal. But most importantly, it will make the parking lot accessible, eliminate any potential safety hazards such as the formation of black ice and help to restore the parking lot to normal operation. Review your snow removal contract regarding the cost of hauling snow and then speak with your snow removal contractor as well as your AM. Treat this as a health and safety hazard and address it with urgency.

- Look around for icicles on balcony edges, and have these removed if possible. If you are not able to remove them, use caution tape to block off walkways to these area(s) and post a notice to warn of the overhead danger.

- The winter can be quite windy; therefore, make sure any recycle bins that are outside are secured and not blowing all over the property or on the road.

- If you have used asphalt patch as a temporary repair for potholes, if not installed properly, there is a strong possibility the patch may get uprooted or become loose when the snow removal contractor plows the parking lot.

- At the end of the cold season as the snow melts, be sure to arrange an extensive winter cleanup of the grounds. This will clean the grounds of any debris that may have been buried in the snow.

- Keep a cold season weather log, winter log or snow log. Whatever your company calls it, this log shows the weather conditions during the cold season for snow, freezing rain, winds, temperature, etc. Check this log when at the building to confirm it is being completed properly. Make sure it is not completed into the future. Some staff will check their smartphones for the forecast for the week or the day and transfer all that information to the log. An example of this is the staff checking the log at the start of the day and then recording the temperature for the entire day, including the evening, or for the entire week. How can that be accurate when the afternoon and evening have not yet come? Bear in mind that weather forecasts are predictions that are subject to change. If there is a slip-and-fall accident, the insurance company will most likely request a copy of the log to see what weather conditions were like and what actions your staff took to maintain safety. That is why it is very important to document where on the property was cleared of ice or snow and how much salt or salt mixture was applied. To drive this point home, you should, if possible, do a call-in with the insurance company your property uses at one of your staff meetings closer to the cold weather season. The call must be planned ahead of time. That way you can speak to the relevant person. This will allow your staff to hear about and understand the importance of the log and why it is necessary for them to prepare it properly, free of falsification.

NB: Your snow removal contractor should document in their own records, every time they clear snow on your property.

Snow Safety Notice

We are now entering the cold season where we can expect to receive varying measurements of snow. As a caution, we would like to remind residents that our snow removal contractor will be on-site from time to time to clear the property of snow. Please proceed with caution when our contractors are on-site, and advise your children to do the same.

For safety reasons, please do not allow your children to play in any snowbank, snow pile or snow mound. While this may look like fun to your children, they can injure themselves. Note also that the snow is mixed with dirt, debris and salt, which can potentially cause harm. In addition, children can fall into the snow piles or slide into vehicular traffic.

Let us enjoy the cold weather by practising safety. Thank you for your co-operation.

Sincerely,

[Name]
Property Manager

E. Entering the Building

When you complete the external inspection aspect of your visit, park and proceed to the rental or building office. If you have supplies to deliver, you may call your staff and have them meet you to collect those items. When you leave the vehicle, your eyes should still be glancing around the property for anything that requires repair and/or correction and for anything that you can commend your staff on. Your ears should be alert to communication over the two-way radio with your staff, if your buildings use two-way radios. Also listen out for tenants complaining, as some may not know who you are. You may have major repairs and upgrades being done in the building, and some tenants in passing may comment on their frustration or the inconvenience of the repair process. Do not take their comments personally. Make adjustments to the general notice if possible, or talk with staff and external contractors about any comments related to the project you heard in passing, so the necessary adjustments can be made to reduce the disruption to tenants.

As you enter the building, look for ways to further enhance the curb appeal and marketability.

- Some tenants have a habit of allowing their dogs to pee immediately outside the building, especially at the entrance door. The smell from this can be stifling and unwelcoming. Be sure to install No Pee signs in those areas. In addition to the signs, a general notice should be sent out informing pet owners not to allow their dogs to pee at the front of the building.

As you enter the vestibule and/or lobby, ensure the following:

- Appropriate designated signs applicable to the building and the company are posted and in excellent condition.
- All light shades are free from bugs, and not cracked or missing.
- Any handicap door opener installed for the entrance door to the building is working properly. The door should not open with any squeaking noise. The push button/push plate switch or automated device for touchless entry should be firmly intact, not loose or shaky. The door should close softly.
- The fire panel box/board, usually located in the vestibule or lobby, is cleared of any trouble signals or sounds, and should read NORMAL if all is well. Report any beeping sound, as this could mean there is a fault or defect somewhere that must be addressed. Any trouble signal or beeping sound should be brought to the attention of the maintenance staff the minute you see the staff. Find out what is being done to address the distress or trouble noise. Is the life safety specialist (LSS) and/or the fire equipment contractor aware of the trouble, fault or distress? Also, when you check the fire logbook, see if the distress is recorded there.
- The fire safety plan box is surface-mounted and padlocked. From time to time, you should check the box to ensure the contents mandated by the fire code are in the box. The required contents may include tagged keys to all utility/service rooms, an approved fire safety plan for the building and extra/replacement unlocked padlocks. Note well, if you have changed out keys to any of the utility/service rooms, you must also update those keys in the fire safety plan box. Note well that all utility/service rooms must be labelled; otherwise, those tagged

keys are ineffective. Some properties will have the box in the vestibule or lobby. However, the fire department usually has information on how far from the main entrance the box should be, as well as how high it should be mounted.

- During the cold weather, the vestibule is heated. If the area is heated by baseboard radiators, are you able to see under the radiators? That area must be clean and free of dirt buildup such as trash, hair and/or fur, and sand or salt. Clean radiators increase air flow and help the unit to operate efficiently.
- The intercom is working. Sometimes tenants will post a note to state their buzzer is not working. Investigate what is being done about the buzzer repair for such tenants.
- Weather-appropriate mats are in place, are clean and are in good condition, not curling at the ends or buckling/rippling.

Always greet your staff by name. Ask how things are going. Compliment or commend them on the cleanliness of the building or even the smallest thing well done. You could also compliment them on handling the formerly angry tenant who finally got her taps fixed and is now happy. Greet your cleaning staff and commend them on the clean glass, fresh-smelling lobby, nicely or stocked cleaning cart. Also ensure all staff are wearing the appropriate uniform. If uniforms are worn, make sure they are clean, not torn or washed out. If your company does not use uniforms, make sure staff are not dressed in pajamas or anything revealing. On your way to the office, look around in the lobby for things that may have been missed by the cleaning staff, such as:

- cobwebs
- scattered mail or flyers
- unauthorized posted notices or old notices that need to be removed

By doing this, you help to train your staff on the standards. They will begin to think the way you think and see things through your eyes. Always commend them for things you have pointed out and they have addressed. They will welcome your visits rather than dread them.

F. Rental Office Visit

When you get to the rental office, greet any staff or tenants you see using their names. Remembering and using tenants' or residents' names will make them feel special and cause them to develop a deep sense of respect for you. If there are no tenants present in the office, a little clean, non-offensive humour can be used to break the ice. A great question to ask that provides all the answers is "How is your day going?" If the respondent says "good" or "bad," ask what is making it that way. Glance around and check if things are out of place. If you are in the office, is there a standard set up to the office and is it being followed? Is the office clean and organized? Is the garbage bin overflowing? If there is a DVR system, check the monitor/screen to see if all the cameras are working. If the cameras are not all working, find out what is being done to address any camera that is malfunctioning.

What is the atmosphere of the office? Are the staff members getting along? Do your staff look happy? Ask what the others are doing. Even if you know, still ask; sometimes your staff may not be where you think they should be, because of different and legitimate circumstances related to the job. Or your staff could be hiding. This kind of behaviour will be addressed under the chapter titled Staffing.

If the property is a community setting, you may want to speak with the building managers or the staff covering the office. To maximize the use of your time, ask to see key staff in any secondary office or room where you can go over things without being interrupted. Thank the staff for meeting with you and get a sense of how their day is going. Are they having issues with contractors or other staff members? Proceed with anything noted on your way from the time your eyes made contact with the building(s) to the time you sat down with the staff. If you are doing a formal building inspection on a form or an electronic device, you can keep it until you have completed the inspection, after which you can leave a copy with the building manager or site staff. Your discussion should note the different aspects of the building inspection. The following inspection areas sum up the operation of the property and dictate how the budget is allocated:

- building structure and exterior curb appeal
- landscaping and grounds
- Systems and routines—cleaning, renting, rent collection, all safety logs
- special or capex projects
- mechanical/utility rooms—HVAC, fire systems, elevators, boiler, electrical, workshops or workstations
- vacant and ready apartments, occupied apartments and apartments being repositioned/renovated or repaired
- tenant requests and concerns
- common areas, including amenities

Pull out your folder for the building and review with the building manager anything you require clarification for or an update on. Discuss the following things with your staff:

1. Any items you delivered to the rental office. These may include:

    a. urgent notices that must be posted
    b. corrected leases/tenancy agreements
    c. letters to be delivered to tenants

2. The vacancy status. Which apartments is the rental office having issues renting? Make sure you go and see any such apartments if entry is possible.

3. Contractors on the property. Are there any issues? Is the project going well?

4. The status of the accounts receivable (AR). Staff should show proof of effort to collect outstanding rent. Depending on the software system your company uses, the rent roll may indicate if tenants have a zero balance or any outstanding balance. If you use a mobile device to access these records, more power to you. Sometimes, poor Internet connection

or signal may restrict you from accessing any information electronically. Hence it is always best to have a hard copy of the current month's rent roll with you for each of your properties. Ask the building manager or whomever you meet with to show you all log books related to Accounts Receivable (AR). Some of these are but not limited to:

a. **Receipt Book**

Your receipt book is your tracking system of the rents, amenities and products or services tenants are paying for directly, instead of through any preauthorized payments. Periodically review the receipt book for any of the following:

   i. Check the carbon or stub copy that is left in the receipt book(s) for consistency, regarding sequence with the receipt numbers and dates.
   ii. Check if the items that were charged and paid for, are authorized by the company and what methods of payments were given.
   iii. To ensure accuracy, check the receipt book against the corresponding log books.
   iv. Post a visible sign inside the rental office asking tenants to request a receipt for all their transactions. A receipt is proof that a tenant has paid. This also forces your staff to record the transaction. If the transaction is not recorded, it may be difficult for you to detect if any fraudulent activities are taking place.
   v. Periodically check the setup of the office including drawers and cabinets. This will reveal if any secondary unapproved receipt books are being used to record "under the table" transactions. In most cases, these transactions are usually paid using cash that is not handed over to the company. If you find any such receipt books, take them with you and report the matter to your AM or branch manager immediately for further investigation.

b. **Parking Log**

When you go to inspect the parking garage, take the parking log and rent roll with you. The parking log should show the following for each tenant:

   i. Apartment number
   ii. Parking spot number
   iii. Tenant's full name
   iv. Make and model vehicle
   v. Vehicle plate number

Randomly pick four or so vehicles. Match the parking spot of those randomly selected vehicles to tenants' names and the apartment numbers on the log. This information should correspond to the rent roll to confirm if the tenant is paying for parking and how much they are paying. If you come across one that is not paying for parking, flag that vehicle for investigation and contact the tenant yourself. You may choose to contact the tenant the same day or at a later date. This will tell you if any transaction is being done off the books. You can even request a parking audit or update the resident information.

For accuracy, you can coordinate the parking audit with a staff from another location. That staff can either be within your portfolio or come from one of your colleague's portfolio. If you see patterns of inconsistencies that goes against company standards such as cash transaction or tenants not paying when they should be paying, probe deeper until you get to the bottom. While the inconsistencies could be due to lack of training, verify if that is the fact. That is why you check to confirm, so corrective measures can be taken. Wherever the investigation leads, take the appropriate action(s) swiftly.

c. **Social Room**

Review the log sheet for the social room to confirm the last used date and the name of the tenant(s) who used the room. You should also confirm the date the room was cleaned. Once they have confirmed that the room was cleaned, check for the following when you go to inspect the social room:

i. Is there leftover food inside the fridge?
ii. Telltale signs the party room was used are, food on top of the stove or food inside the oven.
iii. Is there garbage in the wastebin? The type of garbage in the wastebin will give you an idea of the kind of party or event that was held.
iv. Are the tables folded away or are they folded out and setup? If they are out, do they have spills?

d. **Guest Suite**

Whether your guest suite is paid or unpaid for each occupancy, be sure to check it periodically when you are at the building for cleanliness and unlawful occupancy. Know and understand the cleaning check list or routine for the guest suite and it will tell you how well the suite is being cleaned and cared for. First, confirm if the suite is occupied or scheduled to be occupied. Before you inspect the guest suite, confirm when the last guest/visitor left and the date the suite was last cleaned. Once confirmed, check for the following signs as evidence the suite/apartment was illegally used/occupied and not cleaned:

i. Check the pillows for facial hair. This will tell if the pillow was slept on.
ii. Pull back sheet and check for wrinkles and waves. These tell if the bed was slept in.
iii. Check bathroom for facial hair on floor.
iv. Check tub surround and bath tub for scum marks from soap.
v. Lift the toilet seat(s) for traces of urine or bowel movement. Glove should be worn to lift the toilet seat.

5. Whether your signature is required for work specification sheets to be sent off to contractors. If so, sign those sheets now, if you are aware of the scope of work and you are in agreement.

6. Follow-up on orders that you have approved with suppliers or contractors but that the building has not yet received.

7. Logbooks (fire, preventative maintenance, boiler room, snow log if in cold season). Ask to see these and check that they have been completed. Make sure they are not completed into the future; otherwise, you'll have a case of falsification of records. If you have a case of falsification of records, this is also an indication that the staff are not following their set routine and are slacking off while on the job. Make sure dates are not missed in the logbooks. If dates are missed, let your staff know that incomplete or falsified logbooks are unacceptable. *Maintain a policy of zero tolerance*, and be very firm and professional about these zero tolerances. Confirm your discussion in a letter with the staff in question and serve that letter the next time you visit the building. As a side discussion, let the staff know the seriousness of such logs. Bring to the staff's attention that with any accident involving people's lives such as plane, bus or ship accidents, and with any apartment fires, the first things investigators usually ask to see are the logbooks for maintenance and so forth. Investigators check to see if records were maintained and who, if anyone, should be held criminally responsible. By doing your due diligence, you will ensure that the person held responsible will *never be you*. Always confirm you have seen the logbooks by initialling and dating the logs you checked. Highlight any discrepancy and take pictures as evidence and take the necessary corrective (retraining) and disciplinary action. The disciplinary letter is addressed in the chapter titled Staffing under the heading Staff Readjustment and Discipline. Systems are designed and implemented to protect everyone. If you always do your part, you will spare yourself any heartache and embarrassment.

Before you start any occupied unit inspection, ask if there is anything you need to be notified about or if the staff need help with anything. Make note of whatever is brought to your attention. State what assistance you will give and the time frame in which you intend to complete the task. Gather any Notices of Entry for occupied unit inspections and then proceed with the unit inspections.

G. Interior Building Inspection

i. Prevacate and Apartment Inspection for Turnover Units

When a tenant gives notice to vacate, whether proper notice (60 days or less as per the RTA or a mutually agreed upon vacate date) or improper notice, always arrange to inspect the unit. Even if you have trained your staff to do the inspections, do not leave this totally up to them. Also, any inspection you do at the property should, when possible, be done with a staff member from the building. It is always good to take your building manager or superintendent along with you. Use this opportunity to continually train the eyes and thought processes of your staff, indicating what they should be looking for to prepare the apartment for the next tenant and what they need to improve on regarding their inspection. This training will come in handy at times when you may not be able to inspect the apartments. As you enter each apartment, keep in mind two key areas inside the apartment: the kitchen and the bathroom. From my observation and experience, when these areas are in relatively good condition and pest-free, the apartment tends to rent faster. And interestingly, it gives you more latitude to push the rent beyond the asking or market price.

Kitchen

The focal point of any kitchen is its cabinets and countertop. The condition of the cabinets and countertops will determine the speed at which the apartment is rented. If you are on a tight budget, then safety should take precedence over cost.

- Cabinets
  - Cabinets that are falling off the wall should, for safety reasons, be neatly repaired or replaced. If the shell or frame of the cabinet is good, then you can get away with doing new facing, such as installing new doors and knobs. Are shelves warping? If so, reinforce them.
  - For drawers that are out of alignment, you may need new drawer banks. Knobs or handles should not be missing or loose. A new set of knobs can even make the cabinets look more refined.
  - Taps and faucets should not be loose or leaking at the joints. Calcifying at joints is a sign of leakage.
  - Countertops should be free of burn marks, and not peeling or bumpy from water damage.
  - If the cabinets are stained, can they be painted with a special paint to give them a fresh new look?

- Appliances
  - Appliances must be in good to excellent working order, not rusting, and with no loose gaskets or rubber. Racks, where used, should also be in good condition.
  - The stove should not be falling apart, rusted or missing knobs.
  - Clocks should be working.
  - If you can see the oven insulation material, it is time to dispose of the stove.
  - All appliances applicable to the apartment should be working, clean and free from offensive odour.

Bathroom

- Tub surround
  - There should be no bowing out of shower tiles. Bowing or bulging tiles is an indication that water is penetrating the grout. In a matter of time, the tiles will fall off, creating a safety issue. The sooner you address this problem, the less it will impact the cost. In some cases, the wall may have to be rebuilt before the tub surround can be completed.
  - What is the condition of the taps or shower faucets? If the tub surround is good but the taps are dated, you will have to replace the taps, which may mean breaking a few tiles. In that case, it may be beneficial to do a new tub surround, instead of using different colour tiles to make a quilt-like pattern on the tub surround. This kind of finish can

look very cheap and tacky and turn potential tenants away. In addition, the new grout will highlight the old grout, giving an unsightly finish. Another factor to consider when authorizing a tub surround is that new taps or faucets should always be used. If you reuse the old faucet in hopes of saving money, this could cost you in the long run. If those pipes go bad, you must break the new tiles to gain access. Since tile patterns are constantly changing, it may be challenging to match the existing tiles. A partial tub surround price is sometimes similar to the price of a full tub surround. Therefore, it may be better to do a full tub surround.

- Shower curtain rod
  - The shower curtain rod should be free from rust, and not warped or broken.
  - If you are only replacing the rod, try to get something similar to the old rod. If you change the style, you run the risk of not lining up the new rod with the screw holes in the wall from the previous rod. An example of this would be from replacing a straight shower curtain rod with a curved shower curtain rod. The curved shower curtain installation is installed more inward toward the tiles, whereas the straight rod is installed more outward. If you cannot line up the holes, it can be very unsightly.

- Bathtub
  - The bathtub should not be peeling or rusting. If it is, it can make for a tricky call or decision for the following reasons:
    - If the tub is peeling, you could reglaze it and address the peeling. The problem is most likely to reoccur down the road.
    - If the tub is rusted and posing a potential leak, you could install a new tub. This new tub is going to create a domino effect and affect the existing tub surround. In some cases, if you can match the tiles, you may have to replace the first row above the bathtub. After replacing the tiles at the first row, the grouting will not match.
    - If you cannot match the tiles, you may have to resort to a new tub surround, installing new faucets and/or installing tiles on the floors to address any gap between the new tub and the floor.

- Vanity and sink
  - The vanity and sink should have no rust marks or cracks.
  - Taps/faucets should not be shaking or leaking.
  - Laminate on vanity tops should not be peeling, broken or missing any pieces.

Bedrooms

What are the selling features or focal point in the empty bedrooms? It could be the large size of the rooms, the large closets or the windows, the view from the windows, or the balcony leading from the bedroom. If it is the windows, make sure the walls and trims around the windows are in excellent condition. If it is the closet, rods and shelves should be in excellent condition, as should the closet doors.

Closets

- These should be painted.
- Shelves should be straight and not warping.
- If the closets have rods, they should be in good condition, not rusting, twisted or warped.
- Any doors on tracks should be in proper working condition.

Lighting and electrical

Lighting, even though simple, is very important and should never be overlooked. When you have proper and adequate lighting inside the apartment, it enhances the other features of the apartment. Brighter, whiter light bulbs give the appearance of a larger room.

- Lighting should not be dated. If you have dated light fixtures and are unable to upgrade them, make sure they are clean and have the correct wattage bulbs.
- Always use whatever lighting fixtures that are standard to your company or approved for your building.
- Make sure the lighting fixtures used are consistent in the apartment.

Electrical

- If you must remove the fuse box and install a breaker, be prepared to do possible cosmetic repairs to the wall around the breaker box. There is also a possibility that the upgrade must be inspected by Electrical Safety Authority (ESA).
- Electrical faceplates are inexpensive. Changing them out in the apartment can make a big difference.
- Missing faceplates should be installed with urgency before the tenant moves out. If the tenant removed them, the plates should be reinstalled for safety reasons.
- Sometimes tenants will change out the faceplates to their liking. They must return those removed. If they do not have them, it doesn't make sense to charge the tenants for a few cents' worth of materials. On the other hand, if there are many missing faceplates that will cost a lot to replace, you can make that judgement call whether to charge or not to charge.
- Do you need to do any upgrades in the apartment such as adding ground fault circuit interrupters (GFCIs or GFIs)? Some older buildings may not have them, but the savvy tenant usually will demand them. After all, one cannot be too safe.
- Be prepared for surprises. Some tenants will have altered the electrical wiring inside the apartment to their preferences. In one case, a tenant altered the wiring to accommodate a washing machine and dryer inside one of the closets. The appliances, unauthorized as per the lease, were hidden inside the closets and were never spotted during any form of suite inspection. They were discovered during outgoing inspection after the tenant had died. The cost to remove the old wiring and bring the area back to its original condition had to be absorbed by the building's operations budget.

- Are speaker boxes and hard-wired smoke detectors altered? If they are, call your fire equipment company immediately and get them repaired. The tenant does not have the right to request or demand that this kind of repair be completed when he or she moves out. No one has the right to compromise on safety. This is a piece of life safety equipment that must be working at all times according to fire code. Take pictures and add the repair cost to the tenant's move-out charges. Try to get the tenant to pay the cost before moving out. You can discuss the matter with your legal department to find out if you can end the notice sooner than the vacate date or let the notice to vacate run its course. Also, make a special note on this apartment. Sometimes tenants who give notice to vacate will change their minds and want to stay by rescinding/withdrawing their notice. If you have one of those tenants, you are not obligated by law to accept that notice of rescind/withdrawal.

Walls and ceilings

If walls are stained with nicotine throughout the apartment or have grease on them, especially inside the kitchen, and your lease/tenancy agreement mentions anything about this condition, be sure to follow through on it and charge the vacating tenant for damages. In your assessment of the wall condition, take into consideration the age of the apartment. Is this normal wear and tear? If it is, you cannot charge for it. Also, regarding any damages, are there work orders or service requests to address any of these damages, and if so, did your staff complete them?

- Check walls and ceilings for major cracks and plaster blowouts or malicious damage. I remember inspecting an apartment that was vacated only to find that the tenant had made a huge hole in the wall of a closet to spy on other tenants. This was repaired immediately. Note carefully that the severity of the damage, including cracks and blowouts, will sometimes determine the contractor who gets the job to do the repairs. Make sure the contractor who is given the job can work with a time-sensitive cutoff date. Unforeseen major repairs, if not completed on time, may affect the move-in or rent date of the apartment. If this ends up being the case, the move-in date for the tenant may have to be changed and the rent amount prorated. An adjustment in the rent amount, including parking, storage or other applicable amenities affiliated with the lease or tenancy agreement for that month, should be refunded to the new tenant. Before you finalize the new move-in date, be sure to discuss it with the tenant. Why? For the following reasons:

  1. To find out if the new tenant is able to stay longer in his or her current location until the apartment at your property is rent ready or in a rentable condition for the new tenant.
  2. If not able to stay where he or she currently is, the new tenant may have to stay at a hotel and put his or her things temporarily in storage.
  3. The new move-in date will also affect the moving truck and the movers, the tenant's time off from work and other, personal affairs.

This is why it is very important for you to allot time in your schedule to check on the status of apartments before tenants move in. That way you can give your staff support and put pressure on contractors when necessary.

- Check also for water marks as evidence of leaks or condensation. You may have to address the root cause of the problem before painting. If the problem has been addressed and the stain is still present, the contractor should know ahead of time so he or she can apply special paint to disguise the discolouration and prevent a bleed-through.
- Once light fixtures are changed, the discolouration underneath from the old fixtures may become visible, forcing you to paint the entire ceiling.
- One coat of paint on the ceiling can create the illusion of a larger apartment
- Determine whether or not you can do partial paint jobs instead of doing full painting.
  - Depending on your tenant base, some tenants will keep their apartments in excellent condition and the apartment may not require painting. That is why it is very important for your staff to choose good tenants and educate the tenants when they view the apartment, as well as upon lease signing and moving in, how they should treat the apartment. Always ask yourself, *Would the apartment look any different if it were painted?* I have been inside vacating apartments where the tenant stayed a year and did not hang a single picture. Hence, the walls had no nail holes and were clean. That apartment was not painted once the tenant left, which saved money allotted for painting on the building's budget. Keep in mind also that even if the apartment may not require paint, sometimes a quick paint job eliminates offensive odour.
  - If you notice the vacating apartment has custom colours, and if the walls are in excellent condition, give the staff the option to rent the apartment with the current custom colour "as is". Of course, the custom colour would have to be carefully noted on any incoming inspection report and the new tenant should sign to that fact. To enhance the paint colour, you can approve to have the doors and trims painted in your company's standard apartment colour.
  - Always take your tenant base/type into consideration before considering any partial paint job. Sometimes one simple coat of paint is sufficient to give the look and smell of a new apartment.

Flooring

- Carpets should be clean and free from fraying, wear and tear, and pet odour. If the previous tenant had pets, such as dogs, it may be wise to replace the carpet. A professional cleaning will only mask the smell of pets, which will resurface and linger after a while.
- When you change out any carpet, be sure to change the underpadding as well. Underpadding traps urine, feces and anything else unpleasant.
- Use transition strips of the appropriate width where necessary to address fraying carpets at entrances.
- Assess the entire apartment and determine if partial replacements can be done. Sometimes you can replace the carpet in one room instead of in all the rooms.

- Tiles and grout should be cleaned. Tiles should not be loose or lifting up.
- If asbestos tiles require removal, this should be done by trained and certified contractors.
- Any vinyl composition tiles (VCT), if used, should be stripped and waxed to accentuate the apartment.
- If you have plank flooring, make sure the planks are not lifting or stained.
- All baseboards and quarter round should be in good to excellent condition. Paint where necessary to enhance the appearance of the apartment.

Doors, trims and baseboards

- All doors must be hung properly, or slide well if they are on tracks.
- Damaged doors should be replaced, not patched or nailed to hold them in place. This latter approach makes your company look cheap. Just replace the doors.
- Look for punch holes in the doors. The holes are evidence of aggressive activity resulting in destruction to the property. This could be the result of children playing or domestic violence.

Be prepared if the tenant denies having caused the damage or says that the apartment was in that condition before he or she moved in. In such a case, check the tenant's inspection report, completed at the time he or she took possession of the apartment, for any notes about the door. Take into consideration the staff you had at the time the tenant moved in. Are or were those staff known for making proper notes? What is the character of that staff? If you know it is/was not good, you may have to give the benefit of the doubt to the tenant.

- Painting and changing out the door handles is another way to enhance the appearance of the apartment. The apartment will be painted anyway, so include the doors, trims and baseboards. These will make the apartment pop or stand out.

- What is the condition of the apartment entry door and door closure? If the door is damaged, the fire-rating integrity may be compromised; hence the door must be replaced. Since the turnaround time for these fire-rated doors can be lengthy, have your staff place the order asap. Sometimes, depending on your supplier, doors can take six to eight weeks to be delivered. Adjust or replace the door closure with urgency. Remember this is part of the life safety mechanism for the building.

- Missing baseboard radiator covers should be located or, if unable to be found, ordered and reinstalled.

Windows and mirrors

- Replace and charge back any damaged mirrors or windows.
- Screen door and balcony doors should be intact and operational.
- Screens for windows should be repaired where possible or replaced with new.

- Are there safety devices or restrictors installed on all windows? Even if windows lead to a balcony, some jurisdictions may require that the devices or restrictors be installed. If not, install them before the vacating tenant leaves.

Health and safety repairs regarding the current tenancy

Before you leave the apartment, note any immediate safety concerns that must be addressed. If you spot any deficiencies, get these things taken care of as soon as possible. If the tenant is home, you can ask him or her about the deficiencies and find out if he or she has submitted work order for the repairs. If the answer is yes, find the work order(s) and make preparations to get the task(s) done. If the tenant is going to or will be taken to the LTB, he or she will find a way to use any deficiencies against you. Give the tenant nothing to stand on or to use to his or her advantage at the LTB. Make any repair(s) without delay.

Units with foul odour

At some point, you will have units that reek with odour to the point where the unit cannot be inspected. In a case such as this, the apartment should be cleaned up once you have legal possession of it. The cleanup can be done by external contractors or your staff, if your staff have the proper personal protective equipment. Apartments that are in this condition will require all carpets and underpadding to be removed and replaced. The floor may require washing and then sealing with the use of a special paint to alleviate the smell.

Check the apartment for any kind of pest. If there are bedbugs, the apartment should be treated, even if the vacating tenant is still living inside the apartment. Treating the apartment will prevent any bugs from being carried in to the hallway and elevator when the tenant is moving out.

ii. Common Area and Utility Rooms

There are two types of common areas, internal and external. The external common area is used or accessible by the general tenants, their occupants, their visitors, contractors, staff and other visitors to the building. These areas include the lobby, hallways, stairwells and garage. Certain aspects of the common areas, such as amenities, including laundry and other amenities, are restricted to the use of tenants and their guests. The internal common areas, such as utility rooms or mechanical rooms, are accessible only by staff and relevant contractors.

When doing an inspection of the building, it is best to start from the top of the building, preferably the roof, and work your way down to the basement. Always inspect what you expect. If you are inspecting for cleanliness, your cleaner or the person who cleans the building should be present with you. Again, use this opportunity to train the eyes and thought processes of your staff, indicating what they should be looking for or what they need to improve on regarding their cleaning.

a. Elevator Cabs

- Fans should be working, and vent covers should be free from dust.
- All lights should be working, and no bulbs should be blown. Flickering lights should be tested with new bulbs. If the light is still flickering, you should report the problem to the elevator company immediately. This could be sign of an electrical problem.
- The ceiling should be clean and free of cobwebs.
- When you enter the elevator cab, check to see if the license displayed is up-to-date. Sometimes the installation number written on the license is also inscribed on the wall panel where the buttons are. Check if the inscribed numbers match those on the licenses that are posted. If there are any inconsistencies, arrange with urgency to have the correct license displayed to match what is inscribed on the wall.
- Elevator walls should be clean.
- Elevator doors and doorframes should be clean.
- Elevator tracks must be clean at all times. Greater care must be taken especially in the colder weather, when salt and sand are tracked into the building. Any buildup of dirt and sometimes one small stone can affect the opening and closing of the elevator door, thus initiating a service call, which will cost you. Daily cleaning and checking as weather conditions worsen will help to keep tracks clean and clear of debris. Clean tracks help your elevator to operate efficiently.
- Any rug on the elevator floor should be in excellent condition. There should be no curling of ends or buckling of the carpet or mat to cause anyone to trip.
- Flooring should be in excellent condition. There should be no popping, shaking or shifting of tiles. If you must replace the flooring inside the elevator, replace same for same. A different type of flooring could change the weight, which may not be safe. A different weight will also require re-inspection by the Technical Standards and Safety Authority (TSSA), which will attract a cost. The floor should be deep cleaned on a regular basis as per the tenant base or type and weather conditions.
- Replace broken mirrors with same for same.
- Is there a smooth stop or does the elevator bounce, jerk or squeak? If you get complaints or experience any of these things, arrange for your elevator company and your elevator consultant to inspect and address the problem.
- When the elevator is at the lowest floor, use a flashlight to look through the opening to see inside the pit. Check to ensure the pit is dry and free of debris.
- If your tenant base is family oriented with many children, I recommend cleaning the elevator pit at least two times each year, six months apart or according to the elevator contract.

b. Elevator Room

- Steps leading to the elevator room should be in excellent condition, firm and not shaking and with no railings loose.
- The door should have a visible sign indicating Elevator Room.

- The door should be in good condition with a proper working door closing device.
- The door should be keyed to prevent free access, for example, of a mischievous tenant gaining access and wandering onto the roof.
- Lights must be working with proper wattage bulbs encased or in a cage.
- Logbooks or log sheets must be up-to-date and not missing months of inspection. If the technician does not sign the logbook, it is an indication that he or she did not show up to do the monthly inspection. Remember your staff should be reprimanded for missing dates in their logbooks. Take a picture of the log with the missing date and forward it to your area manager (AM). Determine with your AM what the course of action toward the elevator company should be. This discrepancy should also be made known to your staff. This shows there are no double standards. I had one such case where during a building inspection, after checking the elevator logbook, I saw that about two months of log reports were missing. I took a picture of the missing information and sent the picture off to the elevator company, copying my AM. In the e-mail, I stated that the missing information was a violation that should never have happened and must not be repeated. I also requested a refund of the maintenance fee for those missed months. Interestingly, a portion of the fee for both months was credited to the building's account. Hooray!
- Fire extinguishers should be in the proper locations and have up-to-date signatures of your life safety specialist (LSS) or fire equipment company.
- There should be no leakage from equipment in the room.
- Based on the type of equipment you have in your elevator room, the room may require an air conditioning unit in the summer to keep equipment cool. If one is needed, do not delay. Speak with your elevator contractor and HVAC team to determine how to proceed.
- The room should be clean and free of all items unrelated to the elevator.
- Listen for any out-of-the-ordinary noise. Contact your elevator company immediately if you hear any.
- A copy of the elevator licenses and all applicable documents required by law should be in the room.
- A working carbon monoxide (CO) detector should be installed if the room is in close proximity to the boiler room.

c. Boiler Room

Some buildings may have two or more boiler rooms, either on the rooftop, in the basement or in some other location. Each room operates a different section or zone of the building. Some of the things to look out for in the boiler room are as follows:

- The entry door should have a visible sign indicating Boiler Room.
- The door should be in excellent condition, not warped or rotted, with a properly working door closing device.
- Does the door need a paint job?
- What is the condition of the floor? Is it flaking? Does it require painting?
- There should be proper lighting.

- The boiler room should be clean and not used as a storage facility.
- There should be no leaks of any kind, such as oil or water.
- There should be no exposed or damaged electrical wiring.
- There should be a working CO detector if one is deemed necessary.
- The room should be properly ventilated. Notify your HVAC technician immediately of all abnormalities.
- Ensure that all applicable certificates are posted and logbooks are up-to-date.

d. Roof Inspection

This inspection should be done internally and externally. It includes, but is not limited, to the following:

External roof condition

- Ensure catwalks are in good condition with properly secured railings. If made from wood, there should be no loose boards or nails popping. The wood should also be free of splinters. If handrailing are made of metal and display any sign of rot, they should be replaced.
- If you have water settling or ponding, there could be a problem with your roof drain that must be addressed to prevent major leaks and repairs.
- Damaged drain covers should be replaced without delay.
- Flashing or metal sheeting used to cover joints must be in good condition. Is the flashing lifting or missing? If so, have this addressed before it creates or turns into something that is costly to repair.
- Make sure roof vents are not cracked or damaged.
- There should be no gaps between HVAC systems and the roof.
- Ensure HVAC systems/units such as fresh air intake vents are not rusting or falling apart.
- Debris should be removed.
- Shrubs or weeds should be removed without delay. That is if your roof is not a green roof.
- Ensure there are no areas with missing gravel. Missing gravel exposes the roof's membrane. The gravel helps to protect roof from elements of the weather and from potential damage when anyone walks on the roof.

Internal roof inspection

- Never rely on the tenant in the apartment immediately below the roof to inform you there is a leak from the roof. If you don't have apartments immediately below, you may have utility rooms directly below the roof. Utility rooms below the roof are better because you do not need a Notice of Entry to gain access.
- Inspect the ceiling and walls of each room directly below the roof for the following:
  o cracks and "alligatoring"
  o bulging or bowing
  o flaking or blistering of paint

- o   water stains or dark spots
- o   obvious mould or mould odour

<u>Exiting the roof and entering the building</u>

- • The door should be keyed to prevent free access, for example, of a mischievous tenant gaining access and wandering onto the roof.
- • The condition of the exit door should be firm not warped or swollen. This allows for easy opening and closing.
- • It should not require painting. Make sure the paint is in excellent condition.
- • The door must have a proper working door closing device.
- • Access to the roof should be limited to Authorized Personnel. Make sure this notice is posted at the entrance on the inside for any at that location to see. If you suspect tampering with the locks to gain entry, try installing a discreet camera to catch the culprit, and then use the applicable law to evict.
- • Examine the walls around the door for signs of water penetration, such as flaking, scaling, swollen doorframe or water stain.
- • Ensure that there is proper lighting inside (and outside for night access).
- • The handrail or guardrails at the landing should be at required or code height. Even though the height may be "grandfathered in" (exempted from the new code by way of a clause) from a safety standpoint, you may be held liable if someone falls over. Therefore, it would be wise to get your contractor to add to the rail and bring it up to the code height. Think about the domino effect of a fall:
    - o   If the fall victim is a staff member, then the claim becomes a Workplace Safety and Insurance Board (WSIB) claim.
    - o   The Ministry of Labour may have to be called in.
    - o   The fall victim will require time off from work, and you must get other staff to cover his or her workload.
    - o   Your building insurance company may have to be notified
    - o   If the fall is fatal, you will have an even greater nightmare.
    - o   You will be ordered to bring the railing up to code to prevent further falls or fatalities.

e.   *Steps and Staircases*

- • Steps should be clean (swept and mopped).
- • If your steps are painted, ensure that the paint is not fading away, stripping or crumbling. If most of the steps show similar signs of paint inadequacy as you complete the building inspection, this could be a possible capex item for painting.
- • Any uneven steps should be painted with a yellow strip or repaired.
- • Handrails should be free of mop strings, cigarette butt-out marks (some tenants "hide" in the stairwell to smoke), fur, hair and body waste (human or animal).

- All applicable signs should be posted, such as No Smoking No Vaping, along with the relevant bylaw numbers. At the very top of the steps, roof anchor drawings and signs for any utility rooms that are located on the roof should be posted.
- Handrails should not be shaking. If they are shaking, arrange with your welding contractor to have them reinforced.
- All spindles of handrails should be in place, not bent or broken.
- Floor numbers signs must be clearly displayed. You should also indicate compass point sign such as east, west, north and south. Replace any that are missing with urgency. It is important to check if your floor number signs should also be written in braille.
- All standpipes should have covers. In some buildings, plastic covers may be best to use (if local code allows), because vandals will remove brass covers and sell them as scrap metal. At one location, I noticed that all the brass caps on every floor in the stairwell had gone missing. As soon as they were replaced, they went missing again. They were later replaced immediately with plastic caps. Thankfully the plastic caps were never removed. It is believed the caps were stolen and sold as scrap metals.
- Ensure there are no obstructions in the stairwells such as shopping carts, garbage or waste. Also, no tenants or animals should relieve themselves in these areas.

f. Hallways

Exit doors, chute doors and apartment doors

- To have a better understanding of what you should look for in light of safety issues, review the chapter on Building Maintenance. It will train and sharpen your eyes and let you know what you should include in the inspection.
- Exit doors and doorframes should be free of dirt. If you open any door and see a dust mark or fuzzy mark that looks like weatherstripping, that is dirt buildup and an indication that no cleaning routine is being done.
- Push and then pull on the exit door handle to make sure the latch is working. The handle should be working too. Then open and close to confirm that the door closes softly on its own without slamming. This is an indication that the door closure mechanism is working. If there is a problem, get your staff to address it with urgency, as this is part of the building's fire safety mechanism. The same should be done for garbage room doors and chute doors.
- Make sure no exit door is wedged open.
- The doors to each apartment should be clean and properly labelled with the apartment number, uniform in sign style, size and positioning (be it to the left, centred or to the right. Wherever you place the labels, placement should be consistent).
- Thresholds should be clean and in excellent condition, not broken or worn. Replace any worn and damaged threshold whether tile, concrete or wood.
- Sometimes only a certain part at the bottom of the exit door or chute door gets dirty. Instead of constantly repainting, you should try installing metal or plastic kickplates on each of these doors. Whatever you choose, be consistent throughout the building if you choose to use them elsewhere.

- Make sure the hallway is free from any form of obstructions. I remember doing a building inspection and observing an extension cord leading from one apartment to another apartment. I thought it was contractors who were using the extension cord because one of the apartments was vacant (this shows the importance of knowing your vacancy report). When I investigated, I learned that the tenant next door to the vacant apartment had no hydro and was using an extension cord to supply hydro to their apartment from the vacant apartment. That tenant was warned and told not to repeat the activity. The incident was documented and added to the tenant's file. That vacant door was then locked and keyed by the staff. I advised the staff to keep an eye on the vacant apartment. Interestingly, a few days afterward, the staff discovered that the tenant had crawled over the balcony and gained access to the vacant apartment again. This was on the 14th floor. The police were called. They went to the vacant apartment and unplugged the cord. The tenant had left the door of the vacant apartment unlocked. When the tenant in question realized the cord was unplugged, the tenant opened the door of the vacant apartment, only to find two police officers waiting for them with folded arms and serious looks on their faces. The look of shock was an understatement. Since the tenant was experiencing financial difficulties, no charges were pressed. Instead an occurrence number was written. We avoided going to court, which would have been too long and drawn out. The outstanding rent was enough to evict the tenant, which was later done. Because we did not know how long the hydro to this tenant's apartment was disconnected, I had to call the hydro company to ascertain that information and avoid any reinspection and or reconnection fee(s).

Other obstructions to be on the lookout for are shopping carts, baby buggies and doorway mats. You can post signs at the entrance of the building stating No Shopping Carts Allowed. To avoid sending mixed messages, do not allow your staff to use these shopping carts as their tool carts or cleaning carts. If your staff are using shopping carts as tool carts, your signs stating No Shopping Carts Allowed will mean nothing to the tenants. The underlying issue that you as the property manager should see is that your staff members need tool carts or cleaning carts. Therefore, you should order the carts from the appropriate supplier. I remember a location where the tenants would leave the shopping carts in the hallways and stairwells. I called the stores whose names were displayed on the shopping carts and was repeatedly told by the managers that they allowed customers to use the carts because not everyone drove or could afford a cab/taxi. They further stated they had a contractor who drove around the different properties in the area to collect the carts. I emphasized the hazards the carts were causing, and the managers said the carts were being picked up. Realizing I was getting nowhere with this issue, I asked a few scrap metal contractors who frequented one of my properties if they would remove some shopping carts that were left on the property. The contractor informed me he could not touch any of the shopping carts unless I gave him a letter stating the shopping carts were a fire hazard in the building and should be removed from the property. The contractor also cautioned me to first write a letter to the store(s) that owned the shopping carts. If the store(s) failed to respond to the letter, then I could give the scrap metal contractor a letter permitting him to remove the carts as scrap metals. *See the sample letter Shopping Cart Letter to Store Owner(s)*, which could be used to convey the concerns stemming from the shopping carts. Letters regarding buggies and doormats are dealt with in the chapter titled Tenant Complaints and Concerns, under the heading Sample Letters Sent to Tenants for Violating the Lease.

Shopping Cart Letter to Store Owner(s)

I am the property manager of [name and location of property]. I am writing to seek your assistance regarding a serious concern we are currently experiencing at our property that could result in injury or even death if not addressed. Our buildings have been inundated with many of your shopping carts used by several of our tenants who shop at your establishment.

These carts, after used to transport the goods purchased at your establishment, are left all over the property of the apartment building. Even though we have posted several signs at the entrance of the building stating No Shopping Carts Allowed, some tenants have disregarded these signs and have left shopping carts in the hallways. Some even try to hide them in the stairwells after they have delivered the goods to their apartments. Shopping carts when left in these locations become a fire hazard. They are potential obstructions that can restrict the escape from a fire or prevent the fire department or other first responders from accessing a fire or other emergency should one occur.

Our company is very safety-conscious and values the life of everyone. We are asking you to please implement measures at your establishment that will prevent these shopping carts from leaving your property. We have observed that some establishments have installed electronic locks embedded in the wheels of shopping carts called "Smart Wheels." These wheels will collapse or lock when they go beyond a certain boundary. This completely disables the cart and prevents it from moving. We strongly urge you to explore this option or something similar that will prevent the shopping carts from leaving your property and keep them from ending up inside our buildings.

Please inform us by [date] of the measures you will be taking regarding our very serious concern. If we do not hear from you by the time specified, you will leave us no choice but to give our scrap metal contractor written authorization to remove *all* shopping carts from our property as scrap metals, as they are potential fire hazards.

We look forward to working with you to resolve this serious concern in a timely and amicable way.

Regards,

[Name]
Property Manager

cc: [Area Manager]

of the lease and use of the common areas should be addressed. Do not attack the tenant's children in the letter, as this could possibly be viewed as a human rights violation or claim. *See the sample letter Children Playing in the Hallway* in the chapter titled Tenants Complaints and Concerns, under the heading Sample Letters Sent to Tenants for Violating the Lease/Tenancy Agreement.

For tenants with muddy boots and dirty bicycles or scooters, follow the trail to their apartments and send these tenants letters about the mess they make in the hallway. Insist that they comply with helping to keep the building clean. Clearly state that if they fail to comply, you will have the floor cleaned by your cleaning contractor and will send the tenant the bill. Your concern and quick action shows your staff that they have your support and you are willing to help them in their effort to maintain cleanliness of the building. Another thing not to overlook on the building inspection is the presence of offensive odour in the hallway. An unusual smell from any apartment should be investigated with a valid 24-Hour Notice of Entry and acted on based on the findings. Always try to get the tenant to remove the source of the smell.

g. Basement Level

Basement hallways can be hard to maintain, especially in the winter and when it rains. If the floor is painted, sometimes it can look tacky or unsightly and be harder to keep clean. Tiled basement hallways aid in the cleaning process. Regular and consistent cleaning of tiles prevents buildup and gives a clean and well-maintained appearance. Full-length mats and runners act as a buffer and reduce dirt, grease and grime tracked in from any underground garage. Upgrading the basement floor from painted floor or vinyl composition tile (VCT) to ceramic tile is another project to add to your capex wish list.

If you have excess flaking or crumbling of basement walls, speak with your construction and property standards department to see how best to reduce or eliminate moisture. Always support your concerns with pictures and follow up to see what is causing the wall to flake or crumble. Whatever the property standards department recommends to fix the problem could be an item to add to your capex wish list. You should also discuss the recommendation(s) with your AM.

Some utility rooms, such as the sprinkler room, generator room, electrical room, boiler room, workshop, pool pump room and general building storage rooms, tend to be in the basement. Also located at the basement level are amenities such as laundry room, storage locker, exercise room, social or party room, guest suite, and cinema room or game room. Periodically check utility rooms, including common areas such as hallways inside storage rooms, for items. Always inspect what you expect. The best way to master an inspection is to look for tasks on the cleaning checklist that must be done. The cleaning checklist will show if routines are being completed. If routines are not being done, it will manifest in the buildup of dust, grime, grease, litter, offensive smell and things being out of place (showing lack of organization). Never let any part of your building get to this level. These are signs of neglect. Sometimes building conditions may reveal that you are understaffed or that there is sickness or internal conflict among staff. Whatever is causing the building to look neglected, always persist and investigate until you find the root cause of the problem.

Your regular inspection with the cleaning checklist in mind and with controlled firmness on standards sends a clear message to your staff and tenants that you have consistent policies that are not up for compromise. Check for the following when you are in the basement hallway:

- All rooms or doors should be labelled. There should also be directional signs to help people find rooms located at this level.
- Doors should be in excellent condition, not rotted and with no peeling of paint. Replace any doors that are in poor condition, or add them to your capex wish list project.
- Where possible install doors with windows leading to stairwells, and certain amenity rooms to promote safety.
- High-traffic doors should have kickplates to reduce scratch and kick marks, normally found at the bottom of the door.

h. Sprinkler Room

- Proper signage should be installed, including a sign stating Sprinkler Room and another stating Authorized Personnel Only.
- The door must be accessible by key to keep out unauthorized persons.
- The room should have proper lighting.
- The room should be clean and not used as storage.
- The pressure gauge reading should be at required level.
- There should be a spare equipment kit with the following: two or more sprinkler heads and a wrench.

i. Electrical Room

- Enter the room only if there is no High Voltage sign posted on the door.
- Ensure there is proper signage indicating Electrical Room and a sign stating Authorized Personnel Only.
- The door must be accessible by key to keep out unauthorized persons.
- The room should be well lit.
- The room should be clean and not used as storage.
- In the room should be a fire extinguisher with an up-to-date signature.
- Do not touch anything inside the room. If you see electrical panels or breaker boxes without coverings or blank brackets, get the appropriate electrical contractor to install what is missing. Do not send your staff to do this in order to save on cost. This kind of work is out of their league and could be dangerous.

No fire door should be wedged open. Fire-rated doors are expensive and should be well maintained. Doors that are wedged open go bad after a while at the hinges. Constant wedging open affects the door closure mechanism and may cause the door to slam. Most importantly, the function of a fire door is to contain smoke and fires or prevent the smoke and fire from spreading before the fire department can arrive to put out the fire. A door that is left open will only spread the smoke and/or fire and may result in loss of life or further damages. Make sure all your staff understand this fire regulation and conform to it daily.

j. *Maintenance Workshop and Storeroom*

An organized workshop or maintenance workshop is a reflection of what is going on in the mind of your building manager or maintenance staff. It is also an indication of what is going on inside the apartments. The maintenance workshop should spell organization and flow of work. How are the work orders or service requests that are submitted by tenants being processed? Are the work orders organized according to the category of work or contractors to be called? For a maintenance workshop to function properly, some of the following should be in place:

- The entrance door should be clearly labelled stating Maintenance or Maintenance Workshop.
- The door should be in good condition with a proper door closing device.
- The room should be clean and free of debris.
- Lighting should be at an acceptable level.
- The room should be properly ventilated.
- The temperature in the room should be at an acceptable level, especially in the cold season.
- PPE should be in good condition and easily accessible.
- The first aid kit should be fully stocked and placed at an appropriate and convenient location.
- The eyewash station should have updated eyewash solution that is labelled.
- The floor should be free of trip hazards. Any drain cover should fit flush over the drain.
- The floor should not be wet. A wet floor can cause staff to slip. In addition, a wet floor can cause damage to supplies being stored at ground level.
- Racks should be safely bolted to the walls.
- Shelves should not be warped.
- Shelves should not have items piled onto them. Items should be neatly stacked.
- Shelves should be clearly labelled.
- Any excess supplies should be flagged, and staff should not order any more until the excess has been used.
- Worktables should be in good condition, not shaking or wobbly.
- Electrical tools should have no broken cords and should have safety guards in good working condition.
- Extension cords being used should not be broken.
- There should be no broken electrical receptacles.
- There should be no loose electrical wires hanging.
- A fire extinguisher should be present with an updated signature.
- Ladders used should be in good condition with no missing rungs/steps and with safety shoes or end caps in place.
- Drawer handles should not be loose.
- If chemicals are stored or used in the workshop, there should be an updated Material Safety Data Sheet (MSDS).
- Any logbook should be updated accordingly.

Always ascertain from your building manager and maintenance staff the current status of work orders that have been submitted. Ask to see them and get an idea of when they will be completed. Find out if the building manager needs assistance in terms of the following:

- tools and materials
- manpower, such as help from other staff
- a contractor for more complex work or because staff have no time / will be busy
- training

Give your maintenance staff the support they need and be sure to follow up with them. You should be more prone to doing this when work orders are coming from difficult and hard-to-please tenants or when repairs stem from court order or an infraction from the city or any other authority. An excellent maintenance system helps with tenant retention and allows you to continue to attract quality tenants. An efficient maintenance system prevents unnecessary trips to the LTB or time-consuming discussions with your boss and his or her boss. It also prevents certain emergencies and lowers your budget eventually. Share the budget with your staff so they can understand how their actions, or the lack thereof, affect the budget. Let your staff know if they are doing a good job and if they need to improve. Maintenance is a key component to your job as an excellent property manager. Make sure you are vigilant where this is concerned. The effectiveness of your maintenance system reflects the kind of property manager you are. Maintenance will be further discussed in the chapter titled Building Maintenance.

k. *Underground Parking Garage*

- All entrances leading from the building to the parking garage should be labelled. You can use compass point directions such as east, west, north or south. If you have multiple entrances, you can choose to alphabetize each door: A, B, C, D, etc.
- All lights should be working with the correct wattage bulbs.
- Audible and visible fire alarm systems must be in good condition, showing no signs of tampering or vandalism. If you see evidence of vandalism, call your LSS, who may notify the fire equipment company and ask them to investigate. Make sure the fire alarm system is not being used as a hiding place for drugs and/or other illegal items.
- There should be no overflowing of garbage bins. Visible signs should be posted above each garbage bin informing tenants not to dump household garbage in the bins. One way to control this is to have smaller bins with self-closing lids or covers.
- Proper signage, illuminating or reflective, should be in place to indicate exits and the direction to different parking levels, and applicable municipal bylaw parking signs should be posted at recommended locations.
- All cameras, if any, must be working.
- No loose wires should be hanging. Wires should be in conduits.
- All junction boxes should be covered.
- Exposed plumbing pipes should not be leaking or cracked.
- Exhaust fans must be working.

Training should be provided for workers who are involved with housekeeping activities. It is important that housekeeping staff be informed about hazards in the workplace, including the risk of injuries to the musculoskeletal system. Therefore, identification of the hazards for such injury at any given hotel is fundamental."

Source: https://ccohs.ca/oshanswers/occup_workplace/hotel_housekeeping.html, November 1, 2016. Reproduced with the permission of CCOHS, 2017.

Your staff, from their training, should know and understand that the cleaning checklist is designed to create balance and promote safe work practices. Any staff going against the cleaning checklist will eventually harm themselves and must be immediately warned verbally and held accountable in writing. Any retraining, where necessary, should be given and follow-up be done to ensure the cleaning checklist is being practised as intended.

I. Types and Samples of Standardized Time Constraint Cleaning Checklists

Sample: 528 Action Road time constraint cleaning checklist for staff

Cleaning checklist
Check cleaning cart for all applicable supplies and replenish where necessary.

Some of the items on the cleaning cart may include the following:

- handheld vacuum
- upright vacuum
- gloves, both latex and puncture-resistant
- garbage bags of various sizes and kinds to fit appropriate bins
- recommended cleaning chemicals in properly labelled bottles
- clean rags (wet and dry)
- extendable duster
- broom and dustpan
- paper towels for cleaning glass, mirrors and windows
- clean wet mop
- clean mop bucket with clean water
- Wet Floor – Caution signs
- doorstops
- squeegee with adjustable stick or pole
- dust/cleaning mask
- other applicable personal protective equipment (PPE)

i. Standardized Daily Building Cleaning Routine

Daily cleaning for lobby

- Empty garbage.
- Put elevators (one at a time) on service at lobby level.
  - Use extended duster or appropriate cleaning tool to clean the vent cover in the ceiling of elevator.
  - Sweep floor and vacuum tracks of elevator.
  - Clean mirrors and elevator cab walls including door(s) and frames with appropriate cleaning chemical.
  - Mop floor. To speed up the drying process, use a dry mop after you have mopped the floor. That way when you take the elevator off service, the floor should be dry and ready for tenants to use.
  - If you do not have a dry mop, place Wet Floor – Caution sign and take elevator off service.
  - Repeat the process based on the number of elevators.
  - Remember to remove Wet Floor – Caution sign when the floor is dry.
- Remove any rugs/mats or runners and sweep the floor. It may be necessary to vacuum mats or runners and then roll them up and put them aside until the floor is mopped and dried, at which point rugs/mats or runners should be returned.
- Use squeegee and paper towels to clean all glass (windows and glass doors) in the lobby.
- If there is a newspaper/flyer stand in the lobby, ensure it is neat and organized.
- Use a damp rag to dust furniture. This should also include any general mailboxes you have in the lobby. Follow up with a clean dry rag to ensure traces of moisture are not left behind. To prevent electrical shocks, use a dry rag to dust lamps and electric fireplace.
- Use extended duster to dust any wall art and chandeliers or exposed bulbs.
- Wipe any radiator covers.
- Mop floor and place Wet Floor – Caution sign in a visible area.
- Vacuum if the floor is carpeted or has a runner or mats. This should extend to any side or back door leading from the lobby.
- Sweep steps leading to the first basement level (B1) and or second basement level (B2) and hallways
- Remember to return any rugs/mats or runners to their respective areas.
- Mop the steps and landing to B1 and B2 and hallways. Leave Wet Floor – Caution sign up.

Daily cleaning for laundry room
Time: 7:50–8:10 a.m.

- Turn on all lights. Report any blown bulbs so they can be replaced.
- Walk around the laundry room and check to see if any washers or dryers are out of order or leaking. Sometimes tenants will leave notes on machines to indicate they are not working. If machines are card-operated, sometimes you will not see any light indicating the price per load. Report malfunctioning machines to the building manager/superintendent immediately. Place an Out of Order sign on defective machine(s). If machines/dryers are coin-operated, check for evidence of tampering to remove coins. Report tampering

immediately to the building manager, and do not touch the machine. This will preserve evidence if the police are called to investigate.

- Sweep the floor.
- Empty the garbage bin and line the bin with a clean garbage bag.
- Wipe the inside and outside of machines with a clean wet rag.
- Clean any lint from lint baskets inside dryers.
- Dust the top of the pop machine with extended duster and then wipe off the front and sides of the pop machine.
- Wash out sink and clean faucet.
- Clean exit doorframe. Remove any wedge used to keep door open. This is a fire-rated door that must be kept closed at all times.
- Check for and remove any old notices or unauthorized signs or notices.
- Mop the floor. Start from the farthest end and work toward the door.
- Remember to leave the Wet Floor – Caution sign in a visible area.
- If the room is air-conditioned, ensure the AC is working in warmer weather. Ensure heat is sufficient in colder weather.
- Remember to turn off all lights if no tenants are inside the laundry room.
- Close the door and proceed to next work area.

Daily cleaning for exercise room
Time: 8:15–8:35 a.m.

- Turn lights on.
- Empty the garbage bin and line the bin with a clean garbage bag.
- Check for and remove any old notices or unauthorized signs or notices.
- Clean any windows and mirrors.
- Report all defective machines and equipment immediately.
- Use a damp rag and wipe off exercise machines and equipment.
- Note any missing weights or other smaller equipment. If necessary, write a notice to request return of equipment.
- Vacuum floor or use multipurpose cleaning machine to clean rubber mat.
- Turn lights off.

8:35–8:50 a.m.   Morning break

8:50–9:00 a.m.   Gather items to go on the floor to clean the hallways. Change mop bucket water, wash out mop or change mop. Get clean rags and applicable PPE.

9:00–9:10 a.m.   Contact super or BM to ascertain if during his or her walk-through he or she spotted any areas that require immediate cleaning, such as places where there were spills. If not, proceed to your work area.

<u>9:10–11:00 a.m.</u> Clean all required floors for the day as per the schedule (average time per floor is 22 to 24 minutes. This building has 8 units per floor).

<u>11:00 a.m.–12:00 noon</u> Lunch

Detailed hallway cleaning

Monday
<u>Floors 26–22</u>

- Sweep the landing at roof access and the steps down to the landing at floor 22.
- Use a clean wet cloth/rag to wipe down handrails and doors and frames.
- Mop the steps. Proceed to the other set of steps on the opposite side of the building and repeat points 1-3a.
- Sweep landing at elevator. Be sure to vacuum elevator track and sweep inside chute room. Remove any cobwebs in hallway.
- Replace blown bulbs where applicable in the hallway and/or clean shades with special equipment if you have it. Bulbs blown in the stairwells can be called in to the maintenance staff or building manager.
- Using wet rag, wipe exit doors and frames, chute room door and frame, elevator doors and frame, fire cabinets (inside and outside), fresh makeup air vent, and the outsides of apartment doors, including thresholds and baseboards. Work in a consistent order.
- If there is a combination of carpet and tile, vacuum the hallway and then proceed to mopping the chute room and elevator landing. Proceed to the next floor using the elevator.
- If the entire floor is tiled or planked, wipe the chute room first then the entire hallway and landing last. Leave Wet Floor – Caution sign and then proceed to next set of floors using the elevator.

Tuesday
<u>Floors 21–17</u>

- Sweep from the landing at floor 22 to the steps and landing at floor 17.
- Use a clean wet cloth/rag to wipe down handrails and doors and frames.
- Mop the steps. Proceed to the other set of steps on the opposite side of the building and repeat points 1-3a.
- Sweep the landing at the elevator. Be sure to vacuum elevator tracks and sweep inside the chute room. Remove any cobwebs in chute room and hallway.
- Replace blown bulbs where applicable in the hallway and/or clean shades with special equipment if you have it. Bulbs blown in the stairwells can be called in to the maintenance staff or building manager.
- Using a wet rag, wipe exit doors and frames, chute room door and frame, elevator doors and frame, fire cabinets (inside and outside), fresh makeup air vent, and the outsides of apartment doors, including thresholds and baseboards. Work in a consistent order.

- If there is a combination of carpet and tile, vacuum the hallway and then proceed to mopping the chute room and elevator landing. Proceed to the next floor using the elevator.
- If the entire floor is tiled or planked, wipe chute room first and entire hallway and landing last. Leave Wet Floor – Caution sign, and then proceed to the next floor using the elevator.

Wednesday
Floors 16–11

- Sweep from the landing at floor 17 to the steps and landing at floor 11.
- Use a clean wet cloth/rag to wipe down handrails and doors and frames.
- Mop the steps. Proceed to the other set of steps on the opposite side of the building and repeat points 1-3a.
- Sweep the landing at the elevator. Be sure to vacuum elevator tracks and sweep inside the chute room. Remove any cobwebs in chute room and hallway.
- Replace blown bulbs where applicable in the hallway and/or clean shades with special equipment if you have it. Bulbs blown in the stairwells can be called in to the maintenance staff or building manager.
- Using a wet rag, wipe exit doors and frames, chute room door and frame, elevator doors and frame, fire cabinets (inside and outside), fresh makeup air vent, and the outsides of apartment doors, including thresholds and baseboards. Work in a consistent order.
- If there is a combination of carpet and tile, vacuum the hallway and then proceed to mopping the chute room and elevator landing. Proceed to the next floor using the elevator.
- If the entire floor is tiled or planked, wipe chute room first and entire hallway and landing last. Leave Wet Floor – Caution sign, and then proceed to the next floor using the elevator.

Thursday
Floors 10–6

- Sweep from the landing at floor 11 to the steps and landing at floor 6.
- Use a clean wet cloth/rag to wipe down handrails and doors and frames.
- Mop the steps. Proceed to the other set of steps on the opposite side of the building and repeat points 1-3a.
- Sweep the landing at the elevator. Be sure to vacuum elevator tracks and sweep inside the chute room. Remove any cobwebs in chute room and hallway.
- Replace blown bulbs where applicable in the hallway and/or clean shades with special equipment if you have it. Bulbs blown in the stairwells can be called in to the maintenance staff or building manager.
- Using a wet rag, wipe exit doors and frames, chute room door and frame, elevator doors and frame, fire cabinets (inside and outside), fresh makeup air vent, and the outsides of apartment doors, including thresholds and baseboards. Work in a consistent order.
- If there is a combination of carpet and tile, vacuum the hallway and then proceed to mopping the chute room and elevator landing. Proceed to the next floor using the elevator.

- If the entire floor is tiled or planked, wipe chute room first and entire hallway and landing last. Leave Wet Floor – Caution sign, and then proceed to the next floor using the elevator.

Friday
Floors 5–1

- Sweep from the landing at floor 6 to the steps and landing at the 1st floor.
- Use a clean wet cloth/rag to wipe down handrails and doors and frames.
- Mop the steps. Proceed to the other set of steps on the opposite side of the building and repeat points 1-3a.
- Sweep the landing at the elevator. Be sure to vacuum elevator tracks and sweep inside the chute room. Remove any cobwebs in chute room and hallway.
- Replace blown bulbs where applicable in the hallway and/or clean shades with special equipment if you have it. Bulbs blown in the stairwells can be called in to the maintenance staff or building manager.
- Using a wet rag, wipe exit doors and frames, chute room door and frame, elevator doors and frame, fire cabinets (inside and outside), fresh makeup air vent, and the outsides of apartment doors, including thresholds and baseboards. Work in a consistent order.
- If there is a combination of carpet and tile, vacuum the hallway and then proceed to mopping the chute room and elevator landing. Proceed to the next floor using the elevator.
- If the entire floor is tiled or planked, wipe chute room first and entire hallway and landing last. Leave Wet Floor – Caution sign.

12:00 noon–12:15 p.m. Check the lobby according to weather conditions, and address where sand or snow is tracked into the building or water tracked in from rain or dripping umbrellas.

12:15–2:00 p.m. Afternoon projects

2:00–2:15 p.m. Afternoon break

2:15–3:30 p.m. Continue with afternoon projects, or report to building manager or superintendent for special assignment, which could include cleaning vacant apartments.

Weekend superintendent or building manager duties when there are no cleaning staff

Saturday Perform building walk-through and sign logbooks.
Clean lobby.
Clean laundry room.
Clean exercise room.
Clean rental office.
Empty garbage, including from underground garage and around property.
Do any common area maintenance repairs.

Prepare vacant apartments.

Sunday   Do building walk-through and sign logbooks.
Clean lobby.
Clean laundry room.
Clean exercise room.
Clean rental office.
Attend to rental office duties.
Empty garbage, including from underground garage and around property.
Do any common area maintenance repairs.
Prepare vacant apartments.

It is a good idea to leave a sign on the door of the laundry room stating the day and times you will be closed for deep/detailed cleaning, example:

"Closed every Tuesday at [time–time] for detailed cleaning."

ii. Deep Cleaning the Laundry Room

- Turn lights on.
- Clean shades or light globes. Ensure blown bulbs are replaced.
- Ensure AC, if installed, is working in warm weather and heat is working in cold weather.
- If you have windows, clean them, including the windowsills.
- Get assistance from other staff to pull machines and dryers out, if they are able to be removed.
- Use the special attachment from the vacuum behind smaller dryers if possible.
- Sweep behind machines and dryers if possible, and sweep the entire room. Behind larger dryers can be swept but the dryer vent cleaning should be cleaned only by professionals
- You may have to get the help of other staff to mop the area behind the washing machines and dryers before putting those appliances back in place.
- Use a special steamer to clean each machine inside, including the lid, top and backsplash.
- Clean each dryer by wiping the inside and cleaning the lint basket. Wipe the fronts and sides of dryers.
- Scrub, wash and rinse sink. Polish faucet. Dry the faucet and the sink
- Dust any wall art.
- If there is a wall clock, make sure it has batteries, is working and displaying the correct time. If not, request replacement. Staff should not forget to adjust the clock for the start and ending of daylight saving time.
- Wipe off tops and sides of all vending machines.
- Wipe off any bench or folding table(s).
- Clean any signs posted that can be cleaned, and remove any posted outdated notice(s).
- Clean door and frame.
- Empty or remove garbage.
- Wipe bin inside and outside and then line it with the appropriate size garbage bag.

- Use the special machine to scrub the floor.
- Mop the floor and leave Wet Floor – Caution sign.
- Turn the lights off and close the door.

iii. Deep Cleaning the Exercise Room

- Turn lights on.
- Replace blown or missing bulbs.
- Ensure light shades are clean.
- Clean vent covers including AC vent covers.
- Clean any windows and mirrors.
- Clean any signs posted that can be cleaned or remove any outdated notices posted.
- Use an approved disinfectant and cleaning chemical to wipe down all machines.
- Report any defective machines immediately.
- Note any missing weights or other smaller equipment. If necessary, send a notice to request return of equipment.
- Dust any wall art.
- Replenish wipes or paper towels.
- Wipe door and doorframe.
- Wipe baseboards.
- Empty the garbage bin.
- Wipe bin inside and outside and then line it with the appropriate size garbage bag.
- Vacuum the floor or use multipurpose machine to clean rubber mat.
- Turn lights off and close the door.

iv. Deep Cleaning the Social/Party Room

- Turn on all lights. Note any bulb needing replacement.
- Ensure light shades are clean not cracked or chipped.
- Walk around the room and check for and remove anything out of the ordinary.
- If there is a dishwasher, check for dirty dishes. If there are any, load them into the dishwasher and run it through its cycle.
- Check the refrigerator for unauthorized items and discard any found.
- Check drawers and cupboards for unwanted/unauthorized items. If any are found, discard them.
- Remove stove top grills, knobs and plates. Place them in a clean garbage bag and spray with approved oven cleaner. Leave the bag open and allow the spray to work on the grime. If the stove has a ceramic top, clean it with the appropriate cleaner.
- Using an approved oven spray, spray stove top and oven. Allow the spray to work on the grime.
- Check for garbage in the room. Remove any you find.
- Clean windows.

- Wipe off tables and chairs. If tables are foldable, put them away in the designated storage area or arrange as per standard setup.
- Sweep the floor, being sure to pull out the stove and refrigerator and sweep behind them. You should also mop before you return the appliances to their respective positions.
- Dust any wall art.
- Wipe cabinets inside and outside.
- Clean the range hood.
- Wipe countertop and backsplash.
- Clean off stove top, backsplash, and sides and front of oven.
- Wash and dry stove top racks and knobs, and then re-install.
- Clean the refrigerator inside and outside. Remove and clean racks. Clean rubber gasket as well.
- Wipe the microwave inside and outside. Wash the rotating plate; dry and replace. Make sure the plate is aligned well when replaced.
- Remove any dishes from the dishwasher. If they are wet, dry them with a paper towel. Place clean dishes in cupboards.
- Wipe inside and outside of dishwasher.
- Wash and dry the sink and polish the faucets.
- Clean the doors and frames.
- Wipe inside and outside of garbage bin. When dry, line with a garbage bag.
- Wipe baseboards.
- Mop the floor or use the special machine to clean the floor if there is vinyl plank flooring. For regular vinyl composition tile (VCT), floor should be stripped and waxed every quarter to maintain cleanliness and luster.
- Place Wet Floor – Caution sign, turn lights off and leave the room.
- Remember to return to retrieve Wet Floor – Caution sign.

v. Deep Cleaning the Washrooms in the Common Area

- Open the door and turn the lights on. Replace any blown bulbs before you start.
- Spray any urinals or toilets. If the toilet seat is down, lift the seat and then flush the toilet to get rid of any waste inside. Flushing the toilet will also let you know if it is clogged and requires a plunger to clear, or if maintenance should be called to snake it with their cable. If maintenance cannot clear the blockage, the plumber should be called in. An Out of Order sign should be placed on the door until the repair is addressed. *If the washroom is close to the party/social room and the party room is booked for use, this blockage should be treated with urgency to return the toilet to normal operation.* Return when the plumber is finished. Then remove the Out of Order sign and repeat the spraying of the toilet for cleaning. After that, proceed to the next step.
- Spray the vanity and toilet or urinals with the required cleaning chemical. Allow it to sit.
- Proceed to remove any cobwebs.
- Sweep the floor.
- Empty the garbage bin and wipe the bin out if necessary.

- Clean mirrors.
- Clean the vanity, including sink and taps.
- Clean the toilet tank, seat, rim, bowl, including urinal(s) and foot or base.
- Replenish the following and ensure that any case that holds these supplies is clean and properly closed after replenishing:
  a. toilet tissue
  b. paper towels
  c. hand soap
  d. hand sanitizer
  e. garbage bin liners
  f. disposable toilet seat paper
  g. feminine napkin disposal bags
- Ensure the baby changing table is clean and safe to operate.
- If there is an automatic hand dryer machine, make sure it is working.
- If a clock is present, ensure it has battery and is reading the correct time. Staff should not forget to adjust the clock for the start and ending of daylight saving time.
- Clean the door and doorframe.
- Mop the floor (leave Wet Floor – Caution sign if there are multiple stalls and door will be left open).
- Close door.

vi. Deep Cleaning the Cinema Room

- Turn on all lights. Report any defective light.
- Ensure light shades are clean.
- Empty garbage bin, wipe it inside and outside, and line it with clean garbage bag.
- Check each chair for food, crumbs and defects. If a defective chair is found, notify the building manager.
- If you have a leaf blower (preferably one that is not gas operated and it is safe to use inside), flip down each seat and use the leaf blower to remove any crumbs or items that maybe stuck in the crevices. Note, there are leaf blowers that are cordless and battery operated or electric. These cause no emissions and produce limited or no noise.
- Remove cobwebs from wall corners.
- Wipe down each chair, or vacuum each chair using the special vacuum attachment (whether upright or handheld).
- Use applicable duster to dust screen.
- Wipe doors and frames.
- Vacuum room, starting from the farthest end and working your way toward the door.
- Turn lights off and close door.

vii. Deep Cleaning the Locker Room

- Turn all lights on.

- Walk the hallway(s), checking for any items stored in the hallway(s). If any are found, report this to the building manager so the tenant(s) in violation can be contacted or a general notice can be sent out to all tenants.
- Call in any blown light bulb for replacement.
- Report any leak or evidence of theft immediately.
- Remove all cobwebs from wall corners and around light shades.
- Wipe entrance doors and frames.
- Sweep the floor. Mop the floor if it can be mopped.
- Turn lights off and close the door

viii. Deep Cleaning the Vacant Guest Suite

- Collect any necessary key for this suite, as it may not be openable by your regular master key for the apartment doors.
- Confirm that the suite is vacant.
- Gain entry by knocking loud on the door two times. If there is no answer, open the door. Once inside, loudly state the name of the company, even if you know the suite is vacant.
- Walk through all rooms and call the name of the company as you go from room to room. This is to make sure the apartment has no guests inside or, if there are guests inside, to alert them to the fact that you are inside the apartment, in case they did not hear your knock. Turn on all lights as you enter each room and open the curtain or blinds.
- Your cleaning cart should block the doorway to the apartment, preventing anyone from entering while you are inside cleaning. However, to prevent any obstruction to the hallway, you can take the cart inside with you once you have ascertained the suite is empty.
- Head to the kitchen and check to see if there are any dirty dishes. Load any dirty dishes in the dishwasher and run the cycle while you proceed to other areas of the apartment.
- If there is a laundry closet, pour the recommended amount of vinegar solution into the machine and run a cycle. This helps to clean any gunk from the washer.
- Clean any lint from the lint basket and ensure the dryer is empty and clean.
- Remove all garbage. Proceed to the bedroom(s) and washroom(s). Flush any cigarette butts found in ashtrays. To avoid fires, never dump cigarette butts in the garbage. If you leave an ashtray, you are encouraging visitors to smoke in the room. If you leave an ashtray, put a sign stating that smoking should be done on the balcony.
- Remove all dirty linen (sheets, pillowcases, mattress pad, towels, and fabric shower curtain or shower curtain liner) and place in a dirty linen bag. Never scoop dirty linen by hugging; this is not safe.
- Using the required cleaner, spray the shower curtain inside and outside (if curtain is plastic) and all walls of the shower stall or the tub-surround tiles. Also spray faucets and bathtub.
- Spray the toilet and the vanity sink, including the faucet, and allow the cleaning chemical to sit and work on the dirt while you attend to the bedroom(s).
- Inspect the mattress for stains, damage and any sign of bedbugs. Check if mattress requires flipping or rotating. Flipping or rotating allows the mattress to have even wear and will

prolong the useful life of the mattress. For health and safety reasons, mattress rotation/flipping should be a team sharing task.

- Make the bed as per company standard with a new mattress pad, sheets, pillowcases and applicable spread or comforter set.

- It is important not to put a pillow under your chin to get the pillow into the pillowcase. The correct procedure is to lay the pillow flat on the bed, lengthwise. Fold the pillow in half lengthwise and hold. Place the folded end of the pillow that is pointing away from you into the pillowcase all the way down. Release the pillow. The pillow will open to fill the corners of the pillowcase. Smooth out the pillow and arrange it as per standard.

- Check the closet for adequate hangers and pillows. Arrange as per standard. Remove all personal items of the previous guest(s). Label these and set them aside on the cleaning cart to deliver to the rental office.

- Open all side tables, all dresser drawers and the chest of drawers. Remove any item you find belonging to the previous guest/visitor. Label with date and time of discovery. Place the item(s) on the cleaning cart and drop off at rental office after cleaning the suite.

- Starting from the farthest end of the room, wipe all furniture down with a damp cloth. Be sure to clean side table lamps and lampshades, inside all drawers, and windowsills, as well as doorframe, closet door, baseboards and baseboard radiator covers.

- Sweep the bathroom and then bedroom floor. If the bedroom floor is carpeted, vacuum it after mopping the bathroom floor. Sweep dirt into a dustpan.

- Proceed to washroom and start by scrubbing plastic shower curtain. Twist and flip the outside inward and place against the wall. If there is a fabric shower curtain liner, replace it with a new liner after you have washed and dried the shower stall or tub surround.

- Scrub all walls and the bathtub of the shower stall or tub surround, as well as the faucets and showerhead. Rinse walls, faucets, plastic shower curtain (if there is one) and the bathtub.

- Dry walls, faucets, shower curtain, curtain rail and bathtub.

- Scrub, rinse and dry vanity sink. Clean sides of vanity. Check under the vanity and ensure only appropriate items are stored.

- Clean towel rack, all mirrors in the bathroom, medicine cabinet, and any picture frames in the bathroom. The bathroom vent should also be wiped off.

- Use a dry cloth to clean exposed lights. Never use a damp cloth.

- Use the approved cleaning chemical and a toilet brush to scrub the toilet bowl. Flush. Use paper towel and approved disinfectant or other chemical to clean the tank and outside of the toilet, including the base, lid and seat. Leave the lid down.

- Restock soap. Fold toilet tissue tip in a *V* shape. Arrange bath mat, hand towels, washcloths and bath towels as per company standard.

- Line the garbage bin with applicable size garbage bag. You may have to knot the garbage bag to hug the wastebin. If so, tuck the knot under and turn the bin around so the knot is out of sight. Do the same for the bedroom wastebin.

- Go to the bedroom and give a final dust with a dry cloth. This should remove any lint caused by linen while making the bed.

- Mop the bathroom floor. Repeat the cleaning process if there is more than one bathroom.

- Mop or vacuum the bedroom floor, starting from the farthest end. Repeat the cleaning process if there is more than one bedroom.
- Turn lights off and close door.

NB: If the suite is going to be occupied for more than two weeks, clean the occupied suite on the same day you would if the suite was vacant and dirty and needed cleaning. While the guest/visitor does the light cleaning, your detailed cleaning prevents buildup and reduces the amount of time the cleaning staff has to spend to bring the suite back to clean and ready status.

Kitchen

- Check the refrigerator for unauthorized items. Discard any you find.
- Check drawers and cupboards for unwanted/unauthorized items. Discard any you find.
- Remove stove top grills, knobs and plates. Place them in a clean garbage bag and spray with approved oven cleaner. Leave the bag open and allow the spray to work on the grime. If the stove has a ceramic top, use the appropriate cleaner to clean it.
- Using the approved oven spray, spray the stove top and oven. Allow it to sit.
- Check for garbage and remove any found.

Balcony

- Sweep the balcony. Do not sweep anything over the balcony. Sweep dirt toward wall and into a dustpan.
- Clean balcony windows with approved cleaner applicable to the weather. Also, clean balcony glass rail or panel.
- Wipe down windowsill.
- Wipe off balcony furniture and the balcony door, inside and outside, including doorframe. In the winter, all balcony furniture should be covered with a special covering. Make sure the covering is well secured over the furniture.
- Close the door and proceed to the living room and dining room.

Living room and dining room

- Start in the dining room by removing cobwebs.
- Pull chairs out from under the dining table.
- Sweep the floor, including under the dining table. If there is an area rug under the table, vacuum the rug.
- Sweep the living room floor, including closets. Remove all cobwebs. Pull sofa cushions from the sofa. If you have no vacuum attachment, use a handheld vacuum and vacuum the base of the sofa where the cushions sit. Pull sofa away from the wall and sweep or vacuum the floor. Sweep under the coffee table, side tables, TV stand and any other furniture in the living room. Sweep dirt into dustpan.

- Return to the dining room and wipe down the dining room table and chairs. If the floor is carpeted, rearrange chairs around the table. If the floor is not carpeted, wait until the floor is mopped and dry to return the chairs.
- Dust all wall art. Clean mirrors. Clean windows inside, including tracks of windows and windowsills. Clean baseboards and radiator covers.
- Go to living room and wipe sofa, coffee table, side tables, TV stand, remote controls and any other furniture in the living room. Also wipe wall art and ornaments or accessories. Be sure to use a dry rag to clean away moisture left from wet rag on furniture. Rearrange things as you go along.
- Return to en-suite laundry closet and wipe any scum out of the washer. Wipe the outside of the machine. Remove any lint from the dryer and from the wall. Sweep behind the washing machine and dryer.
- Clean out any other closet.
- Mop floor throughout, except in the kitchen.

Return to kitchen

- Sweep the floor. Be sure to pull out stove and refrigerator and sweep behind them.
- Wipe cabinets inside and outside.
- Clean the range hood.
- Wipe countertop and backsplash.
- Clean off stove top, backsplash, and sides and front of oven.
- Wash and dry stove top racks and knobs, and then re-install.
- Clean refrigerator inside and outside. Remove and clean racks and drawers. Clean rubber gasket as well. Fill ice tray and put in freezer.
- Wipe the microwave inside and outside. Wash the rotating plate, dry and replace. Make sure the plate is aligned well when replaced; otherwise, it will rumble and move about when in use.
- Remove any dishes from the dishwasher. If dishes are wet, dry with paper towel. Place dishes in cupboards.
- Wipe inside and outside of dishwasher.
- Wash and dry sink, and polish faucets.
- Wipe inside and outside of garbage bin. When dry, line with a garbage bag.
- Wipe baseboards.
- Mop floor, including behind refrigerator and stove, and then return these appliances to their proper places.

Final walk-through and check before leaving suite

- Check the bathroom to ensure everything is in place. There should be no hair on the floor.
- Use a dry dustmop to go over floors throughout the bedroom(s), living and dining room, and closets, including laundry closet. Dustmop the kitchen if the floor is dry.
- Rearrange all curtains or drapes so they hang properly. Make sure all windows are closed.
- Close doors to all closets.

- Depending on the season or time of year, check that AC is working or that there is adequate heat in the suite.
- Stand back and see things from the visitor's viewpoint. Adjust anything that is out of place, including the literature basket.
- Place remotes for the AC and/or TV in their proper places.
- Turn off lights as you leave each room.
- Close the door and return the key.

Freshening up vacant and ready suite

Time: 15–20 minutes

Your guest suite may not always be occupied. However, it should always be clean and ready for any visitor who wishes to use it.

On the same day the suite is schedule for cleaning, your assigned staff should go in and do the following if the suite is clean and ready:

- Turn all lights on.
- Flush all toilets. This is to keep water in the P trap and prevent sewer smell from coming up into the suite.
- Run all taps: vanity sink, shower and kitchen. This also prevents any drain smell from coming up into the apartment. Be sure to dry any water in bathtub and all sinks.
- If the suite has not been occupied for an extended time, note any special care from your company or municipality regarding the prevention of legionnaire disease.
- Dust all furniture.
- Check temperature in cold season to ensure the room is adequately heated and in warm weather to ensure the room is adequately cooled.
- Check for leaks and anything out of the ordinary.
- Turn lights off, lock door and return keys.

Word of Caution

Once the guest suite is cleaned and setup to accommodate visitors or guests, take a picture of how each area or section in each room should look or be arranged. Have the pictures laminated and show them to the cleaning staff. This will serve as a guide to the cleaning staff to maintain standard and consistency. If you fail to do this you will have inconsistencies in the arrangement and setup of the guest suite every time it is cleaned. Ensure the pictures are kept on the cleaning cart at all times.

Letter to Visiting Guest

Dear Guest(s),

Welcome to our [building name] guest suite. We are pleased to have you as our guest(s). Our staff at this location are as follows:

- Building Manager(s), [Name(s)]
- Superintendent(s), [Name(s)]
- Cleaner, [Name]

To add to the joy of your stay with us please, note the following amenities:

- Laundry room [state location or indicate if available inside the suite]
- Exercise room [state location]
- Cinema room [state location]
- Indoor/outdoor pool [state location]
- In-room literature basket, which has a city guide to help you find your way around and brochures of various attractions, including restaurants and supermarkets

We do not have a housekeeping department, but the suite is fully stocked and equipped with basic supplies for your use, such as the following:

- dishes and cutleries
- dish soap and dish scouring pad
- dishwasher
- broom and dustpan
- toilet brush and cleaner
- iron and ironing board

Please help us to keep this suite clean. Our staff will check on the apartment once per week to replenish supplies. If there is a maintenance concern in the suite, please call our rental office at [telephone number] and we will attend to the matter.

Please remember to take all your personal items with you when you vacate the suite.
Should you have a medical emergency, please call 9-1-1. Your location is [address and unit number].
We trust you will enjoy your time with us. Let us know if we can do anything else to enhance your stay.

Thank you,

[Name]
Property Manager
[LAMINATE AND POST ON REFRIGERATOR]

ix. Weekly Afternoon Deep Cleaning Project Schedule

Monday	Tuesday	Wednesday	Thursday	Friday
Garbage chutes, five per day Clean globes on select floors Wash blue recycle bins in the summer and wipe them out in the cold weather	Guest suite cleaning	Garbage chutes, five per day Clean globes on select floors Laundry from guest suite Or do cleaning or other assignment from BM	Social room Or do apartment cleaning	Garbage chutes, five per day Clean globes on select floors
	Swing day to clean apartments if there is no suite checkout cleaning	Tenant laundry room Team sharing for health and safety	Storage locker rooms (if multiple locker rooms)	Storage locker rooms (if multiple locker rooms)
		Cinema room		

- When possible, laundry machines should be moved to gain access behind them for cleaning. For the safety of each worker, have a cleaner from another building team assist with moving machines.
- If the secondary amenities are not in individual buildings, the workload should be shared to distribute the duties in a community setting.

Before you discuss or implement workload sharing with your staff, consider doing it from a health and safety standpoint. Your staff may be more inclined to embrace the idea or concept.

How can team work reduce the risk for RMI?

Team work can provide greater variety and more evenly distributed muscular work. The whole team is involved in the planning of the work. Each team member carries out a set of operations to complete the whole product, allowing the worker to alternate between tasks. This approach reduces the risk of RMI.

Source: https://ccohs.ca/oshanswers/occup_workplace/hotel_housekeeping.html, November 1, 2016. Reproduced with the permission of CCOHS, 2017.

Once you have completed the building inspection, do the following:

Before you leave the property do a final meeting with the building manager(s) or office staff and briefly review what should happen between your current visit and your next visit. Ensure you do the following:

1. If your company uses a building form system for the building inspection, be sure to leave a copy of the form at the building.
2. The building manager should make copies of the completed inspection form and give one to each staff member at the building, so they can address the section or tasks that apply to them or will be assigned to them by the building managers.
3. Sit with your building managers or superintendent and sign off on any work planners or work authorization forms to be submitted to external contractors.

Be sure to follow through on any task you assigned yourself. This may include sending e-mails to any contractors you indicated you will be contacting regarding the inspection. Also, note any letters that must be sent to tenants or N5 notices that must be served. Allow the staff a few days to complete the tasks on the inspection form. Once these tasks are completed, the building managers should sign and date the inspection form to indicate all items have been addressed. When you are at the building next, ask to see some of the items the staff have completed. Have a habit of randomly following up on work you have assigned. You are simply inspecting what you expect. Your staff will know this about you and will be more inclined to follow through on their tasks. You should also lead by example and show that you have completed your tasks on the inspection form.

Word of caution

To avoid feeling overwhelmed by the various inspections that must be done, consider doing "bite size" inspections. You can do this by training your eyes to focus on one aspect or category of the inspection when you visit each of your buildings. For example, if you choose to do exterior inspections, then do that at all your buildings. By the time you visit all your buildings, you will have put the skills into practice several times. Your eyes will become sharper and you will be more attuned to the job. Whatever category you choose, as you do more visits and inspections, these will automatically become part of your routine, to the point where it becomes second nature to you and takes less time to complete. You can do it!

Staffing

Most of your time as a property manager will be spent on issues and concerns related to staffing in your portfolio. This can drain your energy if you are not on top of things by being alert to the overall operation of your buildings. As we have discussed earlier, the best way to know what is happening at the buildings is to physically visit them. Each location will have its own set of challenges. The key to succeeding at a difficult location is to put trained and experienced staff who have a teachable attitude at the location. It can make that location a breeze. Remember your staff is the lifeblood of the properties in your portfolio. The best way to keep your staff pumping or moving is by motivating them, powered by emotional intelligence. Your application of emotional intelligence hopefully will lessen the stress and worry at your properties. Listen to your staff. If they come to you with a complaint, never shut them down by telling them to "suck it up" or "you are being emotional because your feathers were ruffled." If they are talking to you about a matter that is bothering them, the matter is important to them. Therefore, you should listen with unbiased ears. Find the time, or else they will go over your head and then you will be forced to give them the time. Remember that your staff have the same options your tenants have, only through different avenues, such as the Ministry of Labour (MOL) and the Human Rights Tribunal, just to name a couple. It is less of an headache giving a listening ear than preparing or defending an application to the MOL or Human Rights Tribunal.

Understand that your budget will revolve around staffing and how your staff execute their duties. Duties fall into what I refer to as the eight core operational areas of property management:

1. building structure and exterior curb appeal
2. landscaping and grounds
3. systems and routines—cleaning, renting, rent collection, completing all safety logs
4. special or capex projects
5. mechanical/utility rooms—HVAC, fire systems, elevators, boiler, electrical, workshops or workstations
6. vacant and ready apartments, occupied apartments and apartments being renovated or repaired
7. tenants' requests and concerns
8. common area inspections, including amenities

Therefore, treat your staff as your best tools and assets, because they are. In fact, they are the most vulnerable of your assets. Polish your staff and they will shine for you. Bring out the best in your staff. Tell them the good you see in them. The more often you tell them, the more comfortable they will feel hearing it, and the more they will believe it when you speak it to them.

A. Building and Leading a Team

A team can be defined as "a group of individuals with complementary skills linked to a common goal or cause." The purpose of a team may be to start or complete a task or improve a situation or project. When the team is highly effective, it can accomplish its goals in a timely manner and a highly productive way. What makes a team highly effective is the shared commitment and responsibility of each team member, which gives rise to the famed acronym Together Everyone Achieves More (TEAM). For a team to be highly effective, it must have a competent and willing leader to guide and influence all members to achieve the desired goals. That willingness in a leader indicates the leader is unconsciously performing competently. That is to say, the skills the leader possesses have become second nature or instinctual and effortless.

In an article titled "6 Ways Successful Teams Are Built to Last," written for *Forbes*, the author Glenn Llopis states the following:

> It takes great leadership to build great teams. Leaders who are not afraid to course correct, make the difficult decisions and establish standards of performance that are constantly being met—and improving at all times. Whether in the workplace, professional sports, or your local community, team building requires a keen understanding of people, their strengths and what gets them excited to work with others. Team building requires the management of egos and their constant demands for attention and recognition—not always warranted. Team building is both an art and a science and the leader who can consistently build high performance teams is worth their weight in gold.

The article goes on to say "that history has shown that it takes a special kind of leader with unique competences and skills to successfully build great teams and companies."

According to Llopis, the six ways successful teams are built to last are as follows:

1. Beware of how you work: As the leader of the team, you must be extremely aware of your leadership style and techniques. Are they as effective as you think? How well are they accepted by the team you are attempting to lead? Evaluate yourself and be critical about where you can improve, especially in areas that will benefit those whom you are leading.

   Though you may be in-charge, how you work may not be appreciated by those who work for you. You may have good intentions, but make sure you hold yourself accountable to course-correct and modify your approach if necessary to assure that you're leading from a position of strength and respectability. *Be your own boss. Be flexible. Know who you are as a leader.*

2. Get to know the rest of the team
   Fully knowing your team means that you have invested the time to understand how they are wired to think and what is required to motivate them to excel beyond what is expected from them. *Think of your team as puzzle pieces that can be placed together in a variety of ways.*

3. Clearly define roles and responsibilities
   Each of your team member's responsibilities must be interconnected and dependent upon one another. This is not unlike team sports, where some players are known as "system players"—meaning that, although they may not be the most talented person on the team, they know how to work best within the "system." This is why you must have a keen eye for talent that can evaluate people not only on their ability to play a particular role—but even more so on whether they fit the workplace culture (the system) and will be a team player.

4. Be proactive with feedback
   Feedback is the key to assuring any team is staying on track, but more importantly that it is improving each day. Feedback should be proactive and constant. Many leaders are prone to wait until a problem occurs before they give feedback.

   Remember that every team is different, with its own unique nuances and dynamics. Treat them as such. No cookie-cutter approach is allowed. Allow proactive feedback to serve as your team's greatest enabler for continuous improvement. *Take the time to remind someone of how and what they can be doing better. Learn from them. Don't complicate the process of constructive feedback. Feedback is two-way communication.*

5. Acknowledge and reward
   With proactive feedback comes acknowledgment and reward. People love recognition, but are most appreciative of respect. Take the time to give your teammates the proper accolades they have earned and deserve. *When people are acknowledged, their work brings them greater satisfaction and becomes more purposeful.*

6. Always celebrate success
   Celebration is a short-lived activity. Don't ignore it. Take the time to live in the moment and remember what allowed you to cross the finish line.

   Hence, leading a team can even be classified as what I call "commercial parenting." Like a parent, you must understand how each staff member thinks or how the workers behave overall. By taking the time to know each person on the team, the leader can tap into the skills of each team member and nurture or harness specific talents through constant motivation, inspiration and giving feedback on how to improve. Grasping that concept can assist in building an effective team.

i. Modelling Teamwork and Leadership in the US Army

Team building is an ongoing process that requires a lot of time and effort both on the part of the leader and the members. By assessing the team and leadership structure of the US Army, one can gain a clearer understanding of how a team should function. In a YouTube video titled *Circle of Safety in the Marines* by Simon Senik, Senik states that *safety* actually means "someone will be there for me." He elaborates, saying that the marines are conditioned to think no more of themselves as "I" but as "we," meaning as a team. Hence, soldiers are strategically allowed to work on their own for a while. The purpose of using this tactic is to set them up to fail as individuals during their first few weeks of training. The training is to condition each soldier to believe that he or she cannot, and will not, succeed on his or her own. Therefore, each will need the support of others. This team approach of the army is a clear indication of how a healthy or highly effective team should operate. Similarly, let your staff know that no single staff or team member, regardless of title or tenure, can accomplish anything on his or her own. If any person attempts such a thing, he or she will burnout and fall to pieces. Hence the importance of teamwork.

The team in a company should be for the good of the company, thereby creating a powerful force. This will only work if the leader views each individual he or she leads as a real person and views all subordinates collectively as a team. Therefore, for the equation to be true and complete, an effective team must be guided by a great leader. In an article titled *Emotional Intelligence and the Army Leadership Requirements Model*, written by Lieutenant Colonel Gerald F. Sewell, US Army, Sewell provides the Field Manual (FM) 6-22 definition of "Army leadership": "the process of influencing people by providing purpose, direction, and motivation while operating to accomplish the mission and improve the organization." Sewell feels what is missing from the definition is a holistic emphasis on emotional intelligence, meaning that leaders should be aware of their emotions and how their emotional competence influences the way they lead and impact their followers.

The article further states that an army leader motivates people both inside and outside the chain of command to pursue actions, focus thinking and shape decisions for the greater good of the organization. A person's training and access to resources does not necessarily make him or her a great leader. Sewell's concluding words are, "The Army's leader development programs will do a great service to its leaders by placing increased emphasis on the emotional intelligent aspects of leadership. The next step for the Army is to incorporate emotional intelligence in its leader and Soldier development programs. If Army leaders study and apply emotional intelligence, they will be more effective and successful in building strong organizations and teams."

ii. Managing with Emotional Intelligence

Learn to lead and manage with emotional intelligence. Having emotional intelligence means recognizing your own feelings and the feelings of others based on circumstances and environment and adjusting your approach accordingly. When you understand the root cause of a certain emotion being portrayed, it puts you in a better position to communicate with your staff member who is projecting that emotion. Leading and managing with emotional intelligence is not a sign of being weak. It is a sign of strength and compassion, and shows you are human. This skill helps you to connect with your staff and even understand yourself. You can only connect with your staff when you take the time to know them and understand them. Who are their children? Do you know their names? Ask about their families. It doesn't have to be personal. Ask how the kids are. If a staff member's child is sick, can you give him or her the day off to attend to the child? Depending on the severity of the child's sickness, that parent is not going to produce much work. If a staff member's parents are sick, say something like, "How are your parents? I heard your mom is in the hospital. How is she doing?" If a staff member has a pet, ensure you know the pet's name. "How is your dog Barney?" Despite what your staff are dealing with personally or professionally, you are able to connect with them and let them know you are there for them. This way they feel they are appreciated and their contribution to the company is valued. Sometimes you may hear comments such as, "I can reason with my boss. She knows and understands me." When you lead and manage with emotional intelligence, it helps to build staff members' respect for you, enhances communication and ensures your presence is not resented. Your staff tend to feel relaxed and comfortable around you. It helps to build morale, and somehow acts as your high-performance multivitamin, thereby energizing your staff and making them want to be at work.

iii. Strategies to Dismantle Dysfunctional Teams

For your team to be effective and perform at its best, the team cannot be broken; otherwise, it will not even function. A dysfunctional team will give you untold headaches, drain your mental and emotional energy and ultimately make you look incompetent. As an excellent property manager, you must be on the lookout for and eliminate a dysfunctional atmosphere at any of your properties by implementing the following:

1. *Build trust.* If there is no trust, team members will not feel at ease and will become unwilling to admit to their mistakes. Without this perceived comfort level, trust is impossible. Trust can be built by getting to know each other through having lunches, having pizza parties or taking in coffee (or another hot beverage) or breakfast for everyone on the team. If it is hot in the summer, cool the team down by taking frozen novelties such as freezes, ice crème cake or bottled water to each building or calling and faxing an authorization to the building manager to make the purchase from petty cash. Use team-building activities and clean, non-offensive humour—and get feedback—to help build trust.

2. *Eliminate fear by encouraging healthy and civil debate at staff meetings.* This makes the team feel comfortable about discussing difficult key issues. Make decisions taking into account the concerns raised by the team and they will feel you have their best interests at heart.

3. *Build commitment and camaraderie.* Great teams unite behind decisions and commit to clear courses of action. Without commitment, team members may become resentful and demotivated. Listen to their suggestions and assess how these suggestions will bring the team closer to the company's goals and objectives without negatively impacting the budget. Suggestions recommended by the team that get implemented are an automatic buy-in / agreement. The team will not tear down what they have built or helped to implement. This

approach builds trust and inspires your staff to go the extra mile. It also reduces or eliminates staff turnover. Moreover, it energizes the team and instills a great sense of pride. I remember that in one staff meeting, I brought in some sample tiles for the team to help select for an upcoming capex project. There was one colour that I recommended to complement the colour scheme of the wall. The team objected and asked if they could do a "water test." I was curious about this water test, so I told them to go ahead. They poured water on each tile and rubbed their fingers along the tiles to see which type was more slippery when wet. I was blown away by their brilliance and went with the tile that was safer according to their experiment. They were excited and I learned something new. After all, they would be the ones cleaning the tiles and would be walking on the tiles a lot more than I would.

4. *Hold team members accountable.* Do not tolerate malice, laziness, excuses or inactivity. These are like an infection of the blood that will slow down the team. Show how inactivity and lack of commitment affects the team and the desired goals. Meet privately with the team member who demonstrates this behaviour, and the building managers, to state what the concerns are. You should include the building managers because it sends the message that you the property manager are not the only one who is aware of the concern. This tells the staff member in question that both you and the building managers are on the lookout for bad behaviour and, on the other hand, positive change.

5. *Clarify the expectations and responsibilities of each team member.* When ideas are not clear, they cannot be supported. Unclear ideas diminish the ability of the team to achieve its goals. Each team member must know what they are doing. They must have the needed resources, tools, training and support to carry out that which they are responsible for or asked to do.

B. Staff Meetings and Goal Setting

Staff meetings are like progress reports and goal-setting opportunities. The meetings show what a team has accomplished and what they need to accomplished. How do you know what should be discussed at the staff meeting? You can build your agenda through a variety of ways, such as the following:

1. Determining what goals you or your AM have for the property and what you and the team are doing to achieve those goals.
2. Personally visiting each department and stating that you will be having a staff meeting at a particular location. This can give you great insight. Find out what challenges each department is having at that location, and be sure to address those challenges in the staff meeting.
3. When you visit the building, note what concerns jump out at you.
4. Determine how the property measures up in light of the eight core operational areas of property management.

Staff meetings should be scheduled ahead of time, so all staff present on the property can attend without interruption. This allows staff to plan and organize work and contractors around the meeting. Since my background is in hotel management, I tend to have staff meetings over a meal: pizza, takeout, fast food, café food or whatever I may allow the staff to choose within budget. Breaking bread is good; it signifies peace, unity and togetherness.

At one location that was part of my portfolio, the staff seemed a little aloof. To get them to warm up, I asked them if it would be ok if I baked them a cake. They were shocked but all agreed. I baked my way into their hearts. It mellowed them down. Cakes then became a staple at our meetings. When my portfolio grew, I resorted to buying cakes instead of baking. Each staff member at each location had his or her own preference of either cheesecake or carrot cake. I made the mistake one day of not taking a cake to one of the staff meetings. At the end of the meeting, the team said the meeting was good, but they were very disappointed that I had not brought in a cake. Prior to the meeting's end, a staff member had to step out for a short time. When this person returned, he asked if any cake was left for him. The group replied in a unison, "She did not bring any cake!" When the staff who'd returned heard the answer, there was a look of horror and disbelief on his face. Everyone in attendance had a belly laugh. I was reprimanded for not bringing in a cake, and I promised never to make that mistake again.

After each staff meeting, I made myself available to meet privately with team members who had personal concerns related to the job. Sometimes these could be very personal family issues and the staff members wanted a listening ear and for me to know what they were enduring. After listening, I would try to offer any commendation in their job despite what they were dealing with. Then I would direct them to the company's EAP (employee assistance program) so they could get the required help to function, not just as a staff member but also as a person.

Even after referring a staff/team member to the EAP, you should follow up on how things are going. Do not dump the person to get rid of the problem. Following up shows concern and gives you a better picture of the staff member and how you should approach him or her for any new developments related to the work. A staff member could just be returning from sick leave. This is a good time to find out how he or she is doing or address any return-to-work plan given to you by your human resources department.

Some of the other concerns addressed could be inappropriate behaviour of staff toward one another. Or there could be concerns expressed about a new staff member not complying with company standards. Depending on how severe the concerns are, that new staff person can be spoken to and given a chance to relate his or her side of the story. Make your Note to File and send a copy to your branch or area manager and human resources.

i. Combined Staff Meeting

Have a combined portfolio staff meeting at the start of the financial year with your staff from all your buildings. Use this meeting to set the pace and expectations for the months to follow. Pump staff up with high-energy music for about two to five minutes. You can use high-energy music similar to what is used in most gyms for workouts. Your meetings should be a mental workout that energizes your team to reach the goals that must be achieved. The Internet has many short cartoons and real-life videos on leadership and team-buildings exercise you could use to assist and "edutain" your staff.

a. *Agenda for Combined Staff Meeting*

- Start off with clean, non-offensive humour.
- Thank everyone for showing up to the meeting.
- State the properties in your portfolio and share something positive about each location.
- Introduce yourself, mentioning how long you have been with the company and the previous properties you have managed. This is a great idea if your portfolio has changed or you have had new locations added to your portfolio.
- Give an overview of what to expect in the meeting.
- Clearly state that monthly staff meetings will be held at the property level. All staff meetings will be positive to build up everyone in attendance and help them work to achieve the goals the company has set out for the financial year. *Never use the meeting to put anyone on the spot or tear anyone down.* If anyone has personal concerns, those should be discussed with you behind closed doors—*never* in public.
- Establish that the main purpose of the meeting is for everyone to know who is in the portfolio and part of your team. This is to build a network and emphasize teamwork. This shows that everyone is part of the pie with the same goal in mind.
- Give a coin to each staff. Have each staff member introduce themselves (name, location, title and length of time with the company) and state something positive that happened to them in the year inscribed on the coin.

After you have broken the tension in the room, get down to business.

- Tell the team a little about your management and leadership style.
- Ask them about what expectations they have of you.
- State the capital expenditure projects that will be done at each location, such as balcony restoration and guardrail installation, garage repair, hallway painting, paving parking lots or drive ways, and painting parking lines and spot numbers. Tell the staff to look around and make a wish list of things they would like to see upgraded at their building. Serve this up as a form of appetizer. Set them up for success by delegating to them and empowering them. They will look at their properties through the eyes of improvement when you allow them to have a say in the property improvement. This is a perfect way to get buy-in and commitment. They will be eager to see their thoughts or suggestions realized. When that happens, they will have a sense of pride and want to surpass their accomplishment next year.
- Shed some light on the areas below and how you think they can be best achieved:

    1. Tenant satisfaction (communication and in-suite preventative maintenance)—keeping tenants happy (through good communication, swift maintenance both behind the door and in common areas including mechanical rooms, and functional equipment)

2. Rent collection—accounts receivables

    "We must collect all rents. That is how we stay in business and grow."

3. Renting vacant or upcoming units

    In the hotel industry we call this "heads in beds." In residential property management we want heads and beds.

4. Curb appeal (interior and exterior)

    Let the staff know that as part of the company standard, you will be inspecting their buildings each month for cleanliness and safety compliance. If your company uses an inspection form, hand each team member a copy and briefly explain each section.

- Hand a copy of the blank performance evaluation to each team member. Review each section and have each one of them indicate how they would like the review to look once you sit down with them. They can keep the filled-out form and check it from time to time to see how well they are doing or measuring up to their own expectation.

b. *Agenda for Monthly Staff Meeting at Individual Properties*

- Welcome and announcements
    - *"It's always nice to see an exciting team together."*
    - *State who is off sick or on vacation.*
- Commendation and recognition
    - *Was there an emergency and the team worked to keep things under control? If so, thank the team.*
    - *Were there a lot of move-outs and move-ins the last month end and the team handled these with grace? If so, thank the team. Point out specific things that were done by the team.*
- Update on capital expenditure work and special projects
    - *"The balcony repair and installation will start soon and additional notices will go out."*
    - *"The elevator repair got approved and will start on [date]. One elevator at a time will be down. I will need your feedback on the anticipated disruption to tenants and how we can keep them happy in the process."*
    - *"In the next four months we will be submitting our list of capital expenditure projects we want to complete for next year. I have completed the list and would like to review the list with you today so we can make any adjustments."*
- Updates from branch office or headquarters
    - *New procedures*
- Health and safety inspection update
    - *"The property is up for inspection. As you do your work, note anything out of place, and any items or things needing repair, and then call them in. Please follow up to ensure they get repaired asap."*
    - *"We have two items outstanding to complete the report."*
- Accounting concerns
    - *"Work specification sheets have not been signed by the property manager to show that the work was approved. Please ensure these are signed before you send them off to the respective contractors."*
    - *"No confirmation of delivery slips are being sent in. We have to ensure the deliveries were made before we can pay for the goods."*
    - *"Physically inspect the work to ensure the contractor did the work. Be sure to confirm the inspection by writing on the work specification sheet 'work completed along with the date.'"*

- Legal updates
  - o "The tenant in apartment [unit number] is taking us to the LTB on [date]. Please clear your calendars. The following staff will be attending court as witnesses [or 'all staff will be attending'], and we will have to get coverage for the building. [List names of those who will be attending.]"
  - o Mention any new forms from the LTB.
- Team-building activity or short Internet video (no longer than 3-5 minutes) on team building. Ask the team what they learned from the video and how they can implement some of the suggestions.
- Upcoming tenant events (seasonal—December holiday social, summer BBQ, and any smaller events as approved by company)
  "Let's think of dates and revise the menus. All staff are required to be present. We will plan the date around vacations."

Any other business and concerns from staff should be addressed, and an update on previous concerns should be provided. Go around the room and ask each team member if they have anything to contribute or add. This is their opportunity to speak about concerns about the job and how these should be addressed or the support they need.

- "Tenants are walking dogs off leash and not picking up after their dogs."
  "If we know which tenants are doing this, we need to send them a letter."
- Cleaning staff: "My eighth floor has a strong odour like cat pee. It's hard to clean the floor when I get there. I feel like throwing up."
  "Book an inspection of all the apartments on the eighth floor to find out the source of the smell. Once the source is identified, I will send the tenant a letter with an action follow-up date. If the tenant fails to comply, I will have the legal department send him or her the appropriate legal document."
- Superintendent" "So-and-So is allowing her dog to go in the south stairwell."
  "Place a concealed camera at the spot where the tenant takes the dog to relieve itself. Review the recording, identify the person, and send her an N5."
- "I hate my vacuum. May I have a new one?"
  Ask the staff to be more specific. Is the vacuum working? What does he or she dislike about the vacuum? If necessary, change the vacuum, but consult with the training facilitator, if your company has one, to determine the most appropriate vacuum to purchase.
- "A tenant asked me if she can get a handicapped door opener on her apartment door . She was just diagnosed with MS."
  "Ask the tenant to write a letter disclosing the disability. She should get her doctor to briefly confirm the disability. Then we'll use the tenant's letter and doctor's letter to request funds for the door opener."
- "I am going on vacation. The last time I went on vacation, the contract cleaner who came made a mess of my building. I had to walk all over to find my things. Can you make sure that person does not clean my building when I am gone?"
  Find out who cleaned the building in the past and ask whom the staff member prefers. If that person is not available, get someone else, but certainly don't get the person who made the staff member upset.
- "When can we get our apartment upgraded like the other apartments?"
  Keep that as a wish list item and discuss the matter with your branch or area manager. Advocate for the staff. They will know you have their best interests at heart.

C. Rewarding and Improving Staff

It has been said that people don't change jobs; they change bosses. If your staff do not feel appreciated, they will not feel the need to stay and grow. Appreciation can be shown to your staff in different ways. As my late aunt advised, "Make your staff better than they were when you got them." Start by always looking for the good in your staff. Tell your staff when you spot that good. Most importantly, nurture whatever good you see in your staff. This is you being of service to the team or individuals on the team. John Maxwell, in his book *The 21 Irrefutable Laws of Leadership*, writes as follows:

Leadership #5, The Law of Addition means leaders add value by serving others. When value is added to the followers, lives are changed. Four guidelines for adding value to others are:

Truly Value Others – effective leaders go beyond not harming others, they intentionally help others. They must value people and demonstrate they care in such a way that their followers know it.

Make Yourself More Valuable To Others – the more intentionally you have been in growing personally, the more you have to offer your followers.

Know and Relate to What Others Value – this can only come by listening to your people's stories, their hopes and dreams. Learn what is valuable to them and then lead based on what you've learned.

Do Things That God Values – God desires us not only to treat people with respect, but also to actively reach out to them and serve them.

The attitude of the leader affects the atmosphere of the office. If you desire to add value by serving others, you will become a better leader. And your people will achieve more, develop more loyalty and have a better time getting things done than you ever thought possible. That's the power of the law of addition.

How do you tell your staff and put it into action that they are valued, appreciated and loved? How do you create an atmosphere or culture that echoes that feeling? By doing the following things:

1. Commend them even for small things they do. Did they drop everything to help you with a quick pop-up project? If so, tell them thank you.
2. If one of them is off sick, get that person a get-well card and have all your staff at the location to sign the card. If the sickness is something the person does not mind talking about (you want to make sure you are not violating any Human Rights code), have all the staff in your portfolio sign the card. If you can get your branch or area manager to sign the card, that would be awesome. This gesture sends a message that you care about the staff.
3. If a staff member is expecting a baby, have a baby shower. Get your staff to sign a congratulatory card. If you do decide to have a baby shower, invite a representative from each of your properties/buildings to attend. If the representatives are unable to attend, have them call in by phone on the day of the shower and wish the parent(s) well.

4. If a staff member is celebrating an anniversary of working with the company, don't let that person wait for the company pin or certificate of appreciation. Those pins, plaques and certificates are great in that they make a formal statement, but what does a staff member have to look forward to in between those milestone years? Smaller gestures are more personal and show you care. They help you connect with the staff and build loyalty, encouraging the staff to make it to that 5- or 10-year milestone with the company.

5. Celebrate with your staff. Do you have an upcoming project, or did you just complete one? Let the team choose the meal they would like to have or the restaurant they would like to go to celebrate. Before you begin the project, ask the team what they want or where they would like to go for a meal.

6. If it is cold outside, take the team coffee and donuts or muffins. If it is hot outside, frozen novelties can cool the team down.

7. The tenants at some locations can be brutal to the staff. If your staff come under verbal or physical attacks from tenants, extend support to your staff.

i. Explore the Possibility of Giving a Second Chance

While I was working at an all-inclusive resort, one of my housekeepers came crying to me one day. In tears, she said the senior managers were going to terminate her employment over an alleged acceptance of tip from a guest. Tipping is not allowed in an all-inclusive resort because gratuity is given as part of the salary. The housekeeper assured me that the allegations were false. She held my hand tightly and pleaded with me, asking if I would please speak to the senior managers on her behalf. She related the importance of the job to her, stating she had kids and bills. In tears, she pleaded with me to help save her job. Having worked with this staff member for some time, I felt I could give her the benefit of the doubt. I calmed her down and told her I would try my best but could not guarantee the outcome. Later I approached one of the senior managers about the situation, indicating the staff had asked me to speak on her behalf. In that brief meeting, I heard the side of the incident that had been reported to the senior managers. After hearing their side of the story detailing the alleged acceptance of the forbidden tip, I focused on the strengths of the housekeeper and her length of service with the company. To the best of my knowledge, I said, the housekeeper had never had a complaint of this kind against her. The housekeeper was one of the top-performing housekeepers. She was fast in cleaning her rooms, she was an excellent cleaner, she had good attendance and she was punctual and polite. Based on these qualities, I recommended to the senior manager that the housekeeper in question be pulled from her assigned work area and be relocated to a new work area. The rationale behind that relocation was that if the matter reoccurred in this new location, then the housekeeper should be dismissed on the basis of mistrust. The recommendation surprisingly was accepted, and the staff member kept her job and functioned well in her new workstation.

Many months passed. I had forgotten about the situation. However, one day several housekeepers called in sick. We had a large checkout and back-to-back check-ins that very day. I had no choice but to call the housekeepers who were on their scheduled time off. Many whom I called said they could not come in because they were either tired or had other plans. The last housekeeper I called told me she was at the beach with her family. Interestingly, without hesitation she said she would go back home and would then show up for work. Her words were "I am doing this only because it's you. I would not do it for anyone else." I was humbled by her comment and appreciative that she was sacrificing her family time to show up for work. In less than an hour she was at work. It turned out to be the housekeeper who had begged me to save her job. I had totally forgotten what I'd done to save her job, but she had not forgotten.

Looking back on this experience reminds me of Leadership 10, the Law of Connection, from *The 21 Irrefutable Laws of Leadership*. Maxwell says, "Leaders touch a heart before they ask for a hand. People don't care how much you know until they know how much you care. You develop credibility with people when you connect with them and show that you genuinely care and want to help them. As a result, they usually respond in kind and want to help you."

Get to know your staff. With good judgement and compassion, reward them with second chances when circumstances call for it. They will thank you by demonstrating their loyalty, sometimes not to the job but to you, the manager. About five years after that experience with the room attendant, I was faced with something similar, this time in Canada. Two staff at one of my buildings acted in a way that did not go against any clearly written company policy, but the principle behind their action was wrong. The matter was investigated, and the findings pointed toward terminating their employment. I was later given the clearance to make the dismissal. That was painfully hard because I really had a professional liking for them. Just like that room attendant, one of the staff begged me to save their job. The staff acknowledged that what they had done was wrong and pleaded for a second chance. The two were a dedicated and hardworking team. I really liked them for their humble, willing attitudes, their respect for me and their passion for the work. Sadly, they had made an unwise decision. My gut told me to give the two a second chance, which I did. Instead of accepting the clearance for the termination, I recommended a transfer. The recommendation was accepted and the two were transferred, not just to a different building but miles away to a different city in another portfolio. I had no control over where the transfer would be. To show I was still thinking of them, I kept in touch with them. I was not mad and wanted them to know that. I was also concerned about their adjustment to and progress in their new location.

The irony of that transfer was that after a year or so, I had difficulty finding suitable staff at one of my larger locations. Who expressed an interest in that location requiring suitable staff? Yes, the same two staff members who had been transferred. I gladly accepted them back into my portfolio. They confessed that they had been shocked by the out-of-city transfer, but said it gave them some time to think, and they learned a huge lesson. They also thanked me for saving their jobs and assured me they were not going to let me down this time. Their words were "We have your back. You helped us, and we will never forget it. We realize you could have dismissed us, but you did not." These two turned out to be my best and strongest staff members. They were not perfect; however, they had a perfect approach to their work. They were like two diamonds that had inclusions but with their value still very much intact. Their loyalty was demonstrated in their high energy and deep desire to work and help to improve the new property to which they were assigned, and they delivered on their promise.

D. Staff Readjustment and Discipline

We do not live in a perfect world, and that includes the people we manage. They will make mistakes, some small and some large in terms of dollar value. If you nag them for every mistake, that makes you a policeman or policewoman. They will feel you are out to get them and therefore they will only make more mistakes. This approach shuts down creativity and growth, stifles potential, takes away self-worth and does damage to overall morale. Never let your staff feel like they are being hunted as if they are wild animals. It is nothing short of assassinating their dignity. It creates an uncomfortable and very stressful work environment, one not conducive to productive work. Under these conditions, as we indicated earlier, staff are prone to making serious mistakes. No one should have to work under those conditions. Discipline or correction should always be done to the proper degree. Anything beyond that is abuse and harassment, thereby making you a dictator or a totalitarian. These characteristics are not part of the makeup of an excellent property manager. Those who choose to go that route are mediocre or average, weak and unprofessional.

I have always expressed to my team that if they follow company policy and procedures, they have my full support and I will fight for them. However, if they deviate from those policies and procedures, they step out of the protective bounds and give me absolutely nothing to stand on if I wish to support them. As a result, I let them know I have to take the necessary corrective action(s) so the policy is not broken again. Having said that, I now ask, at what point do you start:

1. Making notes to yourself?
2. Making notes and adding them to the employee's file?
3. Writing letters and adding them to the employee's file?
4. Or worst of all, terminating the employment of an employee?

From my experience, which of these to choose depends on the seriousness of the violation and on whether or not the team member keeps making the same mistake after you have spoken to him or her. People respond to things in writing differently than they respond to a verbal warning. Take for instance the falsification of the logbook mentioned in an earlier chapter. That was pretty serious and had to be addressed immediately. (*See the sample of a disciplinary letter to address such a scenario.*) What if the staff repeats the behaviour? Initially he or she was warned and retrained. At this point, you need to inform your branch or area manager and recommend a dismissal. Why so drastic? Because this type of staff member is risky to keep. Such a person has demonstrated that he or she cannot be trusted or does not intend to follow company policy and procedures. Your failure to act on this particular case may land you in hot water or, worse, in jail. If something were to happen, the authorities will want to know if you, the property manager, did your due diligence to try to prevent whatever happened.

Safety cannot and must never be compromised. Advertise zero tolerance when it comes to compromising safety. Remember the definition of a team: people working together toward a common goal or to improve a situation. If that staff compromised on safety, how can such an action improve a situation? Can that person be rightfully called a team member? Is he or she risky to keep? It is very important for you to know what must be checked and to do random checks or follow-ups whenever you visit the properties so as to ensure consistent compliance with policy and procedures.

Sample Letter for Missed Dates or Completing Logbooks Ahead of Time

Hi, [Name],

This is to confirm our discussion on [date] regarding the [specify which type] logbook. While doing my routine inspection on the aforementioned date, I observed that the following date[s] was/were missed [or completed into the future]. We regard completing future dates as falsification, which is a very serious safety violation. During our discussion, it was emphasized that maintaining accurate logbook records is part of our company's health and safety policy, which cannot and must never be compromised.

Failure to follow the building routine and physically check this equipment and sign off at the appropriate time shows not only a disregard for maintaining the equipment but also gross insensitivity to human life and to the integrity of the company. Please note that we maintain zero tolerance on this matter. We trust it will not be repeated. Any repeat will be viewed as a demonstration that you do not share our safety protocol, and for this we will have no choice but to end the employment relationship. To clarify any misunderstanding you may have regarding the logbook[s], we have arranged further mandatory training with [name and department], which must be completed within one week from today's date.

If you have any questions, please feel free to contact me.

Regards,

[Name]
Property Manager

cc: [Area or branch manager]
     Employee file

E. Dealing with Disruptive Staffing Situations

Missing work or showing up late

You call the rental office and certain staff members are never in the office and are not cleaning. Or the telephone rings and no one answers. One team member covers for the other. "She is in the washroom" or "He is out doing a work order," one might say of another. "They just stepped away. They are showing and apartment." Follow your intuition or gut feeling. Be sure to alert your branch or area manager about what you suspect might be happening. Are the tenants complaining that the staff cannot be found? Are work orders or service requests being done? The best way to address this concern is to visit the building unannounced. That is why you need your own set of keys to the building, including garage keys. At two different locations I had, every time I visited the property, a certain staff member was always missing. When I asked where that person was, I was *always* told that she was in the washroom/bathroom or with a tenant. Regardless of the time of day I called the building, the answer was *always* the same. I changed the times I visited the property and was *always*, without exception, given the same answer.

To verify if the statements were correct, I conducted my own investigation. One day, on a day I would normally be at the office, I visited the property unannounced. I waited outside the apartment of the staff member and allowed some time to elapse by checking some e-mails. I then called the building's phone and requested for him to meet me in the rental office. The staff member who answered the telephone told me he was with a contractor and would be right there. Of course, the person in question came out of his apartment. When he saw me in the hallway outside his door, he told me he had stopped off to quickly use the washroom. When I inquired about the other staff, I was told *again* that person was in the washroom. Well, these games did not sit well with me. These were telltale signs of laziness that reflected itself in the poor upkeep and lack of cleanliness at the building. During my inquiry, I learned the other staff was actually off the property conducting personal affairs. Now, if that staff had been injured while conducting personal affairs, would that be considered a workplace injury? This was a serious matter. What the staff did not know was that I was making notes every time I called or visited the property and was told one of them was in the washroom. What anyone does in the washroom/bathroom is their business. However, I am not sure what was so special about the washroom. I strongly felt it was an excuse. This behaviour and approach to work was not tolerated. The staff were confronted, and the progressive appropriate actions were taken.

I had a case of MIA (missing in action) where I kept calling the building the entire day and no one was answering the phone. I got concerned and went to the building. The staff who was on duty could not be found, so I contacted the staff who were off duty. Those staff had no idea where the on-duty staff was and related to me that tenants were also knocking on that individual's door as well as their door. I finally called the personal cellphone of the on-duty staff and told him I had been trying for hours to contact him. The staff told me he was in another city. Another what?! Yes, another city, one that was not even close by. It was not even for a family emergency, to which I could say ok. This person was not thinking logically. He was in another city for personal frivolous reasons. If there had been an emergency at the building, such as a fire, who would have assisted the fire department? Any staff who exhibits this kind of behaviour is not serious about his or her job and is a major liability if kept around. I made detailed notes regarding the MIA, and the staff member in question was dealt with appropriately.

Even if you are unable to visit the building one week, what are your tenants calling to report to you? When you get to the building, what is its condition in terms of cleanliness and upkeep? When the tenants see you, what are they complaining about? If it's a community, are the other staff complaining? If you do your routine inspection or check the logbooks, this will help you monitor what is happening at the properties. If you missed that building in your last inspection, do the inspection as soon as possible. Let the staff in question come with you, and listen out for the excuses. If they tell you they cleaned an area last week or a few days ago, you will know whether or not that is the truth. During my time in the hotel industry, I learned that fresh dust blows in the wind when you touch it or run your hand along any surface. Fresh dust also comes up as thin film. Stale or built-up dust rolls or drops, too heavy and grimy to be carried by the wind. Therefore, if the staff cleaned or missed a day cleaning, you will know. They may have been busy. If they have not done any cleaning for some time, you will also know.

If after your building inspection you determine that the building is in poor shape in terms of cleanliness and upkeep, sit and have a discussion with the staff. This is a discussion you should take notes during, and you should send those notes off to human resources, along with a copy of the building inspection. Indicate the date, time and location. Share all your concerns with the staff and ask probing questions to see what is causing the decline in the cleanliness standard. Do they need more tools or better equipment? Are they sick? Are they having issues with other aspects of the job? Do they need help, and if so, why? Is the location a stand-alone building or a community? Have you increased the workload? Do you have an upgrade project happening in the building? Be realistic. Or is the staff just being lazy? What if anything in the building has changed in terms of workload or projects? Do your follow-up inspection to confirm if the staff completed the item(s) or area(s) you have pointed out in your inspection. Let them know you will be confirming your discussion in the form of a letter. Serve that letter within a week of the meeting. Do not delay. During your follow-up, if you see improvements, commend the staff. If there are no improvements and no known external factor to account for the deficiency, follow your progressive discipline procedure. Be sure to work with your AM and/or HR regarding this particular case.

Timing

Sometimes the timing to administer discipline may not be convenient. You may have to delay or change the plan. During one building inspection, I observed that a top-performing staff had noticeably dropped behind in her cleaning. The staff member was not present for the inspection, and the superintendent could give no reason for the substandard cleaning. This was not within the character of the cleaner, so I scheduled a meeting with her. She later called to cancel the meeting, citing a family emergency, which progressively got worse. When the staff returned to work, the timing was still not correct. There were indications that she was trying her best, but her work was barely meeting the standard. A meeting was still held with the staff to ascertain how she was doing personally. I had other staff check in on the staff in question to let her know that she was still part of the team. I pointed out to the staff that I could only imagine how difficult it was for her and said that the fact that she showed up for work was quite encouraging. I thanked her for the areas that showed improvement and told her that in due time the building would be up to the sparkling standard again. In addition to those words, I broke down the work for her so she could focus on "bite sizes" of the job. This helped her to realign her focus. Not long after this, the staff was back to her old self, following the cleaning standard. The incidents were documented just in case the staff were to come back and say she had gotten no support when she was dealing with a very serious family emergency.

Other issues you may have to deal with are staff who do the following things:

- *Drink alcohol, take recreational drugs or use medical cannabis/marijuana on the job.* Know and understand the signs of impairment from recreational or prescribed substance. Impairment is a hazard to everyone, including the one that is impaired. Both you and your company have a duty to provide a safe environment for all workers. An impaired site staff is a huge liability to the property and, by extension, to the company. Being under the influence or dependence of a recreational or prescribed substance will affect the staff's ability in different ways to respond to emergencies or carry out the job in a safe way. Recreational or prescribed substance may also slow down a person's ability to work at what may be considered a normal pace. This can also cause tension on the job among other staff who have to pick up the slack.

  Sometimes when staff are engaged in the use and dependence of recreational substance, they may not show up for work and hide under the guise of calling in sick. Other signs to look out for are hair looking dishevelled, fatigued, offensive body odour mixed with alcohol and or drugs smell. The quality of their work will most likely be affected. In some cases, there could also be incidents of volatile domestic issues that are carried over into the work environment. Make sure you document all these observations and work carefully with your AM and or HR department on how you should handle these cases so that no human rights code is violated.

  What if you have a staff who is taking "medical marijuana/cannabis"? This is such a grey area that could lead to violation of the staff's human rights if not handled properly. If a staff discloses that they have been prescribed (in whatever form) or they are taking medical marijuana, are there repercussions for disclosing that information to you? What policies and procedures does your company have in place through its human resources department, Joint Health and Safety Committee (JHSC) or what can you the property manager put in place to accommodate the staff? Can the staff safely carry out their duties while under the effects of this "medication," or will they have to be put on modified duties? In extreme cases will the staff have to be off work for a period of time? Make sure you get legal advice before you implement any policy.

Once the Cannabis Act comes into force on October 17, 2018, the recreational and medical use of marijuana is expected to increase. It is important for you and your company to conduct training on impairment and establish acceptable standards of behaviour, performance as well as possession and use of recreational substance or medical marijuana. The training of your staff will show you have done your due diligence. To properly address behaviours, assess and document the employee on performance. You can also refer to your company's employee handbook. If you do not have one, speak to your AM or HR department about how to proceed. In most cases these personnel are given legal advice on how to help you and your other colleagues proceed. HR's approach may not necessarily mean dismissal but may mean getting the staff the correct help through any employee assistance program (EAP) and where possible, take appropriate progressive disciplinary steps. In Canada, you cannot ask the staff to do a drug test, as this could be getting into a plethora of human rights violations. This situation could be a form of "disability"; hence, you want to ensure you are following any human rights code or local laws. For your benefit, I recommend you take the initiative and do online e-learning courses offered by Canadian Centre for Occupational Health and Safety (CCOHS) on impairment and cannabis related topics. It may also be necessary to obtain legal advice on the matter and update any employee handbook after the fact.

- *Engage in or are victims of domestic abuse.* No property manager likes dealing with supers or a building manager couple who fight. What kind of example are they setting for the tenants? No tenant will respect staff who fight. Hence you may find yourself with a vacancy issue. Even if tenants have their own personal issue of domestic abuse to endure, they do not want to hear your staff fighting. This also kills morale of the other staff. Once you are aware of this kind of abuse, you are, under the Occupational Health and Safety Act, expected to implement measures to protect the staff. Do not forget, too, that the apartment where the superintendent or building manager couple lives is part of the workplace. If your company has an employee assistance program (EAP), the staff should be referred to the program after you have had a conversation with the staff. Also, some cities have crisis centres and organizations that can offer assistance. Be sure to tap into these resources and seek help for the staff at risk. Always document what you have done to assist the staff, as this will be evidence of your due diligence. Make sure your company has strategic interventions so that it will not become a legal issue if the employment has to be terminated.

However you discipline your staff, you should do so in a way that does not demoralize them. Their dignity should *always* remain intact, so much so that they should have the moral energy to correct that which has been pointed out to them. If you fail to handle this matter properly, it could have a greater demoralizing effect on your staff. Do it properly and this may also increase the respect and trust your other staff have for you. If training is needed, provide the necessary training in a timely manner and document it. Does the staff need counselling? If your company offers this service, make sure the staff in question is referred to receive the necessary help.

F. Performance Evaluations

Evaluations are done in every aspect of our lives for different reasons. Your first set of evaluations occurred during the different stages of your development inside your mother's womb until you were born. Evaluations will continue until you are no more. Remember when you were in school and the school would send a report card every term or semester to your parents or guardians? That was also a form of performance evaluation. However often it was done, that report card gave your parents or guardians an idea of how you were performing or doing in school. The process that your teachers used when completing the report card required that you meet certain criteria or standards for your age and grade level in select subject areas. The report card gave a summary of whether you were at, above or below your grade level for your age in select subject area(s). Some schools and communities had programs that provided needed assistance if students were not performing at grade level. Some of these programs may have included extra classes and after-school tutoring in math and various subjects so those students could improve.

This reporting system follows you even when you get to college or university. At this level, you do not get a report card, but you are given grades, and those grades determine whether you complete your program of choice and get your diploma. When you apply for a loan, banks and other financial institutions conduct a performance evaluation in the form of checking your credit score, confirming your employment and determining a possible guarantor. In the medical field, the evaluation of a patient is called a complete physical examination. In the workplace, the evaluation may be called a performance appraisal, performance review, performance evaluation or performance assessment. Regardless of what it is called, the purpose of a performance evaluation is to let others know, or to give them an idea or a sense of, where they are and what they have or have not accomplished. Even before you begin new employment, an evaluation of some sort is done of you in the form of reference checks and a police background check, and in some cases a drug test (not done in Canada as it could be viewed a violation of human rights on the basis of disability or perceived disability), all to determine your suitability for the new job. When you start to work, the criteria change to reflect the goals and culture of the company or the established standards unique to the industry. Unlike your school report, the performance evaluation is not sent to your parents, or your mate if you are now married. It is discussed with you in a meeting with your immediate supervisor.

When you are given the responsibility of preparing a performance evaluation for staff you supervise, it is not something that you should take lightly. The performance evaluation is a very important document that must be honestly and properly prepared, using all factors and variables applicable to the company and the staff's job responsibilities. Performance evaluations become part of the employee's file and can determine if and how a staff member moves on with the company. If for any reason you must go to court regarding employment-related issues, the performance evaluation is sometimes brought into question. Therefore, when you prepare a performance evaluation, do so in a way that, if need be, it can stand up in a court of law.

i. How to Prepare a Performance Evaluation

As a property manager, you may ask yourself, *What goes into writing a good performance evaluation?* Following are four things to remember about writing performance evaluations:

1. Do not use the performance evaluation to tear team members down. It should not be seen as an opportunity to unleash your wrath on the staff. If team members are broken, or made to feel that way, they cannot stand and feel like they are part of your team.
2. The purpose of writing a performance evaluation is simply to narrate what the staff has been doing to assist in achieving the property's goals and by extension the company's goals. This includes what the staff did well and what they need to improve on.
3. It is an opportunity for the staff and company representatives to sit down together and see how well they were both able to meet the assigned company goals.
4. The performance evaluation indicates what support you, the property manager, have given to the staff to achieve those goals.

Each company is different and will use different criteria that are unique to the company or its industry. Regardless of what standards are used to measure the performance of your staff, below are some factors you could consider to assist you in capturing what the staff member has been doing in his or her role.

1. Review the job description of the staff member if you are new to the company. The job description will give you an idea of what the staff should be doing.
2. Review the performance evaluation form before you begin the review. This will give you an idea of how to summarize the information.
3. Review the most recent performance evaluation for the staff. This will give you an idea of the staff's previous performance so you can compare it to their current performance to determine if the staff is improving.
4. How does the staff address concerns highlighted on the monthly building inspection reports or other inspection reports? When you do follow-up inspections, are previously noted items addressed?
5. When you visit the property, what kinds of feedback do you give the staff regarding the upkeep?
6. What kinds of feedback do you get from tenants regarding the upkeep of the property, or work orders or service requests tenants have submitted?
7. What kinds of conversations do you hear over the two-way communication radio? The tone of the conversation gives insight into staff relationships. Is the conversation professional? Do you detect anger or frustration?
8. Does the staff member follow systems and routines? Does he or she follow your instructions as well as company policies and procedures?
9. Is the staff on the property during working hours, or is he or she elsewhere when he or she should be on the property?

10. What kind of feedback do you get from the other staff, external contractors and departments who work with this staff?
11. What is your rapport with the staff?
12. What value does the individual bring to the property?
13. Are there any unresolved concerns with this staff? Do you have previous notes on file for this staff?
14. If you are evaluating, for example, a superintendent couple/team, do you know and understand each team member? If you don't, then you cannot give a true evaluation.

In your evaluation, include only concerns you have spoken to the staff about. Do not spring anything new on the staff in the evaluation. The evaluation should also include any improvement the staff has made in light of areas you have pointed out to him or her. Always state the facts. The evaluation should not be written out of fear of the employee's anger or retaliation. If the staff has that attitude, he or she should be given the opportunity through training or counselling to correct it and/or make the necessary adjustments. In fact, it is wise to have someone else with you to review the performance evaluation with this person.

If the staff is not strong in a particular area of the job, does the company have a system in place that can assist that staff to improve? Remember schools have after-school programs to assist students who are performing below the recommended standards. If your credit is bad, there are credit counsellors who can assist you in repairing your credit. If your health is poor, your doctor may recommend lifestyle changes and refer you to a specialist. Hence, what does your company have in place to help staff whose performance is below standard? Make use of any programs designed to help staff improve. Recommend those programs where necessary. Be sure to note those recommendations on the evaluation. Use action dates to ensure recommendations or goals are met.

On the following page, find the evaluation form I designed to reflect the responsibilities of staff at the property level.

ii. Site Staff Performance Evaluation Form

Name(s) of Employee(s): _____

Job Title(s): _____ Location: _____

Date: _____ Evaluation Period: From _____ To _____

Type of Evaluation: Probationary: _____ Annual: _____ Job Change/Promotion: _____

Name of Supervisor/PM: _____

Performance indicators are: excellent, good, meets standard, needs improvement and not applicable or N/A

Customer service

We are in the business of attracting tenants. All our tenants deserve to be understood and treated with respect. This adds to their happiness and satisfaction. It makes it easier for them to call their apartment home.

Area of performance	Excellent	Good	Meets standard	Needs improvement	N/A
Prompt and efficient service to tenants					
Polite, friendly and professional					
Ability to deal with difficult tenants					

Comments: _____

_____

_____

Work attitude

Your approach, behaviour and mindset toward your duties

Area of performance	Excellent	Good	Meets standard	Needs improvement	N/A
Punctuality					
Attendance					
Team player					
Approach to training					
Work at own initiative					
Ability to deal with feedback					
Ability to meet deadlines					

Comments: _____

_____

_____

Maintenance

This helps us to preserve the useful life of the property. A well-maintained and cared for building attracts and keeps happy tenants.

Area of work	Excellent	Good	Meets standard	Needs improvement	N/A
In-suite					
Common area					
Carpentry repairs					
Cleanliness of utility rooms					
Cleanliness and organization of workshop					
Ordering supplies					
Receiving and storing supplies					
Plumbing repairs					
Instruct and supervise contractors					
Electrical repairs					
Miscellaneous					

Comments: _____

_____

_____

General common area cleaning

Cleaning adds to the curb appeal of the property. It is a very important aspect of property maintenance. A clean property attracts and keeps our tenants. There can be no compromise in any of these areas as they all complement each other.

Area of work	Excellent	Good	Meets standard	Needs improvement	NA
Laundry room					
Amenities: gym, pool, storage room, theatre, etc.					
Fire cabinets					
Doors, doorframes and baseboards					
Stairwells and hallways					
Elevator cabs and tracks					
Light shades					
Garbage chute					
Garbage room					

Area of work	Excellent	Good	Meets standard	Needs improvement	NA
Recycle room/area					
Lobby					
Move-out area/room					
Garbage removal around the property					

Comments: _____
_____
_____

Vacant apartment and guest suite cleaning

Providing a clean apartment for a tenant to move in to shows we delivered on our promise. It is a beautiful way to start off the tenancy. It shows our company has standards and tells tenants how we want them to treat the apartment. We do well to extend those clean surroundings to our guest suites so that guest of tenants or our staff can feel comfortable if they wish to stay over.

Area of work	Excellent	Good	Meets standard	Needs improvement	N/A
Bathroom / en suite					
Bedrooms					
Living room					
Balcony					
Kitchen					
Cabinets					
Appliances					
Light shades					
Windows					
Doors and doorframes					
Closets and storage					
Miscellaneous					

Comments: _____
_____
_____

Reception and administration

This is the binding agent or glue. It helps to paint a clear picture and gives direction to all the other areas of the property.

Area of performance	Excellent	Good	Meet standard	Needs improvement	N/A
Telephone communication					
Report writing					
Filing					
Renting apartments and upselling amenities					
Incoming and outgoing inspection					
Planners and delivery notes/slips					
Desk and office organization					

Comments: _____
_____
_____

Rent and revenue collection

Collected rent and other revenue sustains the building. This helps us to operate a safe building by paying our utilities and contractors. No one should owe any rent. Collected rent helps us to keep our staff happy and fulfills our promise of compensation to you or other staff. Strive always to meet the target for the community.

Area of performance	Excellent	Good	Meets standard	Needs improvement	|N/A
Lawful rent					
Storage locker audit					
Parking audits					
Guest suite					
Social or party room					
AC form/addendum					
Ability to communicate with legal & accounting department and serve documents					

Comments: _____
_____
_____

Logbooks and safety

Physically checking equipment to ensure it is working properly is of utmost importance to the preservation of lives. Monitoring weather conditions and responding to emergencies also shows respect for life.

Area of performance	Excellent	Good	Meets standard	Needs improvement	N/A
Emergency response					
Maintenance log					
Snow log					
Snow blower and tractor log					
Fire logbook					
Wears personal protective equipment					

Comments: _____

_____

_____

Current personal job-related goals	Current company goals for staff
	Training: Areas to improve:
Previous personal job-related goals	**Previous company goals staff**

Supervisor's summary of performance:

_____

_____

_____

_____

Employee's assessment of the evaluation and opportunity to comment on performance:

_____
_____
_____
_____

Verification of review

Signature of Employee: _____ Signature of Employee: _____

Signature of PM/Supervisor: _____ Signature of Branch Manager: _____

Signature of Human Resources: _____

iii. Sample of a Building Manager's Performance Evaluation

Name(s) of Employee(s): _____ Team _____

Job Title(s): _____ Building Manager _____ Location: _____ Motivation Community _____

Date: _____ Evaluation Period: From _____ To _____

Type of Evaluation: Probationary: _____ Annual: __X__ Job Change/Promotion: _____

Name of Supervisor: _____ Excellent Property Manager _____

Performance indicators are: excellent, good, meets standard, needs improvement and not applicable or N/A

Customer service

We are in the business of attracting tenants. All our tenants deserve to be understood and treated with respect. This adds to their happiness and satisfaction. It makes it easier for them to call their apartment home.

Area of performance	Excellent	Good	Meets standard	Needs improvement	N/A
Prompt and efficient service to tenants	X				
Polite, friendly and professional	X				
Ability to deal with difficult tenants		X			

Comments: Team knows the tenants by name. They both understand the tenant base and care about the satisfaction of the tenants. An example of this is when general notices are posted, the team ensure older tenants and the physically challenged who seldom leave their apartments are given a copy under their door. We appreciate their high level of personalized customer service.

Work attitude

Your approach, behaviour and mindset toward your duties

Area of performance	Excellent	Good	Meets standard	Needs improvement	N/A
Punctuality		X			
Attendance	X				
Team player	X				
Approach to training	X				
Work at own initiative	X				
Ability to deal with feedback		X			
Ability to meet deadlines		X			

Comments: <u>Team have a very good work attitude. They bring a vibrant energy to the community, which adds to the positive team spirit. This approach is appreciated especially during a heavy month-end. Team remain calm and are able to help the group focus on the work at hand.</u>

Maintenance

This helps us to preserve the life of the property. A well-maintained and cared for building attracts and keeps happy tenants.

Area of work	Excellent	Good	Meets standard	Needs improvement	N/A
In-suite				X	
Common area	X				
Carpentry repairs			X		
Cleanliness of utility rooms		X			
Cleanliness and organization of workshop			X		
Ordering supplies		X			
Receiving and storing supplies			X		
Plumbing repairs			X		
Instruct and supervise contractors			X		
Electrical repairs			X		
Miscellaneous repairs			X		

Comments: <u>[Name] is very proactive in his approach to maintenance. He quickly addresses any repairs in the common areas of the community. We encourage [name] to take the same approach to work requests inside occupied units. [Name] does not call contractors unnecessarily. Whenever contractors are called, he gives very clear directions and supervises their work to ensure it meets company standards.</u>

General common area cleaning

Cleaning adds to the curb appeal of the property. It is a very important aspect of property maintenance. It attracts and keeps our tenants. There can be no compromise in any of these areas, as they all complement each other.

Area of work	Excellent	Good	Meets standard	Needs improvement	N/A
Laundry room			X		
Amenities: gym, pool, storage room, theatre, etc.			X		
Fire cabinets			X		
Doors, doorframes and baseboards			X		

Area of work	Excellent	Good	Meets standard	Needs improvement	N/A
Stairwells and hallways			X		
Elevator cabs and tracks			X		
Light shades			X		
Garbage chute			X		
Garbage room			X		
Recycle room/area			X		
Lobby		X			
Move-out area/room			X		
Garbage removal around the property			X		

Comments: <u>When minimal staff are on duty, especially on weekends and holidays, team ensure the basic cleaning is done so tenants wake up to a clean building. During regular business hours, the team is not afraid to help the cleaners if they are busy doing other things throughout the community.</u>

Vacant apartment and guest suite cleaning

Providing a clean apartment for a tenant to move in to shows we delivered on our promise. It is a beautiful way to start off the tenancy. It shows our company has standards and tells tenants how we want them to treat the apartment. We do well to extend those clean surroundings to our guest suites so that guest of tenants or our staff can feel comfortable if they wish to stay over.

Area of work	Excellent	Good	Meets standard	Needs improvement	N/A
Bathroom / en suite	X				
Bedrooms	X				
Living room	X				
Balcony	X				
Kitchen	X				
Cabinets	X				
Appliances	X				
Light shades	X				
Windows	X				
Doors and doorframes	X				
Closets and storage	X				
Miscellaneous					

Comments: <u>[Name] ensures apartments are cleaned before tenants move in. She will physically check and follow up on the cleaners to confirm that work is going as planned. She is very good at co-ordinating with contractors working in vacant apartments and new tenants to stagger the</u>

move-in process so tenants can move in to clean apartments. Guest suite is always clean and ready for the next person to use.

Reception and administration

This is the binding agent or glue. It helps to paint a clear picture and gives direction to all the other areas of the property.

Area of performance	Excellent	Good	Meets standard	Needs improvement	N/A
Telephone communication	X				
Report writing			X		
Filing				X	
Renting apartments and upselling amenities	X				
Incoming and outgoing inspection				X	
Planners		X			
Desk and office organization			X		

Comments: [Name] has great administrative skills and is great at renting apartments. If the office is busy, she still answers the telephone and asks the caller if they will hold. She returns to them after dealing with her previous task. Planners are always written with clarity. She also sets aside a day with her property manager to have planners signed before they are sent off to contractors. This helps to facilitate a smooth month-end procedure. She would do well to file work orders once they are completed. She needs to be more detailed with incoming and outgoing inspection reports.

Rent and revenue collection

Collected rent and other revenue sustains the building. This helps us to operate a safe building by paying our utilities. No one should owe any rent. Collected rent helps us to keep our staff happy and fulfills our promise of compensation to you or other staff. Strive always to meet the target for the community.

Areas of performance	Excellent	Good	Meets standard	Needs improvement	|N/A
Lawful rent		X			
Locker audit	X				
Parking audits			X		
Guest suite	X				
Party or social room	X				
AC forms		X			
Ability to communicate with legal & accounting department and serve documents		X			

Comments: <u>The apartment rent collection for the building is low and sometimes within the target. While effort is put forth, we believe more persistent and continuous door knocking can exceed the target for the community. Team conducts annual locker room and parking audit to ensure all spots are accounted for and paid for by tenants. If they are doing a work order and observe an air-conditioner unit inside the apartment, they will follow up to see if the tenant completed the AC addendum form and paid.</u>

Logbooks and safety

Physically checking equipment to ensure it is working properly is of utmost importance to the preservation of lives. Monitoring weather conditions and responding to emergencies also shows respect for the life of everyone on property.

Area of performance	Excellent	Good	Meets standard	Needs improvement	N/A
Emergency response	X				
Maintenance log	X				
Snow log	X				
Snow blower and tractor log	X				
Fire logbook	X				
Wears personal protective equipment	X				

Comments: <u>Team are very safety-conscious. If they are off duty and an emergency occurs, they show up to assist the team on duty. An example of this is the recent flood in the rental office. They helped the team on duty to move the furniture and then vacuum the office to minimize the damage.</u>

Current personal job-related goals	Current company goals for staff
	Training: • AR reduction strategies • Incoming and outgoing inspection report Areas to improve: • Work on reducing AR for apartments • Completing detailed inspection reports • Work orders for apartments to be completed 48 hours after submitted • File work orders once they are completed
Previous personal job-related goals	**Previous company goals for staff**
	• Planners sent to contractors with signature of PM. Achieved.

Supervisor's summary of performance:

Team is a great fit for Motivational Community. Their positive attitude helps the rest of the team to deal with challenges in a calm and focused way. They are respected and loved by the tenants and the staff they lead. Team take great pride in the job and take personal ownership of the property. They embrace change with a positive attitude. It is a sincere pleasure working with them. I look forward to continuing this work relationship and helping them in their growth with the company.

Employee's assessment of the evaluation and opportunity to comment on performance:

_____
_____
_____
_____

Verification of review

Signature of Employee: _____ Signature of Employee: _____

Signature of Supervisor: _____ Signature of Branch Manager: _____

Signature of Human Resources: _____

G. Job Interviews and Staff Selection

When you take on the job of property manager, you may already have staff in place. However, at some point in your role, you will have to conduct job interviews either for your own portfolio or for that of a colleague. Depending on the size of your company, you may not be the one to conduct the initial telephone interview and arrange an in-person job interview. Obviously if a candidate made it to the in-person interview, something about him or her must have stood out. Since the prospective employee will be working for you, hire based on the following:

- The needs of your portfolio and the personality of the other staff and the tenant base or type. In other words, will the potential staff fit in with the existing staff and tenants at the building?
- The needs of the location for which you are hiring. Is it a building or a community? Those needs will gauge how the interview is conducted.
- The kind of energy the prospect projects.

If possible, always do a job interview with a property manager colleague or human resources representative. Whoever will co-interview with you, ensure you inform that person of the date and time of the interview. This allows the person to clear his or her calendar to accommodate the interview. Meet with the colleague who will be conducting the interview with you before you begin the interview. State clearly to your colleague, the location and vacancy you are trying to fill and what you are looking for in the potential staff. Your co-interviewer will likely see things you may miss. After the interview is finished, you can sound your opinions and observations off each other. This other person will be your co-pilot or spotter. Always thank your colleague who conducted the interview with you at the end of the interview.

The actual interview

The assessment of any potential staff for an in-person interview starts the minute the person steps foot on the interviewing location. How is the person dressed? How does he or she smell? Is he or she too early, like by one hour? This can throw you off. It is nice to be early, but if the person demands to be seen before the scheduled time, don't waste your time to see him or her. This is not a good attitude and indicates that the person doesn't respect your time. This person is all about himself or herself. People like this potentially will go above you rather than work with you to get what they want. If the prospect discussed with you beforehand the possibility of an earlier interview time, fine. If not, stick with the agreed upon time. If you go to see the potential candidate and he or she tells you he or she cannot stay long for the interview, find out why. Is the person on the job, having come in for a quick interview? Never interview in a hurry. Use probing questions to determine what the person is trying to escape from at his or her current place of employment.

During the interview

Most candidates are usually nervous for an interview. Calming their nerves with humour will help to relax them and make them talk more than they normally would. Once they are comfortable, it is easier for you to probe for answers. Start the conversation the minute you greet the candidate. Be sure to greet with a firm but not a killer handshake.

"Hi, [candidate]. I am Simone, the property manager. Thank you for coming. How was the drive? Is this your first time in the area?" Wait for an answer. This will let you know if the candidate has friends or family in the area. If he or she does, you will sense any deep desire for the job. The person may tell you he or she grew up in the area or once lived in the area and is quite familiar with it.

When you interview to fill positions of vacancy within your portfolio, you have to be prepared for anything and everything in the interview. This includes being flexible and accommodating. For one interview I did, the candidate brought her preschool-age child into the interview room. She came on her day off, which meant the sitter, who was a relative, was off. Like the parent, the child was nicely dressed and well-spoken. I had a brief child-friendly conversation with the child to get him comfortable and put the parent at ease. The child told me about school and about his grandmother, who was the sitter. That brief conversation also confirmed the parent's earlier comment. The child agreed to do some paperwork while I spoke with his parent. I wrote the letters of the alphabet and had the boy rewrite those letters, twice. Surprisingly the child kept quiet and completed the work I gave him. Once the interview was over, I had to give the child check marks and a high-five as a reward for being a good child. My skills as a teacher and a tutor came in handy. I also wanted to demonstrate to the potential staff, the child's parent, that the company was family-oriented and show the compassionate side of my ability to lead. Given the nature of the business, where some staff lived on the property with their family members, this was acceptable. It was within reason to accommodate this person with her child in the interview.

Find out who the candidate is first before you tell him or her about the company. This will let you know if you wish to continue with the interview. If you are satisfied, ask the person questions related to behaviour. This will tell you how he or she will act in similar situations.

Confirm the position for which the person is applying by asking, "What do you know about the position and the company?"

Say, "You have a very impressive resume. Tell me about yourself." This question allows the person to provide personal information you may not ask because of human rights laws. The person will open up to you. If it's a team position, you will know how long the couple have been together, how many children they have (if any), which of their relatives live in the area, how long they have been in the industry and any future plans they have. The answer to this question reveals things not written on the resume.

"Tell me how you start your day." You are looking for structure and the individual's ability to follow a system or routine.

"Explain how you prepare for month end." This lets you know if the person is organized or chaotic.

Pose a real-life scenario. "Let's say today is month end with 10 tenants moving out and 10 more moving in. Walk me through how you manage the process." Listen out for the person's ability to prioritize, organize and work with vacating tenants and new tenants to stagger the move-in dates and times to make the process smooth and seamless.

"Tell me about two of your difficult and very challenging tenants. What kind of customer service do you extend to calm them down?" This gives you an idea of the person's ability and willingness to work with difficult tenants and remain calm and focused.

"It's dinnertime and you are in the middle of your meal. A tenant calls to say they have a fire or a sewer flood. What would you do in either situation?" This gives you an idea of the person's ability and willingness to handle an emergency. He or she may tell you about something similar he or she has dealt with before.

Let the person know the rough side of the job. That way, he or she will never be able to say that you hid that from him or her or that he or she did not know what he or she was getting into.

The person's ability to do the work and to fit in to the location being interviewed for

Scenario A

"At this location, we have *x* number of apartments. The amenities are [list them]. The tenants at this location are professionals, which means they are very demanding. They are not afraid to call here or our executives to report any concerns. They are high-maintenance and expect every problem to be resolved before they even complete the sentence describing it. Does this sound like somewhere you want to work? Remember that you will be living here as well. What would you be bringing to this company that makes you the correct fit for this location?"

Here, you have given the candidate(s) an escape route or an opportunity to state their ability to deliver.

Scenario B

This will scare the candidate or reveal his or her substance.

"At this location, we have *x* number of apartments. It's a fast-paced environment with an average of 10 to 15 move-outs each month. During busy seasons, that amount is doubled. At this location, we have a major pest problem—roaches and bedbugs. Some tenants can be very rude when they find out they have bedbugs or cockroaches. In some cases, you may have to do emergency work orders inside any of these units should an emergency arise. We have two other teams that we have interviewed for this location. Why should we consider you over them?"

This is a tricky question. You have given the person an opportunity to hop out of the interview and run away from the problem. The answer you are listening out for includes the information that the person has dealt with bedbugs before and knows exactly how to book treatments and ensure tenants are prepared for treatments. The person is not afraid. Look for a willingness to work with tenants, contractors and others to address the problem.

The candidate's ability to work with you and the current staff at the location

"What did you like about your previous property manager or supervisor?"

This will tell you the kind of relationship the person had and what he or she is not looking for. Can you work with such a person?

"Tell me about the last disagreement you had with your property manager. What did you do to improve the relationship?"

This will tell you if the person is a peacemaker or peace disrupter. It will let you know if he or she is needy or, on the other hand, has a willing attitude.

At this point you can state your management approach and style. State also the kind of person or team you are looking for to fill the vacancy. Ask the candidate if this is something he or she can work with.

Engage the candidate and ask if he or she has any questions for you before you move to the section of the interview where you telling him or her about the company and benefits. Or you can end the interview at this point.

Request the person's authorization to conduct any necessary checks such as background check and reference check. Thank him or her for coming.

While the candidate is doing the paperwork, excuse yourself to speak with your colleague who conducted the interview with you in a separate office. Share with this colleague what you observed during the interview. If your branch/area manager is present, include him or her in the discussion if he or she is available. One area/branch manager once told me, "Always ask yourself the question, If it did not work out, would I be surprised? If you say you would not be surprised, then do not make the hire. Follow your gut feelings."

If you like the candidate, ask if he or she would like to see the location being interviewed for and meet some of the staff. Prior to your interview, you would have informed the staff at the location that you may be sending a potential team or candidate to view the property. If the potential team is not able to make the visit after the interview to the site with the vacancy, immediately make arrangements for another, convenient time. Obviously, you may want to conduct the interview on the days your key staff at that location are at work. If you are interviewing for a superintendent team, the building manager team should do the tour with the hopefuls. They should show the potential staff the main areas—utility rooms and the apartment where they will live if they are employed—plus give them a brief tour of the whole property. Have your staff call you the minute the potential team or candidate leaves.

The question you should ask of your current staff is, do you like them? Why or why not? Your staff will be working with these new hopefuls. Listen to your staff and share only what you are permitted by law and company policy to share about the candidate with the current staff. By including the current site staff in the process of hiring, you will help to build a team of people who can work together. In most cases, the new hopefuls will be more relaxed while viewing the property, since they are in an informal setting, and may share information they may not have disclosed to you.

Once clearance is obtained and the reference check is completed, touch base with your branch/area manager and agree on a salary. Arrange any orientation and training before you call and inform the hopefuls who will become part of your team. If an apartment is part of the salary package, that apartment should be cleaned and any necessary repairs done before the hopeful(s) move in. The condition of that apartment will be seared into the new hires' minds as to the standard you expect of them.

Pest Control Management

The location and the tenant base of your properties will sometimes affect the type and frequency of pests you have and must treat. Some cities will be famous for bedbugs, some for cockroaches, some for mice, some for fleas, some for mould and some for a combination of all of the above. The pests I had the most gut-wrenching challenges and experiences with were bedbugs and cockroaches. I dealt with other pests, but they were secondary when compared to the magnitude and volume of bedbugs and cockroaches. In this chapter, references will be made to how these pests (bedbugs and cockroaches) were dealt with at properties where they posed a significant problem.

Controlling pests inside your buildings can be very challenging. A pest of any kind can affect your bottom line. Pests will drive tenants out faster than any legal proceedings. However, bear in mind that this method of eviction *is not* the wisest route to take to get rid of your tenants. In the long run, it can be very costly from a legal standpoint and can ruin the reputation of the property, ruin the company brand beyond repair and destroy your ability as a property manager to effectively address the problem. If you allow a pest problem to get out of control, remember it is not a good reflection on you as a property manager. Therefore, as a property manager, you should do everything necessary to get rid of all pests in buildings that you suspect of having pests, whether those buildings are new additions to your portfolio or existing buildings within your portfolio.

If your tenants live with pests, it takes away the "reasonable enjoyment" to which they are entitled under the RTA. People associate pests with dirt and an unclean environment. An excellent property manager is proactive and vigilant when it comes to pest control management. An excellent property manager will also work co-operatively with his or her staff, area manager (AM), tenants and pest control company—and health department if necessary—to eradicate pests of any kind from the buildings in his or her portfolio.

A. The Consequences of Not Treating Pests

Regardless of the type of pests, early detection and quick action are key to eradicating them. If not treated aggressively, properly and timely, pests can make your job as a property manager gruelling, resulting in the following domino effect:

- You will have to make multiple trips to the Landlord and Tenant Board (LTB). Your trips to the LTB will be like a revolving door, meaning you will be in and out of the LTB trying to settle and prove your cases with unhappy and miserable tenants.
- Your time at the office will be spent addressing concerns from angry and unhappy tenants who are affected by the pests.
- Pests affect availability by eating away at your revenue. No one wants to live in a pest-infested apartment. Vacant apartments spell no rent. No rent means no profit.
- Your building will have a bad reputation and will also be labelled as a bedbug or cockroach building. Never forget that we live in a world of reality TV. The various social media allow people to put information out as events are happening, for the world to see. Think about what an upset tenant can do if he or she has pests such as cockroaches and or bedbugs.
- Pests affect the level at which you can set rents. Even if your product normally commands above-market rent, you may have to settle for below-market rent just to fill the vacant apartments.
- Pests affect the quality of tenants you will attract, creating another headache if you end up with undesirable tenants.
- Pests affect staff morale at the building. Unhappy tenants will vent on the site staff, and this can drain staffs' mental and physical energy and kill their desire to get through the day or even remain on the job.
- Pests affect staffing by increasing turnover and the quality of staff you can employ. You will have to settle for who you can get and *not* who you really want or need.
- Not only do pests affect staffing, but also you may be forced to overcompensate the staff you settle for in order to keep them at the building.
- Pests affect maintenance, as some contractors may not be willing to accept or perform work at your building or inside the apartments if that is where the pests tend to be.
- Pests also affect you the property manager. You will not feel comfortable when you are at the building. Dealing with pests can be a very stressful and draining part of being a property manager.
- Pests create a cyclical administrative strain for the following:
  o those who must prepare the lease/tenancy agreement
  o the accounting department, who must close off the account of the unhappy tenant who is vacating/leaving for reasons that may have stemmed from legal proceedings. Then the accounting department will have to establish a new account for the new tenant who is moving in and who may be moving out before he or she unpacks.
- Having pests increases your AR (accounts receivable), as some tenants will take matters into their own hands by withholding rent, feeling that the apartment is not worth paying for and that the withholding of rent is compensation for their discomfort.
- This may spark the formation of a tenant association.
- If you are fighting a losing battle with pests, your company may have to part ways with the building by disposing or selling it.

No one wins when you have pests. That is why it is very important that you take the treating of pests very seriously, treating them aggressively and swiftly.

B. Effective No-Nonsense Approach to Treating Cockroaches

i. Treating Common Areas

A proper and consistent cleaning routine is a key ingredient to keeping *some* types of pests out of your buildings. If you have inconsistency in your building's cleaning regimen, or if the cleaning is not being done, the problem can snowball and the building can become a coveted buffet for cockroaches and other pests to feast on, giving them reasons to lurk. Before you know it, your building is heavily infested with cockroaches and/or other pests. Another thing that may contribute to an infested building is the lifestyle of some tenants. Also, you could inherit an infested building when you have changes to your portfolio. Complaining about the infestation or trying to swap out buildings will not get rid of the pests. The best way of controlling and treating a heavy cockroach infestation is to come with an aggressive action plan and ensure both the common areas and individual apartments, vacant and occupied alike, are treated. When treating the common areas of a heavily infested building, the following should be considered:

- ✓ hallways
- ✓ elevator pits
- ✓ garbage chutes
- ✓ recycle bins
- ✓ garbage and compactor bins
- ✓ compactor room
- ✓ garbage rooms
- ✓ move-out room

The areas listed above should be cleaned regularly as part of your preventative maintenance program. It can be a challenge to treat common areas; however, if you have a proper cleaning routine, it will serve you well when it is time to administer the treatments.

Step 1

It may be wise to treat the compactor room first, before any other locations gets treated. This allows some time to pass so the treatment can work or take effect. The time frame could be one to two weeks, or as recommended by the pest control company. You want the treatment to get rid of any pests behind the compactor before the compactor is moved. That way, when you are ready to clean the compactor room, you can move the compactor and any dead pests can be cleared away. At one of my properties where the compactor was moved before the treatment was applied, cockroaches and rats were seen running away. At another location, I decided to treat first and then move the compactor after. The result of the latter was much better.

Step 2

Whatever treatment (gel, dust, spray, freezing or steaming) is safe and acceptable to be used **AS PER LOCAL LAW(S)** in the common areas should be administered. *That is why you need trained technicians from a reputable pest control company who will know the best treatment to administer in the common area—to keep everyone safe.* Each common area location may require a different treatment. Based on the treatment being used, it may be necessary to post a notice and close access to hallways for a few hours. This means no in and out access to apartments by tenants, unless for emergency reasons. To properly achieve this goal, it would be best if tenants left their apartments. That way you know for sure tenants are not in their apartments and are less likely to go in the hallway. Decide ahead of time what you will do with the tenants who are unable to leave because of medical reasons.

Step 3

The elevator pit and move-out room should be treated with the appropriate treatment. To treat the pit, you must get the elevator company to be present and give the pest control technicians access to the pit. Make sure the pit has no standing water and is free of garbage.

Step 4

Clean chutes and compactor bins. Staff should clean chutes on a weekly or monthly basis depending on your building's traffic level and tenant base. Further measures should be taken by having all chutes professionally cleaned at least one to two times each year. I personally recommend professionally cleaning all chutes before any pest control treatment is applied. On the other hand, compactor bins should be treated first and then cleaned after. This allows for the treatment to sit for a while.

Another time you could schedule the cleaning of the chutes is the middle to the end of May, or just before the warm weather approaches. Start from the top and work your way to the bottom, being sure to include the compactor room. This deep cleaning removes grime missed by your staff and helps to eliminate smell caused by summer heat and flies. It is also necessary for you to rotate bins, including compactor bins, and have them professionally cleaned. Let these measures be part of your preventative maintenance program and you will be less likely to deal with the headache of eradicating pests.

Any professional cleaning of the chutes to administer pest treatment should be done after the time period has expired for the first treatment of the compactor room. Co-ordinate the compactor room cleaning with the pest control contractor and the contractor that repairs your compactor. The professional cleaners may have tools and equipment necessary to move the compactor to clean away any debris that may be lodged behind and under the machine, as well as any pests that may have been affected by the earlier pest treatment.

This is a great time to treat the areas behind and under the compactor before the compactor is returned. Your compactor room should have a smooth finish to the walls and the floor. Smooth finishes make for easy cleaning. If your walls and floor are damaged, fix them. Your failure to repair these damages will cost you more in the long run in lost rent and damaged reputation. These repairs may not be a quick fix. You may have to get your general contractor to repair the floor and the walls before your pest control contractor can administer treatment and the compactor can be returned.

These are areas you would have highlighted in your monthly building inspection and know ahead of time that they need repair. If you are aware of what is happening inside your buildings, it will help you to properly plan the repair. Hence the co-ordination of the work may be in the following order:

1. Treat in habitat area or critical area first.
2. Clean.
3. Repair.
4. Reapply treatment if and where necessary.
5. Return compactor where necessary.

Always remember to have your staff post a notice before any major chute cleaning (which may involve chute closure) and/or compactor work that is being done. I recommend not doing this work close to any major holidays. Friends and family tend to visit during holidays. Think about the pride of the tenants who may not want visitors to their apartments when they have limited access to the garbage disposal. Notices must be posted advising tenants/residents of the work to be done a minimum of two to five days before the actual work is started. If the repairs or renovations will be extensive, based on local laws, you may have to give the tenants longer notice such as, weeks or months ahead of time before the repairs or renovations to the garbage room or chute room(s) begins. *See sample notice regarding chute closure.* In addition to posting the notice, ensure all chute rooms are locked and tenants have no access to them until the entire job is completed. For added safety, ensure the safety slide above the compactor is engaged. This will stop anything from falling through in case a chute door above gets missed or a tenant forcibly gains access to the chute.

Keep recycle bins clean by washing them regularly, weather permitting. These bins can also be a source of food supply for various pests. Eliminating the food supply will deter pests from showing up at this area because they will have nothing to feed on. Clean bins and clean common areas sends a message to your tenants that you have high cleaning standards and they should help to keep the area clean. Make sure you have adequate garbage pickups. Depending on your tenant base, you may have to arrange additional garbage pickup. This may also require the purchase of extra bins.

ii. Treating Inside Apartments

Cleaning and treating the common area alone will not be effective in treating your heavily cockroach-infested buildings. It may also be necessary for you to do a full *building cleanout*, which means treating all the apartments for cockroaches. The apartment treatment should be done immediately after or before the common area is treated, or concurrently. The aim of this approach is to prevent any refuge or safe haven for the pest. If you think treating the common area was tough, then get ready for battle when you treat inside the apartments. May I remind you, these are occupied apartments. Before you treat inside the apartments, each tenant should ensure their apartment is cleaned and prepared according to the specifications of your pest control company's preparation sheet. Once you tell tenants to clean up, it is automatic that you will have to contend with extra garbage. To accommodate this extra amount of garbage, you can rent a bulk garbage bin to facilitate the cleanup. This will help tenants to dispose of any unwanted items they may have lying around inside their apartments that they deem as garbage. Both you and the bin rental company can determine the size you will need, based on the size of your building, to accommodate the cleanup.

Remember no building gets infested overnight. To prevent any form of infestation in your buildings, be vigilant about any complaints you get from tenants who may call you, as well as complaints you get from your staff. Your annual in-suite inspection is a key indicator of what is happening inside your apartments. That is why you should act immediately on complaints of pests. Your other indicator is complaints from contractors who may enter an apartment to do repairs but realize it has pests. If you are getting complaints from a certain *line or riser*, have that line or riser inspected. Find out what is below and near that riser. What riser do you have to the left and to the right? Instead of doing a full building cleanout, you can treat the one or two risers that are affected. Regardless of what you decide, the treatment can be a success if you serve to each tenant a general notice that is properly detailed and timely, with a list of places that may offer preparation services to get the units ready for treatment. Getting the co-operation of all tenants is very important; otherwise, the treatment will not work. After you post the notice, be prepared for opposition from tenants and determine how you intend to address those oppositions. For sure you are going to have tenants tell you the following:

- They have a disability and are unable to prepare their unit.
- They are allergic to the treatment.
- They are unable to leave the apartment (if the treatment requires the tenant to be out of the apartment for a certain amount of time).
- The apartment is cluttered and you cannot access anywhere inside it.

That is why you need to include in the notice about the cockroach treatment any volunteer organization that will offer preparation services, which include cleaning of the apartment. It is also wise to contact your local municipal health department and ask for assistance with tenants who have any form of physical or mental disability and who may require help. Or ask if the city can identify and direct you to some of these organizations.

Doing a full building cleanout requires proper planning and co-ordination. If you serve the general notice to the tenants at least two to three weeks before the treatment dates, this will give your tenants who have special needs time to contact any of the organizations you listed for them to call or contact their caseworker if they have one. It may also be necessary for you to foot the bill under "duty to accommodate" and prepare some units yourself if any of those organizations cannot do the preparation. You want to be able to treat *all* the affected units when the date arrives for the treatment. One untreated unit can defeat the purpose and cause the pest problem to linger. Therefore, in your notice regarding the treatment, state clearly the consequences of not preparing for the treatment. And be sure to follow through on legal proceedings such as serving any N5 notices. After the treatment, you must have an ongoing pest control management program for tenants to follow. I have included a sample letter you can send to tenants indicating how they can assist in keeping the building pest-free. This letter can be sent every season on different colour paper or be provided as a newsletter to your tenants. File all notices and letters or newsletters you send out. Remember—if you are taken to the LTB, this is evidence you have done your due diligence.

Sample Notice for Chute Closure

On [date(s)] between the hours of [times], our contractors will be doing a detailed cleaning [and/or repairs] of the garbage chute and garbage room.

Because of the nature of the work, all chutes will be closed for cleaning [and repair] and application of pest control treatment. Please take your garbage to the bin outside behind the building [or other designated area]. We kindly request that you do not leave your garbage in the hallways or stairwells. Also, do not stockpile the garbage inside your apartment for the duration of the closure, as this can potentially attract pests.

We regret any inconveniences this temporary closure may cause. Thank you for your patience as we complete this project.

Speak with the building staff if you have any questions.

Thank you.

[Name]
Property Manager

Tenant Pest Control Tips

Dear Residents,

Thank you for your co-operation regarding the recent cockroach treatment. We take great pride and quick action to ensure our property is pest-free. Treating any pest requires continued co-operation of both tenants and management. We recommend that you continue to help by doing the following inside your apartment:

- Empty garbage daily, especially garbage from the kitchen. Never sleep with garbage inside your apartment. When you are sleeping, that is when the cockroaches have their dinner. If you have leftover food as garbage, then you have created a buffet for these cockroaches and other pests.
- If you are going to be away for a day or more, do not leave any garbage inside your apartment.
- Wash garbage cans/bins weekly. It is best to line bins with garbage bin liners or used grocery bags. Garbage containers should have fitted lids.
- Use small containers with lids to store leftover meats, gravies, pizza or other foods. Since some containers are kept inside the refrigerator, containers can be emptied every other day to avoid buildup. Depending on the size of your family, it may be advisable to empty the container every day.
- Clean stove tops each time you cook. In addition to helping to keep away pests, your regular cleaning helps to preserve the useful life of the appliance. Clean spills on the stove top such as gravies and sauces immediately. If this is not done, the spills can cause fires.
- Clean the oven after each use and the microwave after each use. It is helpful to use a microwave-able lid to minimize or prevent spatter from food that is being warmed/heated in the microwave. Spills and spatters inside microwaves, if not cleaned, are a great source of snacks for pests.
- When cleaning your kitchen, pull away the stove to ensure no foods are trapped behind it. If you have no unwanted food lying around, pests will have nothing to feed on.
- Clean all spatter from kitchen walls when you cook. Oil on walls not only is unsightly but also serves as a constant food source for cockroaches and ants. You can also be charged for any paint or plasterwork needed to help restore the wall.
- Do not leave dirty dishes on the counter or in the sink overnight.
- Clean all spills on the floor immediately.
- Store food properly.
- Report any pest you see inside your apartment immediately by submitting a work order.
- Do not use any store-bought remedy to address the pest. Our pest control technicians are trained to administer the correct treatment with the required concentration of the active ingredient. While your intentions are good, applying your own treatment could counteract the treatments our pest control technicians are using and the efforts they are making.
- Report any cracks or holes in walls via work order immediately.

Thank you for your continued co-operation.
[Name]
Property Manager

C. Bedbugs

Bedbugs are no respecter of persons, career, age, race, religion, gender, salary, social status or zip or postal code. Bedbugs do not discriminate. Bedbugs are equal-opportunity bloodsuckers. Bedbugs love blood, and it's not the drink Bloody Mary. A sincere apology if that is a favourite drink of yours. Bedbugs need blood to survive. That blood could be yours. They are interested in feeding on anyone as their main source of food. Bedbugs do not care if you are rich, poor, educated, clean or dirty, or even if you worked more than one job to purchase your furniture. These suckers only care about surviving on your blood. Bedbugs will camp out in your furniture to have a party and feast on your blood. Bedbugs don't fly, but they are great hitchhikers. Bedbugs will never ask you or anyone else for a ride. They will just hop onto your clothes or your body discreetly to get a free ride to your home. Bedbugs can be picked up from anywhere, such as schools, hospitals, health centres, libraries, movie theatres, public transportation or even hotels. I have seen bedbugs in apartment elevators, lobbies and laundry rooms, and in occupied and vacant apartments alike.

If you visit someone who, or somewhere that, unknowingly has bedbugs, or if you use an infested moving truck, you can take these suckers home with you. If you take one bedbug home with you, it can make your life miserable. The bedbug's saliva contains a form of anesthetic that is injected into the target area of your body before the creature feasts on your blood. Therefore, when a bedbug bites you, because of that anesthetic saliva, you most likely will not feel anything. Some people may notice skin irritation a few minutes, a few hours or a few days after they are bitten by bedbugs. The skin irritation maybe in the form of bumps, blisters, rashes, or bite marks along with itching and pain. Sadly, not everyone will know they have bedbugs. Simply put, not everyone reacts the same to the bites of bedbugs. Some people don't react at all. That is why some tenants who have bedbugs have no idea they are serving as meals to the bugs. Therefore, those tenants who do not react to the bites are unable to report any bedbug activity. Some tenants will associate bedbug bites with allergies. Others who have bedbugs are embarrassed to talk about it or admit they have bedbugs. As a property manager, how can you know you have bedbugs in your buildings?

i. Clues Your Properties May Have Bedbugs

What are some of the signs you as a property manager should be looking out for to determine if you have bedbugs in your buildings? My experience shows that some of the indicators can be (although they are not limited to) the following:

- Your staff may inform you that some tenants are complaining of bites.
- The frequency of invoices being generated for treatments and of treatments being applied to certain apartments. Your staff will follow the instructions to book treatments for apartments and, at the same time, neglect to inform you, the property manager, that there is a bedbug problem at the building. How many invoices are you seeing? And does your contractor state the level of preparation the tenants have done? What is the housekeeping condition

of the apartment? Are the apartments being treated scattered, or are they confined to a certain riser, line or floor?

- Some tenants will call you to complain.
- During the annual in-suite inspection, you may notice the presence of bedbugs or the tenants may confide in you because they feel ashamed of the problem. You may also notice self-treating being done.
- There are several bulk garbage disposals, such as furniture that appears to be in excellent condition, but you have no scheduled move-outs.
- Mattresses or other soft furniture is placed on the balconies of apartments. Yes, this could be a case of bedwetting, but we live in modern times where diapers are available for both children and adults. When you see these types of items on the balcony, it is most likely, as my experience has shown time and again, a case of bedbugs. However, based on your geographic location, it may be something else. When in doubt, check it out. *Do not forget that mattress and falling cigarettes are also perfect companions to start fires.*
- The city refuses to pick up bulk garbage and informs you that you have bedbugs.
- Applications to the LTB by tenants who did not notify the building staff they had bedbugs, or your staff did nothing when the tenants notified them that they had bedbugs, or the tenant's apartment keeps getting re-infested.
- Contractors who are sent to perform work in apartments inform you that you have bedbugs.
- During your monthly building inspections, you notice a white powder at the thresholds of apartment entry doors, which is an indication of self-treating.
- Based on complaints or multiple invoices, you request a K-9 inspection and a visual inspection to confirm where the bugs are.

These are some very common indicators that you should be on the lookout for. If you visit your buildings and see or hear of any of these things, remember to investigate and treat without delay. Your treatment for bedbugs in most cases will be concentrated in the apartments. If bedbugs have been left undetected and untreated, you will have to do some treatments in the hallways and other common areas. When the infestation gets to this level, it becomes more expensive and complicated to treat.

ii. Dealing with Multiple Bedbug Complaints

Shortly after receiving an additional building to my portfolio, I observed one day during a routine visit, while in the rental office, several tenants coming in one after the other to report to the building manager they had bedbugs. The staff at the new location informed me that tenants/residents were complaining about bedbugs. The staff said they were overwhelmed with complaints from tenants who were getting bedbug bites. They were booking treatments, but the problem was only getting worse. I could see that the staff were really booking the treatments based on the invoices I was signing. Since the building was a new addition to my portfolio, I did not know much about its history. Some invoices were still in process, and I had not received the bulk of the invoices until sometime had elapsed. I contacted the pest control company and requested and obtained a one-year history of the treatment of bedbugs and other pests for all the apartments in that building. On that report, I saw that the invoices matched up to apartments that were being treated. What I did not see were any notes on inspection regarding the surrounding "block" or any "block treatments" to protect the surrounding units. Some of the invoices I'd signed did not state preparation level or housekeeping condition of the apartments that were treated. Some invoices stated, "This was the fourth treatment." That meant the problem was not going away. I did not know what was happening inside the apartments.

A block treatment, as illustrated below, includes inspecting and treating the infested unit in addition to the immediate surroundings units: the unit above, the unit below, the unit to the left and the unit to the right. This approach is necessary because bedbugs can travel through electrical outlets, in holes in walls and around pipes such as plumbing or heating pipes (radiators) to other apartments. It is also necessary for these holes to be sealed to prevent insects from passing through them. Sometimes if you are administering heat treatment in the infested apartment, the bugs will travel along the plumbing lines in the kitchen or bathrooms to escape the heat. Therefore, even though the surrounding units may not have bedbugs, the heat treatment will send bedbugs to those units.

Block Treatment for Bedbugs and Cockroaches

	Above – prevent	
Left – prevent	**Bedbug/cockroach infestation**	Right – prevent
	Below – prevent	

I was shocked that the pest control company had neither raised an alarm nor recommended the standard block protocol to the staff. No inspections of the surrounding apartments were even done. No one knew what was happening inside the surrounding units. That was critical. The surrounding units could be the main factor that was contributing to the rapid spread of the bedbugs. By this time, the building was not merely infested; it was grossly infested. Bedbugs were in the lobby and elevators. Bedbugs were along the baseboard lines in the hallways. I saw bedbugs walking about as though it were a busy thoroughfare or a subway full of commuters hurrying to catch the next train. This graphic explanation may sound like a joke, but it was very much a frightening reality. Yes, bedbugs come out at nights, but those bedbugs were up and about in broad daylight. That is how grossly infested the building was. From one apartment, I could see bedbugs crawling out in droves from under the door as if it were a spring. Out of curiosity, I knocked on the door of that apartment. When the tenant of that particular apartment opened the door, I saw that the walls were *completely* covered with bedbugs. It appeared as if the walls had been painted in bedbugs. At one point, the bedbugs all moved in one direction as though in a well-choreographed dance. Listen, this is no exaggeration. This happened. *I witnessed it.* I could not believe my eyes. Was this for real? My body itched all over. How had the infestation gotten to this level? How many more units were there like this? And how many apartments were affected by this grossly infested apartment? Had I found the root cause of the problem? No wonder my vacancy was so high and I could not find staff to work at the location.

Having this many bedbugs, I learned and experienced firsthand what can happen to a building when pests are not treated immediately. Because it hadn't been effectively treated, the building suffered and struggled with the consequences. If the stigma were to be removed, the bedbugs had to go—and fast. The only way to resolve this problem was, first, to meet with the pest control contractor immediately and seriously voice the frustration of the tenants, discuss the many court visits in the name of bedbugs, mention the frustration of the few staff I had and the inability to keep staff at the location, and vent my own frustrations as the property manager. Based on the volume of complaints, a building cleanout *had* to be done fast. That is to say, all the apartments had to be treated. I had some knowledge from dealing with bedbugs before, based on a previous building I had successfully treated. However, this level of infestation was way beyond the scale of the previous location. It was at this new location with the gross infestation that I was educated on bedbugs. I learned how bedbugs behave. I learned how tenants react when they have bedbugs, don't want bedbugs, can't prepare for treatments because of some form of disability and/or refuse treatments, and I discovered the overall toll a pest-infested building can take on the operation of that building and by extension the company. I became "bedbug savvy" not by choice but by circumstances. My work was cut out for me.

To compound the problem, the city refused to pick up the bulk garbage. At first it was frustrating when the city refused to pick up the bulk garbage. However, the city's refusal to take the bulk garbage worked to the benefit of the property. The city only collected bulk garbage once per week. It was observed that some tenants were putting bedbug-infested furniture out for disposal and, sadly, other tenants from the building were taking those same bug-infested pieces of furniture back into the buildings. Can you imagine the headache I had? I was then forced to arrange alternative bulk garbage pickups. This arrangement worked to the benefit of the building and helped to curtail the problem. As soon as tenants threw out their bulk garbage, that garbage was removed immediately from the property, by a private contractor, before other tenants could carry the infested furniture back into the building and inside their apartments. Tenants who were caught rummaging through the garbage—also termed "dumpster diving" or "dumpster shopping"—were verbally told by the staff not to do so, as the items they found could very well be infested with bedbugs and as the tenants were unknowingly re-infesting the building. Those tenants were not allowed to take anything from the dumpster into the building. Those tenants were also sent letters demanding that they desist from doing so, or else face eviction.

Treatment methods used at this location varied according to the infestation level inside each apartment as well as what was happening in the surrounding apartments. Some apartments required the following:

1. spraying
2. cryonite freezing
3. heating
4. dusting
5. a combination of treatments

iii. Hurdling Roadblocks to Treating Apartments

To successfully treat these apartments, I was met with several challenges and obstacles along the way and learned the following:

- **You may have to do some repairs.** Apartments that were grossly infested had to have all their wooded baseboards completely removed and carpets ripped out to properly administer treatments. After the treatments were administered, new carpets and baseboards had to be reinstalled. In some cases, instead of replacing the carpets inside the apartments, ceramic tiles and or plank flooring had to be installed throughout some apartments. This was to prevent bedbugs from borrowing or hiding in the flooring if for any reason they were reintroduced inside the apartments. If that were to happen again, the process to treat the bugs would be less challenging.

- **Be flexible.** Tenants were complaining that the preparation for some of the treatments, especially the spraying, was too much. Some of the preparation required vacuuming of floors and mattresses and other soft furniture, as well as washing and drying of clothes and other linens. To assist everyone in the preparation for the mandatory treatments, and to increase the compliance rate, I requested complimentary laundry for all tenants. This assistance proved very valuable, as many tenants prepared for the treatments without paying to wash or dry their clothes. Tenants who choose not to prepare for the treatments were served legal documents to start the eviction process.

- **Get involved and be prepared to extend compassion.** Heat treatment had to be used in the apartment mentioned earlier that had the walls covered in bedbugs. Due to the severity of that infestation, the heat treatment took the entire day and went on into the late evening. I had to call the fire monitoring company and the fire department to take the building off fire test, once the heat treatment was completed. The tenant of that apartment was elderly with no known next of kin. Therefore, for the benefit of all, I took on that responsibility as the property manager. If that tenant were my relative, I would want someone to treat her with dignity and compassion. I could not allow the tenant to go back into that apartment, which was like a literal oven. I had to arrange transportation and accommodation with meals for the tenant. In addition, I had to get contract cleaning staff to rid the apartment of those dead bedbugs. Now with that many bedbugs in the apartment, a second heat treatment was necessary, so the accommodation process had to be arranged all over again. Thankfully it worked. The second heat treatment rid the apartment of all the bedbugs. In addition, the outside of that apartment no longer had bedbugs in the hallway because it had been treated with the appropriate treatment.

- **Listen and be persistent.** There were several other apartments that required heat treatment. One of those apartments had to be heat-treated and then sprayed a few days after the heat treatment. About a month after both the heat and spray treatments, the tenant complained of more bedbugs. How was that possible? The technicians went back, inspected the apartment and found bedbugs. However, the technicians could not understand why the tenant still had bedbugs. After a careful inspection of the apartment, the technicians realized the tenant had two scooters. The scooter the tenant used when each treatment was being done had not been treated before she left the apartment. Therefore, that untreated scooter kept introducing bedbugs back into the apartment. Wow! For the next treatment, the technicians went to the tenant's apartment the day before and treated one scooter, which the tenant could use the following day, and the second scooter was treated when the apartment was being done. That approach solved the problem.

- **You may have to compromise.** In another of those apartments that had to be heat-treated, the technicians had to cancel the heat treatment in the setup stage. The tenant of that apartment had pets and could not locate one of the pets on the day of the heat treatment. Out of concern for the missing pet, and out of the fear of baking the pet inside the apartment, we cancelled the treatment and booked a new date. On the new date, the tenant insisted on going back into the apartment immediately after the heat treatment, even though overnight accommodation had been arranged for the tenant. The underlying factor in this case was that the tenant had a disability. Before treatment could be administered, several attempts were made to contact the caseworker of that tenant, but none of those calls were returned. A neighbouring family of the tenant convinced the tenant to stay with them, saying the pets could also stay. The tenant was more comfortable with that arrangement and stayed with the neighbouring tenant. That neighbour's apartment was later inspected to ascertain if bedbugs were present inside. Thankfully no bedbugs were found.

- **You may encounter cluttered and hoarding apartments.** The toughest apartments in which to administer the treatment for bedbugs are cluttered or hoarding apartments, apartments that are so packed you cannot get past the front door. One way of preventing apartments from getting to this level is to ensure you conduct your annual in-suite apartment inspection and be firm that tenants keep their apartments in a state of cleanliness as per the Residential Tenancies Act (RTA).

"The tenant is responsible for ordinary cleanliness of the rental unit, except to the extent that the tenancy agreement requires the landlord to clean it" (*Residential Tenancies Act*, 2006, c. 17, s. 33).

Hoarding apartments are tricky to treat because hoarding is considered a mental illness. Therefore, under the Ontario Human Rights Code, you as the landlord or representative of the landlord have a "duty to accommodate" this illness, meaning that you have a legal obligation to provide service to these tenants without discriminating up to the point of undue hardship. A few apartments in buildings I inherited were cluttered and hoarding and were very much infested with bedbugs. Those apartments had to be prepared room by room, and item by item, to reduce the clutter. This preparation was done through special contracted services that took days to complete before any appropriate treatments could be applied. Yes, the service was expensive; however, when I analyzed the benefits, it made financial sense because the bedbug-free apartments were no longer infesting the surrounding units. This approach made the treatment of bedbugs in the apartments that were once cluttered and infested, the surrounding units and the building manageable and successful.

In an effort to cut costs at the different locations where bedbugs were an issue, I decided to reach out to the health department and ask for help. I wanted to know if the different municipalities had programs that could assist tenants who were mentally or physically challenged, especially tenants who had hoarding or cluttered apartments. If the municipalities told me they could not help, I asked them to refer me to the relevant organizations or agencies that had programs that could benefit the tenants who fit the profile to which those organizations catered. Through that approach, I learned there were layers of resources that were available in the community through non-profit organizations (NPOs) or non-governmental organizations (NGOs). Tapping into those resources helped tremendously.

iv. Getting Rid of Bedbugs

Bedbugs by nature reproduce in an aggressive way. The female bug is stabbed by the male bug so she can be inseminated. This is called "aggressive insemination." Hence, if you want to get rid of bedbugs, the treatment should be just as aggressive. Use trained contractors who understand the nature of bedbugs and will use the recommended concentrated dose of the treatment to get rid of them. Many pest control professionals agree that tenants who choose to self-treat may create additional challenges when it comes to bedbug control. The reasons for this are as follows:

- Domestic products purchased at a local hardware store have a low concentration of the active ingredient that is approved for bedbug control. Unless the appropriate application is applied directly to the bedbug, it is unlikely to have any type of effect other than to serve as a repellant.
- The repellant affect then causes the bedbugs to relocate further into the building's structure, where they become more of a challenge to eliminate.

As a property manager, you must first understand that the treatment of bedbugs will not be an overnight/quick fix. It is going to take a lot of your time, patience, effort and money. *Do not try to cheap this pest out!* I repeat, *do not try to cheap this pest out!* It will only cost you more. Do the treatment aggressively, do it properly, and save your building as well as your building's reputation. However, before attempting to treat an infestation of this magnitude, it is wise to know the following:

1. what apartments have bedbugs
2. what level of infestation is inside each apartment
3. the required treatment to use or administer
4. what units need a preventative treatment
5. what any necessary follow-up treatments will be
6. how willing and competent your pest control company is in helping you to win the battle

7. the physical and mental limitations or capabilities of the tenants living in the infested apartments, and if they will need help to prepare the unit if necessary

Treating bedbugs is a form of relentless warfare. Like with all wars, you must first assess the battlefield and strategize how you will attack or treat to win the war. You also must be willing to change your strategies according to the latest industry standards and methods. Knowing the answers to the above questions will help you to come up with winning strategies to win the war on bedbugs. Another factor to consider is that if you have bedbugs in a community setting, your staff will have to play detective. They can ask tenants who report bedbug activity if they *visit other apartments* in the neighbouring community building(s). If they do, you may want to have your pest control technician inspect those apartments, or place bedbug sliders / glue traps with bedbug pheromone in those apartments and monitor them for activity. The sliders are similar to glue traps for mice or cockroaches but they are not the same. Sometimes they come in the form of a power bar, or a surge protector with a strip of glue as an insert not easily detected by the tenant. When placed inside the room where the tenants sleep, the slider should attract bedbugs that are supposedly in the room. Once activity is confirmed, treat without delay, and get all tenants to comply, meaning the affected unit and the surrounding units if necessary. Sometimes these sliders are not very accurate. I have personally seen where this method did not work even though bedbugs were present inside the apartment. A visual inspection and the use of a trained dog is your best option as long as the tenant is not self-treating, and that is because self-treating throws off the scent-detection capability of the dogs, which could result in the dog not picking up the scent of the bedbug.

a. *Canine (K-9) Inspection Combined with Visual Inspection by Trained Technicians*

Given that everyone reacts differently to the bite of bedbugs, what is to be done about those who have the bedbugs and do not know it? One of the most effective ways to identify those apartments is to have a bedbug-detecting canine (K-9) go through all the apartments in addition to having visual inspections performed by trained professionals. If you are inspecting the entire building, do not leave this responsibility up to your staff. It is too great an undertaking for them to manage on their own. Co-ordinate this with the pest control company and be present at the building on the day of the inspection. Be sure you have enough staff to assist in the process. You can request help either from within your portfolio or from other colleagues. If it is not possible for you to get additional staff, you may have to hire contract staff to assist you according to your building needs. Why the use of additional staff? They can go ahead of the K-9 handlers and alert tenants of the inspection. You want this process to go smoothly. In addition, your own staff can help to calm down any tenants who may want to make the inspection difficult. While the inspection is in progress, the extra staff will help the other operations of the building to continue.

Your K-9 company doing the inspection should be able to generate a report for you on the same day the inspection is completed. The findings from the report will help you to begin the co-ordination of treatments for the affected units before the infestation gets worse. If you decide to use the K-9, you must be prepared to treat once the infested apartments are discovered. Plan your course of action properly. You want to treat in a timely manner. Before you even get the K-9, it is best to do the following:

1. Set a K-9 inspection date and arrange to get the report from the handler or company on the same day of the inspection.
2. Set tentative treatment dates. That way, as soon as you receive the report, you can just send out your general notice and roll in the treatments. Since tenants are already anticipating the treatments, it is best to carry them out with urgency, as tenants will be more willing to comply after the canine inspection.
3. Arrange notices according to floors and the appropriate time slots on your Notices of Entry. Some handlers have stated that their canine should always remain alert or active. Therefore, they may want to have a steady flow to the inspection. Hence, the Notice of Entry should reflect a continuous flow, according to your building type and needs of the building. As an example, the general notice could reflect the following:
    a. Floors 18–14 to be treated from 9:00 a.m. to 1:00 p.m.
    b. Floors 12–8 to be treated from 10:00 a.m. to 2:00 p.m.
    c. Floors 7–2 to be treated from 11:00 a.m. to 3:00 p.m.
4. Have extra staff on hand to accompany the pest control technicians. Staff also serve as witnesses if you must serve an N5.
5. Arrange with the locksmith to do any possible lock change for tenants who do not want to comply. The locksmith can show up at the building closer to 12:30, that is, only if you have units you were unable to access during the first session of the inspection. Just make sure you have replacement keys for the tenants. This is in keeping with section 24 of the RTA: "A landlord shall not alter the locking system on a door giving entry to a rental unit or residential complex or cause the locking system to be altered during the tenant's occupancy of the rental unit without giving the tenant replacement keys" (*Residential Tenancies Act*, 2006, c. 17, s. 24).
6. Arrange with your legal department to serve any N5 notices to violators or non-compliant tenants after the inspection.
7. As soon as you receive the report, chart the information in Excel similar to the Sample of Charted K-9 Report in the chapter. At a glance, this chart gives you a better understanding of what is happening inside the building and where your efforts should be concentrated.
8. Confirm the treatment dates with the pest control contractor.
9. Make arrangements for tenants who have a disability and have no one to assist in any necessary preparation.
10. Serve your notices, being sure to include the information that treatments are mandatory and the consequences of not complying.
11. Follow through with all treatments and any second treatments.
12. Serve N5 or applicable eviction notice to tenants who did not comply with any treatment, be it first treatment or otherwise.

Notice of canine inspection for bedbugs. Letter to be given door-to-door. Do not post in the building.

Dear Residents,

We are receiving reports that some tenants have observed bedbug activity inside their apartments. We thank you for bringing this matter to our attention. Note that we are doing everything necessary to resolve the problem. On the other hand, some tenants/residents are afraid or feel embarrassed to report they have bedbugs. Rest assured that bedbugs do not care if you are clean or dirty. Bedbugs can be picked up anywhere and by anyone. Bedbugs suck the blood of both clean people and dirty people.

To accurately determine which apartments have bedbugs and which apartments need treatment, we have arranged for a mandatory inspection of all apartments by technicians using a specially trained canine (K-9). This inspection will take place on [date]. Once we have completed the inspection, we will arrange to treat the apartments that have bedbugs, including neighbouring apartments to prevent the bugs from spreading. This treatment will take place approximately one week after the K-9 inspection. Failure to comply with the treatment will result in legal actions being filed for impairing the health and safety of others and yourself.

If you have changed your lock without written consent from the property manager, this is a violation of your lease. Ensure the building manager has a copy of your new key(s). Be advised that if we are unable to gain entry to your apartment because of a lock change, we will have our locksmith change the lock at your cost. You may collect your new key at the rental office with proper identification between the hours of [time]. If you have a home alarm security system on your door, please disable the alarm on the date of entry or have someone there to do it for you. If you will be out of town, please prepare your apartment before you go and have someone check later to discuss any treatment your apartment may need for any bedbugs found.

Please prepare your apartment as per the attached preparation sheet for the upcoming inspection. Do not move items from your apartment and leave them on your balcony. Keeping items where they are will allow the canine to accurately identify where the bugs are hiding. We caution you not to take furniture off the road regardless of the neighbourhoods where you see them. Also, be careful where you purchase secondhand furniture, either in store or online, as it could be infested with bedbugs. Note carefully the time slot when your apartment will be inspected [the following are examples]:

a. Floors 18–14, 9:00 a.m.–1:00 p.m.
b. Floors 12–8, 10:00 a.m.–2:00 p.m.
c. Floors 7–2, 11:00 a.m.–3:00 p.m.

If you have any questions, please speak with your site staff before the inspection. Any refusal will generate chargeback and immediate legal action. We thank you for your co-operation as we work to address this issue.

Regards,
[Name]
Property Manager

b. *Overcoming Challenges from Tenants Regarding the K-9 Inspection*

After being served the aforementioned letter along with the schedule, some tenants may call you upset and inform you of any or all of the following. They may even come up with different stories.

1. "I am allergic to dogs."
   Inform these tenants that you are willing to accommodate them if they can present a doctor's letter or a doctor's note attesting to their allergy to dogs.

2. "I just had an operation" or "I am sick."
   You can let these tenants know that they can sit in their bathroom/washroom quietly while the inspection is being conducted. In most cases, the inspection takes only a few minutes. Usually, 20 minutes to 45 minutes for a thorough inspection, is recommended for a one-bedroom apartment depending on its size and content. But, what if the tenant is sick and bedridden? I recommend you talk to the handler and find out if the inspection can be done while the tenant is still in bed. You can also try to place a bedbug slider / glue trap ahead of time in that unit and then check it on the day of the inspection. ***Please note if the tenant is allowed to stay inside the apartment, this is only for the inspection <u>and not for any chemical bedbug treatment</u>. When the unit is being chemically treated for bedbugs, all the preparation instruction sheets that I have seen or worked with, always request that tenants leave and remain outside of*** the apartment for a period of time, sometimes up to 4 or 6 hours, or longer if tenants have any underlying medical condition. If the unit is heat treated, the tenant may have to remain outside of the apartment for up to 24 hours. This much time allows the apartment to cool down to a safe and comfortable temperature before the tenant can return.

3. "I have a dog and do not feel comfortable leaving my dog locked up."
   You can refer these tenants to any doggy daycare centre in the area. This is also an opportunity for you to contact any dog- or pet-sitting services in the area and ask for a special rate for any tenants you refer. Obtain any brochures from the pet-sitting service so you can distribute if necessary. Emphasize to your tenants that the inspections are mandatory and that if they refuse entry, you will charge them for the bedbug inspection service, as you may have to rebook. In addition to this, tell them you will be filing against them for preventing you from performing necessary maintenance service inside the apartment. I had several tenants who called stating they could not accommodate the treatments because they had pets. Referring them to a pet-sitting service seemed to resolve the problem.

4. "My religion forbids me from allowing dogs to enter my place of dwelling."
   This one is very tricky and hard to verify. To avoid any human rights claim, you will have no choice but to take the tenant's word. A visual inspection must be done, and sliders may have to be placed ahead of time in that unit and then checked on the day of the inspection. What is happening around this apartment will also determine what kind of treatment should be administered.

5. Your staff may contact you indicating some tenants do not speak English.
   Ask your pest control company ahead of time to provide pictorial instructions, and give these to the tenants who do not understand the language.

6. "I just had a baby."
   Speak to the handler about how to approach this case.

c. Sample of K-9 and Visual Inspection Report

Unit no.	Finding
1801	Evidence on mattress and baseboard in all three bedrooms
1802	Baseboard alert in bedroom
1803	No evidence
1804	No evidence
1805	Clusters of bedbugs around the entrance doorframe. Evidence of dead bugs at the inside entrance. Not able to access rooms in the apartment. Heavy hoarding. Unit is dirty.
1806	Heavy clutter. Tenant appears to be self-treating. Found several dead bedbugs on floor.
1807	Sofa and mattress alert
1808	Baseboard alert, and carpet alert in bedroom 1
1701	Evidence on mattresses in bedrooms 1 and 2
1702	Evidence on baseboard in living room
1703	No evidence
1704	Visible evidence on mattress in bedroom 1
1705	No evidence
1706	No evidence
1707	Mattress alert in bedroom
1708	Mattress alert in bedrooms 1 and 2
1601	Visual evidence of fecal matter on mattress in all three bedrooms
1602	Mattress alert in bedroom and mattress alert in living room
1603	Mattress alert in bedroom 1 and mattress and crib alert in bedroom 2
1604	Baseboard alert in bedroom 1
1605	No evidence
1606	Sofa alert
1607	Alert in living room carpet and baseboard
1608	Sofa alert in living room
1501	Heavy infestation. Visible activity in ceiling, walls and mattresses of all three bedrooms. Tenant appears to be self-treating.
1502	Several dead bedbugs; tenant appears to be self-treating. Also found one live bedbug.
1503	Inconclusive; tenant is self-treating.
1504	No evidence
1505	No evidence
1506	No evidence
1507	Mattress alert and bedroom chair alert
1508	Fecal matter on mattresses in bedrooms 1 and 2
1401	Baseboard alert in living room and all three bedrooms. Mattress alert in bedrooms 1 and 2

1402	Baseboard alert in living room and bedroom
1403	No evidence
1404	No evidence
1405	Sofa alert in living room
1406	No evidence. Poor housekeeping
1407	Baseboard alert in bedroom
1408	Baseboard alert. Sofa alert in living room. Evidence on mattress in bedroom 1

1201	Evidence on mattresses in all three bedrooms
1202	Sofa and suitcase alert
1203	No evidence. Tenant was present at time of inspection and complained of bite marks. Tenant has family in unit 1408.
1204	Hoarding and evidence of dead bedbugs. No access to bedrooms. Hallways are cluttered.
1205	Inconclusive. Tenant is self-treating.
1206	Evidence on mattress and bedroom chair
1207	Heavy infestation on mattress
1208	Baseboard alert in bedroom 1

1101	Baseboard alert in living room
1102	Carpet alert in living room
1103	Backpack alert in bedroom 1
1104	Fecal evidence on mattresses in bedrooms 1 and 2
1105	Fecal evidence on mattresses in bedrooms 1 and 2
1106	Fecal evidence on mattress and baby crib
1107	No evidence
1108	Inconclusive. Tenant denied access and was aggressive. Evidence of self-treating at the door.

1001	No evidence
1002	No evidence
1003	Baseboard alert in living room
1004	Fecal evidence on mattresses in bedrooms 1 and 2
1005	Hoarding. No access beyond entryway. Visible clusters of bedbugs around the entrance doorframe.
1006	Alert in large sofa
1007	Inconclusive. Tenant is self-treating. Tenant said no activity.
1008	Hoarding. Mattress is covered in fecal matter with evidence of live bedbugs.

901	No evidence
902	No evidence
903	No evidence
904	No evidence
905	Baseboard alert in living room

906	Mattress and baseboard alert
907	Mattress, baseboards throughout and sofa alert
908	Hoarding. Evidence of squashed bedbugs on walls. Access only to one of the bedrooms. Mattress has fecal matter and signs of heavy infestation.

801	No evidence
802	No evidence
803	No evidence
804	No evidence
805	Mattress alert in bedrooms 1 and 2
806	Visual evidence on mattress. Baseboard alert in bedroom
807	Inconclusive; tenant is self-treating.
808	Inconclusive; tenant is self-treating.

701	Mattress alert in bedrooms 1 and 2. Backpack alert in bedroom 3
702	Baseboard alert in bedroom and living room
703	Office chair and baseboard alert in bedroom 2
704	Sofa and love seat alert in living room
705	Visual evidence on mattress in bedroom 1. Side table alert
706	Tenant admits to self-treating, stating contractor's treatment is not working. Tenant has visible bite marks. Visual inspection was done. Mattress is covered in dark spots, which indicate feces. Box spring has multiple live bedbugs. Found live bedbug on living room sofa. This is a heavy infestation. Tenant was told to stop using their treatment.
707	Headboard alert in bedroom. Sofa and baseboard alert in living room
708	Sofa and love seat alert in living room

601	No evidence
602	No evidence
603	No evidence
604	No evidence
605	No evidence
606	Fecal evidence on mattress in multiple areas. Headboard alert
607	No evidence
608	Visual inspection only. Tenant has medical note stating dog allergy. No evidence.

501	Inconclusive. Hoarding. Not able to get past the entrance.
502	No evidence
503	No evidence
504	No evidence
505	No evidence
506	Mattress alert and baseboard alert
507	No evidence
508	Tenant refused K-9 inspection, citing religious reasons. Visual inspection done. Inconclusive.

401	No evidence
402	No evidence
403	No evidence
404	No evidence
405	No evidence
406	Two night stands and baseboard alert in bedroom
407	No evidence
408	No evidence
301	Sofa, love seat and recliner alert
302	Computer desk and office chair alert in living room
303	Mattress alert in bedrooms 1 and 2
304	Mattress alert in bedrooms 1 and 2
305	Mattress alert in bedroom 1
306	Baseboard and mattress alert in bedroom
307	Sofa and baseboard alert
308	Sofa and baseboard alert
201	Mattress alert in bedrooms 1 and 2 only
202	Recliner in living room alert
203	Two twin mattresses alert in bedroom 2
204	No evidence
205	No evidence
206	No evidence
207	No evidence
208	No evidence

d. Importance of Charting the K-9 Report

Charting the information from the K-9 and visual inspection report is a great way to understand the report at a glance. Charting gives a picture of what is happening in the building, but note that charting on its own *does not and will not* get rid of the bedbugs. Charting shows where you need to concentrate your effort and begin treatment. At a glance, you can see from the sample chart that you have scattered cases of bedbugs throughout the building. The chart also shows all apartments on the third floor and seventh floor display evidence of bedbugs. However, most of the problem is located on the upper half of the building. Therefore, it is a strong possibility you will have to do some form of preventative treatments to neighbouring apartments that do not show signs of bedbug activity. Thereby preventing the bedbugs from travelling to those apartments.

Based on the findings from the inspection, the pest control technician may recommend that tenants who have furniture that are heavily infested with bedbugs, to throw out those infested furniture. It is very important to inform tenants who were given that recommendation, that it is mandatory for tenants to wrap infested furniture properly, in large size furniture plastic bags and seal those plastic bags before they dispose of any such furniture. Those plastic bags can be purchased at moving supply stores. Information on where to obtain those plastic bags should be passed on to the tenants. The use of the plastic bag, is to prevent the bedbugs from escaping into the hallways and in the elevators. There should be a designated area on the property where tenants must put infested furniture that were removed from their apartments. Make sure that designated area is not up against the building wall. Otherwise you would be reintroducing bedbugs back into the building. My experience shows it would be wise to have a private contractor remove those infested furniture from the property, before other tenants take them back inside the building. If your tenant base can afford to hire someone to remove their own junk from their apartment, consider posting the names of reputable junk removal companies inside your laundry room and or your move out room(s), that will remove bug infested furniture from apartments. Be sure to mandate that ALL items being disposed of, MUST be properly wrapped in the specified material before they leave each apartment.

Apartments with tenants who are hoarding will require special and swift treatment. Since hoarding is considered a form of mental disability, you may have to work with family members and/or caseworkers, if any are of the latter assigned, or organizations that are designed to assist in cases such as these. When all these fail, call the health department or some form of social service. In some cases, and notice I stress *some cases*, I have personally observed that once you serve legal papers, every resource hiding in the woodwork comes out to help the tenant to avert an eviction. Therefore, you win and the tenant wins. Some tenants may get aggressive and defensive, not wanting to allow anyone inside their apartment to do anything. This behaviour, while understandable, is preventing you the landlord from performing necessary work inside the rental unit. Also, a tenant with this kind of disability did not get the apartment on his or her own, unless the disability occurred after the tenant moved in. Check the tenant's file, because there must be some information on record about next of kin or caseworker. Do not stop until you make contact with one of these people. If you must evict the tenant, you have to show you have made every effort humanly possible to assist. The longer you wait to treat the bedbugs, the harder and more expensive it will be to treat them.

You can develop your own key system according to how you are going to treat the various activity levels. Work with your pest control contractor to determine how the various levels of bedbug activity or infestation will be treated. Once you have completed the chart, give your staff a copy of both the chart and the report. Your staff should know that the information on the chart is not to be passed on to the tenants and is not to be posted in the rental office for tenants to see. Do not add to the tenants' stress.

A copy of the chart should also be given to the pest control company. Regarding the building mentioned earlier that was heavily infested, when the K-9 report was sent to me, I found it was hard to visualize the many pages that were sent. It was at that point I realized I had to chart the data in order to fully grasp what it was saying. After the chart was completed, the pest control contractor was also presented with a copy of the chart. They were very surprised by the big picture and thankful for the chart. When you have this level of infestation, the teamwork becomes more intense and aggressive to prevent other units from becoming infested and to rid the building of this ravenous pest.

e. Sample of Charted K-9 Report

29 TLC		3 BR	1 BR	2 BR	2 BR	2 BR	1 BR	1 BR	2 BR
Risers		1	2	3	4	5	6	7	8
Floors	18	1801	1802	1803	1804	1805	1806	1807	1808
	17	1701	1702	1703	1704	1705	1706	1707	1708
	16	1601	1602	1603	1604	1605	1606	1607	1608
	15	1501	1502	1503	1504	1505	1506	1507	1508
	14	1401	1402	1403	1404	1405	1406	1407	1408
	12	1201	1202	1203	1204	1205	1206	1207	1208
	11	1101	1102	1103	1104	1105	1106	1107	1108
	10	1001	1002	1003	1004	1005	1006	1007	1008
	9	901	902	903	904	905	906	907	908
	8	801	802	803	804	805	806	807	808
	7	701	702	703	704	705	706	707	708
	6	601	602	603	604	605	606	607	608
	5	501	502	503	504	505	506	507	508
	4	401	402	403	404	405	406	407	408
	3	301	302	303	304	305	306	307	308
	2	201	202	203	204	205	206	207	208
	Ground level	Office and utility rooms							

Bedbug alerts = 72

Total units = 128

Key		
Bedbug infestation level	**Treatment type**	**Units to treat**
Bedbug evidence		64
Preventative		49
No evidence		6
Heavy infestation		2
Hoarder and evidence		6
Hoarder and inconclusive		1

Sample Notice or Letter After Receiving the Report of Canine Inspection for Bedbugs

Dear Tenants,

Thank you for co-operating with the recent canine inspection. Based on the report, it has now become mandatory to treat some apartments for bedbugs and administer preventative treatments to surrounding apartments in hopes of preventing bedbug infestations in those apartments. These treatments will take place [date–date], between the hours of [times].

To effectively treat these apartments, we are asking for the co-operation of all. In our attempts to treat apartments in the past, we encountered some challenges. The following type of behaviour will have to change going forward:

1. Tenants/residents self-treating. Note that your treatments interfere with the chemicals that our approved contractor uses, thereby defeating the purpose of the process.
2. Some tenants/residents are not prepared. When tenants report bedbug activity, we not only treat the bedbug-infested apartment but also sometimes treat the neighbouring apartments to prevent the bugs from travelling to those units. Everyone needs to be prepared for the treatment to work.
3. Tenants/residents turn the contractors away and do not accept the treatment.
4. Tenants/resident change their locks without written consent from the property manager and without providing the building managers with a copy of their new key(s). This is a violation of your lease.

Please note that if we encounter any of the above, you may incur chargebacks to treat your apartment and possibly other apartments within your block of treatment. In addition, we will start eviction proceedings through the Landlord and Tenant Board on the basis of impairing the health and safety of yourself and tenants around you. One failed or missed treatment defeats the purpose and prolongs the infestation or makes it worse. Please co-operate with us.

Note carefully the type of treatment that will be attached to your Notice of Entry. If you are given a preventative preparation sheet, it means you are within the perimeter of an affected apartment and that yours must be treated to prevent the bugs from entering your apartment. If you are given a preparation sheet for full bedbug treatment, it means you have strong evidence of bedbugs inside your apartment and your apartment must be treated.

We thank you and look forward to your co-operation as we strive to bring the issue under control.

Regards,

[Name]
Property Manager

f. Treating Tenants Vehicles for Bedbugs.

Advice tenants who report bedbug activity inside their apartments and who will have their apartments treated for bedbugs, to have the interior of their personal vehicle(s) professionally steamed and detailed at an automotive shop that provides car detailing services. Why is this necessary? In addition to removing salt and grime, the service most time involves vacuuming, shampooing and steaming of seats, carpets, mats and seatbelts. This steam cleaning of the vehicle, involves high pressure steaming that should kill any adult bedbugs and their eggs.

While the tenant is out of the apartment for the day, that is a good time for them to have their vehicle detailed. This detailed cleaning of the vehicle can take up to 5 or more hours, depending on the automotive establishment and or the level of any bedbug infestation inside the vehicle. Why so long? Because bedbugs have a high resistance to heat, there is a possibility the vehicle may have to be steamed multiple times. In some cases, the automotive establishment may have to remove all the car seats and steam them individually outside of the vehicle. Removing the seats also allows for proper and a more thorough steaming of the vehicle's carpets. Hence, it would be wise for tenants to schedule the steaming and detailing service ahead of time, preferably on the exact day of the bedbug treatment.

I recommend that tenants take with them fresh clothes to change into once they drop the vehicle off for detailing. Those clothes should be bagged and tied then laundered immediately and separately as the circumstances allow. The idea is the clothing worn to drop the vehicle off, MUST never be worn to pick up the vehicle, unless they have been laundered and dried on the highest cycle on the dryer. *This avoids reintroducing bedbugs to the vehicle when tenants return to pick up the vehicle.*

Tenants should not try and treat any bug infested vehicle themselves to cut cost. They should know that any chemical they spray inside their vehicle(s) could harm them and their family including pets. That is because the chemical will circulate through the air conditioning/heating system in the vehicle.

Tenants should know that the detailed cleaning of their vehicle(s) is at their own expense and NOT an expense that will be reimbursed by the property. Detailing is more than a precaution. Detailing is to avoid tenants and their occupants reintroducing bedbugs to the apartment. In addition, steaming and detailing save tenants from purchasing new/used car seats which can be very expensive or worst purchasing a new vehicle.

To reduce the headaches of tenants calling around to the different automotive companies regarding professional detailing services and bedbug removal, have those contact numbers and addresses available for your tenants. In addition to the preparation sheet provided by your individual pest control contractor(s) that your staff should serve along with any Notice of Entry, you could add a supplementary sheet for tenants indicating the following categories:

Preparation services and cleaning: *Approved companies that charge a fee or volunteer/government organizations that can* prepare the apartment as per the preparation sheet, along with doing any necessary laundry. Some treatments may require a second or a follow-up and reorganization of the tenant's personal items/belongings.

Off site pet sitting/pet daycare service: Approved companies that offer pet sitting service which may include pick up and drop off of pet(s). Each company can state the type of pet(s) they specialize in or care for.

Automotive detailing and steaming:
Detailing interior of vehicles which should include vacuuming, shampooing and steaming of seats, carpets, mats and seatbelts. It would be beneficial if they have experience removing bedbugs from vehicles.

Be sure to clearly state that the list is **only a recommendation. Tenants who choose to use any of the services, do so at their OWN expense.**

v. Effective No-Nonsense Approach to Treating Bedbugs

Treating bedbugs is not an ordinary task. You will have to be vigilant in observing and acting. It is a type of warfare you must be determined to win, not just with the bedbugs but also with your tenants and your staff. Regardless of how good your intentions are to treat these bugs, not all your tenants will want to co-operate with your plan. To win this battle, you *must* establish firm and consistent measures so tenants, staff, pest control contractors, other contractors and management will comply. The infested building mentioned earlier in the chapter saw its bedbug activity reduced to a significant degree, after which other buildings with similar issues were assigned to my portfolio and treated with the same success rate. The only way those results were possible was by using the no-nonsense approach as stated below:

✓ **Educate.**

    ○ Tenants need to know what bedbugs are, how they are spread and that they are not necessarily associated with being dirty. You can obtain posters or brochures about bedbugs from your local municipal health department. Even if you have your own newsletter on the topic of bedbugs, be sure to still circulate materials from your local health department. This shows the pest is not necessarily confined to your properties—it is a city or public problem—and that you are taking necessary steps at the building level to address the problem. Also, on those brochures will be the URLs for Web sites that tenants can visit to get further information. If you are doing a full building cleanout, you should send tenants a notice similar to the one for the canine inspection for bedbugs along with the Notice of Entry. This should be handed out door-to-door and not posted in the building.

o   Emphasize that tenants must not take furniture off the side of the street, regardless of the condition of the furniture or the neighbourhood where the furniture is found.

o   Discourage tenants from leaving unwanted items in the laundry room for others to take. Those could also be infested with bedbugs. Be sure to post a sign for all tenants to see in the laundry room indicating that tenants are not to leave items for other tenants to take.

o   Mandate that tenants wrap bedbug infested furniture properly, in large size furniture plastic bags and seal those plastic bags before they dispose of any such furniture. Those plastic bags can be purchased at moving supply stores. This is to prevent bedbugs escaping into the hallway and elevators.

o   Staff should be educated on what to look for and the urgency to act by booking treatments for any bedbug-infested apartments and any necessary preventative treatments for surrounding units. They should also keep their property managers informed about any reports of bedbug activities.

o   It is also necessary for you the property manager to know as much as you can about bedbugs. Start by obtaining a history from your pest control contractor of treatments done in the building. Know what resources are available to you in the wider community or city and from your company and how you can access them. Also familiarize yourself with any organizations that provide training on bedbugs. You can never know too much about bedbugs. Learn about what treatments are available, how they are administered and the frequency of treatments if more than one is necessary. This makes for better negotiation with your pest control contractor.

o   When your contractors understand your tenant base, it makes for smoother treatments and better organization. Remember knowledge alone is not power. It is what you do and how you use the knowledge you have that gives the power.

✓ **Collaborate.**
   Treating bedbugs requires the joint effort of the following:

o   *All tenants*, must comply with the pest control company and carry out any necessary preparation for treatment. If units are not prepared or the building manager has no access to the apartment to treat it, the infestation will get worse. Be firm with tenants who insist on treating when they are at home. You are legally required to give proper 24-Hour Notice of Entry; you do not need their consent, and they do not have to be present. The treatment is mandatory on your terms.

o   *Building staff*, who should book treatments in a timely manner or arrange to have the pest control company inspect and assess what kind of treatment is appropriate for the infested apartment. If the tenant is disabled and requires assistance for the preparation of his or her apartment, this should be communicated to the property manager immediately.

o *The property manager,* should be observant and knowledgeable on the bedbug indicators and do follow-ups to ensure treatments are done and building or site staff are given the support and training they need. An excellent property manager empowers and guides his or her staff in the booking of treatments. An excellent property manager also listens to the suggestions of his or her staff and the tenants who call. Most importantly, an excellent property manager keeps in touch with the pest control company. If there is a full building cleanout, these dates are booked by the property manager, as are follow-ups to ensure treatments are working.

o *Senior managers,* who must be notified of any major bedbug problem and what the property manager and his or her team are currently doing to address the problem, as well as what kind of resources are needed. Sometimes the effort to eradicate the bugs may be above your bracket of authority and you need the support of those above you. Be open-minded about their direction and suggestions. Also, when you start following through with the non-compliant tenants, they are going to run to your boss to complain about you and the process. Your boss must support your decision; otherwise, you will become nothing but a fool to the tenants. Not only that, but also the process of getting rid of the bedbugs will linger and frustrate you to the point of inactivity, which is not a characteristic of an excellent property manager.

o *A reliable and competent pest control company,* which is an integral part of the equation to resolve the bedbug problem and any other pest outbreak or infestation. Your pest control company and the technicians they send should respect your dates and times for treatment. If you are doing a thorough inspection for bedbugs or a full building cleanout, the company must send an adequate number of technicians so the time slot on the Notice of Entry to each apartment can be honored. The pest control company must also have enough K-9s. That way, the dogs will not get tired and give inaccurate alerts of bedbugs as a result of fatigue. Technicians should also do visual inspections to confirm the alerts of the dogs. Technicians should do a thorough job both in their inspections and with their treatments. It should not be a quick in and out. Some tenants who have surveillance cameras inside their apartments have complained about technicians who come in and do shoddy jobs. The thorough professional approach of the pest control company helps to build respect and compliance among the tenants. If you are using the same company and your building's bug problem is getting worse or not going away, tell the pest control company to shape up or ship out. There is no sense in paying for a service you are not benefitting from. It is always good to have more than one pest control contractor. That way, each company knows it must "stay on top of its game" if it wants to keep your business.

o *Any outside organization, such as a health department or volunteer organization.* You will encounter roadblocks in your efforts to treat apartments. These organizations may have the necessary tools or resources to assist you in your efforts to treat units that are occupied by tenants who may be either mentally or physically challenged. Remember that one untreated apartment can cause the problem to linger or get worse. Find out what these organizations are ahead of time. Invite them to your meetings at your building if necessary, or introduce them to your AM. The more support and resources you have, the better equipped you are to win the bedbug war.

✓ **Strategize by detailing your plan from start to finish.**
You should arrange for the treatment to be done without interruptions.

o Depending on the size of your building, a thorough treatment may require more than one day to complete. The treatment dates should not be close to the end of the month. The aim is to have the treatment be the priority, and not part of the month-end activities.

o Know how many apartments the pest control technicians can treat within the window of opportunity as stated on the Notice of Entry. Does your Notice of Entry specify 8:00–12:00, 10:00–2:00, 12:00–5:00, 1:00–5:00 or 2:00–6:00? These time slots all have a four- or five-hour window of entry. Therefore, ask your pest control company how many apartments its technicians can successfully treat within the time frame indicated on your notice.

o Strategy is part collaboration. Some tenants will not have the mental or physical ability to prepare their apartments for treatment. Therefore, as an excellent property manager, you must ensure these apartments get prepared.

1. In most cases, the tenant will have a social worker or caseworker. Try to make contact with that individual, as he or she may have the resources to assist the tenant. I recommend serving both the tenant and the caseworker, or a relative, any notice pertinent to the apartment. Of course, you want to work within the bounds of privacy laws.

2. You can contact your local health department for a referral. If the tenant is on a fixed income or has limited income, he or she *may* qualify for any special program your local health department may have. If your health department has a long waiting list, you may have to absorb the cost to prepare the unit so the other units are not left at risk.

✓ **Treat** according to the bedbug activity or infestation level. As soon as you receive the K-9 inspection report, contact the pest control company and finalize the treatment date(s). Send with the Notice of Entry a letter about the treatment and what tenants can expect (as indicated in the sample letter). Unless the eradication of bedbugs requires one treatment, ensure all units follow the necessary second treatment. In Canada, a full or complete chemical bedbug treatment requires two full spray treatments. For the treatments to be effective, most pest control professionals recommend that the second treatment must be done 2 weeks after the first treatment. It is very important that you state on the Notice of Entry if the treatment is the **first of two treatments**. If that fact is stated on the preparation sheet, it should be highlighted or printed in bold for the tenant to see. The date for the second/follow-up treatment should also be included on the Notice of Entry to alert the tenant. This information is crucial because the tenants will reorganize their apartments after the first treatment. By the time the Notice of Entry is served for any second treatment, the tenant will be tired and upset and probably unwilling to prepare for the follow-up treatment, which is necessary. Remember—when you treat, consider the surrounding units; otherwise, you may be fighting a losing battle. You want to increase the compliance rate. Since most preparation sheets for the chemical treatment of bedbug requires tenants to leave and remain outside of the apartment for up to 4 to 6 hours or longer if they have medical issues, if possible, try to schedule the chemical treatments mid-mornings. That way, tenants can return in the evening to their apartments after the mandatory absence from the apartment has elapsed.

✓ **Evict non-compliant tenants.**

This calls for drastic action that may seem insensitive to some. However, do not be afraid to utilize N5 notices. Tenants who refuse to comply with the treatment for bedbugs or any other pest pose a major threat to your effort to controlling the pest and restore the efficient operation of your building. Do not tolerate the laid-back approach some tenants take toward treatment. I suggest you review the information underneath the previous subheading, "The Consequences of Not Treating Pests." If you have included in your general notice regarding the treatment for bedbugs "Failure to comply will result in legal actions," you must follow through on your word. Never make empty threats/promises. Your tenants will see it as a joke. Also, your desire to treat pests is in accordance with the RTA, which states, "A landlord is responsible for providing and maintaining a residential complex, including the rental units in it, in a good state of repair and fit for habitation and for complying with health, safety, housing and maintenance standards" (*Residential Tenancies Act*, 2006, c. 17, s. 20 [1]).

Every tenant is entitled to reasonable enjoyment of his or her apartment. One untreated apartment can interrupt the reasonable enjoyment of other tenants. Treating pests is mandatory. Tenants must know that they do not have the option to refuse the treatment. If you evict at least one tenant who did not comply, even after you served notice well in advance, the word will spread and the other tenants will know you are serious about your pest control measures. If a tenant says he or she is allergic to the chemical used to treat the bedbugs and is refusing to comply, then it is your judgement call whether or not to evict that tenant. Is the tenant on oxygen, is the tenant elderly or does the tenant have some special needs? What information does your staff have about this tenant that you do not have? Remember your staff know more about these tenants than you do. You may have to offer the tenant temporary accommodation. If the tenant is one of those difficult, hard-to-please people, an immediate release from the lease through an N11 may be something you can offer. On the other hand, this could also be one of those tenants who wants to play the system. What is the tenant's current rent balance? If he or she has an outstanding balance, he or she might see this situation as an easy way out of the lease. For treatments to be effective, all affected apartments must be treated. If you move that tenant to another building, you have not addressed the bedbug problem; you have only transferred the problem. In some cases, I had to put one or two tenants up at hotels, simply because they had just been released from the hospital. And again, it is strictly your decision to make whether or not to evict a non-compliant tenant who cites an allergy to the chemical. Remember—weigh the hotel cost against any liability cost and the consequences of not treating pests. You will see the hotel cost and the liability cost pales in comparison to the consequences of not treating the bedbugs.

Other steps to take

Think of other ways how bedbugs could be introduced or spread throughout your building and how you can curtail them.

1. Replace soft office furniture provided for tenants in your rental office to hard plastic furniture. This is a practice implemented by some doctors' offices, hospitals and organizations that have significant dealings with the public where bedbugs are an issue.

2. Be sure to provide your staff with bedbug covers for their box springs and mattresses. This adds some level of peace of mind and shows that you care about them.

3. Have the canine (K-9) inspect and clear all vacant units before new tenants move in. The pest control company should give you a confirmation of clearance, which must be kept with the apartment file. Request a special rate for these clearance inspections. You give a large volume of business to your contractor, so they should be able to provide you with a special rate.

4. If you have carpet inside the apartment and common areas, consider changing to another type of flooring that will make it difficult or impossible for bedbugs to burrow and hide.

5. If you use padding to protect the inside of the elevators when tenants are moving in or out, know that bedbugs can hide in these pads. Therefore, find out from the company that manufactures these protective pads or curtains how they should be laundered or if they can be steam-treated. Some protective pads are treated with a fire-retardant; you want to ensure any flame rating is maintained.

6. Depending on how serious or severe the bedbug problem is in the region where your buildings are, you may state that new tenants must have bedbug covers before they move in. The best thing is to work with your local health department regarding some of the preventative measures they are using.

Remember that vigilance and speed are important. If you are not vigilant and quick, then the cost you will bear will be more than a financial cost. The bedbug fight will be an ongoing process and a collaborative effort. For this reason, as the property manager, you cannot let your guard down. It is very important that you work with your local municipal health department. And do not be afraid to ask them for help. If possible, form a partnership with them. This partnership will help you to keep abreast of the most current information and possible access to appropriate resources. You should also understand that bedbugs are not necessarily a property/building problem; they can also be a city or regional problem.

Another factor to consider is the efficacy of your pest control contractor. Contractors should be swift and thorough in treating pests and should be abreast of industry changes related to chemicals and other methods of treating pests. It may be wise to invite these contractors to your staff meetings at the affected buildings. This approach will allow staff to share their personal experiences and opinion of various bedbug cases, with the aim of broadening the understanding of the contractors and the staff.

The war against bedbugs is real and requires a lot of work. Stay informed, be vigilant and do not be afraid to act with speed. You can do it.

9

Tenant Complaints and Concerns

After staffing, the next most time-consuming task in your role as a property manager will be dealing with the complaints and concerns of your tenants. Once a complaint is brought to your attention, the tenant(s) making the complaint want(s) it to be addressed. Having a good understanding of your tenant base will prepare you mentally for some of the complaints and concerns that will come your way. Some complaints and concerns from your tenants will be seasonal or year-round. Complaints and concerns may come from one building or all your buildings. Sometimes all the complaints and concerns will come from one tenant. If that tenant is unhappy, he or she will rally the other tenants in the building to join in his or her unhappy state and make your life miserable. Whatever the complaint, one tenant can take up an entire hour, an entire workday, and even an entire workweek or more of your time. Therefore, you may have to spend your time managing the bickering and nuisance from that one unhappy tenant in hopes of quieting all the other tenants.

A. Common Types of Complaints and Concerns

In general, tenant complaints and concerns usually fall into any or all the following categories:

1. other tenants' behaviour
2. the complaining tenant's apartment
3. the complaining tenant's rent
4. your staff or contractors
5. you the property manager and/or the property manager before you
6. company policy and procedures
7. common areas and amenities
8. activities requiring the intervention of the police

Regardless of what is brought to your attention, always listen to the complaints and concerns of your tenants. Your tenants, as annoying as they sometimes can be, will give you tremendous insight into the operation of your buildings. Depending on what the tenant shares with you, determine the best course of action to take. Try to resolve immediately all complaints that land on your desk. Remember any unresolved complaints have the potential of doing the following:

- going "viral" on social media or the Internet; we now live in a reality-driven world
- appearing in the traditional media—television and newspaper
- landing on the desk of your immediate superior or his or her superior
- resulting in an application to the Landlord and Tenant Board (LTB), the Human Rights Tribunal or some other court
- resulting in the formation of a tenant association (tenant associations are discussed later in the chapter)

Let us examine how these complaints could manifest themselves and how they may be addressed.

1. **Complaints about other tenants**

   At times, one or more of your tenants will bring to your attention troubling things that are taking place at the property where they reside. You will receive calls and visits from tenants regarding the behaviour and lifestyle of other tenants, their occupants, their guests and/or their pets. As you grow in your role as a property manager, you will know the tenants who are calling just for casual conversation, the ones who are chronic complainers, the ones who are impossible to please and the ones who are overly sensitive, feeling that they own the property and every potential project at the location should be discussed with them. Train your tenants to put their complaints or concerns in writing. This makes it easier for you to resolve any matter should it go before the LTB. When there are several formal complaints about a tenant, it adds weight to the case against that tenant. Therefore, insist to your staff and tenants that individuals making or lodging complaints do so in writing, with dates and times of the occurrences.

2. **Complaints about the tenant's own apartment**

   Such a complaint could be about any repair or maintenance inside the tenant's apartment. Delegate the inspection of minor repairs to your staff. However, you yourself should inspect the apartment prior to granting approval regarding any request for major repairs.

   a. *Tenants may want permission to do their own upgrades.* If a tenant wishes to do his or her own upgrades, and if your company policy or lease/tenancy agreement allows for this, proceed with caution. Before you give the consent for the upgrades, do or consider the following:

      i. Get a copy of the scope of work that will be done inside the apartment. This will also let you know if there will be any interruption to the building's operation, such as plumbing or electrical system. Does the building have proper shut-off systems to prevent disruption to other tenants? Be careful of giving any tenant access to your building systems. Certain work requires different or higher grades of licensing. If there are major disruptions, will your insurance cover this work? Who will absorb the cost?

      ii. Ask to see a copy of the contractor's insurance. This will tell you if the contractor the tenant wishes to use is reputable and has lability insurance. Anything is possible; you must make sure things are in place to absorb any cost from potential damages.

iii. Will the tenant need an elevator to go on service?

iv. Does the building have to go on fire test?

v. If you are doing a project in the building, your timing and the tenant's timing may conflict.

vi. How will the work inside the apartment affect other tenants in terms of noise and dust?

vii. Will the upgrade be of similar quality or better than the existing finishes inside the apartment? The intended upgrades should not be a lower quality than what is already in the apartment.

viii. What will happen to the apartment in the event the tenant moves out?

ix. If you have to break open walls to access pipes for repairs, who will pay for the cosmetic cost to match what the tenant does?

These are some of the factors you should consider before giving consent or approval for tenants to do their own upgrades.

b. *Your tenant may also want you to do upgrades he or she sees or hears that other tenants are getting*, especially if he or she is a friend of those tenants.

i. Is the upgrade that is being requested warranted? Is it the result of wear and tear or neglect on the part of the tenant? Is the upgrade needed for health reasons?

ii. If your tenant is determined, he or she will find a way to get that upgrade without moving to another apartment. So how do you handle this? You may have to physically go and check what is being requested. If it is not warranted, tell the tenant you regret to inform him or her that what is in place is the standard for his or her apartment type.

iii. You can offer options, such as transferring to another apartment that is upgraded.

iv. If the tenant tells you that his or her friends have the upgrade, let the tenant know you are not able to discuss another tenant's apartment with him or her, even if that friend is present at the time of the inspection.

v. Do not speak with the friend unless you have something in writing from the tenant authorizing you to do so. Friendships can go sour, and you do not want to be caught in the middle. Do not inform the tenant that in order for you to speak to his or her friend, the tenant must put things in writing. You are not the tenant's legal counsel. There is nothing wrong about telling the tenant that you will not grant the request. When you do this, the tenant may go above your authority to get it done. That is why you need to be sure you have ruled out all the factors that could warrant an upgrade. Depending on who the tenant is, alert your area manager (AM), because you are going to need his or her support. After all, you do not want to look like a fool. An excellent property manager will also make a note in the tenant's file. If the building is given to another colleague, the tenant will be sure to approach the new property manager about the upgrade. Some tenants will even say you promised them the upgrade. Your paper trail will be there to assist the new property manager should the tenant approach him or her.

c. *Be prepared for tenants who want their apartments retrofitted to accommodate sickness and disability.*

    i.   Some tenants may want door openers installed on their apartment entry door.

    ii. Other tenants may want grab bars, detachable showerheads, faucets with levers and/or door handles with levers instead of knobs.

    iii. You may get a request to slow down the force of door closures to give tenants more time to complete their entry or exit without being hit by the door.

Do whatever you can to accommodate these requests. If you refuse, there is a strong possibility the tenant could force you to grant his or her request by applying to the LTB or Human Rights Tribunal. In the long run, it will cost you more in time and preparation. Calculate the financial, time and emotional costs of approving versus not approving a request. Also, when you approve these requests, you show you are human and compassionate.

d. *The lifestyle of some tenants will wreck the apartment; nevertheless, those same tenants will demand that you repair what they have damaged.* These are cases you should discuss with your legal department and determine if N5 notices should be issued for damages.

    i.   Some tenants will ask for their walls to be painted. If the tenant smokes inside the apartment, the walls and ceiling may be discoloured with nicotine stains. Agree to paint the walls only if the tenant can remove the nicotine stain. If the tenant is willing to pay for a special paint to cover the nicotine stain, by all means go ahead.

    ii. Some tenants may demand a carpet change after their pet has damaged the carpet. If the carpet was new when the tenant moved in and it has not completed its useful life, the tenant should pay for any replacement. This is in accordance with Section 34: "The tenant is responsible for the repair of undue damage to the rental unit or residential complex caused by the wilful or negligent conduct of the tenant, another occupant of the rental unit or a person permitted in the residential complex by the tenant" (*Residential Tenancies Act*, 2006, c. 17, s. 34). So, who determines useful life? On average, how often do you change out a carpet, or what lifespan did the contractor/manufacture state you would be able to get from the carpet? If the carpet requires cleaning, that should be the responsibility of the tenant as long as cleaning is not covered in the lease/tenancy agreement.

    iii. Some tenants want new appliances. Is the current appliance dirty and grimy? That is an indication of neglect on the part of the tenant. Before you decline a request for a new stove, have the stove repair contractor check the stove for defects. Regardless of the condition, you may have to supply a replacement stove to prevent a kitchen fire. If there are no electrical problems, you can replace the current stove with a used stove that is clean and in good working condition. The tenant should be warned about doing proper upkeep on the replacement stove. If the tenant fails to do the upkeep, you may have to charge for the next stove he or she requests. This should be stated in a warning letter to the tenant. This apartment should be flagged when doing the annual in-suite inspection and the appropriate follow-ups done.

e. *Complaints about pests, heating or cooling*

i. Pests

As soon as pests are reported, inspect if necessary and treatment should be scheduled based on findings from the inspection. Tenants who refuse to accept treatments for pests that were found should be evicted. Have a zero-tolerance policy on tenants who refuse pest treatments. For further information, review the chapter titled Pest Control Management.

ii. Heating during cold weather

Tenants who complain they have no heat should have their apartments inspected for the source of the interruption to the heat. Before your staff visit the apartment of the tenant complaining of no heat, if possible they should go on the outside and check if the complaining tenant or the tenants in neighbouring apartments have any windows opened.

Scenario 1

I had one case where the tenant complained he had no heat. The tenant was a chronic complainer. After every heat complaint from this tenant, the staff would check the apartment but could never find the source of the heat interruption. It was suspected the tenant was opening the windows, but no one had ever caught him doing so. One very cold day as I was leaving the property, I decided to drive in the direction of the apartment rented by the chronic "no heat" complainer. I saw where the tenant had opened not only the windows but also the balcony door. I stopped, pulled my camera out and immediately zoomed in and took pictures. I then called the staff and told them what I had seen. The next day when I was at the office, I received a call from the tenant complaining that his apartment was very cold and saying that my staff were doing nothing to assist him. I thanked the tenant for calling and reporting the concern. I agreed with the tenant that the apartment should be warmer. I also added that this could be accomplished if he kept the windows and balcony door closed. The tenant told me his windows and balcony door were always closed and my staff were lazy and had something personal against him. The tenant ranted that he paid his rent on time. The tenant added he was seriously thinking of calling the city. I allowed the tenant to finish venting. Afterward, I told the tenant that no one would stop him from exercising any of his legal rights. I also related to the tenant what I had seen the day before, including the time, and said that I had taken pictures and alerted the staff. I also drew the tenant's attention to the section of the lease that spoke about tenants leaving their windows open for an extended time when the heat was on. Since this was a violation of the lease, I further stated that if the behaviour was repeated, the matter would be settled in the LTB. That conversation was noted in the tenant's file. The tenant never complained about another heating situation for the rest of his tenancy.

Scenario 2

At a different location, another tenant did the same thing. She even called the city to report she had no heat. When the city arrived to check the heat in the apartment, the radiators and temperature was below that recommended by the pertinent by-law. The bylaw officer was given the evidence in the form of a picture of the open windows. The bylaw officer indicated he would speak to the tenant about not opening the windows. The heat was checked a second time and was found to meet the required bylaw.

Scenario 3

One tenant who immigrated from a hot climate complained of low heat and demanded the temperature be increased inside her apartment. The staff had checked the temperature inside the tenant's apartment multiple times. Their readings showed the temperature was always above that required bylaw. The tenant was upset and threatened to call the police and withhold her rent. I indicated to the tenant that this was not a police matter but she could still go ahead and call the police, and also call the city's property standards division. I even provided the telephone number to the tenant. The tenant called the police and also contacted the city, who visited the apartment to determine if the temperature was below what the bylaw stipulated, and then they contacted me. The bylaw officer related that he explained to the tenant that the temperature was above what the city recommended and saw no issue; thus the case was closed. The tenant called back and was very dissatisfied, demanding that something be done, saying that she had come from a hot country and had a baby. Even though the bylaw-stipulated level of heat was met, the tenant was given an oil-filled space heater for added heat, the type that would shut off when it reached a certain temperature. The reason for giving the tenant a heater was that it was the tenant's first winter in Canada after immigrating from a hot climate. It was a situation to which I could personally relate. The heat was centralized. It would be impossible to increase the temperature in the tenant's apartment without affecting the other apartments. The tenant felt better about the space heater but would have preferred the heat in her unit turned up. The complaint and results of the complaint were summarized in a letter to the tenant, and a copy of this was kept in the tenant's file.

Scenario 4

One tenant called indicating he was on special medication that made him too hot. The tenant was asking if the heat inside his apartment could be turned off. Regret was expressed to the tenant regarding his illness. He was then informed that the heat inside his apartment could not fall below the temperature specified in the bylaw. Since heat and hydro was included in this tenant's rent, the use of an air-conditioner generated an additional monthly cost. The tenant was told that if he had an AC, he was permitted to use it without being charged. The tenant was also informed that having no heat inside the apartment could result in frozen pipes, which could cause flooding.

If you have a building with faulty windows, heat complaints from your tenants can be a blessing in disguise. How so? Think capex. Yes, compiling or totalling all these reports can serve as leverage to get funding for those windows and, if possible, balcony doors. Make sure you do what you can to temporarily solve the tenants' complaints. If your attempts to resolve their complaints fail, document the situation and notify your AM and heating, ventilation and air conditioning (HVAC) department/contractor. Also, if your tenants are cold, they will use their ovens to add extra heat or else overload the circuit with multiple space heaters. If tenants are paying their own hydro, that is good in one sense. If you are paying the hydro, that does not make financial sense. Compare your hydro bill to the one from the same time the previous year and you will see if there is an issue. This should be noted as well. On the other hand, regardless of who is paying the hydro, an overloaded circuit can cause electrical problems such as blown fuse boxes or, worse, cause a fire.

iii. Air conditioning in tenants' apartments, if included in the rent.
When the summer heat gets sweltering, not having a working AC is enough to drive your tenants to their boiling point. Treat no AC like you would treat not having heat. If the AC in a building in your portfolio is always breaking down, when possible consider servicing the AC before the start of the warm weather. This is something you may want to discuss with HVAC and your AM. Also, consider putting a new AC unit on your capex wish list.

3. **Complaints about the tenant's rent**

a. A tenant may complain about rent in order to get the rent increase frozen or to reduce any rent increase. Some of your tenants who are on a fixed income or have a low income, or who may be sick, will from time to time request that their rent not be increased or if they may have a partial increase instead. There is no law stating you must accept from tenant(s) any request for a freeze on the rent increase or partial increase. You should note however, there are instances where applications regarding serious maintenance issues, from tenants that are brought before the LTB, that could affect the rent increase. In situations such as these, the Board may issue an Order called, Order Prohibiting a Rent Increase (OPRI). Should the landlord fail to uphold the Order if one is issued, the landlord can be heavily fined by the Board. *If there is no such Order at any of your properties*, any approval for the request of rent freeze or partial rent increase, should be at your own discretion and in line with the policy of your company. In addition to the company policy, what kind of tenants are requesting the freeze on the rent increase? Are they troublemakers for you and your building staff? What is the condition of their apartments? Pull their files and see who exactly you are dealing with. Now this could be tricky. You can choose to deny the request and serve the full rent increase notice in hopes that the tenant will move out before the new rent takes effect. Such a move-out can be a big relief if this is a problem tenant. Some tenants who request a freeze on the rent increase will feel entitled and go above you to try to get what they want. That is ok. If your boss comes to you, let him or her know the following:

i. if the tenant's current rent is below the market rent

ii. if the condition of the apartment is below the acceptable standard. (To determine this, once the request is made, have your staff inspect the apartment on a 24-Hour Notice of Entry.) If there are any outstanding maintenance work orders/service requests for the apartment, ensure they are completed with urgency.

iii. if the tenant has a laundry list of questionable incidents that have happened at the building to cause disruption to other tenants and the building staff

iv. if the tenant have something against you. Does the person give you a headache? Your strategy on this could be to approve the rent freeze and win the tenant over. If the tenant is a good tenant and you can accommodate the freeze, either full or partial, approve the freeze and make the tenant happy. Take your emotions out of the equation. Is it in the best interests of the building to keep the tenant or to let the tenant fall under the strain of the rent increase? The rent increase in itself is not wrong. Your decision boils down to a matter of either finances or sense.

b. *The tenant can't pay his or her rent and feels he or she should pay whenever he or she so chooses.* Such a tenant will sometimes bring up sad stories and stories about incomplete maintenance requests and repairs as a way not to pay the rent. I remember a tenant who was an expert at this and tried consistently for about five years to evade paying his rent or buying time to pay his rent.

Year 1
The previous record on file showed that the tenant complained of a flood inside his apartment and was compensated for damages through the LTB.

Year 2
The tenant contacted me about his sick pet, stating he was behind on his rent because the rent money was used to care for the pet. While I sympathized with the tenant, he was still taken to the LTB regarding late payment. It took some months to bring the account to zero, but it was accomplished.

Year 3

The tenant fell behind on rent again. When he was served papers for the LTB, he claimed he had been physically attacked by the building staff. The tenant stated he could not work, which resulted in him falling behind in rent by about two months. The tenant did not report the alleged attack to the police, not even when the staff who he claimed attacked him insisted that the matter be reported. The tenant said he had a phobia of the police and begged that the alleged incident not be reported. The tenant was given a payment plan outside the LTB until the internal investigations were completed. The investigations proved the allegations were false. The rent balance was eventually brought to zero.

Year 4

The tenant said he had been in the hospital and had fallen behind on his rent again. The tenant was still served papers regarding the late rent. The rent was eventually paid in full. After discussing the matter with the building staff and the legal department, I voiced my concern, stating the tenant had developed a consistent pattern around the same time every year. Everyone agreed. As soon as the tenant was served the L1 every year around the same time, he would come up with a story. We agreed to be on the lookout the following year. All maintenance repairs that were reported by that tenant were given priority. That way he could use nothing related to maintenance if the matter ended up at the LTB.

Year 5

As was anticipated, the tenant fell behind in rent and came up with another sad story. The tenant complained about the staff again. This time it was about a staff member who was new. When I received the call from the tenant, I listened, thanked the tenant for calling and promised to investigate the complaint, which I did. The staff member was new, but as I have indicated in the chapter on staffing, if you get to know and understand your staff, you will know how to process complaints against them. Regardless of this fact, an investigation was still done. The investigation proved that the allegations regarding the staff member were not true. I contacted the tenant and related that the matter had been investigated and it was concluded that there was no merit to the allegations. The tenant said he was going to the LTB. I told the tenant that he was free to exercise his legal right and said that it was actually a good idea, because I'd thought of doing the same thing on the basis of harassment. The tenant was shocked and asked why I would go to the LTB. I related all the incidents over the last five years and asked the tenant if he noticed anything. The tenant said no. I replied there was indeed something to be noticed—it was called a "pattern," and a consistent one at that. I told the tenant that next year I knew for sure he would come up with something. I was not sure what it would be, but I knew he would be coming up with something. The tenant became quite hesitant and said he had to go. I never heard from the tenant again.

There were no complaints from that tenant. His rent was never again in arrears.

c. *Tenants may inform you their rent is going to be late and request a payment plan.* Their honesty is good but cannot be taken to the bank. If the tenant defaults, what do you have to file at the LTB? Make any payment plan at the LTB, where it is in black and white and formalized. This makes it more likely for the tenant to commit and follow through on the plan or his or her promise to pay. Regardless of what the tenant says, issue the N4. Once the rent is paid in full before the N4 expires, the N4 becomes void.

4. **Complaints about your staff or contractors**

The conduct of your staff and contractors may sometimes come into question. Some situations can be embarrassing if you learn that your staff brushes aside the company policy by engaging in dishonest activity. When your staff steps into the realm of dishonesty, they step out of protective care. For this, they must be dealt with swiftly and appropriately to the proper degree. Dishonest behaviours can manifest in several ways, including but not limited to the following:

a. *Complaints against your contractor for poor workmanship.* Contractors though external, are considered as part of your team. They represent you (your company) when they are contracted to perform work on your behalf. Not all your tenants will notice the difference, unless the contractors are in uniforms. Since the contractors do work on your behalf, tenants will most times see the contractors as an extension of your company. That is why it is important to check on contractors as they complete the work they have been contracted to do to ensure it is of acceptable quality. If your contractor produces poor workmanship, it should be corrected at the expense of the contractor.

b. *Complaints against a contractor regarding sexual misconduct:* When one of your tenants calls to say your contractor has made a sexual pass at him or her, this is a matter that should be given *urgent* attention. I had three such incidents at three different locations that I had to deal with. You should notify your AM asap, and you should follow your company policy. Get as much information from the tenant as he or she is able to give. In addition to telling you, the tenant should notify the police immediately if he or she has not yet done so. The company where the contractor or trades person works should be notified and that contractor pulled immediately. Co-operate with law enforcement and do whatever is necessary to protect the tenant. Is a no trespass order sufficient to keep the alleged perpetrator off the property? Does the tenant want to relocate to another building? Does the tenant want out of the lease/tenancy agreement? If the tenant does want out of the lease, he or she could file an N15 and end the lease in 28 days. Also, do you want to continue doing business with the company where the alleged perpetrator works? These are factors that you and your AM must consider. Going through the process can be time-consuming. Your approach must always be professional and given your undivided attention.

c. *Security charging for parking spot.* A few days after an event, tenants reported that the security person who had been contracted to man the property was charging for parking on the property and pocketing the money. The only reason that this was reported was that the tenant who reported the incident had had a letter sent to him for violating a section of the lease. Even though the comment was said in anger, not long afterward other tenants called to complain that security had approached them about obtaining a parking spot for a small fee. The incident was reported to the security company, and the guard who worked that event was not allowed on any of the properties within the portfolio. That security company was never used again for that annual event.

d. *Staff charging to do repairs.* When you have new staff at any of your locations or you take on a new property, it is customary for some tenants to call and report that they were promised things by the staff or the property manager who is no longer with the company or who got transferred. When those complaints are reported to you, do not dismiss them and treat them as nothing. Listen and investigate. Shortly after the employment of a superintendent team ended at a new location in my portfolio, several tenants called to say they had unfinished work inside their apartments for which they had paid the superintendent to do. The apartments of all the tenants who called were inspected. Inside those apartments was a common theme:

    i.   unfinished tiling in the bathroom
    ii. unfinished painting
    iii. items that had been purchased in anticipation of apartment upgrades that had yet to be done

The superintendent was doing all that work on his work time, with building materials. Sadly, the departing staff were new staff. In addition, the building had not done the annual in-suite inspection for quite some time. (That is why it is important to do your annual in-suite inspection. Please review the subhead "Annual In-suite Inspection" in the chapter Building and Maintenance.) Because of the many complaints, this situation became public knowledge at the building. To avoid a joint application to the LTB, I ensured that the jobs in the apartments of all tenants affected were completed using external contractors. After the work was done, those affected tenants were given letters confirming that all outstanding work had been completed in their apartments and the matter was settled. That letter also stated that it was a violation of the lease for a tenant to compensate any staff to complete maintenance repairs inside apartments. Any repeat would result in termination of the tenant's lease.

Based on the reports of other tenants, those same staff had also collected cash for parking. This shows the importance of conducting annual parking audits and checking your receipt books when you visit the properties. After a parking audit was conducted, it was revealed that some tenants were given free parking but that this was not stated on their lease. Those tenants had nothing in writing and had to pay the current parking fee after the audit was completed.

5. **Complaints about you (the current property manager) or property managers before you**

If tenants were promised anything by the previous manager, check the tenants' files for evidence of this and also ask the tenants to produce their copies of documents indicating what was promised. If you fail to give them what they want, some tenants, perhaps feel they know your job better than you do, will be bold enough to tell you what to do and then rally other tenants to join in with them. Even if a tenant is also a property manager and works with another company, he or she does not have the right to tell you how to do your job. Each company is different, so the policies and procedures of each are different too.

6. **Complaints about the company policy and procedures or the lease/tenancy agreement**

   a. Some tenants will try to dictate how projects should be done and managed at the building. A lot of so-called experts will come forward when you start a project at any of your buildings. Some tenants will tell you that their husband (or wife, or son, or daughter or other relative) is an engineer, or a painter, and so forth, and relate that this person says the project is taking too long.

      i. Regardless of which expert your tenant may know, that expert does not know your building's needs or the details of the project, including the scope and specifications. Therefore, such a person is not in a position to dictate what should be done. You can always listen, but keep in mind that the tenant and the so-called expert do not have all the information to dictate what should or should not be done.

      ii. Delays in projects could be for different reasons: strikes, delayed material delivery, a waiting period before receiving additional funding, sickness on the part of the contractors, weather and so forth.

      iii. An emergency can arise within the building operations and impact the project being done.

      If there are delays with any project, you should communicate that to the tenants. You can relate that the delay is due to unforeseen, or due to necessary adjustments in the scope of work.

7. **Complaints about common areas and amenities**

Complaints of this nature may be about the cleanliness and upkeep of the common areas, such as the following:

a. Hallways and stairwells—not cleaned and with stains in the carpet on the complaining tenant's floor

b. Laundry room—machines not working, not enough machines, inconvenient hours of operation, not clean, too hot in the summer and in need of AC

c. Pool—not clean, inconvenient hours of operation

d. Garage—not clean, garbage overflowing, improper parking

e. Grounds—inadequate snow removal

Complaints in these areas usually tell you what your staff are doing and not doing. Are they cleaning? If so, are they doing it properly? Do they need further training? Do they have proper tools? Who or what is contributing to the unclean state?

8. **Concerns that require the involvement of the police**
    If for any reason the complaints require the involvement of the police, the tenant reporting the complaints or concerns should be told that. Some information will be confidential and anonymous, and some will be confidential but not anonymous. Whichever of these categories the information falls under, you must relate that to the tenant. Complaints of this type include but are not limited to the following:

a. physical or sexual assault of tenants by staff or contractor

b. physical or sexual assault of staff or contractor by tenants

c. theft

d. arson

e. damage/vandalism to property, including fire equipment

f. illegal activities, such as drug use or peddling

g. selling of guns or renting of firearms

Once these concerns are brought to your attention, the matter must be handed over to the police, who will contact all parties involved. Be sure to follow company protocol and document as you go along. You will most definitely have to inform your boss, who will alert HR, legal administration and any executives. Co-operate with law enforcement as best as you can.

The well-being of the whistleblower or tenant making the complaint will have to be ensured. Matters such as this are things that must be discussed with the police. For further information on working with the police, see the chapter Government Organizations and Regulatory Bodies, section C: Police Department.

B. Dealing with Difficult and Irate Tenants

Dealing with difficult and irate, angry or hard-to-please tenants does not have to be draining and upsetting for you. Whether you deal with difficult tenants on the phone or in person at the office or at the buildings, be resolved always to remain respectful, calm and in control of whatever the situation is. Remember the Human Rights Code is there to protect everyone, including you, staff and the tenants. Even if a tenant has valid reasons to be upset, it is not a license for him or her to be rude, disrespectful, abusive or violent. Gone are the days of "The customer is always right." Many people have lost their jobs over this very motto. For that reason, many have fought back, putting the responsibility and pressure on organizations to protect their front-line staff from customers who are threatening or who choose to be verbally or physically abusive to staff. This could explain why when you call or when you go into certain establishments, including government organizations, you see warning signs posted to the effect of "If you choose to be rude or use abusive or threatening speech, your call will be terminated or you will be asked to leave." Remember—under the Occupational Health and Safety Act, workers/staff are entitled to work in a safe environment free from violence, abuse (physical or verbal) and harassment. As the employer or representative of the employer, you must implement measures to protect the safety of your staff. *Your employer also has that responsibility toward you the property manager.* Therefore, your company should post a notice indicating the expected behaviour of tenants/customers for them to see and should include the consequences for failing to adhere to those expectations.

In addition to safety programs, your company should offer training on how to de-escalate any situation involving an irate tenant. When a tenant is upset, he or she is not thinking rationally. The tenant's main concern is to have his or her needs met. The greater the perceived need or value to the tenant, the greater the aggression. By employing proper conflict resolution techniques, you can help to defuse an intense and heated situation with an irate tenant. Think of a time when something caught you in one of your eyes. You probably quickly removed the foreign object that was in your eye. If you could not remove it, you probably asked a friend, a love one or in some cases a perfect stranger to help you—whomever was close by. Think of the last time you burned your finger, cut your finger or hit some part of your body. No doubt that you screamed to indicate the agony you were experiencing? You did everything you could to stop or lessen the pain. Think also of children. When they fall and get a bruise or a scratch sometimes not even the bandage that is put on the bruise will calm them down. All the parent needs to do is to kiss the child's bruise or, as it is called, "boo-boo" and life is good and dandy again. If the father, for example, doesn't kiss the boo-boo, the child will keep going around in tears to the mom, grandparents, et al., until someone kisses the boo-boo. Most often, it is better if one of the parents kisses the bruise or scratch. Once the boo-boo is kissed, the child's tears usually stop. Similarly, when a tenant is angry or irate, he or she is also in pain—in situational emotional pain or emotional distress—and wants that pain to stop. That is why such a tenant turns to you for help. Like the child who wants his or her boo-boo to be kissed, the tenant wants his or her figurative boo-boo to be kissed, meaning attended to. (Please do not kiss your tenants. If you do, you may be charged with sexual harassment. This is only a figure of speech.) If the tenant thinks you cannot help, he or she will go to the very top of the chain of command until that need is met or the pain has stopped.

Solving the complaint

You can resolve the complaint by first contacting the tenant if he or she has left you a message. Do not commit to anything until you have gathered all your background information and the facts, either from your staff or witnesses (where possible). Give the tenant a time frame for when you will return his or her call, and honour that time. If the complaint requires the involvement of the police, tell this to the tenant making that complaints. If the complaint is technical in nature, you may want to discuss your ideas with your AM or legal administrator if they are around. If you cannot make contact with either your AM or the legal administrator/representative via phone or e-mail, you may want to discuss the concern with one of your colleagues. Ultimately, the decision will be yours to make.

These are some techniques you could use to try to stop the pain or kiss the figurative boo-boo of an angry or irate tenant, as follows:

1. Listen.

    a. Remain calm. Regardless of what the tenant says, do not let him or her get you upset. If you get upset, you will lose the tenant. If you get upset, you are no longer in control of the call or situation and cannot resolve the problem. The tenant may not even want to speak with you at that point.

    b. Acknowledge that the tenant wants to be heard, feel validated and be understood. Whatever is making the tenant upset is dear to the tenant or is an irritant. Even if the tenant knows he or she is wrong, he or she still wants to be heard. Let the tenant express what is on his or her mind. Try your best not to interrupt. Bear in mind there may be times when every other word is a curse word.

        i.   Cursing can be difficult to listen to. The tenant should be notified at such a point that he or she is using curse words. Politely and calmly let the tenant know that you will continue to listen only if he or she refrains from using those swear words.
        ii. If the tenant is screaming to the point where you cannot understand his or her words, politely let the tenant know that you cannot understand properly because he or she is screaming. You can calmly tell the tenant, "I see that you are upset and I want to help you, but I am unable to decipher what you are saying."

            •   If you can put the phone on speaker, this will allow you to take notes as you talk to the tenant.

2. Own up to the mistake.

    a. Accept responsibility and apologize to the tenant if you or your staff are in the wrong.

        i.   This shows your maturity and demonstrates that you have a genuine interest in the tenant.
        ii. The tenant become less defensive and, in most cases, begins to calm down.

iii. The apology validates the tenant's reason(s) for calling, allowing you to connect with the angry or irate tenant. Your apology could be something like, "We are very sorry. This was an oversight on our part. Thank you for bringing it to our attention. Please allow us to address the problem for you."

iv. Even if you are not in the wrong, tell the tenant you are sorry that he or she is upset.

v. If the tenant is in the wrong, you should still apologize. You could mention, "I am sorry about what has happened. That is why we have measures in place to prevent situations such as this one."

3. Solve the problem.

a. Get the tenant involved. Ask the tenant, "How would you like for us to solve this for you?" This approach helps you to understand exactly what the tenant wants and what you may have to give up to win the tenant over.

b. Negotiate by letting the tenant know what options you have within the bounds of the lease/tenancy agreement and the company to resolve his or her concerns. If you are presented with an idea that is beyond your bracket of authority, you can say to the tenant, "Thank you for relating that idea. These are the options I have to work with. Which one do you think will best suit you?" If the tenant insists on his or her own grand way of solving the problem, you can say something to the effect of, "I will have to discuss that with my area manager. This is something we have never done before. Therefore, I am not sure what the outcome will be. I will try my best. Is there a number where you can be reached?" This statement implies no promises, and it puts the tenant on notice that the answer could be "no."

c. If you are in the wrong, be prepared to bend the rules a little. Based on the nature of the complaint, and if you (meaning the company) are in the wrong, you may have to give the tenant a little more than what he or she deserves. At this point you may have to get your AM involved and ask for his or her suggestions.

The following are other factors to consider:

i. If the matter goes to the Tribunal, what are your chances of winning?
ii. The costs of going to the Tribunal, which include the following:

- time to prepare the case
- time to be at the Tribunal (you will be away from the office and have less access to the bulk of your work)
- any disruption to building operations if staff must go to testify (you may have to pull staff and work with fewer staff on the day of the case)
- any necessary replacement staff members or security officers at the building
- taxi service for staff who do not have transportation to get to and from the Tribunal

4. Follow through on and fulfill any promises made. Whatever you have promised in response to the complaint that the tenant has reported, get it done and do so urgently. If it involves repair or maintenance inside the tenant's apartment, speak with the contractor who is involved or arrange to have a new contractor carry out the job. Once the job is completed, inspect it yourself and take pictures. If the job is to your satisfaction, ensure contractors clean up. Then follow up, sending the tenant a letter stating the following:

    a. confirmation of the complaint that was reported, along with the date
    b. a thank-you to the tenant for bringing the situation to your attention
    c. an apology for what happened
    d. a description of how the complaint was addressed, along with the date(s)
    e. an indication that you personally inspected the work on [date] and that you consider the matter closed
    f. another thank-you to the tenant for giving you the opportunity to address the complaint
    g. a closing greeting
    h. an indication of Note to File for the tenant's and the building's records

5. Share the story with your staff so there are no repeat incidents.

There is something to learn from every complaint. Share the complaint with your staff at the next staff meeting, or take or fax a memo to the building staff along with the letter you prepared for the tenant. If you choose to send the fax, reiterate the incident and outcome at the next staff meeting. Always ask, "How could we have prevented this?" Establish a going-forward plan that everyone can agree on. If a particular staff member deliberately caused the incident, that individual should be addressed and the appropriate actions, if any, should be taken.

C. Sample Letters to Tenants for Violating the Lease/Tenancy Agreement

When a tenant violates the lease/tenancy agreement or any rules and regulations or addendum to the lease, said tenant must be notified in writing of the violation. You do this to prevent the violation from reoccurring. If you choose to inform the tenant verbally, follow up by confirming the conversation in a letter to the tenant. Do not allow too much time to pass. A letter of this type serves not only as your paper trail for you to build on but also as foundation for any colleague who may take over the portfolio permanently or who may have to deal with the tenant during your absence for any reason. Most of the letters you send to your tenants may have a similar pattern and may follow the following format:

a. State the problem or violation. If you have the information, state the date(s) or approximate times the incident(s) occurred.
b. Quote the section of the lease/tenancy agreement or addendum that is being violated. It is also good to copy the page of the lease or addendum that the tenant signed agreeing to this fact.
c. Warn the tenant, and state the consequences for not complying.
d. Include any date for re-inspection or follow-up.

e. End the letter with a firm and polite tone.

f. Indicate copy to tenant file and any pertinent individual or department.

Once the letter is finished, serve the tenant the letter and alert your staff to be on the lookout for repeated behaviours of this type from this tenant. You should also follow up with the legal department if the problem persists.

Note that sample letters 1–9 are included in this publication.

Sample Letters to Tenants for Violating the Lease/Tenancy Agreement

1. Dog urine or feces
2. Aggressive or out of control pet
3. Pet off leash and waste pickup
4. Offensive odour coming from apartment
5. New dog
6. Barking dogs
7. Throwing garbage off balcony
8. Throwing things from balcony
9. Children playing in the hallway
10. Poor housekeeping in apartment
11. Improper parking
12. Violence against site staff
13. Violence and aggression toward other tenants
14. Loud music / loud talking
15. Smoking in the stairwell
16. Laundry on balcony
17. Foil on window(s)
18. Items stored on balcony
19. Lock change without giving copy of key
20. Damage to property
21. Baby buggy in hallway
22. Overgrown plants on balcony
23. Not prepared for pest control treatment
24. Cigarette butts
25. Requested repairs

Dog Urine or Feces

Attention, [name of tenant],

We have received several complaints that you are allowing your dog to [defecate and/or urinate] [on and/or in] [location]. The most recent incident took place on [date].

This practice violates section [list section] of the pet addendum/lease, which states, "Pet owners must ensure their pets do not relieve themselves inside the apartment or anywhere inside the building, including hallways, stairwells, garage, lobby, amenity rooms or anywhere in the common area."

Please discontinue this practice immediately. Be reminded that your balcony is also part of the apartment. In addition to the addendum, the Residential Tenancies Act states, "The tenant is responsible for ordinary cleanliness of the rental unit, except to the extent that the tenancy agreement requires the landlord to clean it" (*Residential Tenancies Act*, 2006, c. 17, s. 33).

Your apartment will be inspected on [date] to confirm your compliance. Any further complaints will leave us no choice but to resolve the matter at the Landlord and Tenant Board.

Please do not hesitate to contact our office if you have any questions.

Regards,

[Name]
Property Manager

cc: Tenant file

Aggressive or Out-of-Control Dog

Attention, [name of tenant],

Our office has been inundated with complaints regarding your [list pet type and its name], who has been aggressively jumping on tenants when in the elevator or lobby. The most recent incident occurred on [date]. This incident was also caught on the lobby video surveillance camera.

Section [list section] of your pet addendum states, "Pet owners are to keep their pets from causing annoyance or disturbance to other tenants." The current behaviour of your pet [list pet's name] is in direct violation of this section of the pet addendum.

Aggressive dogs pose a serious concern and threat to the well-being of tenants, their occupants, staff and visitors. Please take the necessary steps to control your pet. In addition, the behaviour of your pet [list name] is interfering with the reasonable enjoyment of the property to which tenants are entitled. Any further incident regarding your pet will leave us no choice but to contact the relevant authorities pertaining to [the animal's name]'s aggressive behaviour.

We hope you understand the seriousness of this matter. We look forward to your full co-operation.

Regards,

[Name]
Property Manager

Pet Off Leash and Waste Pickup

Attention, Tenants,

During a recent inspection of the property, it was observed that some tenants are allowing their dogs to play in the hallway and urinate at the front of the building and are not clearing their dog's droppings. This is not only unsightly but also unhygienic. This is a good time for you to review your pet addendum and reacquaint yourself with the rules. In the meantime, pet owners are reminded of the following:

1. Pets should be on leash at all times once outside their apartments.
2. Pets are not allowed to play in the hallway or lobby.
3. Dispose of pet waste immediately and properly.
4. No dogs are allowed on the grass.
5. Pets are not allowed to pee at the entrance of the building or inside the elevator.

We are confident that if you practise all the above, it will add to the curb appeal of the property and the reasonable enjoyment of the property to which all tenants are entitled. No tenant is exempted from these rules, which are clearly stated in the pet addendum. Violators will be served legal documents to start eviction proceedings.

We look forward to your co-operation.

[Name]
Property Manager

Offensive Odour Coming from Apartment

Attention, [name of tenant],

It has been noted that a strong offensive odour is coming from your apartment. Because of the on-going complaints about this odour, on [date], our staff conducted an inspection of your apartment on a 24-Hour Notice of Entry, which you were served. During the inspection, it was noted that the apartment reeked from a combination of cat and dog urine, even though it appeared air freshener was used to mask the smell.

Please take the necessary steps to rid the apartment of the source of the smell. Section [list section] of the pet addendum/lease states, "Pet owners must ensure their pets do not relieve themselves inside the apartment or anywhere inside the building, including hallways, stairwells, garage, lobby, amenity rooms or anywhere in the common area." In addition to the addendum, the Residential Tenancies Act states, "The tenant is responsible for ordinary cleanliness of the rental unit, except to the extent that the tenancy agreement requires the landlord to clean it" (*Residential Tenancies Act*, 2006, c. 17, s. 33).

For health and safety reasons, our staff and contractors will refrain from entering your apartment to address any maintenance concerns under these circumstances until you have addressed the poor cleanliness standard. Your apartment will be re-inspected on [date] to confirm your compliance.

Should we receive any further complaints about this smell, you will leave us no choice but to start legal proceedings to terminate your tenancy.

Sincerely,

[Name]
Property Manager

New Dog

(This can be included in the move-in package for tenants with pets *or* when a tenant signs the pet addendum.)

Moving to a new apartment or getting a new pet can be both exciting and stressful for the entire family, including the pet. As a result, dogs may bark several times throughout the day when left alone. While we understand that settling and adjusting to a new location can take some time, neighbouring tenants can find barking dogs or puppies quite irritating and upsetting.

Remember your neighbours are entitled to a reasonable enjoyment of their apartment. Please consider them. Section [list section] of your pet addendum states, "Pet owners are to keep their pets from causing annoyance or disturbance to other tenants."

Please take the rules listed in the pet addendum seriously.

Barking Dogs

Attention, [name of tenant],

We are not sure if you are aware that your dog barks several times throughout the day. This excessive barking can be heard on different floors throughout the building. Needless to say, many tenants find this upsetting.

Remember your neighbours are entitled to a reasonable enjoyment of the apartment. Please consider them. Section [list section] of your pet addendum states, "Pet owners are to keep their pets from causing annoyance or disturbance to other tenants."

You may find a dog collar helpful. Or you might talk to your veterinarian about your barking dog or puppy. Please take the necessary steps to address the problem. Should we receive any further complaints, in the interest of the other tenants, we will have no choice but to take further action.

Regards,

[Name]
Property Manager

Throwing Garbage off Balcony

On [date], our staff witnessed you throwing garbage from your balcony. The garbage fell close to the garbage bin at which you were trying to aim. Items thrown from your balcony pose the risk of injuring someone below. This is an improper way to dispose of your garbage. Please stop this practice immediately.

The building is equipped with a garbage chute on each floor and bulk garbage bins at the back of the building. In addition to the chute and the bulk bin, there are recycle bins located at the back of the building. We urge you to use them.

Should you repeat this practice, we will have no choice but to start eviction proceedings against you for impairing the health and safety of tenants and staff. Please take this letter seriously.

Regards,

[Name]
Property Manager

Throwing Things from Balcony

[Tenant's name],

It has been brought to our attention that you have made it a habit of throwing things over your balcony daily. The last two occurrences took place on [dates], when you were seen throwing dirty diapers, and later unwanted food, over the balcony.

Items thrown from your balcony pose the risk of injuring someone below. This is an improper way to dispose of your garbage. It is also unhygienic, promotes pest infestation and affects the curb appeal of the property. This practice is unacceptable and must stop immediately.

The building is equipped with a garbage chute on each floor and bulk garbage bins at the back of the building. In addition to the chute and the bulk bin, there are recycle bins located at the back of the building. We urge you to use them accordingly.

Our property has a zero-tolerance policy on this kind of unhealthy practice. Any repeat will result in legal actions to terminate your tenancy.

Thank you for your co-operation.

Regards,

[Name]
Property Manager

Children Playing in the Hallway

[Tenant name],

As you are aware, section [list section] of the lease prohibits playing in the hallways, stairwells, lobby, garage or elevator of the building. These rules were put in place to protect the safety of all. To this effect, we have received several complaints that you are allowing your children to run and play in the hallway of floor [insert number] on a daily basis. Under no circumstances can we tolerate this practice.

Please understand that your neighbours are entitled to a reasonable enjoyment of their apartments. The noise that comes from playing in the hallway compromises that reasonable enjoyment.

At [name of property/company], we always welcome families and are pleased to have them move to our community and make it their home. We are also proud that our property is centrally located near [name of park], libraries and several municipal recreational centres. By visiting the city's Web site at [provide URL], you will find a list of other facilities and recreation activities that may be of interest to your family.

Please do not hesitate to contact me if you have any questions. Thank you in advance for your co-operation.

Regards,

[Name]
Property Manager

cc: Tenant file

D. Tenant Associations

A tenant association is also called a tenant network, tenant union or tenant solidarity. Regardless of the name it is given, the meaning and intent is the same. A tenant association is made up of a group of tenants living in the same building that has the sole purpose of advocating for the rights of tenants, giving a collective voice and collective confidence to tenants by putting pressure on landlords about things happening in the building or on the property and hoping to improve the living conditions. Some of the matters attended to by a tenant association are as follows:

1. repairs and maintenance inside the apartments and in the common areas, including amenities, and the cleanliness of the property
2. eradication or treatment of pests
3. rent increase, such as above guideline increases (AGIs)
4. relationship with building staff, property managers and owners
5. harassment
6. safety

Do not underestimate what these associations can do. The number of tenant associations are on the rise because tenants are more aware of their rights now than ever before and they have more visibility. This visibility is the result of the use of social media, which allows tenants to share information and express themselves freely within the network. What you need to understand about these associations is that they have become a movement. When a tenant association is formed in a building, it links up with other tenant associations in neighbouring buildings, regardless of who owns those buildings, to form a chapter. This chapter, now consisting of several tenant associations, allows tenants to share ideas and results of actions they have taken in the past and their success rate. Your tenants do not have to shop for these associations, as the associations are constantly seeking members and are not afraid to do door knocking and post flyers to reach your tenants. Tenants will gravitate toward these organizations if they feel in any of the following ways:

- neglected and shut down by building staff or management
- unappreciated
- their living conditions are not up to standard, especially when work orders are not addressed and the building is infested with pests

Should you fail to address the needs of your tenants, they will have a greater desire to form a tenant association. As an excellent property manager, your approach to property management must always be a balanced, integrated approach. Your focus will be in the interests of the following:

1. your tenants
2. your staff
3. the company

The interest in your tenants, if demonstrated in the following ways, may reduce or eliminate the need for tenants to form an association:

- Attend to service requests or work orders submitted by tenants in a timely manner.
- Try to be accommodating of tenants who are elderly or have some form of disability.
- Return calls to tenants promptly and listen to tenant concerns.
- Investigate complaints when they are brought to your attention.
- Conduct annual in-suite inspections and follow through on findings.
- Maintain clean buildings by enforcing a cleaning regimen with building staff.
- Monitor and support site staff to ensure they are acting within company standard.
- Maintain a strong presence at the property.
  - Show up for inspections.
  - Greet tenants and address them by name.
  - Support tenant events and participate in them.

When you consistently conform to these standards, you reduce the likelihood of a tenant association being formed in the building. Also, if one is formed, it will have less ammunition to use and have no fertile ground to grow any grievances. The association becomes a weak and toothless dog.

If you attend a tenant association meeting, including a start-up meeting, it will give you tremendous insight into how a tenant association operates, what the thought process of the members are like and what approaches they take. How do you attend the meeting? As soon as you hear about the meeting, arrange to have one of your staff from another building, preferably from another location, attend the meeting. The purpose of attendance should be discussed with this staff member prior to the meeting. When this person is at the meeting, even if he or she hears bad things being said about the company or any staff, it is not his or her duty to defend the company or staff. This individual needs to find out the underlying reasons for why the association is being formed.

When you can attend the meeting in person, it is a different ball game. You will learn so much that it will scare you. I personally attended one of these start-up meetings and learned the following:

- A tenant association is an underground network, meaning that it is secretly formed. Organizers distribute flyers to apartments or post them on light posts close to the apartment buildings stating the intent of the association. Once a contact list is generated, the organizers use social media, restricting access to members only, to communicate with and stir tenants to action.

- They meet off-site within close proximity to the property, at a facility that requires little or no fee for use, such as the following:

  - a municipal recreation centre
  - a religious hall
  - a school when not in session

- If the tenant association is legally registered, it can obtain funding or grants to assist in financing its mission.

- The members' strategies are well calculated. Sometimes when advocating for issues, the association will instruct its members to call the property manager at the beginning of the month about a particular issue. The purpose of this timing is to inundate the property manager with calls at this busy time in hopes that the calls will be ignored. When you the property manager fail to respond to these request(s), the association takes the next step. The association terms this "measured escalation." The next step could be one or more of the following things:

  o To increase publicity by going to the media.
  o To subtly harass you the property manager, such as by obtaining your personal phone number or home address either to call you or to send the media to your home. This information can easily be obtained if you have staff whom you don't get along with, or if former staff live in the building.
  o To send work orders collected from tenants to your office or to the headquarters of the company.
  o To instigate a rent strike, where tenants withhold paying their rent. They can strategically look for faults inside their apartments by damaging their apartments, use the bylaws to their advantage and delay paying their rent for as long as they are able to.
  o To send letters to the headquarters of the company or a joint application to the LTB.

- The association benefits from the pooled knowledge of volunteers. People who contribute to this pool of knowledge are the following:

  o tenants who may have lived in the building for decades and know the ins and outs of things
  o former employees who are now tenants
  o tenants with a legal background

- Tenants are urged to be part of the association *before something happens.* That way they are in a state of readiness and can act as one when the need arises.

- If they do not like you or your staff, they will work as one to get rid of you. Some even bragged about whom they got terminated and what they did to make it happen.

Make sure you have a system in place for completing submitted work orders and filing the proof that repairs were completed. Work orders and annual in-suite inspections are further discussed in the chapter titled Building Maintenance.

Your tenants joining an association is not just cause for eviction. That is, joining a tenant association is not a violation of the lease or any section of the RTA. Keep in mind that tenants who join a tenant association tend to be well aware of their rights and may quote Section 2 of the Canadian Charter of Rights and Freedoms, as follows:

> "Everyone has the following fundamental freedoms:
> (c) freedom of peaceful assembly; and
> (d) freedom of association."

Source: Content and courtesy of the Department of Canadian Heritage © All rights reserved. Department of Canadian Heritage. Reproduced with the permission of the Minister of Canadian Heritage, 2018.

Therefore, you cannot evict any tenant for wanting to join or for actually joining a tenant association. If you do, or if you target any tenant who is a member of or wants to be part of the association, you could be hit with a harassment application. You also cannot charm tenants and dissuade them from forming an association. What you can do is direct your energies toward finding out who or what has triggered the need for an association and to act in a way that shows you have your tenants' interests at heart. If you hear of an association being formed, do not get nervous. There is always a whistling bird waiting for the opportune time to blow his or her whistle to alert you to what is happening. Until you find this bird, the first thing you should do is to inform your AM. Remember what you learned from the start-up meeting: that tenants are urged to form an association *before* something happens. That way they are always ready to attack when they presume their rights or another member's rights have been violated. As a property manager, you should meet with your AM and follow the steps below to look objectively at the property where the association is being formed.

- Be proactive by anticipating the reaction of tenants regarding the upkeep of the property.

- Determine what you can do to improve the common area, which may include the hallway, lobby and parking garage. For these, you may also want to include your staff to get further insight. If you are going to apply for an AGI because of any needed upgrades/improvements, be sure to take pictures before and after the upgrades. Tenants will always try to find ways to justify why the increase is not warranted.

- Ensure amenities are maintained so tenants can enjoy their use.

- Make sure you do preventative maintenance on essential services. For example, service chillers and boilers so they perform at optimum capacity when they are in use.

- If you are doing balcony repairs and tenants will not have access to their balconies, consider waiving the AC charges if you charge extra for AC. Make sure you post a notice or send a notice to each tenant informing them of this goodwill gesture. Try to follow time lines as best as possible regarding any upgrades. You can also do a full cleanup of the property grounds and clean the windows after the balcony repairs or upgrades are completed, provided that your building has fall-arrest roof anchors.

- Determine the turnaround time for completing work orders inside apartments. In other words, find out how long tenants typically have to wait before repairs are completed. Consider reducing the turnaround time when realistic and necessary.

Some tenants may feel and act as if their affiliation with the association gives them a license to violate sections of the lease/tenancy agreement. Do not be intimidated by these tenants. Your consistent approach toward accepting complaints from other tenants in writing can help to add weight and evidence to your claims should matters go before the LTB. These written complaints will help to dismiss any harassment claim, which will help to protect the reputation of the property, the company and you the property manager. If you are attuned to your properties by doing what is stated above, any association formed may eventually lose its teeth and eventually die. If the association is formed to put pressure on the landlord to maintain his or her properties and you are doing a great job of maintaining the property, the association will gradually dissipate.

E. Tenant Appreciation Events and Their Importance

Expressing gratitude to your tenants brings a wealth of benefits to your properties, the company and you the property manager. Demonstrating your appreciation through an event is a great way to connect with your tenants. Tenant events should be something your tenants look forward to enjoying. Tenant events should be budgeted so they can be executed with ease and organization. Your tenant base will determine the type of event, the menu and any activities. Why should you have any form of tenant event? To answer that question, consider the following benefits you stand to gain by having various tenant events in your portfolio:

- They melt the aggression of some tenants.
- This results in fewer complaints.
- They put a face to your name so tenants get to know you as the property manager and address you by name.
- They give you a better understanding of the tenant base, as some tenants will introduce you to members of their families.
- They allow tenants to see you and your staff bonding as a team.
- They allow tenants to see you with other members of the community, such as police officers and firefighters.
- They enhance connectivity.
- They encourage a sense of belonging, which aids in tenant retention.
- They increase pride and satisfaction.

- They encourage positive interaction with other tenants.
- They break down communication barriers and make you appear approachable to the tenants.
- They foster creativity. Some tenants will share ideas with you about what they hope to see happening, or they will express their satisfaction or lack thereof with projects that have been completed or that are currently in progress.

These benefits tend to accrue on a gradual basis. You will not see these benefits overnight. That is why these events should be held consistently. Tenant events help you as the property manager to have a proper vision of and appreciation for your properties, including the tenants and staff who live and work there, respectively. Make it your aim to have at least one event every year. If you hold the event in the same month each year, it makes it better for tenants to plan around the event and gives them something to look forward to. Sometimes circumstances beyond your control may affect whether a tenant event can or cannot take place. Some of these factors include but are not limited to the following:

- projects, whether planned or emergent
- inclement weather or natural disaster
- lack of staff

As the properties progress or show improvement, you can add other events if you are able to financially accommodate them. Should you fail to put on any event, or an event is delayed or postponed for valid reasons, your tenants may secretly organize one on their own. The sad things about secret events are as follows:

A. You are responsible for anything that happens on the property. If there are complaints of noise arising from the event, the city will send the noise disturbance complaint to you, the property manager.
B. An accident may happen at the secret event on your property and you learn about it on the news. This gives the impression that you are not attuned to the property. Be observant of unauthorized notices advertising any such event that may be posted throughout the building in places such as the lobby or laundry room.

Some examples of gratitude or appreciation events are as follows:

1. *A seasonal celebration in the form of an holiday brunch, tea party or breakfast*
   This is best held on weekends and may be better between the hours of 9:00 a.m. and 1:00 p.m. For this event, catering would be better than having your staff do the work. If you have fewer staff on the weekend, an event of this magnitude is the last thing they may want to do. Also, what time would they start to prep? You could host this event in your party room or lobby if it is convenient.

2. *Munch and Learn / Snack N Safety*

As the term implies, this event does not include a meal. It provides a snack to refresh tenants as they learn about safety. You can incorporate this with Fire Prevention Week and partner with your local fire department, asking them to stop by and share fire prevention tips with your tenants while they snack on cookies or sandwiches and drink juice, water or pop.

You can also invite to this learning event any low-cost insurance company, asking them to set up a table where tenants can have questions answered and be given the option of purchasing contents insurance for their apartments. The cost of cookies and/or sandwiches along with beverages is much lower than the cost of restoring an apartment or a building that is damaged by a fire. View it as increasing awareness and serving as an appreciation for life. Do not fool yourself and say a fire will not happen at any of your buildings. You never know. Prevention is better than cure. In your case, prevention is better than restoration of property. What will you do if a life is lost? Speak with your fire department about partnering with you.

3. *Outdoor barbecue*
   Promote this as a family event. Find a day when everyone is able to come out. On that day, both you and your staff can serve the tenants. It adds to the feel of togetherness.

4. *A promotion of healthy living*
   Depending on your tenant base, contact organizations that deal with diabetes, heart disease or other such conditions and find out if they are willing to hold an information session at your property. This can be held in the lobby or party room. Your local library is a good choice to partner with for this type of information session.

Each of your properties should have at least one event each year. The main event should be a summer barbecue. This allows for tenants to come out and enjoy the property and each other. If you do not have the open space for a barbecue and the property has a party room, then tailor the event for the party or social room. Whatever method you choose, make sure you provide all the food for the event. Depending on the policy of your organization, some contractors may want to assist by contributing to the event. If that is something your company allows, determine ahead of time which event and location you want your contractors to contribute to. Some tenants with great intentions may also want to contribute to the event. Even if the tenant asking is in a financial position to contribute, remember that his or her circumstances can change. It is best not to have any of your tenants contribute to the event for many reasons, such as the following:

- You do not know the cleanliness and housekeeping condition of all the apartments. You want to ensure meals are prepared in a clean environment.
- A contributing tenant may later tell you he or she used his or her rent money to purchase items for the tenant event, which is something you don't want to have happen.
- If there is any case of food poisoning, your company may be held liable.
- Not all your tenants will get along. Therefore, some may find it offensive if the tenant they do not like prepared anything for the event.

If your main event is going to be an outdoor barbecue, consider the following factors.

- **Location**

  Where will the event be held? Is there an outdoor lawn or space to accommodate the tenants? Is the location accessible to most of the tenants? If you have a large enough lobby or party/social room, you could consider holding the event in there. Wherever the event is held, make sure there is a constant supply of food to serve. Regardless of the location, the area will be on display and should be cleaned ahead of time. Lawns should be mowed or manicured and free from dog droppings. If the event is being held in a parking lot, the lot should be swept clean and free of cigarette butts and other litter.

- **Parking**

  Do you have to relocate any vehicles to facilitate the event? If so, the owners of those vehicles should be notified ahead of time and given alternate parking. Any paid visitor parking should be suspended for that day.

- **Menu**

  How many tenants are you expecting to attend? How will foods be kept warm or cold? Keep the foods simple and varied so that as many tenants as possible can participate in the event.

Sample Menu 1

- Burgers: beef, chicken and vegetarian
- Hot dogs (great if the property has many kids)
- Salads: tossed vegetable, potato, pasta
- Roasted corn
- Dessert: cakes, tarts, frozen novelties, fruit cups or melon slices
- Beverages: water, pop, iced tea, Tetra Pak juice
- Condiments: ketchup, mustard, mayonnaise, hot sauce, relish, pickles

Sample Menu 2 (Catering is optional)

- Chicken (baked, fried, barbecued or jerked)
- Barbecue ribs
- Baked beans for those who are vegetarian
- Roasted vegetables
- Steamed rice or rice and peas
- Baked or boiled potatoes served with sour cream and chopped green onion (bacon is optional)
- Garden salad, coleslaw, Greek salad, potato salad, pasta salad
- Dinner rolls
- Dessert: cakes, tarts, frozen novelties, fruit cups or melon slices
- Beverages: water, pop, iced tea, Tetra Pak juice

- **Seating**

  Set up chairs and tables (round tables encourage more conversation than rectangular tables). This allows tenants to linger and talk, giving a family setting and imparting a strong sense of community togetherness.

  Rent a tent (optional). Bear in mind that renting a tent helps to buffer the heat and reduce the glare of the summer sun.

  These items can be rented from a reputable party supply store. They can be delivered the morning of the event and returned the next day. If you have a tenant base of people who enjoy taking what is not theirs, renting may not be a factor you should consider.

- **Time and duration**

  What time do you want the barbecue to start? I remember that after holding a barbecue at 12:00 noon, I received some angry messages from tenants who normally left work at 4:30 or 5:00 p.m. They told me they had mouths too. I apologized and thanked them for their suggestion. I could not help but laugh at the frank and humorous comments. Some suggested holding the event between 4:00 p.m. and 7:00 p.m., thereby allowing the majority who had to work to enjoy the event. After I shared the feedback with the staff at the staff meeting that followed, it was agreed that this time frame was reasonable. That is exactly what was done the next year. The event was well attended and everyone loved it. More than twice the number of attendees expected, turned up. Additional food had to be purchased. The hours between 4:00 p.m. and 7:00 p.m. became the standard time for all events in the portfolio. This time allowed tenants who left work at 4:30 or 5:00 p.m. and who "had mouths too" to attend the event.

  An event of this magnitude is best held in the middle of the month, away from month-end activities. The middle of the month is usually the calm before the storm. If you have major projects, you should take the day of the event into consideration to prevent or avoid disruptions.

- **Outside invitees**

  Be sure to invite local organizations and individuals from whose services you have benefitted. These may include police officers, firefighters, your member of Parliament, your city council members or staff from the local library. Once you have confirmed the event date, invitations should be sent out at least one to two months ahead of time via letter or e-mail. This much notice allows for these individuals and organizations to make room for your event on their calendars.

- **Activities**

  Entertainment and activities will vary depending on your tenant base and your budget. You can choose simple music or choose to have nothing. At one hotel where I worked, I needed entertainment for a function but did not have the budget. I contacted the dance teacher of the local high school who had previously performed at the hotel. I asked the teacher if her team would perform at the function in exchange for dinner. The teacher agreed, and on the night of the function, she showed up on time with her students. The school gave the performance of their life. The guests loved it. I was thrilled I had asked.

You can also take the "edutainment" approach, where you educate and entertain the tenants. Do you want your tenants to be more appreciative of the property? Do you tend to have issues with children? If so, what age group? Consider holding an essay or poetry competition with a title such as "Action Drive Community Is My Home." The purpose of this exercise would be to change the mindset of children who create mischief on the property. Your panel of judges could include a member of the police department, a member of the fire department and a library staff member. Contestants should write on the following topics:

o   respect for self, family, neighbours and staff
o   how they (the contestant) contribute to keeping the property clean and safe
o   what they enjoy about living at the property

Who can enter the competition?

•   only children of tenants who reside at the particular building where the event is being held
•   children who fall within the age ranges of 3–6 (Where necessary, you may use age appropriate drawings or colouring of pictures instead), 7–12 and 13–17

Prizes for this contest could be the following:

•   First – A tablet and $400 off the rent (select month) where the winning contestant resides
•   Second – $300 toward back-to-school supplies and $300 off rent (select month) where the winning contestant resides
•   Third –$200 toward back-to-school supplies and $200 off rent (select month) where the winning contestant resides
•   Fourth – $150 toward back-to-school supplies and $100 off rent (select month) where the winning contestant resides
•   Three participation prizes – $100 gift certificate to a local restaurant

Depending on how challenging your issues are with children at the property, you can choose a set of winners from each of the buildings within the community, if your properties are within a community setting. Do not be scared by what the prizes amounts add up to. You should be more afraid of the ripple effect of graffiti, the formation of gangs, the behaviour of unruly children and how their behaviour can drive good tenants out of your building. The ripple effects of the aforementioned activities will cost you a lot more than what the prizes add up to.

- **Staffing**

The choice to cater or not to cater depends on your budget and is up to your company. Utilizing the services of a caterer is always great. It takes the pressure off your staff and allows them to interact with tenants. The other approach you can try is to purchase bulk ready-to-use foods and have staff serve the tenants. If you choose not to cater and your staff will be setting up and serving the tenants, determine what their work hours for the day will be. You may want to plan the day so that your staff get an extra day off or you bring contract workers or staff from other properties to work part the day. Additional staff allows your building staff to not feel burnt out. It also helps your staff to focus on the event with joy and without feeling tired. These are topics that should be discussed at the staff meeting prior to the event to ensure smooth operation.

A few days after the barbecue, assess the event with your staff to see what went well and what you could have improved. Some tenants may want to voice their opinion of how things went. Do not ignore their suggestions, as outlandish as they may sound. Always thank your tenants for any suggestions they make. You may not be able to accommodate all the suggestions, but you should yield to the ones that may seem more practical for the property for the next event. If your tenants request a time change and that time change can accommodate most of the tenants, then go ahead and implement it. To indicate that you have been considering some of the suggestions, you could include them in the thank-you notice as shown on the next page.

Never underestimate the effects and benefits of tenant appreciation events. Treat your tenants well. Remember they do not have to stay with you. Give them reasons to stay and they may just do that.

Thank-You Notice

We would like to express our sincere appreciation to our tenants who supported the Annual Tenant Appreciation Barbecue. It was nice to see everyone interacting positively with each other while enjoying a meal. Your attendance and participation made the event a success.

After a careful review of your suggestions and feedback, we are happy to inform you that next year's barbecue will be held on [date] between the hours of [times], provided the circumstances are favourable.

Thank you again. We look forward to another successful event next year.

[Name]
Property Manager

10

Capital Expenditure (CapEx) Projects

Capital expenditure (capex) projects increase the value of the property. Capex budget is different from the budget to address your weekly and monthly repairs and maintenance, which tends to be operational and short-lived. A capex project is a major or significant expense that is used to "improve the useful life of an existing physical asset or upgrading/renovating the usefulness of that asset." That improvement could be something done to the external aspect of or shell of the building called the building envelope (roofs, walls, foundation, doors and windows). The improvement could also be internal to other areas of the building or be done to conserve on energy, either water, electricity, air (heat and air conditioning) or fuel. Projects to address the building envelope and any garage restoration normally are the responsibility of your property standards department. However, your inspections, along with any complaints from tenants and staff that have been investigated and validated, can help to initiate any of these projects. These projects can also be initiated by any relevant external organization that inspects and issues an order to the property. If you are attuned to your buildings and take decisive action when you spot an issue, this can eliminate any such organizations from giving your property an order.

Your company may look to do capital expenditure projects yearly. Before you begin to make your list of capex items, you may want to meet with your area/branch or regional manager and find out if there are plans to reposition any building within your portfolio. Another proactive approach you can take if you wish to change the tenant base at a property is to show your area, regional or branch manager your list of potential capex projects. Let this person know that you think you have significant items and would like to do an above guideline increase (AGI). If you have several projects at one location, that building may be selected as a candidate for an AGI. To further bolster your claim to do an AGI, you could do a rough calculation based on quotes you have gathered. This approach will have to be carefully thought out. On the other hand, do not allow the property to deteriorate or become run down in hopes of doing major upgrades. That will not reflect well on you the property manager.

Your job as an excellent property manager is to objectively look at the properties within your portfolio and find ways to improve or upgrade different areas of these properties. Capital expenditure projects can sometimes come about because of emergencies. An excellent property manager will always be on the lookout for ways he or she can improve and upgrade the buildings and properties he or she manages each time he or she visits them. This approach will minimize emergencies that may pop up. Another factor that will tell you or give you a hint as to where the next capex project should be is the signing of invoices. As you sign invoices, are you seeing regular invoices to repair a certain item such as a broken garage door? If your garage door keeps breaking down and you have to keep calling the contractor to repair the door, maybe it is time to have a new complete garage door installed. Since each property is different, each will require different upgrades based on the physical needs of the building(s), the tenant base and the trends in the industry.

An excellent property manager includes his or her staff in the capex selection process. Share your capex ideas with the staff at the location where you want to do the upgrades. Make it a team event and ask them for their input. You will be surprised by the ideas and areas your staff come up with and their reasons for why those areas should be attended to. When your staff gives you ideas, commend them and build on the idea when possible. This is an exercise you can do in one of your staff meetings. You can prepare your staff days before the staff meeting by sending a memo or making a phone call indicating that the meeting is a follow-up at the individual property level stemming from the combined portfolio staff meeting on the matter of capex projects. Ask your staff to look around the property to determine which areas they think need upgrading and why the upgrade is needed. Let them know their ideas could be submitted as capex projects. When you meet with your staff on this matter, share your own project ideas that you have for the property along with the rationale for each project. In your staff meeting, you can have each staff member state what his or her idea is. No one should laugh at any of the ideas. Someone can build on the idea, but never laugh. Everyone's contribution is valid. Type the capex list for the property and post it in the rental or back/side office for all the staff to see and keep in mind. If their idea for a project gets approved, they will feel a great sense of pride. Cross off each project that gets approved, and always feel free to add new ones. This prevents a good idea from slipping to the back or being forgotten.

Once you have made your capex list, contact your contractors and request quotations (quotes) to determine the cost to do each project on your list. Whatever price you are given by the contractors for each job, add an extra 10 to 20 percent to the amount. Most quotes given will stay valid for 30 to 60 days. Therefore, this difference in the added price will act as a cushion in case there are any changes in material costs from the time you formally submit your list to the time the project gets approved and is completed. Because of your familiarity with some of the prices, you will have an idea of the cost to do some of the work and you may not require immediate quotes. However, it is always easier to return excess funds than to request extra funds if the project was underquoted. Hence, always try to obtain official quotes and any necessary current photographs of the areas to support your capex list.

A. Areas for CapEx Consideration

The scope of work will affect the budget for each location. If you are unsure of what the scope of work for each area will be, speak with your area manager (AM), your building managers, your superintendent or even one of your contractors, once you put your list together. Some ideas or areas at your properties you can consider for upgrade as capex projects are as follows:

1. **Balcony restoration**

   A number of residential property management companies are upgrading their balcony guardrails to glass railings. Although glass railings seem to be the current trend these days, balcony restoration is due mainly to significant signs of deterioration in a building's balcony slabs and its railing systems. The deterioration could be due to metal guardrails that have become loose and shaky or even severely corroded, they easily flake or separate. In some cases, the advanced corrosion eats away at the foot of the guardrail where it anchors to the slab. The restoration could also be due to concrete slabs that are crumbling, have major cracks that cause leaks on the underside of the slabs and have exposed rebars or reinforcing steel. Balconies in these conditions are not safe. Their structural integrity has been compromised. If left in these conditions, over time and under ideal circumstances, they are bound to collapse and cause injury and or death. Should you come across any balcony at your buildings in this condition, it is very important that you notify your AM and your construction and property standards department immediately. Property standards will conduct their own investigations and do what is necessary to bring the balconies up to pertinent building code. Hopefully the construction and property standards department along with you and your AM can select a railing design, colour and material that will enhance the curb appeal of the property.

   Balcony restoration is a huge project that may be undertaken by your construction and property standards department, in conjunction with a reputable external balcony restoration company. As the property manager, you can help to guide the progression of the project from onset to completion. Balcony restoration work is a very noisy, dusty and lengthy project. The best way to manage the impact of the project on the tenants, is to keep tenants informed through timely notices. Ensure your initial or first general notice informing your tenants of the upgrade or restoration, clearly advice tenants to remove all personal items from their balconies. **Ensure the notice period is <u>more than or within</u> the number of days specified by the local bylaw or tenancy law.** This much notice ahead of the balcony work, gives tenants adequate time to rearrange any storage they may have on the property, or find alternate off-property storage for the duration of the balcony work, if your property does not have on-property storage facilities or adequate storage facilities.

   Giving tenants a few days notice before the start date of the project to remove their personal items from balconies, shows lack of compassion for your tenants and lack of vision or proper planning regarding the project. This is also more ammunition for a tenant association to use against you. Remember, in addition to safety, you are probably doing the upgrade in hopes of applying for an AGI. The psychology of appeasing your tenants starts long before you get to court with that AGI application. Your aim is to get that desired amount of increase without your tenants tearing it down or reducing the amount you are hoping to get. In my experience, tenants will try everything possible to reduce the increase you have applied for. Hence, serving proper and timely notices is part of the paper trail in your supporting documents in the AGI process. Also, if your property has lockers and you make it a practice of conducting annual locker audits, you will know the status of the locker count and what you have available.

If the balcony restoration project will start in the spring and prolong into the in the summer or beyond, tenants will not have access to their balconies. Therefore, you may want to waive any air conditioning (AC) fee, if your company charges extra for AC use. In addition, if you have an outdoor swimming pool that is in close proximity to any balcony work being done, complete the set of balconies that are close to or directly located over/above the pool area **first** or **last**. This will allow tenants to enjoy the pool while the work on the other balconies are being done and hopefully reduce the stress level of the tenants. Note carefully, if you have any pool repairs to be done on your swimming pool, you should also keep in mind that no logical thinking pool restoration contractor, will perform any work on your swimming pool, while you are conducting any balcony work above. **Safety is always first and should never ever be compromised.** Therefore, I strongly recommend that you coordinate such work with both sets of contractors, or the property standards department and your pool restoration contractor for the good of the tenants.

Do not forget that, once the project gets started, the loud jackhammering and other noise associated with the balcony restoration, will drive tenants outside of their apartments. For your tenants who are at home in the days, they will have nothing to do with their day. That is because their routine has been completely disrupted and will most likely be that way for weeks or months. As the property manager, you can try to create a sense of calm and hopefully reduce some of the anxieties your tenants may have by diverting their attention away from the restoration work. How?

Some tenants may not be aware of recreational activities and facilities offered by the city or activities offered at their local library. Before and during your balcony restoration, be sure to build tenants awareness on these programs offered by any local library and your municipal office or region. That way, while the balcony restoration work is being done, some of your tenants are hopefully out during the day, enjoying one or more of the facilities offered by the city.

A cost you can request property standards to squeeze into the quote for the balcony restoration work, is the cleanup of the balconies and windows once the work is completed. This cleaning will eliminate any dust buildup associated with the balcony work.

2. **Replacement of Windows and balcony doors**
Faulty windows and balcony doors, increase maintenance cost if they are not able to open and close properly. Windows and balcony doors are means of egress in case of emergency. Therefore, if they are not able to function, they should be replaced. Windows and balcony doors should also keep intruders out. Buildings with drafty windows and balcony doors are likely to have heat loss and many complaints stemming from lack of, or low heat inside tenants' apartments. Tenants with no heat or low heat will react in different ways. Some

tenants will react by calling the city to report the issue, others will use multiple space heaters or use their ovens to warm their apartments. Regardless of how the tenants react, it will still cost you. Do not forget that you have a legal obligation under section 20 of the RTA "to keep units in a good state of repair and fit for habitation." In addition, when there are heat interruptions, tenants cannot have reasonable enjoyment of their apartments to which they are entitled. Heat is also a vital service that must be provided at a minimum temperature as stipulated by the local bylaw. Another indication that you have faulty windows and balcony doors is flaking and peeling paint around the window sills, doorframes and thresholds. These are all evidence or signs that you should replace your windows and balcony doors. While replacing the windows and balcony doors can be expensive, some benefits the building could gain by replacing the windows and balcony doors are:

a.   They prevent water leakage during heavy rain or snow melt.
b.   Because there is no more air leakage, it reduces energy consumption in heating and cooling.
c.   The new windows and balcony doors reduce complaints from tenants especially in the winter where faulty windows and balcony doors cause draft and increase heat loss.
d.   The new windows and balcony doors enhance curb appeal.
e.   They improve safety. Windows and balcony doors are means of egress in case of emergency.

The replacement of windows and balcony door are projects that will be undertaken by your construction and property standards department. This department should also include cosmetic repairs of plastering and painting around the windows and balcony doors.

3. **Roof**
    Are you seeing leaks in the stairwells at the top? Are the tenants on the top floor complaining of leaks? Are tenants complaining of leakage during rain or during the spring when the snow is melting? Are the leaks severe? Sometimes the source of the leak could be metal flashing on the roof that is loose or missing. In any event, have your construction department inspect the roof and provide recommendations, or have two of your roofing contractors inspect the roof and provide recommendations.

4. **Underground parking garage restoration**
    This kind of project is normally undertaken by your construction department. However, you can alert your construction department to potential problems after any building inspection to assess the structural integrity if you see any of the following:

a.   excess flaking of the concrete from the ceiling (if you do not see anything of this nature, your tenants may complain about falling concrete on their vehicles)
b.   crumbling walls, with holes where you can see through the other side
c.   exposed steel bars
d.   excessive moisture or leaks either from the ceiling or the walls

e. excessive cracking and weeds

If this project needs to be done, you and the property standards department may have to find alternative parking for your tenants while the project is in progress. You can secure alterative parking from neighbouring parking lots or neighbouring businesses. If you are close to a school and the garage repair is to take place over the summer, find out from the school if their parking lot will be utilized over the summer. If not, propose to use and pay for the parking spaces. That is extra income for the school. In addition to these parking arrangements, be prepared to accommodate a few tenants on property who may be sick or have some form of disability and find it difficult to walk to the temporary off-property parking. If the project does not allow for those spaces, to help these tenants, *you may have to pick up pockets of parking around your property.* Stay in touch with the construction team and keep your tenants informed to minimize stress. The decision to cancel any parking fees during the garage renovations is up to you. My rule of thumb is, do not cancel the tenants' parking fee, because you will have to pay a lot more to secure off-property parking for your tenants. A continued tenant parking fee can help to offset the off-site parking fee.

5. **Plumbing riser repair or replacement**
   Depending on where the repairs will be, this may require more than the usual cosmetic plastering and painting work. You may also require two different contractors to carry out the work. One contractor will be the plumber, and the other contractor will be a general contractor who will do the other installations and cosmetic repairs.

   a. If you are doing repairs in the bathroom, it may affect other areas. Therefore, you may want to get a quote to install the following if they are affected:

      i. tub surround with taps
      ii. bathtub
      iii. vanity with taps

      You may have to address any gaps between the old floor and the new tub. Hence, a complete floor installation may have to be done.

   b. If the repairs are in the kitchen, you will have to do cosmetic repairs under the counter and above the counter.

      Be sure to give the tenants plenty of notice. If you give at least 30 to 60 days' notice, that is more than reasonable. Even better is 90 days' notice, or if local code or law stipulates otherwise. A 90 days' notice allows the tenants to prepare for the project and find suitable accommodation if they choose to move out. Be very clear in the notice as to what areas will be repaired and in what order, as well as the time frame. Be as methodical as you can. Work with the plumbers and the other contractor(s) to minimize the impact the repair will have on the tenants.

It is best to work on certain risers first. The most logical thing to do is to repair the worst riser first. This kind of work should be done long before or after any major holidays, as this shows respect for tenants who have family and friends visiting for the holidays. There is also another approach or method, where a special coating is used to line the pipes. It can be expensive as a one-time cost. However, because it requires little or no breaking of walls to access pipes, it is considered less disruptive to the tenants. If you have few or no walls to break, you then have fewer or no cosmetic repairs to address.

6. **Parking lot paving**

   Be sure to include in the scope of work the parking lines and numbers for parking spots. This project should be done in late spring to early summer when the temperature is not too hot. Also, doing this project in the summer allows you to request one-day parking from any nearby schools or churches. If that is not possible, call your municipal/city office and request a one-day roadside parking exemption (authorization to park longer than the maximum parking time) to accommodate the one-day project.

7. **Swimming pool sandblasting and painting**

   The quote should also include depth marking around the pool. Get the quote for this job as soon as the pool season is finished. The best time to start this project is the middle of spring, or as soon as the weather allows for it. This will allow any cement work to be cured before it can be painted. The paint will also need time to cure before the pool can be filled with water. Depending on the size of the pool, this can take days to reach the required level, after which the mandatory inspection can be done by the municipal health department. Be sure to include any applicable signs that must be posted as per code. Also, is there a fence to enclose the pool? What is the condition of the fence? This is another area you can include for the pool quote.

8. **Lighting**

   If you would like to save on energy, you may want to investigate any energy-saving program in your area. Check with your local electricity transmission and distribution utility company to see if they have a retrofit program in which you can participate to receive incentives for lighting upgrades and other upgrades done inside your buildings. Some will even offer workshops to educate companies who participate in the program. Following are some areas were light upgrade could be done:

   a. Upgrade in-suite lighting if hydro is included.
   b. Common area indoor lighting includes stairwells, hallways, chute rooms, lobby and any amenity rooms such as laundry room, exercise room, locker rooms and game room.
   c. Common area outdoor lighting includes the parking lot and underground garage.

   When you have proper lighting on property, it gives tenants a sense of security. Your tenants and others can clearly see around them at night without fear. Proper lighting enhances your curb appeal and makes you stand out from the competition.

9. **Common area hallway painting**

    a. Included in the hallway painting is the following:
        i. walls
        ii. ceiling
        iii. fire cabinets
        iv. unit doors and frames, exit doors and frames, and chute room doors and frames, as well as any utility room such as electrical or cable room

    b. In the stairwell, the scope of painting work may include the following:
        i. ceiling
        ii. walls
        iii. railings
        iv. floor and steps
        v. doors and frames

10. **Hallway carpet**

Contractors should include in their quotes ,any necessary adjustment to doors that may be affected by the newly installed carpet. This is to ensure the new carpet does not interfere with the opening and closing of any doors. If you are installing carpet tiles, *you may not need the adjustment in doors*, since carpet tiles come with their own backing. The current trend in carpet installation is leaning more toward carpet tiles or carpet squares, especially in hallways. This is due largely because carpet tiles are durable and stand up to foot traffic very well. Carpet tiles are good on maintenance, in that if the carpet is stained or damaged, you can easily replace the section that is damaged. Whereas, traditional rolled carpet that gets damaged, if they are not able to be cleaned, the entire carpet will have to be replaced, which can be expensive. Carpet tiles also gives you a wider selection of colours, patterns and designs which allows for mixing and matching. On the other hand, the carpet square/ tiles may not look as uniformed as the traditional rolled carpet. If the carpet is not a standardized colour, choose a type and colour that will stand up to the tenant base, that helps to reflect light and that cleans well.

11. **Hallway tiling**

The following areas are included:

    a. elevator landing
    b. elevator wall
    c. elevator floor (if applicable)

        Be sure to consult with your elevator company about installing tiles inside the elevator cabs. The rule of thumb is, whatever is removed should be replaced with something similar, or same for same. If you remove vinyl composition tiles (VCT) and replace them with ceramic tiles, this could create a problem because you have now increased the weight. Before you install ceramic tiles, you need to know if the new tiles will affect the weight capacity. Any change in weight will require inspection and approval from the TSSA (Technical Standard and Safety Authority).

    d. hallway floor

Contractors should include in their quotes any necessary adjustment to doors that may be affected by the new install. This is to ensure the new floor does not interfere with the opening and closing of any doors.

12. **Laundry room upgrade**

If the laundry equipment is outsourced, you will have to contact the company at least one month before the project begins to co-ordinate the removal of the machines from the laundry room and their return once the renovations are completed.

Include in the laundry room upgrade the following:

    a. tiling of floor (contractors should include in their quotes any necessary adjustment to doors)

    b. you may require a new drain cover for any floor drain(s) that may be affected by the new tiles

    c. tiling four to five feet up the wall behind washers and wash sink area (this allows for easy cleaning)

    d. painting of walls and ceiling

    e. lighting upgrade

    f. wash sink upgrade

    g. wall art

    h. dryer enclosure, including plastering and painting

    i. laundry-folding table

    j. bench or chair

    k. wastebin

    l. applicable new signs (old, dated and damaged laundry room signs will detract from the décor of the laundry room)

    m. applicable carbon monoxide (CO) detector

13. **Laundry equipment**

The size of your building will determine the number of machines you need in your laundry room. Also, the tenant base can affect the type of machines that are installed. If you have elderly tenants and/or tenants with physical disabilities, the possibility of having one or a few front-loader washers for accessibility should be considered. If the dryers are gas-operated, they will need to be connected by certified technicians if you do not have a heating, ventilation and air conditioning (HVAC) team. The washers may require the services of the plumbers. If your dryers are not boxed in or enclosed, you may want to enclose them. Be sure to take these factors into consideration when you request your quotes for this project.

14. **Automatic door installation**

This project will require the actual automatic door and an electrician to provide the power supply. It may also require minor plastering and painting.

15. **Garage door**

Signs that you need a new garage door are that the garage door is not closing and opening properly; there are worn springs that need to be replaced; and/or there are frayed cables. Once you have decided to replace the door, always add an extra eye or sensor for safety reasons to detect pets or small children when the door closes. Most contractors will also inform you of this safety fact.

16. **Mailboxes and mail rooms inside your buildings**

You will have to co-ordinate this project with the supervisor of your local post office. While this work is being done, all mails will have to be removed from the mail room on the property by the post office. Therefore, tenants will have to collect their mail off the property at the closest designated post office or postal point. To manage tenant stress and frustration, I highly recommend that this project be undertaken in late spring or early summer, when it is not too cold and not too hot. The last thing your tenants want to do is collect their mail in the blistering cold, trod through snow or broiling summer heat to receive their mail.

a. Your company's approved design, style and material for the mailboxes. Check if mailbox numbers must also be written in braille

b. Your scope of work for the mailboxes may include cosmetic repairs such as the following:

   i. plastering and painting once the mailboxes are installed (you may have to paint the entire wall where the mailbox is located instead of painting around the mailbox)
   ii. installing of decorative trim around the mailboxes

c. If you are renovating inside the actual mail room of the building, the scope of work may include the following:

   i. floor of choice or as indicated by the company (contractors should include in their quotes any necessary adjustment to doors)
   ii. painting of walls, ceiling, door, doorframe and baseboard
   iii. lighting

   FYI, whether you have a capex project for the mail room or not, I strongly recommend you get a 24 hours emergency contact number for the post office. Remember the mail room located inside your building is off-limits to you and your staff. You do not have a key to this room, which usually has a special lock and a special key that you are not given a copy of. If there is an emergency like a flood in the mail room, how do you address the flood? A possible situation like this is why you need the emergency contact. You should have the number, and the number should also be available to the building staff. I remember receiving a call about an early morning (1:00) major flood at one of my locations that affected the mail room. Sadly, I did not have the emergency contact number for the post office. All the locksmiths whom I called in the early hours told me they *could not and would not* attempt to open the door to the mail room. They warned me it was "federal property" and said they could get into serious trouble for opening the door. The only other option I considered was to call the police and ask them if they had contact information for the post office. In Ontario, since some pharmacies have a post office inside them, I made a call to a nearby pharmacy that happened to open 24 hours. Thankfully, the pharmacy made a call to the emergency contact they had, who contacted us and stopped by that early in the morning at the property to allow us access to the mail room. The plumbers were able to shut the water off to the affected riser and stop the flood. Make sure you have an emergency contact, because you never know when you will need it.

17. **Surveillance camera installation**

    Cameras should be installed where they are needed the most. If you have problem areas, your cameras should be placed in those areas. Before you get a quote for the proposed camera locations, speak with your site staff. They know where the problem areas are. Your consultation with them will add pride and value to their work. They will also feel you are listening to them and to any tenant who may have complained to them about safety and security. Some areas where cameras can be placed are as follows:

    a. in the lobby, either the entrance or near anything of value, such as furniture (including a fireplace)
    b. in the rental office
    c. inside elevators (You may require your elevator company to allow the camera technicians access. This access from the elevator company will entail an additional cost. You will have to call and get the quote for this access and add it to the overall cost to do the installation)
    d. in amenity rooms such as the laundry room, pool room/area, game room, exercise room and party room
    e. at the garage entrance (This will allow you to see when someone damages your garage door or photo eye/safety eye. Cameras can also be placed at the entrance to each garage level)
    f. any back exits to the building
    g. any other location your staff may suggest

18. **Convert general storage area(s) or empty room(s) to tenant storage, social room, game room, exercise room or cinema room.**

    When converting a space into a useful room, some factors that will affect the budget and must be considered are as follows:

    a. tenants' easy access to the room
    b. water supply

c. power supply

d. HVAC

Also, you want to check if the conversion requires any permit. If it does, the cost of the permit should be included in the quote. Will the newly converted room require changes to the building plan, and if so is there a cost for this? Social rooms must have the load capacity (maximum number of people that should be in the room at any one time) posted on the outside and/or inside. The fire department should be able to provide the formula to calculate this number for you. Be sure to include all applicable signs in the quote.

19. **Major elevator repair or modernization**

Is the elevator slowing down? Is the elevator taking occupants to the floors they have selected? Is your elevator not levelling when it reaches a floor? Is it always breaking down, with people getting stuck inside? Now if all these things are happening with any of your elevators, get them repaired before you are given an order to make the repair. If you have *any outstanding orders* to repair your elevator as per the 2017 amendments to the Ontario Residential Tenancies Act (RTA), you will not be able to include the cost to address that repair resulting from the order as part of the AGI, regardless of the cost. Try to avoid having any order to repair the elevators, as that will make the process of the AGI application less complicated. You do not want this cost to be thrown out by the adjudicator.

Is your elevator company telling you that you have to do any major replacements, such as door or cab upgrades? Are your tenants complaining about the elevator? Have your elevator consultant check out the concerns without delay. Elevator and escalator engineer consultants at KJA in Toronto, Ontario, state, "Sometimes it is suggested that the existing equipment be modernized since it is 'getting old' and therefore impossible to maintain." KJA further states, "In the near future there are not always enough personnel capable of keeping the older systems running reliably at their full potential. All of these factors tend to force building owners to examine the question of modernization. It becomes not a matter of whether to modernize but when to modernize bearing in mind the length of time the modernization program will take." Have the elevator assessed by an elevator consultant. Your consultant can determine if a major repair or a replacement is needed. An elevator modernization project can last five to six weeks per elevator. You should also consult TSSA regarding the time line for your elevator repairs.

Based on the anticipated length of the project, the project should probably be done during your slow season. This will better accommodate your few move-outs and will not tie up the elevator. Be sure to send your first notice about this major project months before or as stipulated by any local tenant law before the work gets started. This will allow any tenant who cannot do without the use or limited use of the elevator to find another accommodation by either moving out or making a plan for the disruption of service.

20. **Landscaping**

   The landscaping is one of the first points of contact people have with the property. Any need for landscape upgrades will come about from your frequent visits to the property. You can also walk the property with your landscaping contractor and your staff. Do you need to improve the gardens or flowerbeds? Are there dry trees that need removal or trimming? Are there exposed tree roots that need to be protected through reseeding or mulching? Are there broken curbstones? Does any area of the parking lot require paving? Is proper signage required? Are posts needed for these signs? These areas of concern should be included as part of the scope of work. If you are not able to do everything, push to do the projects in areas that present safety concerns.

21. **Lobby and vestibule upgrade**

   Following are components of this type of upgrade:

   a. floor upgrade (contractors should include in their quotes any necessary adjustment to doors)
   b. painting of wall, ceiling, doors and doorframes
   c. lighting upgrade
   d. new furniture (metal or hard plastic to keep bedbugs out), wall art and accessories (as per local fire code)
   e. possible window treatments (blinds, shutters, shades, curtains, draperies, swags and valances) as per local fire code
   f. new and updated signage
   g. entrance door upgrade
   h. miscellaneous (may include heating radiators)
   i. intercom system applicable to your company

22. **Rental office upgrade**

   The following are components of this type of upgrade:

   a. new furniture (desk, chairs and filing cabinets), wall art and accessories (remember any chairs for tenants should be metal or hard plastic to keep bedbugs out)
   b. window treatments (blinds, shutters, shades, curtains, draperies, swags and valances) as per local fire code
   c. painting of walls and ceiling
   d. lighting upgrade
   e. heating or air conditioning if possible
   f. flooring upgrade (contractors should include in their quotes any necessary adjustment to doors)
   g. entrance door upgrade

23. **Compactor bins**

   If your compactor will not start and you have garbage piling up in the chutes, you have an issue. Say you get the compactor to start but it does not compact or run. Say the door will not open or close. If your contractor cannot repair the compactor or the cost to repair is almost equal to the cost of a new compactor, it is time to replace the compactor. Before you submit your quote for the compactor, powerwash the area (walls and floor) around the compactor and then assess if the area needs to be repaired. Include the powerwash along with any necessary repair to the location of the compactor as part of the budget for replacement of the compactor.

24. **Exit doors and frames**

   Quotes should include painting, door closures and any signs that cannot be reused but should be on the door. From a safety standpoint, get quotes to install doors with windows. The window in the door allows anyone using the door to see on the other side. If you use these doors in the stairwell, it can help to deter loiterers and vandals. Verify if glass for the window doors should be wire meshed. Wired glass is an added form of safety in case the glass on the door gets broken.

25. **Fire equipment**

   Consult with your life safety specialist or your fire safety equipment and protection company to determine what is needed. In most cases, these needs will become apparent during monthly inspections or your annual Fire and Life Safety inspection. You may need to upgrade the sprinkler system, install a new generator or repair a generator.

26. **Special equipment**

   Special equipment can range from bin tugs, also known as bin pullers for large garbage compactor bins, to any floor cleaning equipment or snow blowers.

Not all the projects you submit to your area or branch manager for capex will be accepted. Never feel disheartened if some are rejected or deferred or if you get less money than what you requested. Sometimes the rejection or reduced funding has to do with overall budgeting for the company. Your area manager sometimes knows ahead of time what projects are most likely to be accepted or be allotted reduced funding and what projects will not be accepted. Push the ones you are passionate about that will be of great benefit to the building or building community. Besides, remember there is always next year and the year after. If your projects get approved but with less funds allotted than you requested, you could look at doing the project in phases. That is to say, you could do a portion of the work each year based on the overall budget you have and request additional funds in the next fiscal year. So, the first year would be phase one, the second year would be phase two, and so on. Be persistent and patient at the same time. Always try your best and work with what you have.

B. Managing Your CapEx Projects

1. Spread your capex projects across your company's financial year according to season. Your schedule will depend on the weather; therefore, focus on indoor projects during the colder weather and outdoor projects during the warmer weather. Be sure to take into consideration what is happening in the buildings, such as move-outs and move-ins at the end of each month, or if you have overlapping projects. Your long-range projection and schedule will allow you to complete projects on time and plan around vacation time off for staff, you and your contractors. This way you will not feel rushed and your contractors will not feel they are overwhelmed with last-minute projects. Do not forget that you and your colleagues are competing for the same set of contractors.

2. Begin requesting quotes if you do not have quotes for your projects. Remember too that the quotes used to make up your potential list or wish list may require some updating of prices. It is also wise to give contractors an idea of when you hope to start the project and when you would like the project to end. You can also provide your rationale for the start and end date of the project. Once you have all your quotes, formally apply for funding as per your company policy and procedures.

3. As soon as you have approval for the funding, contact the contractor(s) awarded the project(s) and confirm start date(s).

4. It is also very important for you to obtain time lines or a projected order of work for how and when the contractors intend to complete the project. For example, if the project will take four days or four weeks, the contractor should break down what they intend to do on days 1, 2, 3 and 4. If the project will take four weeks, what will be done in week 1, week 2, week 3, week 4 and so on? This information is for you and your staff. It will give you and the site staff an idea of how the work will affect the operations of the building. You may feel it is necessary to include some of that information in your general notice to the tenants. This is totally up to you.

5. After start dates are confirmed in writing from the contractor(s), prepare tenant notices (either notices handed out door-to-door or a general notice to be posted in critical locations in common areas) to the respective buildings/properties indicating the following:

   a. the anticipated length or duration of the project
   b. the time frame for each day if the project requires multiple days to be completed
   c. the location of the project on the property
   d. how the tenants will be affected and any temporary measures in place to accommodate those disruptions (For example, say you are doing elevator projects. Contractors could work on one elevator at a time until the project is completed)

e. any warning or notification before the work starts and any adjustments or delay to the project (a delay could be the result of an industry strike, weather conditions, an emergency on the property or internal elements/factors within the contractor's company)

Where possible, additional notices/signs may be needed, such as the following:

   i.   Wet Paint sign
   ii. Caution tape
   iii. Danger Overhead sign
   iv. Watch Your Step sign
   v.   Other applicable signs

6. Do not forget that this is a collective or team project with your staff. Make sure they have a copy of the approved scope of work for the project. That way your staff can keep an eye on what is supposed to be done and alert you if there are any deviations.

7. Manage tenant stress by listening to tenants who call to complain about the project. Be prepared to make adjustments to notices or to the project to reduce the impact on tenants. Ensure the contractor works within the guidelines noise bylaw or any other applicable bylaw.

8. Monitor the project by taking your time line or the projected order of work with you when you visit the property.

   a. Physically check on the project every time you are at the property. If you are allowed on or in the work area, walk around and see what is happening. Be sure you are using any required personal protective equipment (PPE).
   b. Give regular feedback by notifying the contractor(s) of any defects before the project ends, and have these corrected as soon as possible without extra cost. If the workers are painting, are they using the correct paint colour? If they are tiling, are they using the correct colour, size and shape, and finish or texture of tile?
   c. If you previously overlooked an area that will incur additional cost, discuss the new finding with your area/branch manager immediately.

9. Enforce health and safety practices by doing the following things:

   a. Ensure contractors are wearing applicable PPE.
   b. Ensure the work area is safe and following safety protocol.
   c. Signs regarding restricted access must be posted. Check if restricted mechanisms that should be installed are in place such as; caution tape, snow fence, metal fence or any other applicable device.
   d. Ensure contractors are following your company safety procedure.

10. Keep the lines of communication open at all times. Do the following things:

   a. Be sure to attend any start-up meetings and progress meetings. If you are not able to attend, your building managers or superintendents must be present. Try to get a copy of any minutes from the meeting and see if there is any action needed on your part.
   b. Have contact numbers for contractors in case there is an emergency.
   c. If any municipal official or other authority shows up to investigate what is happening, be sure that you or the contractor can answer their questions satisfactorily.
   d. If applicable notices and permits are posted at designated locations, this can eliminate questions.

11. Ensure contractors clean up as they go along. If you are paying for removal and disposal of the old material, debris from the project should not be dumped into your wastebin. If there is a final cleaning to be done, know ahead of time who is supposed to take care of the cost.

12. Do a final inspection of the project to see if it satisfactorily meets the work scope or specification.

13. If the project is part of an AGI application, do the following things:

   a. Keep a copy of all notices to show you did your due diligence to give clear and timely notice to tenants.
   b. Always confirm satisfactory completion before you sign any invoice to pay for the capex project.
   c. Keep a copy of the invoice. This shows the cost of the project
   d. Take pictures of the AGI projects before and after. This is important.
   e. Evidence that the work was paid for during the specified time. This will correspond to the time frame on the AGI application.

Capex projects if carefully planned and organized can go smoothly. The expectation should be set before you request the quotes. That way the contractors know what the job entails before they submit their quotes. The chapter titled External Contractors and Trades Persons will shed more light on how to select and work with contractors.

Sample Notice for Hallway Painting

On [date] between the hours of [hours], [days of the week], our contractor will be painting the hallway walls, the ceilings, apartment doors and frames, elevator doors and frames, chute room doors and frames, and fire cabinets on each floor. This project will take approximately three weeks to complete. The project dates may be affected by extreme weather conditions such as heat [or deep freeze].

Please expect some dust associated with plastering and sanding, as well as a strong paint smell, when the painters are on your floor. Kindly refrain from touching any of the painted areas when wet. We ask that you exercise caution when you enter the hallways and be mindful of the Wet Paint signs posted by the painters.

We apologize for any inconveniences this project may cause. Thank you for your patience and co-operation while we carry out this project. Please speak with the site staff if you have any questions or concerns.

Regards,

[Name]
Property Manager

Accounts Payable

Accounts payable (AP) involves paying the bills for services used by the properties within your portfolio so they can operate efficiently. Your company may have a cycle of 14, 30 or 60 days to process bills or invoices received from contractors and suppliers who rendered services within your portfolio. Whatever the cycle, you will have to review and sign off on invoices associated with repairs and maintenance or projects that were completed within your portfolio. As you sign invoices, you will see that some contractors are not as detailed with their invoices. For the benefit of the company and the contractors alike, advise contractors that invoices must be clearly written with details. Details does not mean just the cost of the job. The details entail what was involved in doing the work. For example, your staff may have had difficulty clearing a clogged toilet. If a plumber was called in to snake/clear that toilet, the invoice should state what caused the toilet to clog—probably a toy, a bar of soap or something else not normally found in this aspect of the plumbing. Whatever is found should be verified with pictures. Sometimes invoices become part of the evidence used in the landlord and tenant court system, especially if tenants are asked to pay whole or part of the invoice. Always back up your work with facts. This puts you in a constant state of readiness.

Make sure you know the ins and out of each building in your portfolio. Establish guidelines and dollar brackets of authority with your building managers and superintendents from day one. Before they call a contractor for certain items outside their dollar bracket of authority, they must call you first. If the cost to do the work is over their bracket of authority, they must consult with you. If your company designates a specific day to sign invoices, let your staff know which day this is. Inform your staff that on the designated invoice-signing or -processing day, you may be calling them seeking answers and clarification of some invoices. If your schedule allows, you can sign invoices at one of your properties and get your building managers or superintendents to participate. They can review the invoices and confirm if some of the work has been completed to company standard. Sometimes if I have an inspection to do or a tenant to visit, I will leave the invoices for the staff to review while I am conducting the inspection or visiting the tenant.

Invoice signing should not be taken lightly. It should be used as an opportunity to do the following:

- Assess if training is needed for your staff, for example, if they are too reliant on contractors.
- Get an idea of how to control spending and cut costs.
- Determine whether invoices should be paid by the company or someone else. For example, who caused the damage?
- Decide how to adjust your budget.
- Gain a better understanding of what is happening in the building in terms of maintenance in the following areas:

  o pest control (if you are getting several invoices for pest treatments, then you have a pest problem that should be investigated and measures should be implemented to control or eradicate the pest)
  o plumbing (if you are getting several invoices for plumbing, then you may need some kind of pipe replacement or may have to explore epoxy coating)

  Whenever you see multiple invoices for similar work or a huge bill, always follow the paper trail. You may be asked by your AM for an explanation, or you may have to give an explanation in your financial review meeting.

If an invoice is billed to any building in your portfolio, it doesn't mean you have to pay all or part of the invoice. This is where attention to detail will come in handy. You pay only for services that were approved by you or your staff and rendered at your properties.

A. Basic Guidelines for Signing Invoices

Some basic guidelines to use when signing invoice are as follows:

1. Ensure the contractor who sent the invoice is an approved contractor. Your staff should have called or used only contractors from the company's approved trades list. Contractors on the approved trades list would have submitted all necessary paperwork such as insurance and special licenses, and their credibility would have been checked and cleared.

2. Ensure the price and scope of work agreed on both match what was quoted, unless you made adjustments, which should be attached to the original scope of work.

3. Check or confirm that work was completed before you sign an invoice for payment. Do you use confirmation of packing slips/delivery slips or work specification sheets? Your staff should write or stamp "completed" on the work specification sheet before they are sent to confirm that work was done.

4. The invoice should be billed to the correct company, your company, and to the correct building at the correct location. Some contractors do work for the competition. The competition may have a building on the same street as one of your buildings. There was one case where major work was done in one of the buildings in my portfolio. As with all major projects and

some minor projects, you should inspect what you expect to confirm if the work was completed before you pay any invoice. The inspection in this case proved satisfactory and the invoice for that work was submitted and paid. About two months later, the same contractor sent another invoice addressed for work done inside an apartment in the same building where the major work was completed. It was quite shocking to receive another invoice for the same work that had been completed and paid for. Upon careful examination, the invoice showed that the listed address was for a building owned by the competition located on the same street and not the building in my portfolio. I immediately placed a call to the contractor, who admitted the mistake. That invoice was pulled and was never paid. If that invoice had not been properly reviewed, my building would have paid the bill for the competition.

5. When you personally do unit inspections and approve the work to be done inside those units, it makes invoice signing easier. One contractor invoiced one of the buildings for both a tub glaze and a new bathtub installation. That apartment only had one bathroom and was only approved for a bathtub reglaze, never a bathtub installation. The tub installation was never done, so that line item was removed from the invoice by a credit note from the contractor.

6. If you are having carpet installed inside an apartment, make sure your staff include the square footage on the planner/requisition for floor installation sheet before it is faxed or sent off to the contractor who is doing the installation. You want to ensure you are not paying for more square footage than you should. Is there an agreed upon unit price and wastage? Make sure that wastage is within the guideline that was agreed. If you are doing carpet installation, does the installation include underpadding? Sometimes contractors will reuse the old underpadding when they do a new carpet installation. Your staff can check on the work while it is in progress and confirm if new underpadding is being installed. Old underpadding must always be removed. Old underpadding contains urine and excrement from any pet the tenant has or had. If the work is completed before your staff get to the location, they can check the old carpet that was removed from the area to see if the old underpadding is with it. That old carpet and old underpadding should not be thrown in to your waste disposal bin for the property. Remember you are paying for removal and installation. The contractor should remove the old carpet and underpadding off-site in his or her own vehicle. If he or she throws it inside your wastebin, you could be billed by the waste disposal company. Then you would be paying for disposal twice. Note also that if you are doing carpet installation for a new tenant or tenancy, it is very important that the old underpadding be removed. Any smell that is trapped in the old underpadding will resurface. You can try as you may to shampoo it, but it will never get rid of the smell. The new tenant will only complain and request to be released from the lease/tenancy agreement, or else you will end up at the landlord and tenant court.

7. If you have an invoice for tile installation, check the planner/requisition for installation sheet for the correct square footage of the area and the correct area or location to be tiled. One contractor was contracted to tile the kitchen inside an apartment. The contractor tiled the bathroom instead. The staff followed up on the work and saw that the wrong area was

tiled, so they raised an alarm and informed me immediately. The contractor returned and tiled the correct area but invoiced for both locations even though it was his error. The contractor was paid only for the work he was requested to do. Based on the volume of work the contractor received from the company, I felt he could absorb the cost, which he did, issuing a credit note. The importance of following up is crucial to reducing spending. The staff was given the credit for that cost-saving measure.

8. Familiarize yourself with the prices of various items. This will prevent the company from being overcharged. One contractor submitted an invoice for a door handle at one of the locations I managed. The red flag about this door handle was the price. Also, the staff had not given me the heads-up that the door was damaged and needed replacement. I placed a call to the staff member, who stated that the door handle had to be changed because the door key was broken. Since the door was a fire-rated metal door, the staff member called the contractor to remove the lock and install a new lock. The invoice that came in was not for a lock but a very expensive door. It was two times the price for that type of fire-rated door. I called the contractor, who stated that the price was for something else at another building and that it had been added to my bill in error. The contractor issued a credit note for the difference, which was over $2,500.

9. Know the layout of each of your buildings. It will help you visualize as you sign and approve invoices for payment. When you review invoices for pest control, look to see if notes are written by the technician regarding the level of preparation in the apartments being treated. If an apartment was not prepared well or not prepared at all, investigate the matter. If the tenant in such an apartment doesn't have a disability, that tenant should be given an N5 for his or her failure to prepare for the treatment. Remember the treatment works only if everyone in the block of treatment complies. Any full bedbug treatment must include any necessary block treatments or inspection. If you are familiar with the layout of the building, you will know the units that must be included in the block treatment, if the infestation is very bad. It will also tell you if you have a potential problem and if a more aggressive approach should be taken to address the problem.

10. Tenants, their occupants or any guests who damage the property, including inside their apartment, should be billed for the repair. This is as per section 34 of the RTA: "The tenant is responsible for the repair of undue damage to the rental unit or residential complex caused by the wilful or negligent conduct of the tenant, another occupant of the rental unit or a person permitted in the residential complex by the tenant" (*Residential Tenancies Act*, 2006, c. 17, s. 34).

    Your legal department can send the appropriate letter or legal document and a copy of any invoices to the tenant.

11. As we have stated earlier when you sign invoices you should get an idea of how to control spending and cut costs. Getting many of the same type of invoice can prompt you to take

corrective measures that will reduce costs in the long run. One location required a plastering and painting job in the hallways every other month. The problem was that tenants were taking shopping carts into the hallways and damaging the corners. The corrective measure taken was to install signs that read No Shopping Carts Are Allowed Inside the Building. While the signs were in production, a discussion was held with the staff indicating that corner strips or corner guards would be purchased and installed in the hallways. The guards would act as bumpers or buffers and protect the corners if anyone was still able to take a shopping cart inside the building. All the staff at the location agreed. They even offered to install the guards themselves instead of calling a contractor to do the installation. The financial impact of the decision to install the guards decreased the common area plastering and painting significantly to the point where it was noticeable on the financial statement. The corner strips were later implemented at other buildings within the portfolio.

12. Remember as you sign invoices, determine whether invoices should be paid by the company or someone else. For example, who caused the damage? Therefore, hold accountable anyone who causes damage to your property. Your staff must be vigilant and alert to things happening on the property. One day a staff member called to inform me that an oversized utility truck was parked on the property and asked if I had given the utility company authorization to park on the property. I had not given any such authorization, and even if I had, that would have been communicated directly to the staff. What was interesting about this case is that the parking lot was paved with asphalt about two days before the unauthorized parking of the truck. Because of the weight of the truck and the fact that the asphalt was not fully set, the area where the truck was parked sank and caused a noticeable uneven section in the parking lot. I now had a massive trip hazard and an unsightly parking lot. I immediately instructed the staff to take pictures of the truck from a distance, including its company logo and license plate, and closeup pictures of the damaged asphalt. I placed a call to the contractor who did the asphalt job and had them repair the area the following day. I then called the company that owned the truck and ascertained the name and contact information of the person to whom the pictures and invoice should be sent to address the repair. This resulted in a cheque to cover the full cost of the repair.

Make notes on any out-of-the-ordinary expenses. You will most likely not remember these items months afterward when you have to explain these expenses during financial review meetings. Another thing to note is that several small expenses to deal with the same issue will add up. Be sure to make your notes. Your notes and explanations will show that you know what is happening in your buildings and that you have things under control based on the strategies you have implement to address the financial hemorrhage to take care of the problems generating that expense.

Accounts Receivable

For our purposes, accounts receivable (AR) is the rent money that is due or owed. Rent for most rental properties is due on the first of each month. Even though every tenant may have signed and agreed to pay on the first of the month, they do not always live up to that agreement. Not every tenant will be able to pay on the first of the month. Some tenants will manipulate the system and try not to pay. Tenants may pay their rent according to how they receive their own pay. Tenants who pay are never your concern. Your concerns and headaches will come from the tenants who do not pay at all or who are always late, not by a few days but by two or more months. To prevent late payment of rent, work closely with your legal department and make sure legal documents are served to tenants who are late in paying their rent. Your accounting department can only update what tenants have paid, either by cheque, online, preauthorization, or payment from organizations that provide subsidized funding for certain tenants.

A. Strategies for Collecting Rent

Excellent property managers alleviate themselves of any headache about rent collection. Remember your job as an excellent property manager entails a joint effort between you, your staff and other departments. The departments you want to keep close to are the accounting and legal department.

1. Try to collect as much rent as possible before any major holidays. You want your tenant to prioritize rent over gifts and other holiday customs. Remember shelter is a basic need.

2. Get your staff involved in the process. Door knocking or phone calling should be done daily to collect outstanding balances.

3. If you have buildings in a community setting, you may want to assign a building to each building manager and/or superintendent if you have more than one. Or you can distribute responsibility for the buildings equally between the superintendent and building manager.

4. Set targets of what you want your closing balance to be for each month at each location. Tell your staff that they can achieve the targets. There should be no excuses. Ask your staff

how they wish to be rewarded (within your authority) for achieving the target. Following is a poem I wrote to my staff to build momentum, increase morale and maintain focus on the rent collection process. This poem was received with much laughter and energized the staff. When the target was achieved, I took the staff as a group to their restaurant of choice. Another approach used with the poem was for the staff to state which restaurant they wanted to go to, and the name of that restaurant was written in place of the word *restaurant* in the poem. Another target was set so the name of the restaurant was changed to "seafood restaurant." That target was also achieved, and so another was set with another name.

Door Knocking

I enjoy doing door knocking.
It helps to keep the rent cheques popping
Even though the tenants keep sobbing.
Our property manager will not be nagging
When we hit our target goal; we'll be bragging.
To the restaurant we'll be rocking
Only if we keep door knocking.

5. Be specific about when the target should be met by stating the month.

6. Call your buildings daily and check on the progress of the rent collection. This can be done when you do your follow-up call to the buildings in the morning or afternoon.

7. Commend your staff on the smallest accomplishment toward reaching the goal. It could be they got the tenant with the largest amount of outstanding rent to pay half or in full. The reward for that could be taking coffee or donuts for everyone the next time you visit the building.

8. Your staff should develop a close relationship with the accounting department. They should feel free to call and request copies of statements for tenants if they do not have access to that information at their building. You should keep in touch with the accounting department as well and know what is happening at the buildings. You can also check the software system your company uses and see the rent balances for yourself. You will also see which tenants' rent is still outstanding.

9. The next time you are at the building, you can knock on the door of that tenant with the high outstanding rent. Leave a note and slip it under the door if the tenant is not home. You can write the note on the back of your business card, asking the tenant to call you. Any other note should be put in an envelope for privacy. I lived in an apartment and once received a note that my rent was outstanding even though my rent was paid long before the first of the month. What was embarrassing about the note was that I had a visitor and she was the one who picked up the note about my "outstanding rent" and handed it to me. I was not pleased

about that note. The purpose of the envelope is to protect the tenant's pride and save you a call from an irate tenant who paid their rent on time. Your being involved with the rent collecting will also tell the tenant that the collection is a combined effort. Whatever you do, be sure to keep the legal department informed.

10. Follow up with a phone call and be sure to keep in touch with your staff so communication is co-ordinated and the tenant is not playing you and/or your staff. In the event you speak with the tenant, do not accept any verbal promises of a payment plan. A verbal agreement will not hold up in court. Accept payment plans *only* at the Landlord and Tenant Board (LTB). If it is legal to do so in your region, whatever filing fee you pay should be charged back to the tenant. Some tenants may be hesitant to go to the LTB because of the filing fee. The choice is not theirs to make. Let them know that it is the practice of the company not to accept verbal payment plans. If you file for eviction, the cost of the sheriff will be a lot more. This step formalizes the agreement and forces the tenant to commit to the decision. If the tenant should falter, you are in a better situation to file other documents to have that tenant evicted and or pay the outstanding rent.

11. For tenants who are consistently late with paying their rent, you can request your legal department to serve those tenants an N8. The N8 forces these tenants to pay their rent on the first of the month.

You may have cases where family members and friends want to pay the outstanding rent for the tenant. You may accept the rent and state in writing to the tenant, including any section of the lease/tenancy agreement that states this fact, that rent, if paid by friend or family on the tenant's behalf, does not make the payer a tenant. The friend or family member does not automatically become a leaseholder if he or she pays a partial or the full portion of the rent and, because of this, is not entitled to any of the privileges or rights a leaseholder has. These privileges and rights may include but not be limited to being entitled to a rent receipt for income tax purposes and to submitting formal requests for repairs in the apartment.

Another common roadblock to collecting outstanding rent is that tenants will tell the staff they do not speak English. Sometimes this is a trick employed by the tenant in hopes of not getting evicted. Regardless of the language barrier, serve any legal document intended for the late-paying or non-paying tenants. Once the document is served, the tenant usually finds someone to translate for them very quickly. Note that if you translate any document into one language, you must translate it into the other languages; otherwise it could be classified as discrimination. The rule of thumb is to serve all documents in the same language as the lease/tenancy agreement is written.

In addition to taking preauthorized rent payments from a tenant's bank account, most companies are now offering online rent payment. Depending on the size of your company, an app for your company is probably the next best thing to assist tenants in paying rent online. Most banks have an app or a page on their Web site that eliminates a trip to the bank and allows customers to do banking from anywhere. If your company or the accounting software system it uses has an app, that app may allow tenants to do the following:

- Pay rent online.
- Send work orders regarding repairs needed inside the apartment and receive confirmation that the repair has been addressed.
- Receive general notices about the building (this in addition to hard copies that are posted in the building). That way, regardless of the tenant's location, whether local or abroad, the tenant will still know what is happening on the property.
- Provide the option to book an appointment either at the office or at the building.

The app can also show you the property manager any trends regarding the repairs, help with budgeting or help you spot potential problems. The app may help the company with marketing by advertising tenant referrals, new locations and in-house vacancies. I have found that there is already an existing market already within the buildings. Some tenants want to keep their family together even though the family is expanding. They would rather the family member rent in the same building or one that is close by. Or some tenants want to upgrade to a bigger apartment or downsize to a smaller apartment.

B. Dealing with an Improper Notice to Vacate

When you are processing vacate notices, some vacating tenants may give less than the 60 days' notice as stipulated by the Ontario RTA. Does your company have a penalty for tenants who give less than 60 days' notice? The reasons for giving less than 60 days' notice will vary and may include one or more of the following:

A. inability to pay rent
B. illness
C. relocation to nursing or retirement home
D. job change
E. immigration

In Ontario, as of September, 2016, victims of sexual abuse/violence or domestic violence can give 28 days' notice to vacate. This short notice is filed on an N15 form, along with official proof from the court or any other authority. Thereafter, this information has to be kept confidential by the landlord.

Apart from the N15, sometimes when short notice is given, you may have to extend compassion. To avoid anyone taking advantage of your compassion, extend compassion only when you have proof that it is needed. Ask for medical proof if your tenant claims he or she has a medical problem necessitating him or her to vacate sooner than 60 days. Clearly state you do not wish to know anything personal about the tenant but that you need confirmation in the form of a letter or a medical note stating the tenant is not able to live on his or her own, or is going in to a retirement or nursing home, or will be moving to live with family. Do this only if it does not interfere with any privacy laws. If your staff knows the tenant very well, sometimes they can confirm what the tenant is saying. You may have to use good judgement and make notes stating, "I have confirmed with staff on [date] that the tenant is sick, for example, in and out of the hospital. The tenant has no next of kin. This information is also supported by information on the resident record." With the tenant's consent, you can also call the nursing/retirement home and ask them to confirm if the tenant will be a resident in the future. The tenant can also have the retirement home send a letter to you the property manager confirming that he or she will be a resident on a certain date. Remember that when you have things in black and white, you will have fewer questions to answer from your branch or area manager or anyone else who has the right to ask them of you.

If the tenant is giving notice because of a job change, use good judgement. Is the tenant behind on rent? In some cases, it makes no financial sense to hold that tenant responsible when he or she cannot pay what is owed. If the tenant wants to leave in 30 days instead of 60, apply the last month's rent (LMR). You can still authorize that the tenant file go to collections so the outstanding rent, if any, can be paid. Sign a release letter along with an N11 and mutually end the tenancy if you are not going to hold the tenant responsible for the 60 days' notice. Does the tenant have a history of mischief? If so, hold him or her responsible and try to rent the apartment before you start losing revenue after he or she moves out.

Collecting rent should be strongly emphasized on the performance review of all the staff involved. It should also be a topic of discussion and on the action plan at all staff meetings. Consistent and persistent door knocking is very important. Door knocking can be a combined effort if you team up your staff within the portfolio. A staff member from one of your other buildings can go and assist your staff at another building within your portfolio. This can be done by setting aside a day where the staff member goes to the location that needs the help, and together with a staff member from that location, focuses on door knocking and collecting outstanding balances of rent for that day. Make sure this day is properly planned so the staff are not too busy and they accomplish their goal. Whatever they collect, they will call you with excitement. If the collection is big, they will excitedly tell you that they want something. It is ok to reward them, even if only for their enthusiasm. Sometimes the reward will not be large monetarily. They could say, "We want pizza and wings." Then give them pizza and wings. That excitement will live on. They will feel highly motivated. If they did not collect anything, you will have to motivate them because they will feel like nothing was accomplished. They must know their presence sends a message that will linger in the minds of the tenants.

I remember when one staff member who went to a building to assist with door knocking said a tenant had told him that she hated the fact he was knocking on her door for rent, so she was going to make sure next month the staff got the money because she did not want him back at her door. The staff member took the comment as funny because he was doing his job. He did not collect the rent that day, but he did change that tenant's mindset. Stories such as this one can be told at staff meetings at any of your properties. The staff will know and feel their work and effort is not in vain.

Once the target is achieved at the location, it is courteous to invite the visiting staff who assisted with the door knocking to the restaurant when the team goes to celebrate. If possible, invite a member of the accounting and legal department to join in the celebration.

Marketing and Renting Apartments

In the hotel industry, we call the selling of rooms "heads in beds." You want all your rooms sold to maintain 100 percent occupancy. In the movie industry it is called, anatomy in seats, (they actually use another word). Meaning, people in seats, equal sold-out theatres. The same is true of renting apartments. You want "heads and beds" in your apartments, because they spell signed leases or tenancy agreements. Meaning, you want all the apartments in your portfolio rented and occupied with good paying tenants who stay beyond their one-year lease and become long-term tenants. If you are hoping to increase your rent roll and the value of your property, you want your long-term tenants to stay sometimes beyond the anniversary date for their lease. Why only sometimes? Let us first explain an important process.

The percentage increase on the rent for occupied apartments is set by the Ontario Ministry of Municipal Affairs and Housing. If you wish to get an increase higher than what the government has stipulated for occupied units, you must do so through an AGI (above guideline increase). An AGI must be approved by the Landlord and Tenant Board (LTB) after an application is submitted based on major capital upgrades or major repairs done in the building or throughout the property to improve the useful life of the asset. You can visit the Website of the Landlord and Tenant Board to see what other factors you could use to apply for an AGI.

Now that we have that explanation out of the way, let us shed some light on "why you want your long-term tenants to stay sometimes beyond the anniversary date for their lease." Once the AGI has been approved, tenants who cannot afford the new rent increase have no choice but to move out. When those apartments become available, you may do other major renovations inside the newly vacant apartments and increase the rent based on what the market can bear. Make sure you do your research so that; (1) you follow all rules and or updated laws regarding any application for an AGI. (2) you do not have a set of empty apartments waiting to get filled. Remember empty apartments cannot generate revenue and thus eat away at your profit. What the AGI approach also does is to change out the tenant base by giving you a new set of tenants at higher rents. This is ideal if you (your company) have bought a new building and you want to bring it up to standard or you want to reposition an existing building in the market.

A. Advertising

Renting the apartment starts with marketing or getting the name/brand of the apartment out there among people who need somewhere to live. This can be done through a variety of ways.

i. Banners and Sandwich Boards

A traditional way to attract foot traffic is to use sandwich boards (or "A" signs), banners and wind banner flags. Banners are either upright and blowing in the wind or tied and secured to walls or railings. I remember flying into Texas and seeing from the window of the plane as it was landing a banner or huge sign with the name of a hotel on the roof of that hotel. The banner was faced towards the sky. The banner had the telephone number of the hotel. Whoever thought of the location of that banner was not just "thinking out of the box"; he or she was also thinking from inside the plane.

Sure, the world is digital, but it doesn't hurt to try the conventional approach. It may prove to be successful. If you are close to an airport, a banner on the roof (upright or laying flat) is something you can try (that is if snow will not cover over the banner). Some people who immigrate first stay in a hotel and then find suitable accommodation for their family. Let any immigrating family think of your apartment first as their choice to call home. What if your apartment is located close to a school, hospital or bus station? Your banner with the word *renting* and the building's telephone number can be placed high along the side of the building facing those landmarks or the flow of the traffic heading toward your building. Visibility helps people to know who and where you are.

ii. Digital Reader Boards

A digital reader board could be incorporated with your building sign or placed beside your building sign. Vacancy types such as "1 BR" and "2 BR" can be displayed, along with any promotions being offered. The great advantages with this method are as follows:

1. The board can be seen and easily read.
2. It is up 24/7.
3. It does not need staff to put it out in the day and take it up at night.
4. It is not affected by the wind and does not need to be anchored.
5. It is not affected by the weather, whether rain, sunshine or snow.

iii. Artificial Intelligence (AI)

This type of intelligence comes from a computer. This is now the way to market things. Computer programming anticipates what you want and makes recommendations. Notice that if you have purchased books online, the system will automatically generate a list of recommended books, even if you were not thinking of those books. You will see a heading such as "Others who have purchased this book also purchased ..." The Internet or other technology acts as a person and makes the recommendations for you. If you watch videos on YouTube, similar videos will keep popping up for you to watch.

I purchased some earrings while strolling the mall. In addition to giving me a hard copy receipt, the store sent an electronic copy of the receipt, as well as a coupon, to my e-mail. The coupon was to be used toward my next purchase. *Who said I had plans to go back anytime soon to purchase more earrings?* Well, they gave me reasons to go back. How? When I opened the e-mail to look at the coupon, those brutes had little images of other earrings that I had not bought but might be interested in buying. They got me! Immediately, I started thinking of outfits that would go well with the little images of those earrings I saw in the e-mail. Clever marketing, I thought.

If you take a property management approach to this kind of marketing, instead of a tenant making the referral, the Internet or other technology can do it for you. The advantage is that it reaches a wider base of prospective of tenants, creating mass appeal. Some of the key words or key information you could associate with your property when searches are done are as follows:

1. apartment
2. rent
3. promotion
4. suite
5. renovated bathroom, kitchen
6. one-bedroom, two-bedroom, three-bedroom
7. upgraded apartment
8. swimming pool
9. laundry room
10. in-suite laundry
11. the name of a school or university in the area
12. rent range, for example: one bedroom, $999 to $1,289
13. underground garage
14. the geographic location of the properties

Hence, every time someone types those words or speaks to use voice activation in order to search for an apartment, the name of your property/company will pop up first. Sometimes these things will tag you, as if to say, *Hey, just in case you forget, remember me.* Therefore, your company needs to make sure its Web site is smartphone- or mobile-device-friendly. It should also include the ability to do an online application on a mobile device.

Another factor to consider is how to set the price for the rent. The price you set plays on the minds of prospective tenants and will determine if they want to rent, especially if those tenants are price-sensitive.

"Avoid pricing ending in $X.000. In other words, $3,499, $3,497, or $3,495 looks more attractive than $3,500. Pricing just below the hundreds figure also helps when prospects are searching online. The search engine might miss the whole figure, but the simple truth is that $3,495 sounds better than multiple listings at $3,500. There are countless studies which have proven this fact and there are whole courses on pricing in business school."

Source: https://www.financialsamurai.com/a-pricing-strategy-to-maximize-rental-income-and-m inimize-turnover/. Reproduced with permission from Financial Samurai, September 5, 2017.

B. Incentives and Promotions

Now that people know about your apartments and are calling, how do you help your staff to do the following:

- Convert those calls to visits?
- Convert those visits to viewings?
- Convert those viewings to applications and ultimately a signed lease/tenancy agreement?
- Get the prospect to complete an online application?

Apart from your amenities and location, which your competition may also have, get your staff to state the unique selling features of the building, including the property. These unique selling features should also be stated on your Web site. In other words, indicate what sets your property apart from the other apartments in the area.

1. Is it the location and accessibility to resources in the neighbourhood?
2. Is it the upgrades in your apartments?
3. Is it the view?
4. Is it your on-site staff?
5. Is it the cleanliness of the building and a well-maintained lawn?
6. Is it the amenities, such as parking, in-suite laundry and heated pool?

In addition to those unique selling features, what will you use to stir the emotions of prospective tenants or prompt them to act and become tenants? Some incentives and promotions you could use are as follows:

- The zero-down method used in vehicle sales (if the season is slow). Indicate that the first month's rent (FMR) is zero ($0). "We will pay your first month's rent." Clearly state that this applies only to the apartment rent and not to amenities. Whatever method you use, it should not affect the anniversary date for rent increase. Speak with your accounting department and get their opinion.

- Employee pricing. Does an employee get a discount if he or she rents with the company? This discount can be offered to prospects in extremely slow periods. Since the colder weather seems to be the slower time, why not advertise something like, *For the month of November only, we are offering to the public our employee discount rent. The offer ends.*

- A raffle for a chance for tenants to win back their rent for (you can pick a month).

- "Who has time to cook on the first day they move in to a new place? Rent with us and receive a gift card in the amount of $[dollars] from [the name of a nearby restaurant that does delivery]." Gift cards can be given on the day tenants move in, or when the lease is signed and keys are given.

- Each month celebrates something. Offer a dollar amount move-in promotion and an extra amount during Teacher's Month for prospects who are teachers; during Nurse's Month for prospects who are nurses; etc.

- Have a back-to-school special if you have a problem renting two- and three-bedroom units.

- Offer seasonal tenant referrals where tenants are paid for referring a prospect who signs a lease/tenancy agreement and moves in.

- Do a promotional rent wheel. After viewing an apartment, the prospect can spin a wheel to see the dollar amount he or she will receive as part of the move-in promotion. If you are able to do this promotional rent wheel online, so online applicants can join in the fun, that would be great.

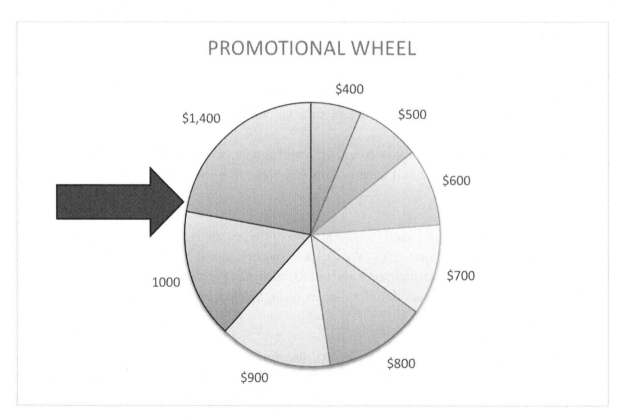

Prospects who receive promotion dollar amounts of $600 and below get a (restaurant) meal card for $50. The card is given on the day the lease/tenancy agreement is signed and/or the keys are given to the tenant.

C. Surveying the Competition

This involves doing a careful examination of other apartment buildings within proximity that offer similar or better amenities. How do your buildings measure up to the competition? Conducting an analysis or survey of similar buildings in the area is a great way to tell what the market looks like and how much people are willing to pay in rent. These surveys or analyses should be done by both you and your staff. You should do at least one building in the area. This will show your staff the importance of doing the surveys. Also, firsthand information of what the competition is about is great to know and understand. Having that information helps to set the rent and reposition your building(s) to gain or maintain a competitive advantage.

When your staff physically visit these buildings for themselves, they can size up the competition and assess the curb appeal. Your staff can physically see the product of the competition and will be in a better position to sell what they have. Continually check with your staff on how the market is taking the prices on the rent map. In addition to the rent, your staff will see how other buildings are cleaned and maintained and will determine any upgrades that are being done. How often one should do the surveys depends on the company. If you want to be excellent at what you do, encourage your staff to conduct surveys quarterly. Have your staff who will conduct these surveys mark three dates on their calendars: (1) at least two weeks before the survey, (2) the week of the survey and (3) the day of the survey. This way they can plan around it. You should do the same on your calendar. The survey keeps your staff alert and focused to changing market conditions. It makes for better leverage in the renting of apartments.

D. Rent Mapping

Rent mapping allows you to set rent and reasonably maximize the price or rent for a vacant apartment based on several factors, such as the following:

1. View – what tenants can see from their apartment that is appealing or breathtaking
2. Location – for example, the higher the apartment, the better the view
3. Accessibility – for an apartment building where your tenant base tends to be seniors, the ground floor or closer to the ground floor may be the most desirable location
4. Size – the building may have different sizes of each bedroom type, such as 1 BR large or 1 BR junior/small. One unit type may have a balcony, and another type may not have a balcony.
5. Unique layout – one type of apartment may have an enclosed kitchen, as opposed to a galley or open kitchen, and another unit type may have a larger bathroom with an oversized linen closet. Another unit type may have a larger living room or more storage space.
6. Upgrades done in the apartment – most apartments are doing upgrades similar to condominiums or hotels and adding other appliances such as washer and dryer inside the apartments. Is that what you are offering? Upgrades sell.

The rent or price mapping idea or principle is employed for pricing concert tickets, sporting events, hotel rooms, cabins on ships and seats on planes. The next time you try to purchase a concert ticket online, take a good look at how the seating arrangement impacts the price you will pay. The site will even show you a chart of the seating arrangement so you can see what you are paying for and the view you will get for that price. The closer you are to the person performing, the more you pay. The better your view of the person(s) performing, the more you will pay. Other factors that affect the price may be any amenities or privileges associated with the particular seating category. Take for example the SMG–Smoothie King Center event seating chart on the following page. The chart shows the different categories of seats that impact the price one pays for an event.

SMG–Smoothie King Center Event Seating Chart

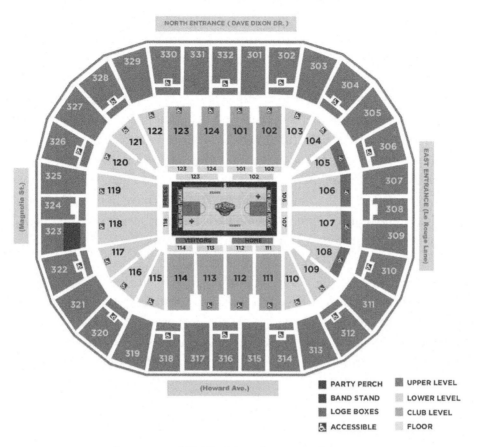

Courtesy of SMG–Smoothie King Center

If you travel on a plane, the person sitting next to you most likely did not pay the same price as you did. In the next hotel where you stay, the person with the same size room as your room will not necessarily pay the same as you paid. What view does that room have? Is it a view of the city? A view of the lake? A view of the beach? A view of the garden? A view of the mountain? What amenities does the room have? All these factors affect how the price is set and how much you will pay. Apply the same concept when setting the price or rent for your apartments and you will increase your rent revenue over time. I have noticed that the average length of time a tenant stays in an apartment is two years to five years maximum. Therefore, the cycle of tenancy is most likely to change within this time. Judging from my experience, the full potential of the rent map can be realized usually within five years. Remember too that once the tenant stays beyond a year, the rent attracts an increase. Rent mapping works only if done properly. As the property manager, you must personally know each apartment type and what is unique to the apartment. I have personally seen increases of 2 to 3 percent added to the rent roll, simply because the buildings were rent-mapped. That increase came from the new rents that were set on turnover apartments.

The rent map on the next page is for properties at Action Drive. It shows how the price is increased every few floors. The price also differs based on the six factors one should consider for rent mapping. The map shows how much monthly potential rent the property will generate according to the rent map. That revenue is matched against the traditional way of setting rent, which is to charge one price regardless of the apartment type or size and of the other factors mentioned above.

Action Drive Rent Map

Floor	Risers	1	2	3	4	5	6	7	8
	View	Lake	Lake	Mountain	Mountain	Mountain	Mountain	Lake	Lake
	Sq. Ft.	700 sq. ft.	875 sq. ft.	975 sq. ft.	800 sq. ft.	800 sq. ft.	1010 sq. ft.	875 sq. ft.	775 sq. ft.
	Type	1 BR	2 BR	3 BR	2 BR	2 BR	3 BR	2 BR	1 BR
PH		3555			3499		3499		3555
15		1265	1449	1699	1409	1409	1799	1449	1334
14		1259	1439	1688	1399	1399	1775	1439	1314
12		1255	1429	1688	1395	1395	1750	1429	1314
11		1249	1419	1677	1395	1390	1725	1419	1294
10		1245	1409	1639	1388	1388	1725	1409	1294
9		1239	1399	1619	1385	1385	1699	1399	1294
8		1235	1388	1619	1375	1375	1675	1399	1274
7		1229	1377	1588	1369	1369	1599	1388	1274
6		1225	1369	1559	1369	1365	1599	1377	1254
5		1219	1369	1539	1359	1365	1575	1377	1254
4		1215	1365	1539	1355	1355	1575	1365	1254
3		1209	1349	1529	1355	1355	1549	1359	1244
2		1199	1349	1529	1349	1349	1549	1359	1244
1		1199	1349	1499	1349	1349	1525	1359	1244
Total		$17,242	$19,459	$22,411	$19,251	$19,248	$23,119	$19,527	$17,886

Rent map rent roll			Traditional rent roll			
Total 1 BR	$35,128		Small 1 BR	14	1200	$16,800
Total 2 BR	$77,485		Large 1 BR	14	1275	$17,850
Total 3 BR	$45,530		Small 2 BR	28	1300	$36,400
Total PH	$14,108		Large 2 BR	28	1350	$37,800
Total rent	$172,251		Small 3 BR	14	1500	$21,000
			Large 3 BR	14	1500	$21,000
			Penthouse (PH)	4	2600	$10,400
			Total rent			$161,250

Difference between rent rolls	$ 11,001
Potential increase (%)	6.82232558

Hope to accomplish within five years based
on apartments that vacate

E. Apartment Repositioning

Apartment repositioning is upgrading by making major renovations inside the apartments to add value to the building and change the perception of how the apartment is viewed by the market. Whether you are upgrading or not upgrading kitchen cabinets and bathrooms, your apartments are still competing with condominiums and with other apartments that are upgrading with hotel or condominium finishes. The type and quality of upgrades will determine the rent you can command and the tenants you will attract. If your company is not upgrading its apartments, it is lagging behind. This repositioning strategy is encouraged by American Terry Moore. "Moore has been an effective apartment broker in San Diego County for more than a generation. He has helped hundreds of investors become millionaires and helped hundreds of millionaires become multimillionaires. His book is *Building Legacy Wealth*. Moore states the following in his article "Repositioning Apartments: A Wealth Building Strategy to Be Proud Of," in part 2 of 4, "Repositioning — Massive Upgrades Grow Equity and Serve Upscale Residents":

Substantial improvements, US$12,000–$20,000 per unit, shift the marketplace's perception of a property. The goal is to upgrade the property and raise rents 20%–30% within two years. New construction can rent for 50%–60% more than a 40 year old product. Repositioning bridges that gap. It is easier, and safer than new construction. And neighbors welcome it, unlike new construction. Good repositioning improves the entire community. Focus on your target resident, not your own taste. Talk with college-educated young adults. How do they perceive the differences between original and new? Estimate the price new residents will pay for each additional improvement.

Source: http://aciapartments.com/2015/05/11/repositioning-apartments-wealth-building-strategy-proud-part-2-4-4/. Reproduced with permission, 2017.

Tenants now want apartments that have a condo-style or hotel finish, and they are willing to pay for the comfort and pride those finishes provide. An upgraded apartment competes better in the market. Apartment owners are upgrading with these types of finishes, and if they are building new apartment buildings, these are the finishes that are expected. Apartment repositioning can include but is not limited to the following areas:

Bathroom

- new bathtub
- new tub surround with accent tiles or an accent wall
- new faucets for the shower and vanity
- shower curtain rod, straight or curved
- new medicine cabinet with double doors
- new vanity and sink set, usually matching the kitchen countertop
- low-energy flush toilets
- new modern energy-efficient light fixtures

- towel bars or rings
- toilet tissue holder
- ceramic floor
- upgraded light fixtures
- upgraded electrical outlet with GFI or USB including Smart Wi-Fi plugs as well as light switches that can synch to electronic devices

Kitchen

- Upgraded cabinets; colour and style depends on the tenant base or type
    - laminate, marble, granite or quartz countertop
    - subway or mosaic glass backsplash tiles
    - double sink with Moen fixtures
    - exhaust hoods usually in the colour of the appliances

- Appliances
    - refrigerator (French doors, side by side or bottom freezer)
    - stove (burners, coil or ceramic or glass top) available in stainless steel, black or white
    - microwave
    - dishwasher

- Doors
    - internal doors that tend to be colonial style with four or six panels, used throughout the apartment on all rooms and closets for balance and uniformity

- Closets
    - multiple shelves for added storage
    - new shelves with closet rod

- Floors
  The increase in bedbug infestation is shifting the trend from carpet to other types of flooring, such as LVT (luxury vinyl tile—looks like ceramic) or LVP (luxury vinyl plank—looks like hardwood). LVP and LVT are durable and waterproof. From an assessment of multiple apartment buildings and companies, I have noted that flooring can be a combination of ceramic, hardwood and LVP/LVT. Some individual apartments may have ceramic tiles at their entrances and in their kitchens. Throughout the other sections of the apartment, other types of flooring are used.

- Baseboards
  MDF (medium-density fiberboard) is primed and ready for painting. Other types are hardwood if you want to stain them and closely match the trim or floor in the apartment. Tall or mid height baseboards are used. Quarter round is also used to cover imperfections in the floor where it meets the baseboard.

- Electrical and lighting
  - o new and upgraded in all rooms
  - o USB plugs, GFIs/GFCIs (ground fault circuit interrupters) usually in kitchens and bath-rooms. Be sure to include Smart Wi-Fi plugs as well as light switches that can synch to electronic devices.
  - o Brush nickel, flush mount, chandeliers, pendant
  - o changing from fuse box to breaker box
  - o square or decorative faceplates

- Paint job
  Usually two colours. The walls have one lighter-shade neutral colour, and the baseboards, doors and trims carry a different colour, which is typically white.

- Some suites may include in-room laundry with washer and dryer combo.
  Unless you have tenants who destroyed the apartment, once these upgrades are completed, the apartments will require minimal repair upon turnover. The most likely repairs you will do in any of these upgraded apartments are painting and cleaning to accommodate the next tenant.

F. Dealing with Excessive Vacant Apartments or Newly Built Apartments

- Pull your market research and assess what apartments similar to those at your properties are renting for.

- According to staging experts, only 10 percent of people can envision themselves living in a new space or place. Before you physically invite prospects to visit and view the new apart-ments, stage each apartment type—a one-bedroom, a two-bedroom and a three-bedroom. Style and arrange furniture and accessories in the apartments as if someone is already living there. The prospects need to have an idea of how to make their personal items fit well in the space. If they are going to rent, your staged apartment will give them an idea of what to buy and how to arrange the furniture in the apartment when they move in. Once the apartments are staged, get professional pictures taken of the staged apartments and use these in your advertising.

- How do you get the word out and reach your target? In addition to your company's mar-keting methods, which may include various Web sites and print, try to maximize how well people are informed about the new apartment building(s).

  1. It doesn't hurt to use other methods such as advertising on the sides of buses in the area, and on the sides of shopping carts in local supermarkets.
  2. Drop flyers off at hair salons and laundry marts if they allow such a thing.

3. Book an area in your local supermarket or local mall and set up a slide show of the property and staged apartments. Make sure you offer incentives for the prospects to visit the property. This is something car dealerships are famous for doing.
4. Drop flyers off at neighbouring apartment buildings. Make sure it is official in that they are delivered to mailboxes.
5. Organizations that assist newcomers or new immigrants to settle

- To prompt your prospects to act, hold open houses, which are the best way to connect with prospects. Open houses should be properly planned and staffed to deal with the invited traffic. This is an event for which you could use other staff within your portfolio to assist. This is another event where you can make it fun and interesting, not just for the prospects showing up but also for your staff. You can have pizza delivered so the team is fed and energized to carry out the task. Open houses should have attractive incentives. If prospects show up and realize the product is not for them, always refer them to one of the other properties in your portfolio or another property owned by your company.

- Teach your staff to upsell the apartments. A prospect may want a one-bedroom; however, by upselling, the staff could persuade the prospect to take a two-bedroom and make the second bedroom the guestroom. One scenario that readily comes to mind involves a prospect who wanted a one-bedroom but rented a three-bedroom instead. A staff member called me one day to excitedly tell me she was able to rent a three-bedroom that the property had been having a hard time renting. I asked what she did, and she replied, "Upsell!" The staff was able to use the three-bedroom to fill an unspoken need. The staff persuaded the couple to use one of the bedrooms as a "man cave." The second bedroom, the staff said, could be a sewing room. And the couple could keep a daybed / sofa bed to use in the second bedroom when they had guests. The couple loved the idea and rented the apartment.

G. Vacating Tenants

Processing notices for vacating tenants is another opportunity to increase the rent or maximize the amount you get on the new rent. If the tenant is moving out just before the next rent increase, make sure the new rent is at or above what the new rent would have been if the tenant had not moved out. Should you drop or reduce the rent below the N1 or notice of lawful rent increase on a vacant apartment, you must wait one full year after the apartment becomes occupied to get any rent increase. Another factor to take into consideration when trying to increase or maximize your rent is the use of your rent map. Your new rent map is based on the six factors previously discussed, as follows:

1. view
2. location
3. accessibility
4. size
5. unique layout
6. upgrades done in the apartment

What if the previous rent had been set using the rent map? Then make sure your rent is at or above your N1. You can also get your staff involved. How much more do they think could be added to the rent? Is it an extra $5, $10, $15 or $20 added to the new rent above the N1 or already-implemented rent map? If you look at the big picture, the impact can be huge. Say you add $5 to each vacating apartment for which you have already implemented the rent map and you have tenants from five apartments moving out from one building. The big picture is $5 \times \$5 = \$25$ combined each month from these apartments. For the year, it would be $\$25 \times 12 = \$300$.

What if the vacating tenant changes his or her mind and wants to stay? If there are no laws requiring you to keep the tenant if he or she has changed his or her mind, let the tenant go. This is another opportunity to get your staff involved before you make your final decision.

- Is the tenant a good tenant, or does he or she cause trouble for other tenants and your staff? Check the tenant file for reports, payment history, cleanliness and condition of the apartment.
- Is the vacating apartment rented?
- Does the apartment have a pending application?
- Is this an apartment that is an ideal candidate according to your rent map to push the rent higher than what you are currently getting?
- What season are you in? Is it a slow season or prime season? This will determine how fast the apartment gets re-rented.
- Do your staff like this tenant and wish to keep him or her?

These are all factors you should consider before you sign to keep or release any tenant who has given notice but wants to stay.

H. Slow Season and Sitting Apartments

If you are in a slow season, a sitting apartment is the last thing you want to have past the move-out date of the last tenant. Ask your staff for feedback when they show the apartment to prospective tenants. There may be times when you may have to rent the apartment without increasing the price. It may make financial sense to reduce the rent in the slow season and set rent high in the busy season when demand is high. You must also have an idea of what the condition of the apartment is like. The staff may relate that the unit is hard to show, meaning there may be a poor housekeeping condition inside the apartment. The vacating tenant could be difficult, not wanting the apartment to be shown unless he or she is home. In any of these cases, always focus the tenant's attention on what is written in the lease/tenancy agreement and the RTA. You can point out that the poor housekeeping condition and/or the fact that the tenant does not want his or her apartment to be shown unless he or she is there is a violation of the lease. Do this by sending such a tenant a tactful but firm letter stating what the issue(s) is/are, as in the sample letters on the next pages.

Review your vacancy report daily with your building managers, superintendents or rental agents, or whoever is on duty. Know which apartments are moving/renting and which ones are sitting

/ not renting. Ask your staff questions and know what attracted tenants to the building and the apartment(s). For apartments that are sitting, find out why the prospects are not taking the apartment. If you have dated apartments, ask probing questions. What in the apartment is preventing prospects from taking the apartment? Is it the floor type or wall colour? Is it the price? Give your staff a floor price and a ceiling price to work with. They can increase the rent by $25 or $50 or reduce it by the same amount. Does the prospect want new cupboards? You may not be able to change the cupboards or cabinets, but you could do a refacing. Find out from the prospects what he or she needs to link or connect him or her to the apartment. Staff should also find out what other apartments the prospect has seen or will be seeing. It is very important to know the competition by conducting market surveys or analysis. When your staff understand what they have and what they are up against, this makes the sales process effortless, and the closing of the sale is converted to an approved application.

If 30 days have passed and the units are still sitting, you may have to reduce the rent by a lot more or offer some form of incentive as stated earlier. Advise your staff to call any tenant they may have on a waiting list. Arrange with your central rental department or marketing department and draft flyers to post in the building, stating the vacancy of a 1 BR, 2 BR or 3 BR for rent. This is where a digital billboard or reader board comes in. Also, if the company has an app where ads can just pop up, advertising what unit types are available for rent. Tenants may know of friends and relatives who want somewhere to live. There could also be families in the building or within the community who want to move out on their own but wish to remain close to or in the same building with loved ones.

Sample Letter about a Hard-to-Show Vacating Apartment

Hi, [tenant name],

We are in receipt of your notice to vacate your apartment [number] on [date]. In accordance with your lease and the RTA, the landlord has the right to show the apartment to potential tenants between the hours of [time] and [time]. Section [number] of the lease also states that the apartment must be clean and in habitable condition. On [date(s)], the staff entered your apartment to view it with prospective tenants. None of the prospects to date have expressed an interest in renting the apartment because of the current condition of the apartment. It was observed that pee pads with animal feces were on the floor throughout the apartment. The apartment also had an offensive odour. The housekeeping standard was below the normally accepted standard and cannot be tolerated.

Please make every effort to clean up your apartment. If we are unable to rent your apartment because of the poor housekeeping condition, note that we will be seeking legal actions for any revenue loss we may incur. To confirm your compliance with this request that you clean the apartment, your apartment will be inspected on [date].

Thank you for your co-operation. We wish you joy and contentment in your new place of residence.

Sincerely,

[Name]
Property Manager

Sample Letter for a Tenant Not Wanting an Apartment Shown Unless He or She Is Present

Hi, [Tenant Name],

We are in receipt of your notice to vacate your apartment [number] on [date]. It has been brought to the attention of this office that you do not wish for our staff to show your apartment to prospective tenants unless you are present. While we respect your desire for privacy, be reminded that your lease, in section [section number], states the landlord has the right to show the apartment to potential tenants between [hours]. Nowhere in the lease does it say the tenant needs to be present. This section of the lease is also in accordance with the Residential Tenancies Act. (*See attached copy of the page of the lease.*)

To alleviate any concerns you may have, we will be providing our staff and all prospects visiting the apartment with disposable booties to wear while they are inside the apartment. Please let us know if we can do anything else to accommodate you as you make this transition.

Understand that if we are unable to rent your apartment because we are unable to show it, we will be seeking legal actions for any revenue loss we may incur.

We thank you for your co-operation and wish you joy and contentment in your new place of residence.

Sincerely,

[Name]
Property Manager

Building Maintenance

When you care about your properties and do upkeep on them, it improves the building's curb appeal and attracts higher-quality tenants. A good maintenance system helps to reduce complaints from tenants and will make your property stand out from the competition. A good maintenance program positions your properties in the market as desirable and helps to create long-term tenants. The best kind of maintenance your properties should practise is preventative maintenance. If you practise preventative maintenance, you tend to have less corrective maintenance to do and will keep your expenses down.

A. Preventative Maintenance

Preventative maintenance is a structured, systemic, consistent routine that preserves the useful life and function of equipment or a building, either wholly or in part. Preventative maintenance is also proactive maintenance. That is to say, things are checked out before something happens to require repair. Preventative maintenance is done by monitoring, cleaning and recording information pertaining to equipment and to the entire building or part of it. Preventative maintenance is vital for the efficient operation and function of equipment and buildings alike. If done consistently, it monitors the normal wear and tear so pertinent repairs can be done to prevent breakdowns, which can be costly and disruptive to the building's operation. Depending on what is involved, preventative maintenance may have to be conducted as follows:

1. Daily
   This may entail a daily building walk-through that includes checking the fire alarm panel box to ensure the system is not in distress.

2. Weekly
   This entails an emergency generator test and inspection of battery-powered lighting, air pressure and the dry sprinkler system.

3. Monthly
   This entails a fire alarm inspection (done by the life safety specialist [LSS]).

4. Quarterly or seasonal

This may entail boilers and chillers as well as other HVAC equipment. These inspections are not normally done by the site staff, they are organized by the HVAC department.

5. Annually

This entails both a Fire and Life Safety inspection and an in-suite inspection.

i. Daily and Weekly Preventative Maintenance

With so many buildings in your portfolio, how can you as the property manager know if your staff are maintaining the buildings as they should? Learning about your buildings by being hands-on is the only way. An excellent property manager must also learn about his or her buildings through the eyes of the staff. This is done by walking through the buildings with the intended purpose of learning from key staff. Arrange in advance to spend half a day with your maintenance staff to conduct preventative maintenance checks with them. This arrangement allows you to conduct the daily and weekly preventative maintenance in one shot. Start the day off with coffee and muffin or whatever your staff want for a quick breakfast. Let your building manager know that the purpose of your time with him or her is to be his or her "apprentice." The staff is the one giving the instructions. Hopefully this will remove any tension or anxiety the person may have about working alongside you for the day.

If the preventative maintenance will be done in a community setting, do only one building. Respect your staff's time. Because you are learning, you will not match the staff's speed and be able to do all the buildings for that day. The last thing you want to do is to tire your staff out and throw them off their schedule for the day. Your time with them will give you a clearer understanding of how the mechanical and life safety equipment is cared for. Wear comfortable clothing and shoes that day because you will be on your feet for the duration. As you walk through the building, note the following:

- Any defective doors and door closures in the hallways. Doors should be latching softly and not slamming when closed.
- Directional signs must be visible in hallways and stairwells.
- Whether or not fire safety signs, such as In Case of Fire and other pertinent signs on the fire cabinets, are in place.
- All exit sign lights must be working and properly installed or intact. The signs should not be hanging or obstructed.
- Whether or not there are mats and boots at tenants' doorways. If so, they should be removed. The hallway should be free from obstruction and combustibles.
- No baby buggies or shopping carts should be in the hallway. These are obstructions.

Also do the following things:

- Run the generator with the staff and check for applicable PPE, such as gloves, earmuffs, ear plugs and face shield. Be sure to note the fuel level and ask about the reordering procedure.

- Go to the boiler room and listen for any noise. Make notes of any satisfactory readings. Look for any kind of leaks.
- Check the sprinkler room and note the satisfactory pressure on any pump.

Know what kind of sprinkler system is in each of your buildings. If you have a dry system, your staff should be draining any water from the valve caused by condensation. This is called routine drum drip draining. This process will continue to be done manually until those valves are digitized and can be drained automatically. Since condensation usually occurs in the fall and winter months, it is essential that this draining be done as often as stated by the LSS during these times. The draining is even more crucial when you are entering a deep-freeze period. Call your staff before the deep freeze and send out a warning, reminder or caution notice about the upcoming deep freeze, asking for their vigilance to conduct drum drip draining. Your staff's failure to do the drum drip draining can result in freezing of trapped condensation, which will trip the system. This very fact is confirmed by the US company Telgian, a worldwide provider of comprehensive fire, security, life safety consulting and engineering/design services. "Removing water from a dry system is an essential part of a good maintenance program. Failure to keep the dry system free of water can result in damage and expensive repairs to both the sprinkler system and building. A program for monitoring the condition of the system and the operation of the auxiliary drains should be instituted."

From personal experience, I can tell you that when this happens, you can expect a domino or accumulated effect. The costs you will face are as follows:

1. Damage to the sprinkler system, which can run into the thousands and become a major capital expense. Since this is considered an emergency, the funds for the repairs most times will get approved. If the funding is approved, you may have to forgo one of your other projects to accommodate this major necessary repair. If the funds are not approved, this will impact your regular budget for repair and maintenance (R&M) because the money will have to come from there. Even though this may be an explainable expense, it says a lot about your staff and their involvement in the care of the building's equipment if they allow the sprinkler system to be damaged. It also speaks to your ability to stay on top of things if you prevent expenses such as this one.

2. When the system is tripped, it activates the fire alarm and monitoring system, which alerts the fire department. You may have to pay the false alarm fee for any fire trucks that show up. Depending on the city where your building is located, the cost per truck can be up to (or sometimes more than) $460. The number of trucks that show up depends on the size of the building or community where the system was tripped. If you have a community of two to four buildings, most definitely more than one truck will show up. I have seen four trucks showing up. Now consider the math: $4 \times \$460 = \$1,840$. Remember this is for the false alarm cost only. You have not yet added the other associated costs.

3. At this point, the fire equipment company must be contacted. You will have their service call fee to pay for the times they show up to repair the equipment. In addition to that service cost, you will have the repair cost for the sprinkler system.

4. If the parts are not readily available or will take a few hours to repair, your fire equipment contractor will ask your staff to conduct a fire watch. For this, the fire monitoring company and the local fire department must be notified. A fire watch requires someone to act as a walking smoke detector and to alert the fire department in the event of a fire. A watch goes in effect when a building's automatic fire alarm system experiences temporary failure. The fire watch requires a person or persons to be appointed to patrol the building once per hour on a 24-hour basis, until the automatic system is restored. That means these people must walk the building from top to bottom, going on each floor, checking every utility room and garbage chute and looking for fire. A log must always be kept of the fire watch activity.

The following are excerpts from the West Allis Fire Department, Wisconsin, USA:

Additional fire watch requirements and documentation

Secondary record-keeping options:
If you choose to generate your own log / record-keeping document the following information must be included:

- The address of the facility
- The person responsible to putting the fire watch in place (Authority Having Jurisdiction {AHJ} or contractor)
- Date and times that the fire watch went into effect and was cancelled
- Name and signature of the person conducting the fire watch
- Dates and times (log in and out times) of each person doing fire watch duty
- The means of communication arranged for the fire watch person to contact the fire department.
- A note field for entry/recording any unusual occurrences or notable items.
- Records of any pertinent information directed to be collected by the person enacting the fire watch condition.

Where a required fire protection system is out of service for more than 10 hours in a 24-hour period, the impairment coordinator shall arrange for one of the following:

a. Evacuation of the building or portion of the building affected by the system out of service.
b. An approved fire watch
c. Establishment of a temporary water supply
d. Establishment and implementation of an approved program to eliminate potential ignition sources and limit the amount of fuel available to the fire.

8) A tag impairment system has been implemented.

Source: Reproduced with the permission of the West Allis Fire Department, Wisconsin, 2017.

Note also that the staff member who does the fire watch cannot perform any other duty at the same time. If that person must attend to other duties, he or she cannot, because the fire watch must be his or her main duty or focus. This shift in focus affects other areas of the building's operation.

Remember—drum drip draining takes only a few minutes and can save you thousands of dollars and many headaches. Do not accept excuses if your staff fail to perform this important maintenance procedure. Do not rely solely on the inspection of the LSS to inform you if your staff are doing the drum drip draining. When you walk through the buildings to conduct your building inspections, look for evidence that the drums have been drained. You will be able to know if drums are being drained if you are trained on what to look for. Evidence of a rust water mark when released should be on the wall closest to the valve or on the ground directly below. Be firm about this necessary preventative maintenance procedure. Share the domino effect of the damages caused by not doing it with all your staff so they will not neglect to carry it out.

At the end of the exercise, commend your staff for their hard work and what you have learned from them. If for any reason you observe any deviation in procedure and/or defect, point this out to the staff in a private setting and highlight the need for further training to make them better at what they do. You can make a note to yourself about this exercise. Sometimes training can also be in the form of teaming up with a more experienced building manager at another location. Before you finalize that arrangement, discuss your action plan with your LSS and get his or her feedback and support. Then the LSS will see that you take this aspect of the job seriously. The learning outcome also reflects well on the life safety specialist. Always follow up with the staff member who received the training and ask how he or she benefitted. Always send any document of training off to human resources for keeping in the employee's file. This is a sign you have done your due diligence on the staff and in the area(s) of concern(s).

ii. Annual In-Suite or Apartment Inspection

One of the purposes of carrying out the annual apartment or in-suite inspection is to comply with the Residential Tenancies Act, regarding the landlord's responsibility to maintain and repair the apartment or suite according to the following section: "A landlord is responsible for providing and maintaining a residential complex, including the rental units in it, in a good state of repair and fit for habitation and for complying with health, safety, housing and maintenance standards" (*Residential Tenancies Act*, 2006, c. 17, s. 20 [1]).

The second purpose for the annual inspection is to assess the physical condition of the company's asset. The in-suite inspection also helps you to understand your tenant base and helps you plan for an effective and efficient operation of the building. The condition of the apartments will also tell you if repairs are being done after tenants submit work orders. This information will come from the tenants you meet during the inspection, who will provide feedback to you.

Before you start the in-suite inspection, have a plan

Decide if you will do half the building in the morning and the other half in the afternoon. Depending on the size of the building, you may have to do the inspection over a two-day period. Whatever you choose, be organized, and be open to and be prepared for anything. Clear your day to accommodate the inspection, and work with your staff as a team. The annual in-suite or apartment inspection is a great team-building opportunity—and the chance for pizza. The inspection should be planned separate from the building's annual Fire and Life Safety testing, the main aim of which is fire safety. This is because the annual in-suite inspection involves much more than fire safety inside the apartment. The results of the inspection should be documented on a special inspection form, either hard copy or electronic. Do not enter a unit and tell the tenant to submit work orders for what you have identified or noted. Also, do not promise tenants anything unless it is an outright safety concern that must be dealt with urgently. The annual in-suite inspection should assess the following:

- safety—smoke detectors, door closure, window restrictors, balcony door and railings
- damages or adjustments to the apartment, suite or unit caused by the tenant, the occupant(s), pets or visitors
- normal wear and tear—any walls, floor, cabinetry, bathroom, lighting, appliances, baseboard radiator covers that are falling apart
- plumbing—leaks, drips, running pipes, taps, faucets and checking for aerators
- good housekeeping—clean and free of odour, with no clutter
- pests—rats, cockroaches, ants and bedbugs
- mould
- illegal or unapproved activities such as a grow operation, daycare or selling chemicals
- other—tree touching balcony

The in-suite inspection should be properly scheduled around building activities. Given the move-out and move-in cycle of the business, the annual inspection is best done in the second week or middle of the month you choose. When planned at this time of the month, the inspection does not interrupt the normally busy month-end activities. The inspection should go smoothly. A general notice should be sent out at least a week ahead of the inspection date, indicating the date of the inspection and what floors will be done during each time slot. This much notice gives tenants the opportunity to clean their apartments or put them in order to accommodate the inspection. In addition to that general notice, individual Notices of Entry should be sent to each apartment.

Make an effort to be present at the building for the inspection and participate. Why? Because the inspection will help you to personally know your building and its layout and to understand the tenants. I had a location that was known for its challenges. It was very difficult to get and keep staff at that location because of the aggressive behaviour of some of the tenants. Through careful selection, I found capable staff who were up for the challenge and placed them at the location. The new staff were given the opportunity to get settled in their roles and were also given the necessary support to function. Once they were settled, the annual in-suite inspection was scheduled. This was my first time conducting the annual in-suite inspection at this location. After completing the in-suite inspection, I had a different outlook on and appreciation for the property. The inspection taught me that the tenants took great pride in and cared for their units. I learned what was unique to each apartment type. The new staff who were added to the location demonstrated that they were very involved in the care and maintenance of the property by promptly completing work orders from tenants when they were submitted. The property had been misunderstood and misrepresented because of a few mischief-makers who were the occupants of some of the tenants. That inspection reshaped my view and vision of the property. The property needed a lot of work, but beyond the work, the property was a goldmine.

At the end of the inspection, I shared my views with the staff and they all agreed. After separating the repairs according to contractors, we came up with and implemented the following action plan:

- Identify the gang members by name, discover where they meet on the property and determine who their parents are.
- Document all activities of tenants, occupants or guests of tenants who cause damages, cause disruption and interfere with the reasonable enjoyment of all. Then issue an N5 where possible.
- Send warning letters to tenants whose teenage children or occupants cause disruptions.
- Refuse to accept verbal complaints from tenants. All complaints should be put in writing. This adds greater weight at the Landlord and Tenant Board (LTB).
- Repair all malfunctioning cameras and DVDs.
- Post 24-Hour Surveillance signs at various locations on the property.
- Rent-map all the buildings in the community in terms of the following:

  1. view
  2. location
  3. accessibility
  4. size
  5. unique layout
  6. upgrades done in the apartment

  The rent map was done with the intent of increasing the rent on vacant apartments and changing the tenant base.

- Get parking lot signs and get the property approved for parking enforcement.

The beauty and the financial potential of the property glowed gradually. The property soared and kept soaring after the plan was implemented and the mischief-makers were evicted. Those who were not evicted were given No Trespass letters to prevent them from accessing other buildings in the community to make further mischief. Since the police were sent copies of the No Trespass letters, those tenants along with their occupants moved from the property. The action plan to improve this community of properties is further discussed in details under the subheading *Legal Administration* in the chapter titled Interdepartmental Relationships.

Safety

Your annual in-suite inspection will show you have done your due diligence. When you check for safety, ensure the following:

- Entry doors should be in sound condition. When the door is closed, you should not be able to see in the hallway or see from the hallway into the apartment. The door should have a working door closure that is in excellent condition.

- The smoke detector should be working, with no evidence of tampering. If the smoke detector is hardwired and is tampered with, it should put the system in distress and show up on the fire panel board and give the exact riser. Today, there are systems that can give the exact location of the defect or distress. The tenant should be billed for all repairs associated with the tampering of the smoke detector, including all service calls associated with the tampering and appropriate legal action(s) taken for impairing and compromising the health and safety of the property, other tenants and themselves. In Ontario, removing the batteries from the smoke detector or tempering with the smoke detector is against the law. What jurisdictions outside of Ontario, Canada has done, specifically New York, USA, is since 2019, to have mandatory hardwired smoke detectors or 10-year non removeable batteries. That is to say, the batteries are built in to the smoke detectors and cannot be removed by the tenant and used for some other purpose in the home or apartment. Ensure all units are in compliance as per your local fire code and any updated code. The audibility or speaker box should not be covered with Styrofoam or show evidence of tampering. In my experience dealing with apartment fires, the fire department always asks and investigates to determine **if a working smoke detector was installed in the apartment.** Therefore, if any of these fire safety devices are damaged, get them repaired with urgency. Tenants should immediately remove any Styrofoam covering the speaker or audibility box. If the tenants are not present at the time of the inspection, your staff should remove anything used to cover the speaker box and then leave a note to the tenant indicating they (staff) removed the Styrofoam and it should not be reinstalled over the speaker box.

- Openable windows should have window restrictors or safety mechanisms installed. The purpose of the restrictors is to limit the opening of the window to prevent children from falling through from height. Window restrictors are required on all openable windows above the ground floor that do not lead to an exterior balcony. Some codes may require window restrictors to be installed on all openable windows, whether they lead to an exterior balcony or not. Each jurisdiction will specify the dimensions of the balcony. Investigate the local building code in your area to ensure you are in compliance.

- Balcony doors should have proper locking devices on the inside. Check the door to ensure the tenant can gain entry from the balcony only if the tenant has temporarily disabled the locking device. If the door is not a sliding door and the door slams while the tenant is on the balcony, the tenant should still be able to get back inside if no one else is home.

- Balcony guardrails should be free from signs of shaking and rot. The railings should not be missing spindles, and if the railing system is made of glass, it should not be sliding out of the frame or have cracked or broken glass. Check the floor slab of the balcony and the ceiling slab of the balcony above for major cracks.

Damages and adjustments to the apartment

Be reminded that the RTA speaks directly to the tenant's responsibility regarding undue damage to the apartment caused by either the tenant or his or her guests or occupants. Section 34 of the RTA states, "The tenant is responsible for the repair of undue damage to the rental unit or residential complex caused by the willful or negligent conduct of the tenant, another occupant of the rental unit or a person permitted in the residential complex by the tenant" (*Residential Tenancies Act*, 2006, c. 17, s. 34).

Some tenants will mistake a rental as their very own personal property. While that can be good if they really care for the apartment, it can also be bad. Tenants will sometimes alter the layout of the apartment to suit their personal needs and preferences. That is why it is important for you to know the layout of each unit type. When you go to inspect the apartments, ensure each apartment is in its original layout. At one building I managed, a tenant felt a wall was needed to separate the living room from the hallway, so he built the wall himself. It was so neatly constructed that it was hard to tell if it was original or if it had been added on. At another location, one tenant converted part of the living room into a bedroom by building two walls and even adding a door. Those tenants were asked to remove the walls and restore the apartments to the original condition. At two other locations, one tenant drilled holes and hung a boxing punching bag from the ceiling. Another tenant jackhammered a concrete wall to allow a steal beam to pass through so he could install a bungee toy for his child. These tenants were sent letters stating that they were in violation of the lease. In addition, the walls that were jackhammered had to be assessed for structural damages. The repairs to both apartments were done through the building repair budget and then charged back to the tenants, who paid the bills.

An apartment can be damaged by aggressive activities such as violence. This type of damage can include punched-in or broken drywall or doors, damaged doorposts or missing door handles. Sometimes you will literally see the fist pattern. These damages will also be consistent with furniture damages in the apartment. If the apartment is not rented as furnished, then there is no need to take the furniture into consideration. If it is legal for you to take pictures and support your claim, go ahead and take pictures of the damages. The tenant should be notified in writing about the damages even if he or she is present at the time of the inspection. In the notification to the tenant, be sure to include a cutoff date for him or her to complete the repair, stating that it should be done with materials similar to what the company uses. If the tenant fails to meet this deadline, your legal administrator should be informed and a N5 done for the cost of the repairs should be served to the tenant. The formal notification sends a message that tenants must conform to the rules of the lease. The letter also provides a paper trail if you get reassigned to other buildings or you leave the company.

Damages can also result from children playing with and damaging a window. Some damages may be caused by children who are mentally challenged. These are very delicate and sensitive cases that should be addressed with your area manager (AM) and legal administrator. There are also some tenants who will allow their pets to destroy carpets, other flooring, screen doors and other areas inside the apartment. These damages should also be brought to the attention of the tenants so they can have an opportunity to make the repairs. If the tenants are not able to address the repairs, the repairs can be completed by one of your external contractors with the building budget and charged back to the respective tenants.

Following are some types of damage caused by lifestyle that may not be obvious:

- walls badly stained by nicotine, the result of smoking inside the apartment
- discolouration to walls in the kitchen caused by oil spatter
- discolouration of walls caused by children drawing on the wall
- discolouration caused by pets rubbing against a wall
- plaster blowout caused by moisture from several plants or from laundry being done inside the apartment (if the apartment does not have an individual in-suite laundry)
- mould caused by excess moisture
- cigarette burn marks in the carpet
- burn marks from pots on laminate countertop, or cracked granite countertop
- unclean carpets and dirty bathroom walls

Normal wear and tear

Signs of wear and tear are indications that a thing is at or near the end of its useful life. Dated items can sometimes be mistaken as wear and tear. Because an item is dated does not mean it is unsafe. However, information regarding wear and tear can help you plan for future upgrades on your capex wish list and for the installation of energy-efficient bulbs and appliances. Some things to look for in terms of wear and tear are as follows:

- signs of threads if the apartment is carpeted
- floor tiles that are lifting, missing, broken or cracked
- plaster blowouts, and paint peeling or flaking because of moisture from a nearby body of water. Depending on the severity of the blowout, the entire wall may have to be drywalled. If an electrical outlet is on the wall that requires the repair, you will need an electrician to replace or readjust the outlet on the new wall.
- windows that will not close properly and allow heat to escape and cold air to enter

- tub surround with bulging or bowing tiles and/or tiles that are missing
- weak and shaking taps
- rotted bathtubs and vanity sinks
- appliances that are missing parts and malfunctioning
- closet doors that can no longer operate on their tracks
- kitchen cabinets falling off the wall. This is not only a matter of wear and tear but also a major safety concern that must be addressed either by reinforcing the existing cabinets or installing new cabinets.

Plumbing

View leaks, drips and running pipes as money going down the drain. If you prolong these repairs, they can lead to greater problems and cost you more. When faucets go bad, a faucet washer may not be all that is required to address the problem. You may have to replace the entire faucet set. That replacement or changing out of the faucet, may require you to break open walls. Once the replacement is completed, cosmetic repairs will have to be done to the walls. Leaking taps, faucets or pipes can also cause countertops to swell and rot, thus requiring replacement. If you come across any leaks or drips ensure they get addressed. You should also remind the tenant of such apartment if they are present at the time of the inspection, that once the leak has been fixed, if the problem reoccurs in the future they must report leaks by submitting a work order. Check to confirm that faucets have aerators. Aerators conserve water by helping to slow down the flow of water through the faucet. The reduced water flow, results in less water usage which in turn reduces water cost.

Good housekeeping and cleanliness

Under the RTA, the tenant has a responsibility to keep the rental unit clean.

"The tenant is responsible for ordinary cleanliness of the rental unit, except to the extent that the tenancy agreement requires the landlord to clean it" (*Residential Tenancies Act*, 2006, c. 17, s. 33).

In my experience, cleanliness is also an indication that the apartment is cared for. Cleanliness results in low maintenance costs while the tenant occupies the apartment. Good housekeeping also means low turnover costs when tenants move out, because the flooring, walls, cabinetry and bathroom are in excellent condition. A clean apartment means that vacating apartments can rent faster and for more money. *Clean and well-kept apartments show well to prospective tenants.* Clean apartments sometimes spell fewer pests or a better ability to control them.

As you check for cleanliness, note if you see a clear path to get from one room to the other. If there are no paths, and if the apartment is cluttered or classified as hoarding, you must be vigilant and persistent with the tenant to get the apartment to an acceptable level. Hoarding is classified as a mental disability. Therefore, be prepared to refer the tenant to agencies and organizations that can offer assistance to help clean up the apartment. If there are no agencies or organizations to offer such assistance, under the Human Rights code, you as the landlord have a duty to accommodate up to undue hardship by providing help to the tenant. Cluttered or hoarding apartments make treating and controlling pests such as bedbugs difficult, frustrating and almost impossible.

If there were an emergency, would your staff or contractor work or refuse to work in the cluttered apartment? At one location, there was a bad leak in a bathroom and the plumbers had to be called to address the leak. When the plumbers arrived, they refused to work inside one of the apartments because the bathroom was so dirty that it was not even safe to enter. The plumbers quickly turned the shut-off valve to prevent further flooding below and then walked away from the job. No work could be completed until that apartment was cleaned. The tricky thing about this case was that the tenants were out of town and I had no idea when they would return. In any event, I could not leave the repairs hanging until they returned. Hence, I authorized that contract cleaners be brought in to clean only the bathroom of that apartment. Of course, pictures were taken before and after. This was to prepare for any legal action the tenants may have decided to take as a result of my approach. The cost was charged back to the tenants, including the service call for the plumbers to return. In the same letter, the tenants were reminded of their responsibility to maintain the apartment, which they had failed to do. The bill was paid in full when the tenants returned.

Pests: rats, roaches, ants, bedbugs, etc.

It is great to have a pest-free building. However, some apartments you enter will show obvious signs that the tenants have a form of pest. Other apartments you enter may not show such obvious signs. The best way to get information about the presence of any pests is to ask the tenants. Some tenants will tell you if they have any pests and what kind of pests they have, as well as what treatments were, or are being, administered. You should also look for evidence of self-treating. If there is a language barrier, look around for anything crawling, anything dead or any traps. Any of these will tell you what kind of pests, if any, are in the apartment. Other tenants may not be aware that they have pests and do not know what to look for. As you go from unit to unit, check the hallway if you see any pest activity. If any pests are reported, remember to act swiftly and aggressively to treat them, and also do any necessary follow-up.

Illegal or unapproved activities such as grow operation, daycare, selling chemicals

Tenants who engage in activities that violate the lease/tenancy agreement may not be welcoming or accepting of any form of in-suite inspection. These tenants will sometimes call you before the inspection and resort to rudeness, violence, threats and intimidation in hopes of averting the inspection. If a tenant like this, or someone authorized by the tenant, is not going to be at home at the time of the inspection, the tenant will not want you there. This does not mean every tenant who refuses entry is engaged in some kind of illegal activity inside the apartment. Even if tenants' behaviour raises a red flag for you, do not tell the tenants that you feel they are engaged in illegal activity. Remind these tenants that the RTA makes it very clear that a valid Notice of Entry is required for the landlord to gain entry. *The Act does not say the tenant or anyone approved by the tenant needs to be present at the time of entry.* Also, the very purpose of your inspection is to comply with the RTA's provisions for maintenance and safety. If the tenant still refuses the inspection and changes the lock, obviously without your consent, address this tenant separately; otherwise, this person will consume your time. Do not let up about the inspection. At a later date, do whatever is legally necessary to gain entry to the apartment. You can serve the tenant with an N5 because he or she is preventing you from carrying out a necessary inspection or doing necessary work in the apartment. Regarding the lock change, you can change the lock and have the tenant pick up the new key(s) at the rental office if you had mentioned the lock change in the notice. In the general notice you send out to the tenants, you may include information about lock change similar to the following: "Any tenant who changes the lock without written consent from the property manager and without giving a copy of their new key to the landlord is hereby informed that the landlord will change the lock at the time of the inspection. *The new key can be collected by the leaseholder with valid ID* at the rental office between the hours of [times]."

If you have changed the lock, *you must* provide the tenant with a copy of the new key(s). This is in accordance with the RTA, which states, "A landlord shall not alter the locking system on a door giving entry to a rental unit or residential complex or cause the locking system to be altered during the tenant's occupancy of the rental unit without giving the tenant replacement keys" (*Residential Tenancies Act*, 2006, c. 17, s. 24).

If you fail to provide keys, you are in violation of the RTA and the tenant can file a T2 application for tenants' rights. Bear in mind that you not being able to enter an apartment might sometimes inadvertently be for your and your staff's own safety. You do not know what is behind the door. Tenants who are engaged in criminal activities will sometimes set booby traps for "trespassers." Hence, serving a tenant an L8 for having changed the lock without your permission may be your best and safest way to proceed.

If the tenant calms down and allows you to enter the apartment, be mindful of any air freshener or incense used to mask the presence of foul odour. If you have strong suspicions about the apartment based on information you get from your staff, send the tenant a letter about any strong offensive odour masked with air freshener observed in the apartment at the time of the inspection. State a re-inspection date of at least one week in the future. If you discover a grow operation or another form of drugs, contact your area manager (AM) when you have a chance, and then follow his or her directions, including contacting the relevant authorities. If you observe any business such as daycare or chemical sales, follow what your company policy and what the lease/tenancy agreement state about these kinds of activities. *Marijuana/Cannabis Grow Operation* will be discussed in details under the chapter titled Emergencies.

Other: tree touching balcony or overgrown balcony vegetable garden

Any tree touching or resting on the building, including windows or balconies, should be trimmed by your landscaping contractor to prevent insects and rodents from coming onto the building. Trees can also come from balcony gardens of neighbouring tenants. If balcony gardening is allowed, the tenants who engage in this activity should not interfere with the reasonable enjoyment of the other tenants.

What happens after the in-suite inspection?

So, now that you have completed the annual inspection, what is the next step?

1. If you are doing a full-day inspection at the property, sit over lunch with your team and separate the inspection forms for the units you completed during the first part of the day. Inspection forms for apartments that have no concerns should be dated, signed and filed away as per your company policy.

2. Inspection forms for apartments that have concerns should be grouped or separated according to how the repairs will be done. The grouping and the separation should also be based on actions required by the property manager and, if possible, the legal department. Repairs should be grouped according to the following:

   • electrical and/or fire repairs—hard-wired smoke detectors
   • plumbing—all pipes, including taps, aerators
   • bathroom—tub surround, bathtubs, vanities, sinks
   • flooring—carpet, ceramic tiles, LVP, LVT
   • painting—walls, ceilings, plaster repairs and drywalling
   • carpentry—cabinets, countertops, doors, doorframes, door closures, baseboards, shelves and closets
   • HVAC—baseboard radiator covers that are falling apart
   • appliances—refrigerators, stoves, and other appliances that may be applicable to the building, such as microwaves, dishwashers, washers and dryers
   • pest control—rats, roaches, bedbugs, ants or other insects
   • landscaping—tree trimming and/or overgrown balcony garden
   • letters from the property manager—to address housekeeping and damages with quotes and/or invoices
   • legal action—N5, L8 or any applicable legal action
     While separating the forms, simply and briefly review the repair and maintenance (R&M) building budget with your staff. Do the following and round off the numbers to the nearest hundred. The exercise is to give your staff an idea of what you have to work with monetarily to complete the repairs.
   • State what must be paid every month for fixed expenses. These expenses most likely include elevator maintenance, fire monitoring, landscaping including snow removal and any other items applicable to your building
   • Variables will include the following:

     o Any scheduled common area plumbing repairs, perhaps to repair a section of pipe, or any other minor emergency repair being done. Regardless of the repairs being done, you should have an idea of how much they will cost.

  o Units turning over for the month. You should have an idea of how much it costs on average to do minor repairs on a unit at the end of a tenancy. You should also be aware of the slow months when you have less move-outs.

  Add your fixed cost and your variable cost. Subtract that amount from the budget for the month. The remaining difference will be the funds you will have to work with to carry out the repairs for the month you are reviewing.

  Explain to your staff that all work will not be done at the same time. Spread the work across each month. Emphasis should be given to safety, plumbing and pest-related issues. Never gamble with safety. Repair first and battle legally with the tenant afterward if the tenant has damaged the fire equipment in his or her apartment. It makes no sense to compromise the safety of the other tenants in the building. This will be an explainable expense on the budget.

After some time, you will have an idea of how much it costs to do each repair in the apartment. Based on that knowledge of pricing, determine how many and what kinds of repairs you can do. You might be able to push through three or four apartments per month tagged by the inspection for repairs. Focus first on the repairs that have an element of safety; the others can be completed after these. One other factor to consider is if the building has an AGI in progress. Make sure each of these units have no maintenance issues to address. If tenants from those apartments raise an issue, resolve those issues with urgency.

Annual in-suite or apartment inspections should not be taken lightly. They should be consistent. If done during a particular month each year, tenants have time to plan around the inspection. Make sure you have enough staff to assist in the process when you decide to have the inspection. Your inspection will reveal a lot of things that you might even use to make a capex wish list and that might be the perfect AGI candidate.

Decide ahead of time what units you must see. These units can include the following:

- hoarding or cluttered units
- units suffering major damages caused by the tenants
- units requiring major repairs due to plaster blowouts, leaks that were not reported, etc.
- units with poor housekeeping
- units with an excess number of animals or pets that exceeds the bylaw
- units with a grow operation or illegal drugs

B. Corrective Maintenance

Corrective maintenance is performed when some aspect of equipment or the building has a defect and requires fixing either immediately or at some other time. Some examples of corrective maintenance are the following:

- work orders submitted by tenants
- repairs ordered by health and safety inspections
- emergency repairs
- building inspections by you the property manager and or other individuals authorized to conduct them

Corrective maintenance can happen in any area of the building, such as common areas or utility rooms. Corrective maintenance may be performed inside apartments to prepare the apartment for the next tenant to move in. If you have a good preventative maintenance program, most of your corrective maintenance should originate with tenants submitting work orders to do repair or to correct defects inside their apartments. Make sure you follow up with your staff on work orders that are submitted by tenants. Submitted work orders that are completed make for happy and satisfied tenants. Your annual in-suite will tell you if your staff are following through with submitted work request/orders. Repairs inside tenants' apartments could be due to the following:

- leaking toilet or tap(s)
- falling tub-surround tiles
- closet door falling off its tracks
- broken cabinet doors
- broken door handles
- appliances that are not working or missing parts
- electrical or breaker problem
- leak in the wall
- lifting floor or damaged carpet
- having no heat or A/C
- missing radiator covers or A/C sleeve
- fire- or flood-related damage
- request for pest treatment

i. Work Orders from Tenants

Most apartment leases or tenancy agreements encourage tenants to inform the landlord of any defect inside the apartment. Hence, when your tenants submit a work order or service request, they are fulfilling their obligations under that section of their lease. Regardless of the method your company uses for tenants to submit work orders, whether it is letter, memo, text message, telephone call or e-mail, your staff must ensure that submitted work orders get addressed in a timely manner. Their failure to do so could result in the company being fined for breaching the RTA. Remember -- under the RTA, the landlord is obligated to keep the unit in a good state of repair. Establish ahead of time with your staff what kinds or categories of work orders require your inspection and or approval before the repair can be done. Some requests are for the following:

- new cupboards
- new tub surround

- full apartment painting due to plaster blowouts or major cracks
- new floor installation: carpet, tile, plank
- repair of major leaks (obviously the staff or plumber would have stopped the leak and call you to discuss pricing and options)

Once any of these requests are brought to your attention, call the tenant and make an appointment to see the tenant and inspect the apartment. Make sure to honour those appointment dates with proper Notices of Entries. After you inspect the apartment for requested repair(s), determine the following:

1. The urgency of the repair
   a. Is it health and safety related?
   b. Will it cause further damage if not done right away?
   c. Will a temporary fix work until a permanent fix can be done?

2. Skill set needed to address the repair
   a. Does this require staff at the current location or from another location? Are those staff available?
   b. Does the repair need a special contractor? If so, how will the work affect the tenant and neighbouring tenants? (I remember a few cases where the tenant complained of a leak every time it rained. I inspected the area within twenty-four hours of the leak being reported and contacted the property standards department. After a thorough investigation, it was determined that some bricks needed replacement. For that work to take place, it required swing-stage setup. Vehicles parked below the work area had to be relocated. In addition, notice had to be posted to tenants along the affected riser advising them to close blinds and curtains for privacy during the repair.)

3. Funds needed to address the repair
   Should this be done with regular funds, or should this be done with capital expenditure funds? If you must use regular funds, what other work will you have to put on hold to accommodate this repair?

4. Availability of materials
   Does the property have the material(s) to do the repair? Do the materials have to be ordered? How long will it take for delivery?

5. The length of time the area needing repair has been in that condition
   Is it neglect on the tenant's part or your staff's part?

6. Who should pay for the repair, either the building or the tenant
   If the tenant damaged the apartment, the cost to address that damage should be paid by the tenant. While you are doing the repair, talk to the legal administrative department about filing against the tenant at the tenant court for damaging the apartment.

7. Whether or not you are receiving complaints from other tenants asking for that same type of repair

   If so, can the repair be submitted as a capital expenditure item? Or is this a case of faulty workmanship from a previous contractor or faulty material?

8. Whether or not the building is up for an AGI

   If so, fix the problem. The last thing you want is a set of angry tenants showing up to an AGI hearing to slam your application because you failed to maintain their apartments after they submitted work orders. Bear in mind that if there is an AGI hearing, your tenants are going to raise the issue whether you address or ignore maintenance requests in an apartment. If your maintenance program is consistent and efficient, these tenants will have less ammunition against you.

9. Who is making the request

   Is it the leaseholder or an occupant? What does the lease or tenancy agreement say about leaseholders making a work order request? Is the request valid, or is the tenant just being difficult?

These are factors that must be considered when a work order requires that you inspect the unit before providing approval. Always enter on a Notice of Entry. If the tenant says you cannot enter unless he or she is present, explain to the tenant what the Act says about right of entry; quote the Residential Tenancies Act, 2006, c. 17, s. 27 (1). The Act does not say the tenant needs to be home.

Regardless of the reason for your entry into any apartment, always check the following:

- Is the door-closing mechanism working the way it should?
- Is the entrance door slamming? (Windows or balcony doors that are open will cause the entrance door to slam due to air suction. If they are closed the entrance door should not be slamming. If the door slams check out the door closure)
- Is the door closure damaged?
- Do you see anything that is in violation of the lease or tenancy agreement?
- Has the tenant removed the smoke detector?
- Is the audibility box covered?
- What is the housekeeping condition of the apartment?
- Is there any other obvious repair the tenant did not inform the staff about? (This may be due to a language barrier.)
- Do you see any sign of pests?
- Is there any sign of illegal activity?
- Is there anything else that concerns you as the property manager?

These are all things you can check for at a glance. As you grow in the role of a property manager, noticing these things will become automatic to you.

Circumstances requiring leniency

When to extend and not to extend leniency is at the discretion of you the property manager. If you are going to conduct an inspection, *sometimes* the name of the tenant will indicate the presumed nationality and language spoken by the tenant. If you have a team member at the property who speaks the presumed language of the tenant, take that staff member along with you on the inspection, to assist with translation where necessary. This shows you are interested in the concerns the tenant has raised or the repair he or she has requested. It is recommended that you never go on an inspection alone. Regardless of the language the tenant speaks, always take someone with you.

If you enter an apartment to conduct an inspection and the tenant does not speak English, what do you do? This can be tricky and may require good judgement. If the leaseholder doesn't speak English and has a child living there who speaks English, you may have to communicate to the tenant through the child. For things that are of a more serious nature, let the child know that an adult who speaks English is needed and that this person, once found, should contact you immediately. Leave your business card with your contact information for the adult to contact you. In some of these cases, these tenants may have caseworkers who have access to resources for obtaining a translator. When appropriate, always try to go that route first. If the tenant has no one present to translate for him or her, the tenant can still point out what is wrong in the apartment. I remember going to an apartment to do an inspection only to find out the tenants spoke a foreign language. They were new tenants and the staff did not remember to tell me of the language barrier until I was inside the apartment. The tenant took his cellphone out and pointed at it, indicating that I should speak into the phone. I did as requested by the tenant, and the phone app translated what I'd said into the tenant's language. We all laughed at the clever use of technology.

When the occupant resides as the tenant

Sometimes children will rent the apartment for their aged parent(s) to live in. You should advise your staff or the rental consultant that relatives who wish to rent such an apartment should consider a joint tenancy. Why is this? While it is a loving gesture on the part of the children renting the apartment, the parents who will be living in the apartment have no right to the apartment. They are only occupants. The agreement is with the children signing the lease or tenancy agreement and the property management company, not the parents. The parents won't be able to collect any new keys simply because they are not the leaseholders. So, how do you extend leniency in this situation? Your site staff tend to know a lot more about what is happening with the tenants than you do. Ask your staff. You may have to accommodate the arrangement with the parents living in the apartment as the tenants. Use good judgement.

Another scenario is when the parents are the tenants but are no longer able to make decisions on their own and their children must make the decisions. If the adult children are not the next of kin on file, in this case you could request a copy of the power of attorney (POA). This is a grey area, but personally I think you should request it early, because if the parents die and these children do not

Emergencies

Emergencies are inevitable. They are not planned. They happen most times without warning. At some point, as a property manager, you will have to deal with various types of emergencies. When emergencies happen, they require immediate attention to prevent loss of life and prevent or minimize damages. The Canada Mortgage and Housing Corporation (CMHC) defines *emergency repair* as "when something in the rental unit has broken and the health or safety of the tenant is in danger or the building or property is at risk until repairs can be made." The Residential Tenancies Act, section 26 (1) (a), allows entry without notice during emergencies. Some emergencies can be seasonal, such as central air breaking down in the middle of summer or a sprinkler valve tripping because of the freezing of trapped condensation during the cold weather. Emergencies can be dependent on your tenant type or tenant base (caused by tenants), the age of the building or the location of the building. The most common types of emergencies you will face as a property manager are as follows:

- leaks and flooding
- fire
- death of tenant on property
- marijuana/cannabis grow operation
- power outage
- catastrophic events or activities such as explosions, bomb threats or terrorism

Even though you hate emergencies, your hatred will not prevent them from happening. The best way to deal with emergencies is to always prepare for them. The preparation manifests itself in the way you go about doing your job as an excellent property manager. Every inspection you do on your own, with your staff, or with the various departments, such as HVAC and Fire and Life Safety, that visit your buildings helps you to prepare for an emergency. How so?

- Conducting inspections with these departments or shadowing their representatives as they visit your buildings gives you a better understanding of your responsibilities as a property manager.
- You come to understand your buildings and how the mechanical systems function.

- When an emergency happens, you are aware of the ripple or domino effect the particular emergency will cause. Hence you know which contractors to call. When you turn to any of these internal departments for help, you already know and understand their language or jargons.
- You are in a better position to guide and support your staff when they need you the most.

Your staff should also be prepared to handle emergencies. Ensure your staff have the proper training and that they are utilizing the training to the point where it becomes second nature to them. For the monthly fire inspection and equipment testing, mandate that a staff member accompany the life safety specialist (LSS). If you have new staff, they should accompany the LSS for up to three months, and rotate every other month if your staffing number allows for it. In addition to training, your staff must have the proper tools and equipment to aid them in their response to emergencies. Do they have a Shop -Vac for minor flooding? Do they have a pump if the Shop-Vac is inadequate for the flood? Do they have a working camera with battery and SD card? Can they write a proper report about the emergency? The insurance company will want details of what happened. Are your staff empowered to call contractors for certain levels of emergencies without contacting you? If the emergency is something your staff cannot handle, are they comfortable and confident enough to call the relevant contractors? When your staff are prepared and empowered, it helps in their confidence. It also helps to reduce damages and eliminate associated costs. It makes you look great and takes a tremendous amount of stress off you.

Always inform your area manager (AM) or branch manager about any emergency as soon as you become aware of it. This is to make him or her aware of the problem and to provide needed support to you and your team. Get as many details as you can about the type of emergency and its exact location. Let your AM know what you are currently doing to address the situation, including whether or not you are going on-site. If your AM has any suggestions to help in the process, he or she will most likely work with you or want to be updated as the time ticks away. Your AM should never have to turn the radio or television on to learn about any emergency that occurred at a building within your portfolio. Firmly insist that you be notified immediately of any major emergency that happened or is happening at the building(s) or anywhere on the property. Your staff should be trained to inform your superior if they are unable to contact you, their property manager. This must be done not hours or days after the emergency, *but immediately,* either while it's happening or immediately after it has happened. Strongly advise your staff not to speak to the media unless an authorized person in the company has given them the go-ahead to do so. The reason for this caution is to gauge the information that goes out about the emergency. It protects the image of the company and also protects the company from any future liabilities related to the emergency. Your staff should not mention anything about the emergency on any form of social media. Until the investigation is completed, the situation is deemed to be fluid, constantly changing.

Remember you will need details about the emergency to submit a report to your AM. Support the details in that report with any necessary pictures. Know ahead of time the recommended procedures you must follow. Start a file on each emergency. In that file keep the following things:

- all quotes
- receipts
- reports from staff, eyewitnesses or any outside agency or government body
- pictures

Make sure you have contact information stored in your phone for the relevant contractors, including restoration contractors, already approved by your company. Since emergencies can happen anytime at various locations, ensure the gas tank of your personal vehicle is never below half full. If you live quite a distance away from your furthest building, this will ensure you always have enough gas in your vehicle to take you to your farthest building and get you back home. Depending on the type and degree of emergency, you may have to physically go to the property and assess the damages or just give support either to your staff and/or the first responders. You must always be prepared, even if it's in the middle of the night or the wee hours of the morning. When you get that call, it is time to go directly to the location, not to pump gas. Let us now take a closer look at the typical emergencies you are most likely to encounter as a property manager:

A. Leaks and Floods

A leak, even though not a gushing flood, should never be underestimated. It may be gentle, but it could also be a giant in another sense. It could be a slow leak that no one was aware of until it reached its breaking point. At that point, your staff may call to inform you that the entire bathroom ceiling in one of the apartments has just fallen. Unable to find the leak, your staff member calls the plumber to locate the leak and repair the damaged pipe. The plumbers locate the leak, but for them to complete the repair, they recommend a total emergency shutdown of the building's water supply. If this is during working hours, you may have to post a notice to the tenants regarding an emergency water shut-off. If this happens in the middle of the night, then notice is not necessary, as most tenants are asleep and would not be adversely affected.

Say the plumbers have located the leak and recommend an immediate replacement of a reasonable section of the pipe extending past two apartments above the one in which the leak was found. Hence under the definition of emergency, they will require immediate access. This simple leak has resulted in major pipe replacement. The plumbers will need access to those two apartments to carry out the repair on the pipe.

Once the plumbers complete this aspect of the job, arrangements must now be made to address all the cosmetic repairs associated with the leak at a later date. Hence walls must be closed with drywall or plaster/mud and then painted. Since this was a slow leak, mould may be present inside the cavity or sections of the ceiling that caved in. The plumbers, your staff or the tenant may inform you that it looks like mould is present in the area. In that case, the ceiling must remain opened until the area can be tested for mould and treated if any is present. Contact your general contractor or one of your approved contractors who is experienced and certified to remove mould. In addition to the mould, the general contractor will take care of the installation of the new ceiling, the necessary plastering and painting, and any electrical work if necessary. Have the contractor assess the area and treat it immediately. If the tenant is not aware of the presumed presence of mould, you must disclose that to the tenant and let him or her know you are aggressively dealing with the problem.

The Residential Tenancies Act does not speak directly about mould; however, you are required under the RTA, section 20 (1), to keep the apartment in a reasonable state of repair. Bear in mind that the tenant can report a mould problem to the city, who will send a bylaw officer/inspector. If the officer shows up, you may be issued an order to address the problem if you are not doing anything about it. Be prepared to answer questions from the city's health department or bylaw officer. If the city shows up, be honest and open with them. Let them know you are dealing with the problem and give a tentative date of completion, or let them know how soon you can give them an update on the progress. The tenant may insist you put him or her up at a hotel until his or her apartment is free of mould. Remember this was caused by a leak. If the lease or tenancy agreement clearly states that the tenant must have and keep in effect apartment contents / tenant's / renter's insurance, then accommodation at a hotel should be covered under that insurance, at the tenant's expense, not the company's. Your responsibility is to repair the structural damage caused by the leak. If the tenant is elderly and has no next of kin, you can use compassion and provide accommodation. However, that is up to you, your AM and your legal administrator. If the tenant decides to withhold rent or deduct the accommodation cost from the rent, speak to your legal department about the options you have regarding the tenant's non-payment of rent. This is not cruel. The tenant may have breached the lease/tenancy agreement by not having contents insurance. In any event, it is very important that you address the repair and the presumed presence of mould immediately. Your due diligence will show you completed the repair in a timely manner. If you feel that this may become a bigger issue than you wish to deal with, you may want to relocate the tenant to another apartment or allow him or her to utilize a clean but vacant apartment in the same building until the repair gets addressed. Your other option may be to compensate the tenant in rent for only the days his or her apartment was not usable. Before you make an offer, speak with your area or branch manager and your legal administrator to see what your best legal options are.

A major flood

Unlike a slow leak, a gushing flood will let you know immediately that you have a problem. Once a flood has been reported to you, always ask the following questions:

1. What is the water source? Is it clean water from the domestic water system, sewer water, overflow toilet, laundry water or bathtub overflow, or is it from the rain?
2. What is the volume, force or intensity of the water? Is it dripping, pouring, gushing or falling? How long would it take to fill a five-gallon keg/bucket?
3. What is the most likely item to get damaged by the water? Does the water pose additional danger?
4. Who or what is responsible for the flood? Is it a frozen pipe? A child's toy stuck in the toilet? An unauthorized appliance inside a tenant's apartment?

The answers to these questions will determine if your staff can handle the job or someone with more expertise must be called in. Depending on the location and the type or category of flood water, the damages caused by the water can be significant in terms of cost and adversely disrupt the lives of tenants and the operation of the building. If you know the physical layout and setup of your buildings, you will have an idea of the impact the water will have on the immediate and extended surroundings of the flood path or area. This information will allow you to track the path of the water and to determine any potential damages that can result along that path. Will the water be in contact with special equipment or an electrical system? You must think about wood in the form of doors and flooring that may swell once it comes in contact with flood water. Having this basic information will serve you well if you must call a restoration contractor. Your conversation with the restoration contractor will dictate the equipment he or she brings on-site for the cleanup. Once the restoration contractor gets to the location of the flood, he or she will conduct a thorough assessment. Follow up with the restoration contractor until the job is completed. Flooding can result from any of the following:

- *Sewage backup*
  This can happen anywhere you have a sewer pipe. The most common places observed are hallway ceilings, basement levels and inside apartments. So where will the water go? If it is in the hallway, it can make its way under any door, enter tenants' apartments, run into utility rooms, go down stairwells or pour into elevator shafts. Is your staff trained to handle this kind of flooding with proper personal protective equipment (PPE)? If not, it is best to call in your restoration company. They will have the proper equipment and chemicals to clean up the flood water and will be able to assess damage to the drywall, doors and flooring. Carpets will have to be removed, including underpadding and probably baseboards. Your restoration contractor may have specific steps regulated by law for what should be done.

- *Failed sump pump*
  This will most definitely affect the basement level. Rooms on the basement level tend to be utility rooms such as generator room, electrical room, sprinkler room, maintenance and storage room for building materials and supplies, and tenants' storage locker rooms. A word of caution is that if you have tenant locker rooms, it is important to have a log indicating who owns which locker. Having this information allows staff to contact tenants if there is an emergency. If you have inherited a new building with locker rooms for which there are no logs indicating which tenants the lockers belong to, try to establish a log and get keys to those lockers as soon as possible. Treat this with urgency. The tenants may have their own keys without you having a copy. It is important that you have a copy of the keys for the simple reason of gaining entry if there is an emergency. These factors drastically affect the cleanup process and the speed at which it is done. To prevent a repeat, find out from your plumber if the pump can be repaired or if it should be replaced.

- *Tap left on by tenant inside his or her apartment after building water shutdown*
  This can happen if there is a building water shutdown to conduct plumbing repairs. Tenants or their occupant(s) will sometimes go to turn on the tap, realize there is no water and

forget to turn the tap off. Another scenario is that sometimes tenants become preoccupied with other things and forget they were catching water to take a bath or do the dishes. Whatever the proven cause of the flood, these tenants should be held accountable and have all charges billed to them. The water will affect their apartment and possibly the hallway or apartments below. Hence, you should instruct your staff to check all the apartments below the flooded apartment until they get to the basement. Sometimes water has a weird way of skipping a floor or two. Your staff may check the floor below, see that everything is dry and end the inspection or investigation at that apartment. However, in my experience, tenants whose apartments were believed to be safe called later to say they had water inside their apartments running down the walls or somewhere else in the apartment. It is also recommended that your staff check those apartments again within a few hours or a day afterward to ensure there is no water penetration. To reduce the risk of tenants leaving their taps on, include in your notice to the tenants for water shutdown "Please remember to turn all taps off during the repair."

- *Contractor failed to turn the shut-off valve inside apartment before turning on the main water supply to the building*
  Whether the apartment is vacant or occupied, the contractor should be held responsible for all damages inside the apartment and outside the apartment related to the flood if he or she failed to turn the shut-off valve. This is negligence on the contractor's part. In such a case, your staff will have to check all apartments for damage, as indicated above. Each hallway should be checked for damages and should be restored to preflood condition. Any damages to occupied units should be discussed with your AM and the legal administrator. Sadly, I had a similar case at one of the buildings I managed.

- *Frozen burst pipes*
  The good thing about this type of flooding is that it is seasonal. However, it can be very costly if it happens and can cause major disruption. When water freezes, it expands. Sometimes the bursting of a pipe may not take place at the point of freezing. This expansion causes cracks to develop in the pipes. A frozen pipe can cause a cascading waterfall; you will wonder if the Niagara Falls was diverted to your building. In addition to the massive cleanup, you must replace any damaged building materials. A flood of this volume will need the services of your plumber. In addition, the water will find its way to the lowest point of the building, which tends to be the elevator pit. Water inside the pit of the elevator can cause system failure. Therefore, it is very important to have your elevator company or consultant assess the pit for any damages to equipment or any of the elevator cables. Work with your staff by giving them the support to restore the building to preflood condition.

- *Aged or deteriorating pipes*
  Sometimes pinholes may develop in older pipes, which can be the culprit of slow leaks, which we mentioned earlier. When these pipes wear on the inside and reach their breaking point, they will command your attention. You may get the call from your staff or from a screaming tenant. Once you have a pinhole leak, it is a sign of more pinholes to come—and you may have

a greater plumbing problem than you believe. Your leak may be a steady flow or a spray like a shower, not necessarily gushing. Sometimes these leaks can be behind walls, ceiling beds and flooring. Wherever they are, these leaks can be annoying. Some buildings that are famous for pinhole leaks may try to eliminate the leaks and the nuisance by resorting to water softener equipment. Usually when this happens, the pipes are already clogged. Other properties may try to enhance the plumbing system with the use of an epoxy coating on the interior of the pipes. Until that happens you must deal with the headaches these pinholes cause. If these pinhole leaks are becoming frequent and you cannot keep up with them, it may be time to consider rejuvenating your pipes with the epoxy coating. Based on quotes that I obtained for buildings I was considering, this procedure can be quite pricy and should be submitted as a capital expenditure project. The advantage to this process is that it eliminates the breaking of walls and pipe replacement, thus reducing the disruption to tenants.

- *Unauthorized washing appliances (machines, dryers and dishwashers) inside individual tenants' apartments*
  If the plumbing for the building system was not designed to accommodate washing machines inside individual apartments, any washing machines inside tenants' apartment may cause major stress on the drainage system and result in flooding. If these appliances are clearly stated in the lease/tenancy agreement as unauthorized, be firm about compliance. Your staff may call to say tenants are complaining of soapy water coming up into their sinks or bathtubs or elsewhere in their apartments. View this as trouble waiting to explode. Under the definition of emergency, your staff should first confirm the complaint by seeing for themselves what is in the tenant's apartment. Once the complaint is confirmed, have your staff enter without notice to investigate units on the same riser. That is the only time you will find the problem. Entering the apartments while the sinks are flooding allows your staff to catch the guilty tenant in action. If you give a Notice of Entry, the guilty tenant will hide the machine beforehand by covering it or storing it inside whatever closet it is able to fit. Your staff will also be able to smell the detergent or fabric softener being used, making it harder for the tenant to deny the use of the unauthorized appliance. Any water damage caused from the use of a washing machine must be charged back to the tenant, as should any plumbing repairs.

- *Washer malfunction in laundry room*
  A broken hose, a loose-fitting hose, leaking valves, clogged drain pipes or worn parts can be the cause of laundry room flood. The flood can also result from unconnected pipes hidden behind the walls of the laundry room. To reduce the damages and expenses that result from laundry room floods, flush floor drains at least once each year. Floor drains that are clean and clear of lint, dirt and other items will allow water to channel freely from the laundry room down the drain. This prevents water from escaping into other areas that are within close proximity to the laundry room. If you have old machines, consider replacing them with new. Before you replace the washers, flush all drains to enhance the efficiency of the new machines. Ensure your staff get machines repaired as soon as they are reported as being out of order. Bear in mind that if you are repairing machines constantly, it may be time to

get new ones. If the machines are on rental or they are being operated independently of the company, consider having them replaced with new machines. The last thing you want your building to be known for is broken machines and a laundry room that constantly floods. Never forget that a flood brings many expenses, such as the following:

- o   the cost of the lost water
- o   the damages caused
- o   the cost to repair those damages
- o   the inconvenience to your tenants

- *Standpipe turned on by vandals*
  When this happens, it can be devastating. This water comes out with great force and will no doubt torrent down like a raging river or waterfall. A flood such as this can force the fire department to evacuate the building. In addition to finding its way into the stairwell, apartments, hallways and utility rooms on each hallway floor, this water will most likely find its way into the elevator pit located at the bottom of the building. The pit usually contains equipment that can be damaged if exposed to water, and damage to this equipment will greatly disrupt the operation of the building. According to KJA, elevator and escalator consulting engineers, a pioneer in the industry, care should be taken to record as much information as possible. To determine if there are damages and the extent of the damages to the elevator equipment inside the pit, KJA recommends asking and recording the answers to the following questions:

1. Approximately how much water entered the elevator shaft?
2. If a pipe has burst what is the flow rate?
3. How high did the water level reach in the pit (if a contractor is on site to provide pit access)?
4. Was there only a puddle of water on the pit floor or was the water 5 feet deep?
5. Where in the shaft was the elevator located when the flooding occurred?
6. Did the elevator continue to run as the flooding continued and if so for how long?

Source: https://www.kja.com/rising-waters-impact-on-elevator-and-escalators-p154285. Reproduced with permission from KJA Elevator and Escalator Consulting Engineers, December 8, 2016.

It is always wise to work with an elevator consultant such as KJA. Elevator consultants have expertise in the repair and maintenance of elevators and escalators. They also offer cost-effective advice and solutions for preventative maintenance to ensure the overall efficiency of elevators and escalators. Your consultant can inspect your elevator and the pit if water has entered the pit. On the matter of water in the pit, KJA states, "The Information you gather from the questions, can assist consultants such as their company when they are called out for an inspection. The information can also help to settle your claim more quickly with your insurance company."

- *Heating radiator pipe leak*

  This is rare and is usually something the staff should be able to handle. Normally it is the tenant whose apartment that is affected who will call the staff. With a leak of this type, your staff may call HVAC directly if they are not able to address the leak on their own. You are normally notified after HVAC has been contacted. Since HVAC is calling the shots on this flood in terms of repair, make sure you stay in touch with both HVAC and your staff. If you have carpets, advise your staff that they should be professionally cleaned. In all the cases I have had, the water was contained inside the apartment.

- *Extinguishing a fire by the fire department or water from damaged fire equipment*

  When the fire department is called to put out a fire, rest assured that you are going to have a flood. The water from the fire hose will come out with great pressure. You can call it both a torrential downpour and a raging waterfall. If you have apartments below, to the left and/or to the right of where the fire was put out, these apartments should all be checked for water damage. Your hallways and stairwells should also be checked for damage.

These are just some types of flooding that can occur. Firsthand information along with quick thinking can help to minimize damages and lessen the repair costs associated with the flood. Whenever a major flood is reported, always go on-site or ask your staff specific questions so you can have a mental picture of what the area looks like. Your staff may also send you pictures, but the best assessment is to personally see it for yourself. For some emergencies, you may not be able to make it physically to the site. Therefore, you will have to rely on your staff and contractors who are on-site. It is also great if they can send you videos or pictures of the situation.

B. Fire

Another type of emergency you may face is dealing with fires. Remember—once you have a fire and the fire department must put it out, you automatically have a flood. Sadly, I have had to deal with many fires in the following areas: kitchen, balcony, stairwell, lobby, laundry room and garbage chute. The first time I dealt with a fire I was nervous. It was a balcony fire. After that balcony fire, the next fire I had to deal with was a garbage chute fire. At that location, security was at the building because I had no staff present at the time. Security called to inform me that there was a fire at the building and the fire department was on-site. Since I had no staff at that location, I immediately made my way to the building. I arrived with my set of keys to the building and identified myself to the fire department. Thankfully the fire was put out. The firefighters requested that I take them to the sprinkler room so they could turn the sprinkler system off, because water was gushing everywhere. Without hesitation, I took them to the sprinkler room. One fireman told me that if the firefighters hadn't been able to gain access, they would have used their "universal key," the sledgehammer. If they had done that, I would have had to replace the door, which was quite expensive. I was later asked to silence the fire panel, which I did. I am so glad I learned how to do that.

While the fire department was dealing with the sprinkler room, I notified the relevant personnel. Then I called the fire equipment company, who dispatched someone immediately. Since I had no staff, I called one of my other locations for backup. The fire equipment company arrived before the fire department left and repaired the broken sprinkler head. Before the fire department left, they told me that since the sprinkler head had been repaired, there was no need to write an infraction. They thanked me for addressing the repair without delay and gave me a thumbs-up. Interestingly, I had done training at that same location with both the LSS and the HVAC team on separate occasions about one month before the fire. Talk about preparation! By the time the staff from one of my other buildings arrived, I had completed all the required paperwork relating to the fire. My staff checked over my paperwork to make sure I had completed it accurately. That was such great teamwork; I thanked them dearly. I am glad I was familiar with the building. Even though the security guard had been given a tour of the building when he first arrived, it was obvious he was startled by the fire. Had I not shown up, who knows what would have happened. This was a small fire, so I made arrangements for a small approved cleaning contractor to immediately clean up the flood water. The other repair was to the door to the room where the compactor bin was kept. A new set of fire-rated doors was ordered. Once they arrived, they replaced the damaged doors. The takeaway lessons from this emergency were as follows:

- Know the locations of all utility rooms at your buildings.
- Have the keys to your buildings.
- Get familiar with all the keys on the bunch and know which room they are able to open.
- Have contact numbers handy for all contractors and department heads.
- Work as a team with the fire department, your boss, your colleague(s), your staff and contractors.
- Remain calm no matter what. That way your thoughts will flow better.

I was hoping that this fire would be my last, but sadly it was not. That was only wishful thinking. This fire only prepared me for many other fires that took place. Even though each emergency is different from the previous, the best way to deal with any emergency is to be prepared. This helps you to be calmer, more focused and less alarmed by surprises. Your response becomes second nature. On the other hand, you will never know how prepared you are for an emergency until you are dealing with one—or one on a larger scale.

Whenever you get a call informing you of a fire at any of your properties, usually the relevant authorities are already on-site. I strongly recommend that you visit the site and see for yourself what the damages are. If your portfolio spans different regions, provinces or states, it may not be possible to get up and go as you wish. However, this should not be an excuse not to visit sometime later. Avoiding the visit is the approach of a mediocre property manager. If you feel the visit is not necessary, take a look at officials who did not visit ravaged areas after a major disaster. They are viewed as lacking compassion and most often lose the respect others once had for them. Usually when those officials visit and survey the disaster areas, people see them as compassionate and caring. Therefore, visiting a property within your portfolio that has an emergency demonstrates you are a concerned and excellent property manager. It shows that you take your job seriously. Immediately after the emergency is also the time when your staff need you the most. While you are on-site, you can answer any questions from the fire department or any other authority. Your physical presence on-site also takes the stress off your staff, who will now be in a better position to address any cleanup or start the cleanup process until any contracting cleanup crew shows up if they are needed.

I was notified of a massive common area fire that happened at around 3:00 a.m. or 4:00 a.m. When the phone rang, even though I was in my deepest sleep, I knew which building was calling. That is because of the ring tone I had given this property. I also knew the call had to be about something big. The staff at that location were seasoned and capable. The fact that they were calling this early meant it had to be something major. Very calmly, the staff member on the phone told me about the fire. I quickly made my way to the property, only to find about ten or twelve fire trucks, police vehicles and ambulances surrounding the property. All the tenants were standing on their balconies. Thankfully it was not during the cold weather. After locating my staff, I learned that the fire had been put out. I then courageously made my way over to the fire marshal and introduced myself to get the details of what had transpired. The fire marshal had a firm and angry look on his face. Based on the look, I didn't know if I should walk away or stay. The fire marshal was so mad that he didn't even shake my hand. He told me the fire was the result of arson and proceeded to reprimand me about an adjustment that had been made to a door. I had no idea what the fire marshal was talking about. I had not done any adjustment to the door in question, nor had I been told prior to the fire that there was an adjustment done to the door. As far as I was concerned, that is how the building was built.

This fire marshal was not buying that explanation. The building may have been new to me, but it was not new to the fire department. The fire marshal was personally familiar with the building and was able to tell me the names of all the property managers before me who were responsible for the building. The fire marshal said that if the adjustment had not been done, the damages would have been much less. Damages were estimated in the six-figure dollar amount. The fire had damaged the fire monitoring system for the building, and for that reason the marshal told me he was considering emptying the building, in which case I would have to find somewhere to put all the tenants. In my mind I said, "*Considering*" *means the decision has not yet been made.* However, what he said vibrated throughout my mind and body. The building had over 140 units. I was wondering if there was an inexpensive way of keeping everyone safe. With my strong hotel management background, I knew that it would have been an overwhelming bill to put all the tenants up in a hotel, plus pay all the incidentals charges (food and beverage, parking, laundry, etc.) that would be added to each room's bill.

This fire marshal was talking down to me with great anger like a dragon with flaming fire issuing from its nose. Beyond his anger and his title, I knew he had a heart. I had learned the art of speaking to people's hearts. Therefore, I spoke to his heart, not to get him to compromise the safety of the tenants but to get him to offer me his assistance. I told the fire marshal, "Please do not empty my building. Please work with me." I guaranteed the fire marshal I would deliver whatever he wanted. In an angry tone and with a mean, grim face, the marshal told me with one finger pointed at me, "You only have half an hour to get the contractor to come and assess the fire monitoring system, or else I am going to empty the building." The marshal warned that if there was any further fire in the building, the fire department would have no way of knowing about it because the system was now disabled. I knew the matter was grossly serious and urgent. Therefore, I acted fast.

As mean as he sounded, I knew he was doing his job. Despite what was happening or about to transpire, I had to remain focused, so I blocked his anger from my mind and called the fire equipment company. I stated the magnitude of the emergency, and the contractor said they would be at the building shortly. I then called the locksmith to repair the locking system to the lobby door that the firefighters had broken to gain access. I also called the electrician to turn off power supply to the fire-damaged section of the building. I updated the fire marshal every step of the way and told him which contractors were on their way. Within twenty minutes, the fire equipment contractor showed up in uniform and was directed to the fire marshal to assess and start the repair. Thankfully, only the monitoring system for half the building was damaged. The other half was ok. Hence, the marshal instructed me to get security for each floor to do fire watch for the half section of the building where the fire system was disabled.

Five minutes after that, two more contractors showed up. Since this was a major fire, I called in a major approved disaster restoration company. Within an hour, I had everyone I needed at the building to assist in the emergency, including security guards to do fire watch. Between calls I notified the relevant personnel within the company, who gave me all the support I needed. After about an hour or so, the fire marshal came over to me with a relaxed face and said, "Well done, Simone." He said he initially thought I would not be able to deliver, but when he saw the first contractor and then the others roll in, one after the other, he knew I was serious. It was at that point the fire marshal introduced himself to me, shook my hand and handed me his business card with all his contact information. He told me that if I needed anything, I should not hesitate to call him. He explained the door mechanism that was missing. He said that if anyone had died, we would be talking about a different story. He told me my staff were excellent and added that the only thing that had messed me up was the door mechanism. I assured him I would have the door installed when the circumstances permitted. He asked if a fire logbook was kept, saying I should have it handy just in case it was needed. The fire logbook was later retrieved, and it was up-to-date. Was I ever happy! I was also glad I made it a habit to check the logbooks whenever I visited the properties.

I must emphasize that if the fire department tells you they are going to empty your building, *do not argue with them. Let them do their job.* I also want to reiterate, in this situation, the marshal said he was "considering" emptying the building. That decision was not yet made. What I needed was help, and I was not afraid to ask for help. What I also came to understand is that the fire department can direct you to organizations and resources that are activated once you have a major disaster. I strongly recommend you find out what these organizations and resources are before you have a major disaster.

I had never experienced an emergency of this magnitude before. My internal system was operating on autopilot thanks to all the inspections I had done in preparation, meeting and speaking with contractors and just knowing and understanding the domino effect of the emergency. Yes, I was experiencing a rush of emotions on the inside, but I had to remain strong for the tenants, my staff and the company I was working for. The reassurance from the marshal was very helpful. I did not feel alone but instead felt I had a large team working for the good of the tenants and the property. When I got the chance, I called all the contractors and thanked them for showing up. Their response was, they could not let me down. One contractor mentioned that when he saw my number on his caller ID that early in the morning, he knew it had to be serious. Once things were a little more settled, I bought the staff breakfast and thanked them for their arduous work. One of the staff was even on her day off but showed up to help as if it were a regular workday. Talk about teamwork when you need it the most.

I later took pictures of the damages and made a report to submit to the insurance company. As soon as the fire department and police handed over the building, the restoration company went into action and cleaned the building from top to bottom. The elevator company was also called in to assess the elevator pit for damages and to clean the hoist way, which had accumulated a lot of soot. The immediate cleaning in the aftermath of the restoration work boosted the pride and morale of all the tenants. Not even one tenant called to complain about the fire. Well, one chronic complainer did call, but only to thank us for caring about the tenants, as evidence by the way in which the restoration company was cleaning the building. The tenant said she did not feel forgotten and wanted me to know the cleaning was appreciated. The tenant's statement was quite comforting and reassured me that I was on the right track. The fire was major, and emotionally it was taking its toll on me. That reassurance was very timely and was something I needed.

My takeaways from this major disaster were as follows:

1. Always keep your work or company's phone close by, and make sure each building has its own ring tone.
2. Show up on-site as soon as possible when you are told of a major emergency. Give support to your staff even if they are seasoned and experienced employees.
3. Find the authorities on-site and see what information they need from you. Be ready to act when the authorities give instructions. As seasoned as these staff were, the fire marshal would have chewed them up. The staff had already done their part.
4. I had to work under extreme pressure amid a major crisis and remain calm and focused. Regardless of the crisis, remain positive, envision the outcome you need and work determinedly to achieve it. Shut out the chaos around you and get the job done. Remember you are in control. Use your resources to the advantage of the company.
5. I had to negotiate and eliminate a necessary cost, namely, the hotel accommodation. Say the fire marshal had emptied the building. I could not tell the marshal that the tenants' apartment insurance should cover their hotel accommodations. I felt he would have told me that was not his business.
6. Notify the relevant personnel within your company and make sure you have all their contact numbers. If those personnel are on vacation, be sure to have all the contact numbers for those appointed to cover during their absence.
7. Have the contact numbers for your contractors and know the degree and level of work they are capable of doing.
8. Do not underestimate the preparation of doing inspections with the various departments.
9. Do not fall apart. My remaining together helped to increase my confidence level. (My comfort level in dealing with the fire department also went up a notch.)

To get the building back to prefire condition, the following things were done:

- The restoration company cleaned the common area of all soot.
- Bricks on the outside were soda blasted.
- The elevator company cleaned the hoist way of all heavy soot. There were no damages to the equipment in the pit or any of the cables.
- The fire-damaged areas were gutted and rebuilt.
- A temporary adjustment was done to the door until the area was rebuilt, after which a permanent door was installed.
- In other areas that had soot damage, walls were washed of soot, treated and then painted.
- Fire watch remained in effect until the heat sensor for the other half of the building was reinstalled.
- All mechanical and electrical repairs were completed.
- Damaged doors and windows above the lobby were reinstalled.
- One apartment sustained minor damages that got repaired.

A project of this magnitude requires the input of your AM. It is wise to follow his or her lead, but remain proactive about getting quotes from general contractors to carry out repairs. Most likely you will require minimum of two, and sometimes three, quotes to submit for insurance purposes. Not all the repairs will require more than one quote. Contractors such as the fire protection and equipment company and the elevator contractor have existing signed contracts to maintain these machines and equipment. Hence, you would be breaching the contract if you were to get another company to carry out the repair. The most logical thing to do with these contractors is to have your respective consultants review the damages and the quotes and then offer their advice. In some cases, you may not have time to call in a consultant.

In the years that followed, I dealt with more fires, small ones and large ones. Kitchen fires were the worst and resulted in a lot more damages than any other type. Three of the many kitchen fires I had in my portfolio resulted in major damages.

When assessing fire damages caused by fires inside apartments, you must do the following:

- Make a thorough check for flood damage resulting from the water used to put out the fire. Check hallways of the floor where the apartment fire occurred for damages. On that floor, you will likely have water from the fire hoses, and shattered glass from the fire cabinet if the fire department used your fire hose. If you must replace any glass to the fire cabinet, you must also reinstall all applicable stickers onto the fire cabinet as per the local fire code.
- Once the apartment door to the fire-filled apartment is opened, soot and smoke will bellow into the hallway. Hence that section of the hallway will require painting. Carpet will require either cleaning or replacement, and flooring will require repair or intense cleaning. In some cases, it may be necessary to replace the carpet instead of cleaning it. When you replace the carpet, you eliminate any potential smoke odour trapped in the carpet that could resurface over time.
- From observation, when it is just a single apartment fire, the fire department *may* set up a post on the closest safest hallway to the fire point and in the lobby. That hallway and the

steps leading to the hallway will have black markings on walls, doors and flooring from gears and equipment the firefighters used. You will have to have those black marks cleaned.

Be sure to include these areas in the cleanup costs that you submit to the insurance company.

Inside the apartment

Once the fire marshal hands the fire-damaged apartment back to you, a series of things must take place to get the apartment back into operation, as follows:

1. Take as many pictures as you can of the damages on or in all the affected floors, affected stairwells and affected units. First take a photo of the apartment door with the apartment number, and then take photos of the damages inside the apartment. Take pictures of all damages in the apartment where the fire started.
2. Most importantly you must immediately address any order or infraction given to you by the fire department. Sometimes the heat may damage the speaker box or smoke detector inside the apartment. These should be repaired asap. Work with your AM and all departments involved to rectify the infractions.
3. To get the apartment back into operation, contact your general contractors to assess the apartment and submit quotes after the tenants have removed their personal items.
4. If the personal items of the tenants are charred and the tenants will not be needing them, have the tenants write a letter authorizing the restoration company or your company to dispose of said items.
5. Give a copy of the letter from the tenant to the restoration company and keep the original in the tenant's file.
6. Your staff should take pictures of the tenant's personal items since these may not have been captured in your set of pictures.

After these basic things are done, the following can take place to speed up the process (if they are not included in the scope of work from the general contractors):

1. Contact your fire restoration company and co-ordinate the removal of the tenant's personal items.
2. Have plumbing shut-off valves turned off or installed so that cabinets with sinks, when removed, will not cause flooding. All exposed drains should be capped to prevent the apartment from stinking.
3. Contact your window company, who will visit assess and measure the windows to determine if they need replacement. Any replacements should be done with urgency since these windows are made to order and can take up to six to eight weeks to be delivered and installed. Be sure to include the cost of cosmetic repairs around the windows that are being installed.
4. If broken windows fall below to the ground outside, you may have to get your landscaping contractor to clean up broken glasses and install a snow fence to prevent people from

walking in that area. The snow fence may be safer than caution tape and should be left up for the duration of the restoration work.

5. Order a new balcony door immediately. The company that does the windows normally will do the balcony door. Have them measure the door when they visit to assess and measure the windows.

6. Have new doors and/or frames, including closet doors, installed inside the apartment.

7. Replace the entry door and the door closure. If the entrance door is damaged, order a new one immediately, as the turnaround time for fire-rated doors can be weeks.

8. Replace any damaged flooring, including baseboards. Carpet and underpadding should be replaced. Ceramic tiles may have to be replaced if they are damaged from the heat or stained black from char.

9. Repair the bathroom, including the tub surround and fittings, the vanity and the medicine cabinet.

10. Call an electrician to disconnect the power supply and do all electrical repairs.

11. Repair the fire speaker box.

12. Complete kitchen cabinets. If you are installing new cabinets in vacated units, this may be a unit for which you may want to install the newer cabinets and other upgraded features.

13. Repair or replace appliances applicable to the unit: refrigerator, stove, range hood, microwave and/or dishwasher.

14. Replace drywall/sheetrock and paint walls, baseboards, ceilings, doors and doorframes.

15. Clean all exhaust vents after the work is completed and just before the apartment is cleaned.

16. Repair any fire damage to other apartments, whether these damages are fire-related or flood-related (the result of putting out the fire).

Calculate any loss of rent monies from the date of the fire to the date the apartment is re-rented and add these to the expenses associated with the apartment loss. Keep all quotes and invoices together, and follow your company's protocol for submitting an insurance claim for all the expenses related to the fire. If the fire was the result of a tenant's negligence, file the necessary legal papers. Before you file the legal papers on the tenant, it is wise to get a copy of the fire report to support your case at the LTB. On the next page is a sample letter requesting the report from the fire department.

Letter Requesting Report from Fire Department

On [date] at approximately [time], your fire department responded to a [state type of fire] fire at our building located at [address], apartment [number].

We are requesting a formal report of your findings about the fire. Your urgency in preparing the report is appreciated.

Enclosed is a cheque [or Internet transaction receipt] in the amount of [list amount] to cover the recommended cost of the report.

Please do not hesitate to contact me if you have any questions.

Sincerely,

[Name]
Property Manager

C. Death of Tenant on Property

Another situation that you may face as a property manager is the death of a tenant. The circumstances surrounding a tenant's death can pose several challenges.

Your staff may call stating that relatives of a tenant called asking to be able to enter the apartment to check on their loved one. Tenants may also call complaining of a foul smell on a certain floor. It could also be your staff are aware that a certain tenant is elderly and lives alone and they have not seen or heard from that tenant for a few days. Out of concern, your staff would like to enter the unit and check on the tenant. While all of the above may seem harmless, advise your staff to do the following:

- Inform the relatives of the tenant that they must contact the police and that entry will be given to the police.
- If the staff would like to check on a tenant, they can serve a 24-Hour Notice of Entry to the tenant's unit.
- Any offensive smell on any floor should be investigated with urgency. Post a Notice of Entry for each apartment on the floor in question and inspect all these apartments individually.

I have seen cases where tenants who did not wish to be contacted or who were away got very, very upset and threatened to file an application for illegal entry at the Landlord and Tenant Board (LTB) upon learning that the staff entered the unit without proper notice. These tenants did not even care that the purpose of the entry was to check on them. In these situations, if the police were called and entered the unit, the unit was entered under "good faith." In other words, the intention was good, with the welfare of the tenant in mind.

The situation becomes more complicated if your staff enter on proper notice or they grant entry to the police and the tenant is found unresponsive in the apartment. If the police are not present at the time of entry with the proper notice, your staff should call the police and then inform you. If your staff calls you first before they call the police, advise your staff to call the police immediately. In addition, advise your staff not to touch anything inside the apartment, not to move the tenant and to remain outside the apartment until the police arrive. If the tenant is dead, the police will arrange for the body to be taken away to the proper place. Note well, if a murder occurred inside an apartment at your building, no staff should speak to the media, put the information on social media or speak with any other tenants about the matter. If the tenant lived alone, you can assist in the process by providing the police with any necessary information such as next of kin or other persons who may be on the lease/tenancy agreement. Other information that may assist in the investigation process is any motor vehicle that the tenant may have on property. This can tell the police whose name(s) the vehicle is registered to. If the police are present at the time of discovery, your staff should still contact you immediately.

Either you or your staff should inform the police of the landlord's responsibility under section 91 of the Residential Tenancies Act (RTA) to secure the property, which includes changing the lock if the tenant lived alone.

"If a tenant of a rental unit dies and there are no other tenants of the rental unit, the tenancy shall be deemed to be terminated 30 days after the death of the tenant" (*Residential Tenancies Act*, 2006, c. 17, s. 91 [1]).

Reasonable access

The landlord shall, until the tenancy is terminated under subsection (1),
(a) preserve any property of a tenant who has died that is in the rental unit or the residential complex other than property that is unsafe or unhygienic; and
(b) afford the executor or administrator of the tenant's estate, or if there is no executor or administrator, a member of the tenant's family reasonable access to the rental unit and the residential complex for the purpose of removing the tenant's property.

(*Residential Tenancies Act*, 2006, c. 17, s. 91 [2])

An immediate lock change prevents any person with a key to the apartment from taking anything from the apartment he or she may not be legally entitled to take. It also protects the company against any liability resulting from the claim of any legal heir to the personal property of the deceased. The locks must be changed even if the tenant's apartment is cluttered or considered dirty. In one case, the deceased tenant's apartment was cluttered. After I informed the police of the landlord's responsibility to change the lock in order to protect the contents of the apartment, the police asked if I had seen the apartment, meaning, the apartment was cluttered and they could not see the value of anything amid the clutter or junk. I was very well aware of the condition of the apartment. The tenant was in the process of reducing the clutter inside the apartment.

Despite that expressed thought of the police, the lock was still changed. When the heirs to the estate showed up to claim the items in the apartment, they stated that their relative had a licensed firearm and wanted to know if anyone had found it. They were directed to the police. There was no further mention of the firearm. Regardless of how tenants carry themselves or keep their apartment, this should not stop you from exercising the law. If the police have concluded that the lock cannot be changed until their investigation is completed, you must comply and hold off on changing the lock until the police grant authorization. Remember the police must do their work and will help to determine the cause of death, whether it was natural or suspicious. The police can also assist in notifying the next of kin of the deceased. If there are no known next of kin, the policed may refer you to the Office of the Public Guardian Trustee (OPGT). "The OPGT protects the interests of potential heirs when an Ontario resident dies leaving an estate and there is no one who can administer it." If the tenant is not dead but is in a state where he or she cannot make decisions, "the OPGT will conduct an investigation when it receives information that an individual may be incapable and at risk of suffering serious financial or personal harm and no alternative solution is available." Be sure to get an occurrence number from the police so that proper follow-up can be done when required. The occurrence number should be kept in the tenant's file.

Once the police grant clearance to change the lock, a copy of the key should be given to the police if they are still conducting an investigation inside the apartment. In accordance with section 91 of the RTA, a copy of the key should also be given to the power of attorney (POA) or any person authorized by the police once he or she presents the proper documents and valid identification. Always work with your legal department and your AM on cases such as these. If the tenant lived alone and received subsidized housing, the housing office should be notified immediately. If the tenant had no relatives or next of kin, work with your legal department and ask for their advice on how to proceed. You and your legal department, along with your AM or RM, may want to contact the Estates Administration Unit of the OPGT. If the OPGT decides to take this on, be prepared to provide and release information about the deceased tenant to expedite the work of the OPGT. The following is an excerpt from the OPGT:

The work involved in administering an estate includes:

- gathering information to determine the nature, location and value of the deceased's assets (bank accounts, real estate, vehicles, investments, etc.) and debts (credit cards, mortgages, loans, etc.);
- applying to court for appointment as estate trustee;
- securing the assets, including maintaining and managing real estate, if necessary;
- collecting any money or benefits owing to the estate;
- liquidating all the assets and disposing of personal effects;
- paying debts;
- initiating or defending legal proceedings on behalf of the estate;
- filing tax returns;
- establishing who the lawful heirs are and locating them; and
- accounting to the heirs and distributing the money in proper shares among the heirs.

Source: https://www.attorneygeneral.jus.gov.on.ca/english/family/pgt/estatesadmin.html. February 22, 2017. Reproduced with the permission of the OPGT, 2017.

The OPGT *may* be able to offer assistance with the disposal of personal items inside the apartment or anything else related to the tenancy, such as storage lockers or a motor vehicle. These form part of the tenant's estate. If you are authorized by the OPGT to dispose of the contents of the apartment, get that authorization in writing and keep it with the deceased tenant's file. Who will pay for the disposal of the items? Try to get everything out of the apartment before the 30-day termination date or other mutually agreed upon vacate date. If the tenant lived alone and there are no next of kin and pets are inside the apartment, contact the closest animal organization, animal shelter or local municipal office for direction on how to proceed with the pet(s). Make sure there are no charges to your company. If any of the organizations take the pet(s), get all the necessary information, such as contact person, address and phone number, and keep this information in the tenant's file. It will help you to direct any relatives or legal heirs to the estate who show up to retrieve the pet(s) from the organization.

After the police hands over the apartment to the company, ask the police if there is body fluid of any kind in the apartment. Body fluid should not be cleaned by any of your staff. Your restoration company should be called immediately, notified of the death and asked to remove the carpet (if the area is carpeted) or clean the flooring of any biohazardous material. Out of respect for the family, you may want to arrange cleanup after the family has removed the personal items and given you the go-ahead. It is also wise to inform the family of the legal time limit they have to empty the apartment. Section 91 (1) of the RTA states 30 days after death. The family may request extra time, which may be granted at the discretion of the landlord. The family may also request some cleanup of any body fluid before any items are moved out of the apartment. If they are going to arrange the cleanup of body fluid, find out if it will be professionally done.

The following is according to Ontario Mediation Services:

> Sometimes, people attempt cleanups for financial reasons. Death is, on top of everything else, expensive, with a funeral and other expenses. For the sake of your mental health, we suggest that cleanup is not somewhere you cut corners. There are sometimes options to help ease the financial burden of death cleanup, and we're glad to go over those with you. In the end, though, it is a personal choice. The death of a loved one is one of the toughest, and most personal, experiences anyone goes through. Everyone finds their own process to cope—or to not cope. We speak from experience, but our experience isn't your own. We just want you to know that help is available. We can't grieve for you, but we can get the cleanup done for you, so you can take care of what's truly important.

> *Source:* http://www.ontarioremediation.ca/2015/11/cleaning-up-a-loved-one/. December 11, 2017. Reproduced with permission of Ontario Remediation Services, 2017.

The last thing you want is improper cleaning to contaminate the apartment and put the health of the other tenants on the same floor at risk. Remember things will be taken through the hallway (and into the elevator if the death occurred on a higher floor). If you decide to take on the cleaning and it is done before all the personal items are removed, a more thorough cleaning should be done once all the items are removed. Obviously, this will incur a cost; therefore, you may want to inform the family of the cost, or you can extend compassion to the grieving family. That decision is up to you and the company. You can take the length and quality of the tenancy into consideration before making that decision. In a case at one of the buildings I managed, the tenant bled out in the apartment on the carpet. The relatives paid for proper professional cleanup of the apartment but asked for assistance with carpet replacement for the surviving tenant who wanted to remain in the apartment. The deceased tenant was a good longstanding tenant, so compassion was extended to the family. The carpet and the underpadding were replaced at no cost to the surviving tenant of the apartment.

As soon as you obtain legal possession of the apartment, as per section 91 of the RTA, carry out all necessary cleaning first. This cleaning may incur a huge cost because it must be done by professionals, most likely your restoration company. The apartment cleaning, repairs or renovation must be done so that the apartment will be returned to livable condition and be rent-ready for the market. The renovation process can sometimes be delayed due to the cause of death, any ongoing investigation and/or the length of time it took to discover the body. Check with your area manager to see if this kind of emergency is covered by the company's insurance. In some cases, the insurance company may still want to be notified of any death on the property regardless of cause. If the renovation is not covered by the insurance, then this should be submitted as a capital expenditure project. Therefore, keep all invoices and quotes, the occurrence number from the police, and any report from staff regarding discovery of the body in a special file. Put the apartment number on the file and add the type of emergency, in this case, death. If possible, get a copy of the death certificate and keep a copy in the tenant file and put a separate copy in the capex file. While this is business as usual for you, make sure you use a lot of compassion in speech and action toward surviving family members, even if the deceased tenant was difficult or not in good standing.

D. Marijuana/Cannabis Grow Operation

The day you suspect or learn that you have weed, pot, ganja, vegetable matter or marijuana—and not humans—living inside one of your apartments is a day you will never forget. With a marijuana or ganja farm or growing operation (grow op) inside one of the apartments in a building you manage, some tenants may claim they have the plants for medicinal purpose. The magnitude at which the marijuana is grown will tell you otherwise. Even if the purpose is of a medical nature, what does the lease/tenancy agreement say? Are other tenants complaining about the smell of weed or marijuana? This could be interfering with the reasonable enjoyment the other tenants are entitled to under the RTA. Also, check out what your building code says. Growing marijuana in a setting like this can be costly to landlords and can be a nightmare for property managers for the following reasons:

- To operate a homegrown farm on this scale requires heavy water consumption and heat from special lamps. Hence, if heat and hydro are included in the rent, you could be unknowingly providing much in the way of needed resources to the perpetrators.
- A marijuana grow operation is beyond the cultivation limit thus making it an illegal act that requires notification of law enforcement. It is possible that you will be issued an order to make the building safe.

  o This will give your building and company unwanted publicity.
  o The police will seize the apartment; hence, you will be sitting on lost revenue.
  o Depending on the laws in your area, you will be forced to gut the apartment and repair everything if there is mould damage.

- The air quality must be tested and deemed acceptable for the apartment to be considered habitable.
- Electrical Safety Authority (ESA) must be called in.
- You must repair any altered plumbing done to irrigate the plants.

- Check your insurance policy. It will most likely rule out compensation for damages arising from illegal activity. Therefore, you cannot submit a claim and must foot the renovation bill and live with the stigma associated with having a grow op in that unit. This can also make it hard to rent the newly renovated unit.

Indicators that you may have a grow op:

- *Windows* covered with black plastic, bed sheets or heavy curtains that are drawn shut and are pressed up against the windows. Look for excessive condensation on the windows, the result of humid air and improper ventilation.
- *Odours* coming from the apartment, possibly skunk-like or chemical in nature.
- *Humming noise* from fans or other ventilation equipment.
- *Frequent visitors*, often late at night.
- *Security cameras* in the front and back of the apartment. Grow ops often have extra security in place to protect them from rivals, as well as police.
- *Bars* on the windows.
- *Garbage* or equipment, such as bedding plant pots, discarded potting soil, piping or wiring, lying about the yard.
- *Hydro meters* that have been tampered with.
- *TV* or radio left on at all times.
- *Flyers* piling up in the mailbox.
- *Signs* indicating there is a guard dog on duty.
- *Lawns* left uncared for.

Source: https://www.squareoneinsurance.ca/. February 14, 2017. Reproduced with the permission Square One Insurance, 2017.

Not all the foregoing points listed will apply to high-rise multifamily buildings. However, if you have town houses in your portfolio, these are definitely things you should know and be on the lookout for.

At one property within my portfolio, some tenants were constantly complaining of a strong marijuana smell from time to time in their apartments. On a particular floor in the same building, tenants at one end of the hallway were complaining of an offensive odour coming from one of the apartments. A warning letter was sent to the suspected apartment and no further complaints were made. However, the cleaning staff for that building informed me they saw someone from the suspected apartment spraying air freshener in the hallway. After a building inspection one day, it was observed that the threshold to the apartment in question was very dirty. A follow-up letter was sent to the tenants regarding the dirt at the entrance. They were also warned in the letter that there may be possible chargebacks for cleaning the hallway if the matter persisted. Not long after, the foul smell returned and the complaints from tenants started again. A Notice of Entry was served for an inspection of the apartment. On the date of the inspection, access was denied and the barking of what sounded like a huge aggressive dog were heard as the animal kept jumping at the door. The voice of someone behind the door told us the leaseholder was not at home and we could not enter. A letter was sent to the leaseholder informing him that under the RTA, a valid Notice of Entry is all that is required, not the presence of the leaseholder or anyone else. Hence, another Notice of Entry was served along with the letter. The leaseholder called very upset and threatened to escalate the matter, which he did, stating that he was being harassed. It was expressed that harassment was not the intent and the inspection was within reason based on complaints that were being sent in from other tenants. The aggressive tenant claimed he was going to give his notice to vacate if we tried to enter. I persisted and served the Notice of Entry a few days ahead of the inspection date. Before the inspection, the tenant responded with a 30-day notice to vacate the apartment. Since the property had an excellent record of renting, the invalid notice was accepted with the understanding that it would be in everyone's best interests. It was also communicated to the tenant that an inspection still had to be done to assess the apartment for repairs. A notice was served, but access was again denied on the date of the inspection. A call was made to the tenant informing him that he was being difficult. He should have given a 60-day notice, as required by law, but gave a 30-day notice instead, which I accepted. The tenant was also told the matter was going before the LTB and possibly law enforcement if he refused to co-operate. The inspection, I told the tenant, was scheduled within 48 hours. That would be my final attempt to work with him.

The inspection was done within 48 hours, but the tenant had moved out before the inspection. On top of that, I was not at work that day because I had prior plans. On my return, I did go and inspect the apartment. The apartment was a big mess. It looked like a junkyard, as if no one had ever lived in the apartment. The electrical outlets were all tampered with and hanging out of the sockets. The pipes in the bathroom and kitchen had no taps. The windows had dozens of small nail holes all around them in the walls. Surprisingly, before the inspection, when I looked at the windows from the outside, they all had curtains. Apparently, what the tenant did was to wrap a board with cloth and nail it over the windows to make it appear as though there were curtains. The ceiling and some walls had mildew. There was no physical evidence of marijuana in the apartment, not even seedlings. If any were there, they must have been in the inception stage. The building never missed the annual in-suite inspection. The red flags were as follows:

- the foul smell emitting from the apartment
- the occupant/guest spraying air freshener in the hallway to mask the smell of marijuana
- the person who denied entry may have been a crop sitter
- an aggressive dog
- the tenant's reluctance to have the apartment inspected and reacting with aggression

The apartment went through a full renovation to get it back on the market. Had it not been for persistence to inspect the apartment based on complaints from tenants and observations of staff, it could have been a greater problem. An N5 could have been issued in the beginning to gain entry, but the tenant was leaving and an N5 would not have benefitted the situation, based on the time frame. If you suspect a grow op in any of your buildings and you are going to inspect the apartment, be on the lookout for strategies to mask the smell of the marijuana. A great and effective mask is bacon. So, if you are overwhelmed by the smell of bacon in every room, the tenant could have more than an appetite for bacon. *Please note that this incident took place long before the Cannabis Act was enforced.*

Navigating your way around the Cannabis Act

From a property management standpoint, let us take a closer look at the Cannabis Act. As of October 17, 2018, it is legal for adults (18/19 years and older, age varies in each province) to purchase and consume marijuana in Canada for recreational use within certain restrictions. The Act allows individuals to grow or cultivate up to 4 plants per household *not per* person for personal use. For individuals wishing to cultivate their own cannabis for medical purpose or designate someone to cultivate the plants on their behalf, those individuals must first register with Health Canada along with supporting medical documents.

So, does that mean Canadians can cultivate marijuana inside rental apartments? What can landlords and property managers do? If the potential grow/production site is not the intended grower's/patient's ordinary place of residence and they do not own the place, they must get consent from the landlord. This is according to section 177 (7) of the *Access to Cannabis for Medical Purposes Regulations (ACMPR)* which states, "If the proposed site for the production of marihuana plants is not the ordinary place of residence of the applicant or of the designated person, if any, and is not owned by the applicant or the designated person, the application must include the given name, surname, address and telephone number of the owner of the site and a declaration signed and dated by them consenting to production at the site."

Source: © All rights reserved. Access to Cannabis for Medical Purposes Regulations (ACMPR) Health Canada. Adapted and reproduced with permission from the Minister of Health, 2018.

The registration certificate form from Health Canada to cultivate your own cannabis for medical purpose, has a section for the property owner to sign, confirming that they are consenting to the growth or cultivation of cannabis on the premises. Therefore, the tenant is not the property owner and cannot cultivate cannabis inside the apartment without your signed consent. While the tenants have rights to reasonable enjoyment of the apartment, landlords also have legal rights and interest on how the property can be used. The tenant cannot interfere with those rights. Before landlords give consent to the cultivation of cannabis inside their apartments, they must consider how the cultivation (small or large scale) of cannabis inside apartments, can adversely affect the inside of those apartments. Let us reiterate the devastating effects of how cannabis can affect apartments.

- The plants will require a lot of water; hence the plumbing system must be altered to irrigate the plants. Sometimes the irrigation may be on a timer and will cause excess moisture resulting in:
  - mould growth.

- plaster blow-outs requiring extensive repair and painting, sometimes with the use of special paint which can be expensive.
- damaged window seals.
- excessive water consumption.
- swollen doors and door frames that will have to be replaced.
- damaged flooring.

- The electrical system must be altered to provide power to heat several special lamps resulting in:
  - excessive hydro usage from special grow lamps with bulbs ranging from 300 to 1000 watt.
  - overloading of electrical circuit which can cause fire.
  - once the tenant moves out ESA will have to be called in to do electrical inspection.

- Environmental
  - the smell (skunk-like) from the plants will emit into the hallways and possible neighbouring apartments thus interfering with the reasonable enjoyment other tenants are entitled to under the RTA.
  - you will have to contend with the possibility of high traffic to purchase cannabis.
  - vandalism from others who want to gain access to the plants.
  - once the tenants move out of the apartment the air quality will have to be tested.
  - the apartment will have to be gutted and repaired at the company's expense.

In addition to the devastating effects and knowing what to look for, state clearly in your lease or rules that are attached to your lease or tenancy agreement that tenants should not interfere with the building's plumbing or electrical system. Tenants interference can compromise applicable building code and cause flooding or fire.

If your company is not allowing the growth or cultivation of cannabis at any of their properties, that fact must be clearly stated in the lease/tenancy agreement along with the consequences for not complying. But what monitoring system can property managers and landlords use to ensure tenants are not cultivating the marijuana/cannabis inside their apartments? As the details and restrictions within each province, territory and municipality become clearer once the Act comes into force, property managers should still be on the lookout for small and large scale grow operation including the sale of marijuana inside their buildings. Therefore, as the property manager, you will have to be vigilant and consistent with your annual in-suite inspections. In between inspections, you and your staff must also know the subtle warning signs or indicators on what to look for, if a single plant or small-scale of marijuana cultivation is taking place inside your apartments.

Do not forget that we are living in a technological age, where clever inventions allow us to do things better and faster. You may enter an apartment looking for the cultivation of cannabis which may not be openly visible to the eyes. That is because tenants can cultivate the cannabis in a discreet way. Instead of being done in the open, the marijuana plants are cultivated in grow boxes/tents/

closets. The outside of some grow boxes is made of special fabric or canvas material often looking like a small portable clothing closet. The grow box comes in various sizes. Some are built to adjust in size to accommodate the growth of the plants. What you should know is that the grow box is equipped with the following to grow healthy cannabis plants:

- Lights that give off heat. The lights are called high pressure sodium lamps (HPS). There is also a timer with adjustable delay system that allows the grower to set how many hours of continuous light they want the lights to remain on throughout the day.

- The grow box is lined with special reflective material, hence there is no need for the tenant to cover their apartment windows with foil or other types of reflective materials.

- Air filter system to intake fresh air and exhaust the smell of mature budding plants, thereby eliminating or reducing the skunk-like smell associated with budding plants. It is recommended that the grow box/tent/closet be placed close to an openable window so the filter system can be vented outside through that window. From the outside this vent may look like the vent hose of a portable air conditioner (AC). You should be more suspicious if you see this vent hose in the colder weather. When in doubt check it out.

- Other features or accessories used to operate the grow tents may include humidity controller, noise reduction or air duct silencer. These accessories help to quiet the noise from any air filtering system. In case there is an apartment inspection, these features aid the grower by not drawing attention to the grow box.

If you suspect that tenants are cultivating cannabis inside your apartments, some other clues you should be looking out for during an inspection are:

- multiple potting mix.
- multiple flower pots of various sizes including hydroponic grow pots ranging from 2 to 20 gallons in size. Note well, if hydroponic pots are used you may not see potting mix. That is because the plants do not use soil, instead they are grown in liquid with added nutrients.
- ozone machine to clean the air and eliminate any lingering smell from the plants.
- air freshener or air cleaning products to neutralize the air.
- some tenants will/may tell you they are growing tomatoes or vegetables inside their grow boxes. While this could be true, the apartment is not a greenhouse so do not believe that garbage.

Regardless of how sophisticated these grow boxes may be, they still use a lot of hydro. If the plants touch the bulbs that give off heat, they could start a fire. If law enforcement officers suspect illegal cultivation of cannabis including the sale of cannabis, under the Act, police are obligated to follow and apply "normal enforcement procedures." Make sure you and your company take the necessary steps to protect and monitor your properties from tenants who wish to use your properties as a production/grow site(s).

What if tenants claim or file a Human Rights application because they are unable to grow cannabis at your properties? Would this be an infringement on their rights to reasonably access cannabis for their medical needs? You could point to the Cannabis Act allowing individuals to grow the cannabis by designating an adult to do it for them off site. You could also point to the fact that licensed producers are available and the tenant requiring the marijuana for medical purpose could obtain their supply from those producers. Do not forget that based on proven facts, the cultivation of cannabis inside apartments causes devastating damages. Make sure you consult with your legal team. What about tenants who choose to disregard your decision and grow cannabis inside their apartment? It could be that these tenants are interfering with your rights and privileges as the landlord as per sections 36 and 64 of the RTA which says,

"A tenant shall not harass, obstruct, coerce, threaten or interfere with a landlord." *Residential Tenancies Act*, 2006, c. 17, s. 36.

"A landlord may give a tenant notice of termination of the tenancy if the conduct of the tenant, another occupant of the rental unit or a person permitted in the residential complex by the tenant is such that it substantially interferes with the reasonable enjoyment of the residential complex for all usual purposes by the landlord or another tenant or substantially interferes with another lawful right, privilege or interest of the landlord or another tenant." *Residential Tenancies Act*, 2006, c. 17, s. 64 (1).

Work closely and swiftly with your legal team if you come across such cases. For that reason, the appropriate legal actions should be taken against such tenants, including eviction as per section 61 of the RTA.

> **Termination for cause, illegal act**
> 61 (1) A landlord may give a tenant notice of termination of the tenancy if the tenant or another occupant of the rental unit commits an illegal act or carries on an illegal trade, business or occupation or permits a person to do so in the rental unit or the residential complex."
>
> *Residential Tenancies Act*, 2006, c. 17, s. 61 (1).

On the other hand, there is no law restricting tenants from using cannabis inside apartments. As the property manager, you should also remember that the Cannabis Act does not diminish or negate the reasonable enjoyment that other tenants are entitled to under the RTA. Therefore, any smoking or other use of cannabis that affects other tenants who do not use cannabis, must be addressed. Hence, you will have to come up with solutions to minimize or stop the transfer or escape of smoke smell to complaining apartments.

E. Power Outage

When there is a power outage at any of your buildings, you should have backup power either from a generator or a battery source to operate the common areas in the building. Some of these areas may include the following:

- stairwells
- hallways or corridors
- underground walkways
- at least one elevator, preferably the service elevator, to accommodate any move-outs, or the equipment of first responders should anyone require medical attention

These are necessary in case the building needs to be evacuated. The National Building Code of Canada provides information on how long your backup power supply should last in your building before normal power is restored. It is very important for the generators at your building to be at least 75 percent or more fuelled at all times. It is good to have 50 percent, but 75 percent is much better. Having this much fuel allows you to provide the maximum time to meet code. The power outage may not be an emergency, but you never know when one will be. If you have a building with mostly senior residents, every power outage should be considered an emergency. The working elevator should be recalled to ensure no one is trapped inside. The other elevator should also be checked for entrapments or whatever floor it is stuck on. If tenants are stuck in the elevator, the elevator company must be called. The fire department should be called if the elevator company is not going to be on-site within 15 minutes of making the call.

Your staff should also check to see if neighbouring buildings are experiencing the power outage, both on your building's side of the street and the opposite side of the street. If it is a widespread outage, your staff should immediately call the hydro company and ascertain when power will be restored. If the outage is only confined to your building or a section of your building, still call the hydro company and inform them. They could be doing work close by and your building may be affected. If the hydro company assures your staff that everything is ok on their end, then you or your staff must contact your electrician immediately and have him or her investigate and address the problem. At this point, you must also notify your RM or AM. If the entire building has no power and the hydro company has nothing to do with the outage, chances are that the cost to repair any issue will be above your bracket of authority.

F. Catastrophic Events: Explosion, Bomb Threat or Terrorism

We live in a fast-changing world and must adapt to how we should respond to the changes and challenges that present themselves. As property managers, some other emergencies that we will face may be different from what we are accustomed to hearing about or handling. Since terrorism in its many forms, from an active shooter to a bomb threat, is on the rise in different countries, both building/site staff and property managers must know what to do if a terrorist attack should ever happen. Schools and other institutions have more than the regular fire drill these days. They now include lockdown drills or active shooter drills as part of their emergency plans. Hence, property management companies should also get with the program. Remember the best way to handle any emergency is to prepare for that emergency. This preparation can take the following forms:

- Have local police do a lockdown drill and training at one of your staff meetings, either an individual property staff meeting or combined staff meeting, to indicate what to do in the event of a bomb threat or active shooter.

- Be prepared to travel to your main office and provide information to law enforcement to aid in their investigation. At one location, the building was put on lockdown because a man went to the door of an apartment with a gun and threatened to shoot. The police requested the staff to contact me for information. That information had to be retrieved from my office. I also had to provide video footage from the building's surveillance camera to aid in the investigation.

The following are excerpts from the San Diego County Apartment Association's "Emergency Response Plan Model for Apartment Buildings," March 27, 2002:

In the event of any injury, follow Company procedures for reporting injury.

Explosion
In the event of an explosion in a/the building, employees and residents should take the following actions:

1. Take cover that will give protection from flying glass or debris.
2. Notify the Fire Department. * (Dial 911)
3. Notify Site Emergency Coordinator.
4. After the effects of the explosion have subsided the Site Emergency Coordinator will determine if evacuation is necessary.
5. Upon leaving the building, proceed to assembly area(s) and await instructions.
6. Make certain building is secured if the order is given to vacate the premises.

* Provide the following information:

1. Name of the property.
2. The Building's address and nearest cross street.
3. The floor number, unit number.
4. Describe the condition clearly and accurately.

7. *Don't hang up!* Let the person you are talking to, end the conversation. Other information may be needed.

Bomb Threat

If a bomb threat is received by *phone*, use the Bomb Threat Checklist and attempt to get information from the caller by asking:

When is the bomb going to explode?

1. Where is the bomb right now?
2. What does it look like?
3. What kind of bomb is it?
4. What will cause it to explode?

Try to keep the caller on the phone as long as possible!

Using the attached Bomb Threat Checklist, record the following information:

1. Time of call.
2. Date of call.
3. Exact words of person.
4. Age, sex, adult or child.
5. Speech pattern, accent.
6. Background noises.

Employees receiving a bomb threat should then notify the Site Emergency Coordinator.

If a bomb threat is received by *mail* the employee should:

1. Not handle the letter, envelope or package.
2. Notify the Site Emergency Coordinator.
3. Site Emergency Coordinator will preserve the evidence for law enforcement officials.

When a bomb threat is received! ! !

1. Be *calm* and *courteous*, Do not interrupt the caller.
2. If possible notify someone else by prearranged signal to listen in on the conversation while the caller is on the line.
3. Keep the caller on the line as long as possible. Ask him/her to repeat the message. Record every word spoken by the caller. Ask the caller why he/she is doing this and ask the caller their name ... they may just tell you.
4. If the caller does not indicate the location of the bomb or the time of possible detonation, you should ask him/her for this information.
5. Inform the caller that the building is occupied and the detonation of a bomb could result in death or serious injury to many innocent persons.
6. Pay particular attention to peculiar background noises such as motors running, background music and any other noise which may give a clue as to the location of the caller.

7. Listen closely to the voice (male, female), voice quality (calm, excited), accents and speech impediments. Immediately after the caller hangs up, fill out the form and then report to the person designated by management to receive such information. Since Law Enforcement personnel will want to talk firsthand with the person who received the call, they should remain available until officers arrive.
8. Report this information immediately by dialing 9-1-1.

If a suspicious object is discovered the employee should:

1. Never attempt to touch, move or open the object.
2. Notify Site Emergency Coordinator.
3. If a decision is made to evacuate the area/building, everyone should keep calm and *all* employees should search their immediate work area prior to exiting the building.
4. Attempt to find possible owner of object.
5. Await further instructions from law enforcement officials.

Source: http://www.sdcaa.com/uploads/3/8/5/1/38511575/emergency_response_ plan_model_for_apartment_buildings.pdf. Reproduced with permission of San Diego County Apartment Association, 2017.

G. On-the-Go Personal Emergency Kit/Bag

It is very important that you are prepared for your own personal emergencies. Your job as a property manager entails travelling in favourable seasons and troublesome seasons alike. Make sure you have a personal survival kit in your vehicle. You can get one of these "go bags" online or make one to your liking or preference. If you were to get stranded on the road, what would you need to survive until help reached you, either within a few hours or the next day? Some things you may want to keep in your bag or keep in your vehicle are as follows:

- bottled water
- protein bars
- first aid kit, fully stocked
- socks
- heavy shoes in case it is cold and snowing and you must leave the vehicle
- warmer clothes for the winter
- matches and lighter
- candle in a jar
- flashlight with battery
- raincoat
- whistle to blow for help
- umbrella (small)

- blanket (small)
- warm gloves
- surgical gloves
- comb and brush
- mirror
- lip balm
- toothbrush and toothpaste
- pocket tissue
- underwear, 3–6 pairs
- feminine napkins, 6–12, or tampons with applicator
- warm jacket
- small amount of cash ($50–$100) in small notes. Hide this away in some pocket. If anyone breaks into your vehicle, it should take them a long time to find it—or they should never find it.
- cellphone charger and cellphone charger pack in case your car battery goes dead
- a small bucket and some bin liners. Yes! Just in case you must "go," you will need to "go" in something. You may be laughing now, but you will not be laughing if you must use this bucket.

NB: Be sure to replace items that are expired and always keep items up-to-date. Put a reminder on your cellphone to prompt you to replace the expired items. Make sure this bag is a backpack. If you must leave the vehicle, you can carry the bag on your back, leaving your hands free to do other things.

Emergencies in their various forms will happen; therefore, make sure you are *prepared* to deal with them. If you do not know what to do in an emergency, it can cause chaos. Have you ever noticed that individuals who have certain allergies carry their medications with them? That is being prepared for an allergic attack. Your vehicle has a spare tire and jumper cables. You may even have roadside assistance. All these are preparation for normal everyday emergencies. Ask yourself as a property manager, *How prepared am I to handle any emergency at any of my properties?* Get the necessary training and know the procedures of your company. In addition, check your municipal Web site or their office and familiarize yourself with the emergency plan they have. Remember being prepared is the best way to handle any emergency.

Interdepartmental Relationships

If managing your staff is like commercial parenting, then the other departments within the company are like your brothers and sisters. Therefore, these departments will be the aunts and uncles to your staff. Learn to work with each of these departments. They form part of your support system and are the soft tools or behind-the-scene teams helping to make things happen. They may be required to report to you on some level. Your good interaction with other departments will increase your knowledge and make it easier for you to do your job as an excellent property manager. Your reputation will precede you. Before long, others will know about you and feel comfortable working with you. The ability to work with other departments will help you connect with your staff and your boss. Most importantly, it will show up in the good results you get.

Approach each department with a win–win team attitude. The purpose of your interaction should always be to enhance that department in its role. Make the employees of that department look good and they will make you look even better. This will manifest itself in your overall function. Remember that in an earlier chapter we learned how some of the birds at the Hamilton Waterfront Trail assist in the grooming of each other, a process referred to as "social grooming." In the human world, we may have other sayings to describe it, such as "One hand washes the other" or "You scratch my back and I'll scratch yours." Regardless of what you call it, this practice of assisting each other helps to build relationships and strengthen bonds. When others sense this in you, their respect for you will grow. They will support you effortlessly, will look out for you and sometimes will take a personal interest in your buildings and your staff. Depending on the season or time of the year and rent cycle, you will utilize one department more than the other.

A. Area Manager (AM) or Regional Manager (RM)

This is the individual to whom you directly report. You must first try to understand yourself and your management style. Your second priority is to seek to understand your AM/RM as a person and come to know his or her management and leadership style. In your quest to understand this individual, observe what is not communicated verbally. Sometimes non-verbal communication is even more important than what is spoken. Seeking to understand your boss is an ongoing process. Remember too that your boss is also trying to understand who you are. Once you have a proper understanding of who this individual is, it will position you to adapt to his or her direction and oversight. If you are not sure about your AM's or RM's style, ask him or her what it is.

I recommend meeting with your area or regional manager at least once per week. This meeting is different from any designated operational/board meetings the company holds. Use your meeting to update your boss on the following:

A. projects you may need assistance with or the status of such projects
B. any concerns, visits or infractions from any regulatory body
C. staffing concerns you may be having
D. any critical concern you may be experiencing with a particular tenant
E. any other topic you feel comfortable discussing with your AM or RM

Clear communication is very important to have and maintain with your AM. Therefore, if you are going to start your day at any of your properties instead of starting the day at your home office, you must notify your AM of this. If you tell your AM you are at your properties, make sure that is where you are. If you are going to a personal appointment, someone should know. Remember you are still on the job and on the company's time. If you are not going to be at work because of sickness, you must also notify your boss by e-mail, phone call or text message. This shows respect, keeps the channel of communication open and transparent, and maintains your image as an excellent property manager. If you have critical tasks to address on the day(s) you are off sick, these should be clearly communicated to your AM, thereby allowing any contingency plan to kick in for smooth operation until you return. Your professional relationship with your AM/RM is very important and must be maintained. If decisions are made in your portfolio that you are not in agreement with, respectfully voice your opinion and offer your support. Don't forget that you can be uncomfortable and still be effective.

B. Fire and Life Safety

All departments are important, but you should make this department your priority, even if the services of the Life Safety Specialist is outsourced or contracted through the fire equipment company. There is no season with this department. This department consist of life safety specialists (LSS). The LSS knows the ins and outs of all your properties. LSS staff are at your buildings once every month and sometimes more than once a month. Your staff have some direct aspect of reporting to this department. Develop a trust factor with this department to the point where they will share any concerns about your buildings or staff with you first. Gain their trust and confidence by seeing the buildings through their eyes. Do not take personally anything they point out to you or bring to your attention. Work with them, be humble and ask for assistance when necessary. The best way to do this is by showing genuine interest. Demonstrate interest by conducting a full building audit or inspection with the LSS when he or she is scheduled to be at one of your buildings. Such an audit or inspection consists of doing the following:

• Ring the bells.
• Learn where the pull stations are and what defects to look for.

- Walk the hallways and stairwells. Check fire cabinets and garbage chutes.
- Learn how to check doors, especially fire separation doors.
- Walk the underground garage.
- Visit all the utility rooms such as the sprinkler room, elevator room and generator room.
- Observe how to recall the elevator in the different phases and know the importance of these phases.
- Know what to look for when you sign logbooks. Ensure your staff are filling them out. You can also initial to indicate you have checked the logbooks.

Regardless of what the inspection reveals, end on a good note. Remember you want to do more inspections with the Fire and Life Safety department. You want them to come to you first about any deficiencies at your properties. These inspections will give you great insight into what your staff are doing and what they are not doing. Immediately address any report given to you by the Fire and Life Safety department about any of your buildings or staff. Discuss any quotes given to you by the fire equipment company with your life safety specialist. The LSS may be able to negotiate price, determine if a repair is necessary or determine the urgency of the repair. If you receive an infraction or order from the fire department, make sure you forward a copy to the LSS. Do not just leave it with them. Work with the LSS assiduously to correct those infractions. If you notice any discrepancies in staff performance regarding preventative maintenance, discuss the matter and arrange further training with this department for the staff in question.

If you audit one building in your portfolio each quarter with the Fire and Life Safety department, it will sharpen your skills and train your eyes to allow you to become a high-performing property manager. This knowledge will help you to do the following:

1. Build a close professional bond with the Fire and Life Safety department.
2. Conduct thorough building inspections because your eyes are trained.
3. Interact better with your staff because you understand the work they do and the physical demands that are part and parcel of their work.
4. Interact better with the fire department, either during emergencies or when they conduct random inspections at your buildings. You will know their language and jargon. The fire department will also develop a respect for you.
5. Have better insight when you sign invoices related to fire equipment and service calls.

Also, your staff will see the interest you have taken in this aspect of the operation and will know they cannot play around because you understand their work and know what to look for.

C. Heating, Ventilation and Air Conditioning (HVAC)

Your need for and interaction with this department will vary according to the weather and temperature outside. You will call this department when apartments at any of your buildings are too cold because of freezing temperatures outside, when the air conditioning unit you supply to the building is broken and it is scorching hot outside or when your tenants have no hot water. HVAC will help you to maintain some vital services as required by law. HVAC tries to maintain a level of thermal comfort inside the buildings. While thermal comfort is subjective, meaning only you can determine how warm or hot you are, each building must have equipment that are able to operate and maintain a minimum temperature as required by law. During the cold weather know the bylaw for the minimum heat in each city where you have properties. Your failure to maintain the minimum heat permitted by law inside the apartments may result in infractions from the city. If this happens, the city may post a copy of the infraction (Notice of Non-Compliance) on the main entrance door of the building for all to see. Oftentimes, this will stir up or incite other tenants in the building to make complaints about the temperature. This is a headache you do not want.

Learn from the HVAC department the same way you learn from Fire and Life Safety. Spend some time with them at one of your buildings. Your training should take place in a familiar setting so you will be more apt to remember what was taught or said to you. HVAC will go to your buildings on a needs-analysis or as-needed basis. They may not be at your buildings as regularly as Fire and Life Safety, unless they are conducting quarterly or seasonal routine maintenance or working on a special project. You may have to book a special time with them to accommodate you at one of your buildings.

Try to have a basic understanding of the make-up air unit (MAU) at your buildings. The make-up air unit is installed on the roof. The make-up air unit draws fresh air from outside and pressurizes or pumps air into the hallways. When you walk the hallways/corridors of your buildings regardless of the time of year, what is the air quality like in the hallway? Is the air quality comfortable? The air travels through ducts and comes out through the grills on the walls on each floor. If you cannot feel the air coming through the grills, you should contact your HVAC technician who will address the issue. Learn about the different boilers for domestic hot water and for heating the building. If you have more than one boiler room, know their locations and which zone(s) or section(s) of the building they service or operate. You should also learn about the different heating pumps and chillers at your buildings. Discover what buildings have central air and central heating with temperature control capability. Do you know what buildings in your portfolio use baseboard radiators for heating?

I remember one tenant called to inform me she was taking us to the Landlord and Tenant Board (LTB) because she had no heat coming from the vent in her apartment. I knew her building very well and confidently brought to her attention that baseboard radiators heated her building. When I asked her to give me the location of the vents, I realized she was referring to the exhaust vents in the bathroom and kitchen. The purpose of those vents were to remove air. I asked her if I could have the staff come check and help her to get proper heat flow in the apartment. She agreed. Since section 26 of the Residential Tenancies Act says that 24-Hour Notice of Entry must be given or, in its absence, consent to enter must be given by the tenant, I informed the staff of the tenant's consent.

Entry without notice

Entry without notice, emergency, consent
26: (1) A landlord may enter a rental unit at any time without written notice,

(a) in cases of emergency; or

(b) if the tenant consents to the entry at the time of entry."

(*Residential Tenancies Act*, 2006, c. 17, s. 26 [1].)

The staff immediately went to the unit and the tenant allowed them in. The staff saw where the tenant's furniture were touching the radiator. The staff advised the tenant to pull the furniture 12 inches away, which increased the heat flow immediately. The tenant was thrilled and apologized. Knowing this information immediately resolved a concern and saved an unnecessary trip to the LTB.

D. Central Rental (CR)

The vacancy level of the apartments within your portfolio will determine the frequency and intensity of your interaction with this department. If you want heads and beds in your buildings, you must forge an unbreakable bond with the rental department. Go to them; do not wait for them to come to you. Discuss any changes in rent for vacant or upcoming vacant units at any of your buildings. If this department does the marketing and promotion of the apartments, make sure you inform CR of any promotions or incentives you want to implement at your properties. Let them know you are open to suggestions. Your close relationship with this department will make it easier for them to understand your thought process and increase their willingness to help you.

Central rental is most likely the department that will process applications of prospective tenants applying for apartments at your buildings. Investigate to ensure they are receiving accurate paperwork from your buildings. Get the names of the staff involved so the proper help and training can be given to those staff members. Arrange with central rental for the staff in question to do any shadowing or observation in the central rental department to improve their skills. The best time to make this arrangement happen is in the middle of the month, once the month-end and beginning-of-the-month cycle of activities are over. Since this arrangement will affect coverage at the building or community where the staff member works, you will need proper co-ordination and co-operation from the other building staff to make this happen. It will benefit all involved and, by extension, benefit the company. If the staff doing the training or shadowing speaks English as a second language, more than one day of training may be required.

If your staff attend any scheduled training with the rental or central rental department, always follow up with the individual who conducted the training. To gain a clearer understanding, you should also ask the staff who attended the training to relate how they have benefitted. This shows genuine interest and will also put you in a position to better understand and interact with the staff when you are at the building.

If you are going to have an open house at one of your buildings, discuss the event with central rental. If this department does your marketing and advertising, they may need to advertise the event for you and give you a sense of what has worked at other locations. If you are offering incentives at different locations or for certain units, let central rental know about this promotion as well. Do not be afraid to ask for help with and suggestions for units you are having difficulty with. Again, CR may give you insight into what has worked at your location in the past if they have been employed by the company longer than you have. Make their job and your job easier through collaborative work. You will have more heads and beds in your buildings, thus eliminating lost revenue in your portfolio.

E. Construction and Property Standards

The projects and the nature of the projects at your buildings will determine the level, depth and length of interaction you will have with this department. During the different phases of projects in your portfolio, you may have to attend start-up meetings or progress meetings being held at your buildings. Your presence and the presence of your staff at these meetings is critical. You will learn how the project will impact the lives of tenants and the operations of the building. This will call for some temporary measures and adjustments. Even though you may not be overseeing the projects done by the construction and property standards department, the projects are happening in your building(s). Hence, you and your staff will get any calls from unhappy tenants. Work closely with the construction crew to minimize the disruption to tenants and to manage tenant stress. Great teamwork will accomplish the job at hand regardless of the size and duration of the projects. When the construction department senses your desire to help, they will be able to focus on the arduous renovation project they have. Some of the projects they may oversee at your buildings are as follows:

- underground parking restoration
- balcony restoration and the replacement railing systems
- window and balcony door installations
- roof repair or replacement
- wall repair or replacement
- foundation repair
- other construction-related repairs or work

    o hire and monitor subcontractors
    o plan and prepare construction schedules
    o investigate technical problems reported by staff, tenant complaints or through scheduled maintenance to keep building in compliance with applicable building code
    o obtain relevant permits and approvals from local municipality and other external agencies as required by law

These projects are not quick fixes, and the impact on the lives of the tenants can take its toll and bring out the worst in your tenants. Always keep tenants informed. Since they are the ones living through the renovations or projects, listen to your tenants and amend your notices when legally necessary to reflect anything that is pointed out to you that you may have overlooked. I remember one tenant called to inform me that the notice did not say that dust was associated with the work and her apartment was full of dust. I thanked the tenant and apologized for the inconveniences caused. I also pointed out that the current notice stated our apologies for any inconveniences caused. Therefore, dust would fall under "any inconveniences caused." The tenant said the notice should be specific. I agreed, thanked the tenant again and then revised the notice to include "Dust is associated with this project. Tenants may wish to close their windows and/or cover their furniture while the project is being done." The following day the tenant called to express thanks for the revised notice that was posted. I also thanked the tenant for her input.

Other projects done by this department may come about as a result of tenants' complaints, your staff's suggestions or your building inspections. For example, a tenant may call to say the roof leaks every time it rains. Investigation by your staff may reveal they cannot locate the source of the leak. Hence, you will have to contact your property standards department and ask them to conduct their own investigation. After their investigation, they may conclude the leak is the result of damaged bricks allowing water to penetrate. Depending on the location of the damaged bricks, the repair itself can be costly. The ripple effects of this repair can be as follows:

- A swing stage may have to be installed.
- A general notice will have to be posted to inform of work that may include dust, noise, or blind or curtain closure for the affected risers.
- Vehicles below the area to be worked on will have to be temporarily relocated to another parking area until the project is completed.
- Any fenced-off area may limit access to the building or certain sections of the property.
- Remove and replace the damaged bricks or section of the wall
- You may have to do cosmetic repairs on the interior wall.

If you are not sure what areas will be affected, ask how the work will affect the tenants and what repairs you may have to do that are not covered by the construction and property standards department. Never leave out the input or contribution of your staff.

F. Legal Administration

This is your big brother or big sister department, always ready to defend you and protect you from harm. To understand how this department can best assist you, make it a habit to read and understand the lease or tenancy agreement that your company or region uses. If you are in Ontario, the lease you should be using is the standard lease which came into effect on April 30, 2018. Most individual landlords and apartment management companies in Ontario, are now required by law to use the standard lease.

The core of any lease should reflect the Residential Tenancies Act (RTA). You can also review the RTA or applicable local laws in your area to better understand your rights since you represent the landlord, which is your company. You must also know the rights of the tenants and manage in such a way that you do not infringe on those rights. Your interaction with the legal department will be on a case-by-case basis, as will the accounts receivable balance at your buildings. Accounts receivable is usually referred to as "AR."

From time to time you must meet with the legal administrator who heads the legal department to review outstanding rent balances and make recommendations on what further action should be taken on certain expired documents that were served. For chronic late payers, I recommend the use of the N8 to get them to pay on time. You and your staff will have to monitor closely tenants who have been served N5 notices to see if they make any violations and determine the necessary follow-up steps to take.

Any incident that takes place at any of your properties should be clearly documented so the legal department can file the necessary documents. You should also practise making and keeping excellent notes in your tenant file or message book. This will be of great support to the legal department when the time arises. Instill this level of commitment in your staff to write reports or take notes about tenants. Their simple and clearly written reports of any incidents that occur will speak volumes. Both you and your staff will be of great support to the legal department. The department will also develop a level of respect for you, for your reliable information and for your staff.

Any legal action that you would like to take place should be supported with proper evidence either through pictures, notes, forms or eyewitness reports, and/or eyewitnesses' willingness to attend court and testify. If the legal administrator(s) must go to the LTB to defend or present a case regarding any of your buildings, be prepared to attend in whatever capacity you are asked. Bear in mind that if you must attend, the process can sometimes be quite lengthy, taking up your entire day. Depending on the location and setup of the tenant court, take along work that you can do while you are waiting. Sometimes these cases may be conducted in a designated room, at a local library with easy parking and quick access to the building. If that is the situation, use your vehicle for an office and do some work until you are called or needed. Some of the work you can do is as follows:

1. Respond to e-mails.
2. Return tenant calls.
3. Sign off on invoices.
4. Write letters.
5. Write performance evaluations.
6. Call contractors and follow up on projects.
7. Or you can choose to review the case material you are there about if you need to refresh your memory. Chances are, you may not need to refresh your memory because you would have already done your preparation with the legal department and your staff.

By doing work inside your vehicle while you are waiting, you make the time pass and are less likely to feel unproductive. You may even be surprised to see the amount of work you get accomplished.

In other instances, the nature of the case may call for all the staff at one of your properties to attend court. Hence, you must arrange coverage for that location. In the same breath, staff who were transferred to another location, either outside or within your portfolio, may need to attend the same hearing at the tenant court. If that be the situation, you must arrange with the property manager for whom that staff person now works, for him or her to attend court, or make arrangements with the building manager if the staff member is still in your portfolio but at a different location.

What if all your staff from one location must attend court? Try your best to use an existing staff from another property to cover the property, even if they are not within your portfolio. The existing staff from the other building will be familiar with the company practice or policy regarding emergencies or regular work routine. This will give you and your staff peace of mind while you are at court. If that cannot happen, you may have to hire outside help for the day. Where possible, request a worker who is already familiar with the property.

Other circumstances for which you can utilize the services of legal administration are when you need to have certain notices or letters written. Legal administration can also review with you, certain letters you have written before they are mailed to the recipients. If you have buildings where rent collection is a challenge, invite legal administration to one of your staff meetings. Allow the legal administrator to speak to and motivate your staff and share tips for door knocking and collecting rent. If you can get assistance with the actual door knocking, that would be great. For buildings where you have a problem with pests, such as cockroaches or bedbugs, use the legal department to assist you in getting tenants to comply with the treatments. If any tenant fails to comply, use the legal system to your advantage and evict them where you can. If these tenants are physically and mentally capable of preparing for treatments, serve N5 notices and have no regrets in serving them. Bedbugs bite, and they can turn your life upside down. This will send a message to the tenants that (1) you are fulfilling your legal obligation by addressing the problem and (2) you are no-nonsense and vigilant. Serving N5 notices does not make you heartless; it means you are practical. One non-complying tenant can intensify the infestation, make your effort futile and drive the good tenants out of the building, leaving you stuck with a vacancy issue. In addition, contractors will refuse to work in your buildings for fear of taking any bugs home with them.

Work with this big brother or big sister department to clean up your buildings if tenants are behaving badly. This will take a lot of effort to write incident reports and act swiftly in serving appropriate legal documents to all involved. This was preached and practised at one location where the older teenage children of tenants and their occupants who disrupted the reasonable enjoyment of the other tenants were evicted. In fact, this was the location where the annual in-suite inspection caused us to rethink the vision of the property. Part of this rethinking strategy was to first identify who the gang members were and then to document every disruptive activity on property. We knew who were causing the destruction, but we had to catch them in the act—and they were famous for running away after they caused mischief. To catch them in the act, I fixed all the cameras and upgraded the DVR.

I remember after one major lobby fight that caused major damage resulting in thousands of dollars to repair the elevator. The staff printed still photos from the lobby camera to show all who were involved in the big fight. After printing the pictures, the staff identified each person in the picture, stated who his or her parents were and mentioned to which apartment he or she belonged. A call was made to the police to ascertain if No Trespassing letters could be sent since the perpetrators were all teenagers and considered minors. The police stated that the letter could be written naming the teenagers in question but must be addressed to the parents and sent by registered mail. They also said a copy of the letter should be sent to their station and a copy should be kept on the property. With that information, No Trespassing letters were sent to every parent of the teenagers identified in the picture. The letter forbade those teenagers from going to the other buildings in the community. They could only stay inside their building and not visit the other buildings. If they wanted to meet, they were free to do so off the property. The parents were very upset, but I had sent many warning letters and legal documents before about the behaviour of their children/occupants. These occupants were out of control, causing vandalism to the property by doing the following things:

1. smashing the glass of the fire cabinets
2. ripping off the stairwell number signs and hallway directional signs
3. setting small fires in the stairwells
4. painting graffiti at different locations
5. smoking marijuana/pot/ganja in the stairwells
6. leaving human feces in the stairwell
7. engaging in horseplay and inappropriate behaviour in the lobby, stairwell and garage

These kinds of behaviours were chasing good tenants away from the property. N5 notices were even issued for many incidents, but the parents of these young adults were so skilled at beating the system that it was almost impossible to hold them responsible. I had done my due diligence. The fight and elevator damage was the breaking point. In addition to those letters, N5 notices were issued to the parents of the teenagers for the elevator damages. Those who could not afford to pay for the repairs moved out. Making use of the Crime-Free Program is an approach I probably could have used. However, I was not aware of this program. The No Trespass letter was the tool I was familiar with, and it proved effective in this case. Please discuss any No Trespass letter you wish to issue with your AM and legal department first. Though your intentions are good in issuing one, you want to be sure you are within your legal rights to do so without any repercussions. Crime-Free Program is further discussed in the chapter titled Government Organizations and Regulatory Bodies, section C: Police Department.

The last of those teenage / young adult gang members left when she hit one of my staff. Can you believe that? What made the matter complicated was that the staff member defended herself. Some tenants were calling for the dismissal of that staff person. When I heard about the incident and watched it on the DVR from the lobby camera, I was as furious as a mama grizzly bear. This disruptive occupant had assaulted *my staff*. After watching the video footage of the incident, I told the staff in question that I would not support a decision to terminate her employment, even though the final decision was not left up to me. I did inform the AM and made it very clear that I wanted to keep my staff. This was saving her job, yes. I wanted her to remain at the same property because she brought order and energy to the property. In addition, I wanted those tenants responsible evicted fast for assaulting my staff. On file at that time was a previous and active N5 that had been served. Finally, the last offending teenager was evicted. Other tenants thanked the staff and expressed their relief that the property had been ridded of the gang. It was worth the time and everything that went into it. Those tenants almost drained the staff of physical and mental energy. This level of success was not achieved by the work of one person; it was a collaborative effort that took a lot of time. For that I threw a celebration as a way of rewarding everyone involved.

The breaking up of the gang and the eviction of the gang members impacted the community in numerous positive ways. When the buildings were finally cleared of those tenants and their disruptive occupants, other tenants expressed how safe and happy they felt. Tenants who had moved out because of the disruptive tenants and their young adults were returning. Upgrades could be done without fear of vandalism. This completely changed the tenant base. I enjoyed pushing the rent at turnover to its highest amount and having room for an even greater increase. Over a five-year period, the rent for vacant apartments went up 86 percent. This is no exaggeration. We added value to the product by creating a safe environment. This also gave us a lot of wiggle room to play with the rent. It was shared beauty, using the rent maps and watching the leap in the net operating income (NOI).

The ripple effect of this cleanup was later expressed about two years afterward by the police. The police department commended us and asked what we'd done to rid the buildings of the problem-causing troublemaker tenants. They were happy that they were receiving fewer calls to the location and that their job was becoming easier, allowing them to focus on other aspects of policing. Their commendation took us by complete surprise, as we had no idea that our efforts would also benefit the police.

G. Accounting

You will work with this department very often and more so toward the end of each month when tenants are moving out of or into apartments. Start out with this department by knowing what deadlines they must meet and what documents they will need from you to meet those deadlines. Honour the deadlines given to you. To close off any tenant account, accounting will need all move-out reports or inspections from apartments that are vacating. You should receive one of those move-out reports from all the apartments moving out in your portfolio. To ensure you have those reports, it is best to have a list of the apartments moving out arranged by building. Contact the building managers of those buildings ahead of time and emphasize the urgency of those reports. As soon as you receive those reports, cross them off your list and forward them to accounting. Keep doing this until you have sent all the reports on your list.

Notify accounting of any chargebacks related to damages caused by tenants, their occupants (which may include children or pets) and/or their guests. You should also be specific with the accounting department when requesting refunds for tenants. Any refund request should state why the refund is being made, and a note to this effect should be left in the tenant's file. From time to time, tenants will request a decrease of or freeze in their rent increase after they receive the Notice of Rent Increase. Usually tenants who are experiencing financial hardship will make this type of request. You are not obligated by law to grant such a request. Your approval of this request is based purely on compassion. Remember—no tenant is entitled to having such a request granted, and if the request was granted last year or this year, it does not guarantee an automatic approval for the next request. Some factors to consider before approving a freeze on the rent increase or a reduction in the rent increase are as follows:

1. Is the increase due to an above guideline increase (AGI)? If it is, it should not be approved.
2. What is the current market rent? If the rent paid by the tenant making the request is below the market value, you may decide not to grant his or her request.
3. Is the tenant in good standing? Is the account always paid on time?
4. What is the housekeeping condition of the apartment?
5. Who is the tenant? Is he or she a mischief-maker?

If you decide to reduce or freeze the rent, be sure to state what the new amount for the increase should be. Once approval for the decrease is processed, forward the new amount to accounting and follow up until completed. Then the tenant should be informed in writing before the new rent takes effect, and the tenant file should be updated.

Accounting works with date-sensitive documents and procedures. Therefore, any paperwork received from accounting should be completed rapidly. This includes accounts payable and accounts receivable documents. Your accounting department should never have to chase after you for any report or document. Work with them and gain their trust and support.

H. Training Department

The purpose of the training department is to help you increase the performance of the staff in your portfolio. Your interaction with the training co-ordinator/facilitator who conducts the training will be dependent on the buildings and the staffing needs within your portfolio. Most times, the training co-ordinator will approach you and ask you to select participants from your portfolio when large training sessions need to be held either for new hires, new methods of doing a procedure or required refresher training. However, try to be proactive by sending a list of the staff you want to be trained, and specify the area of training. This approach will make the co-ordinator think of you first when large training sessions are being planned. This is an approach you should develop over time that will serve you well.

Before you interview any new staff or make an offer to potential staff, meet with the training co-ordinator and predetermine a start date. The date should take into consideration the activities at the building where the new staff will be assigned so the staff being trained can devote their full mental faculties, without interruption. Confirm the date in writing via e-mail. This arrangement will allow for proper planning to conduct orientation of new staff in the new role. At some point, you may also meet with the new hires and get a sense of what they are learning. You should also meet with the training co-ordinator/facilitator, who can sometimes give you feedback about the attitude and approach of the new hires. This feedback should serve as any alerts or red flags regarding the new hires. Do not forget that Work Attitude is a category on the performance evaluation in the chapter titled Staffing.

As you interact with all your staff, you will come to know and understand who needs training and for what purpose. Always inform your staff of any mandatory training you are planning or have planned for them. Explain why you think they need the training and when it should be done. One comment normally voiced when you recommend further training is "I already know how to do that." You can mention that it is great that the staff member has some idea of how to do the procedure. The company believes in continuous improvement for all staff and that policy dictates the procedure must be done the company's way. Every burger restaurant makes its burger its own special way. Another comment you may hear is "I don't like how the training co-ordinator does the training." While the latter comment could be true, be careful how you probe for answers. Ask the staff to be more specific about what he or she does not like. This could reveal a weakness in the delivery of the training co-ordinator. Investigate tactfully if other staff are commenting and have the same concern. Or perhaps the problem is a reluctance on the part of the staff. That is why it is very important to follow up with your staff after each training. A simple question to ask is "How was the training?" The staff will either elaborate or say "good," "ok" or "bad." Whatever response you get, always ask follow-up questions such as "What was good [or ok or bad] about the training?"

Do not forget that the training co-ordinator/facilitator is there to assist you. If you do not see any improvement in the performance of the staff who were trained, suggest to the training co-ordinator/facilitator to implement a buddy or mentoring system. This system allows another, experienced staff member to participate in the training as a mentor to the staff who needs the training. Sell the mentoring idea to your staff so they can be more at ease and receive the training with the proper mindset. Once the training is completed, the employee file should be updated.

Depending on the responsibilities of the training co-ordinator, his or her duties may involve health and safety training or inspection. Learn how a health and safety inspection is conducted and what you should be looking for. If there is a committee, get involved and train your eyes. This will put you in a position to better spot potential safety concerns within your portfolio and repair any problems in a timely manner. Any health and safety inspection assigned to you must be completed with urgency. Action dates to correct the defects may be extremely time-sensitive. You can also sign up with the Ministry of Labour (MOL) to receive their newsletter on health and safety. The MOL also offers courses that you can take to broaden your knowledge on the subject. If you are an average property manager, you do not need to know all this. However, an excellent property manager knows that this information is crucial to his or her growth. An excellent property manager will make the time and embrace this new opportunity. Health and safety is further discussed in the chapter titled Building Maintenance, under the subheading *Repairs from Health and Safety Inspections.*

Do you notice your rental office lacks some level of organization? Arrange for the training co-ordinator to visit that location and demonstrate to the staff by working with them to organize the office. The training co-ordinator should not tell the staff what to do but should show the staff and work with the staff on how to organize the office. This will ensure things are properly done and the staff know exactly what they should do. Once the training is completed, spot-check when you get to the building to ensure the staff are maintaining the office the way it should be kept. You can check by asking simple questions such as "Can I have a look at your parking log and receipt book?" You might say, "I need to quickly review something on my rent-roll." When the staff retrieve these items, notice from where they are taken. You can observe as the staff deal with tenants who come in to the rental office for information. Always commend the staff on any improvement after training. Follow up with the training co-ordinator, mentioning what you have observed. Thank the training co-ordinator/facilitator for the training given, as it is really to increase efficiency in your portfolio.

Another area where you can utilize the training co-ordinator's assistance is in the purchasing of certain tools and equipment for staff to do their work. The training co-ordinator can recommend or help to source special tools and equipment. In addition to learning how to source and purchase tools and equipment, the staff will have to be trained on how to use and care for these special tools and equipment. Some of this equipment may be floor machines or outdoor motorized equipment. Arrange for initial training and any refresher training needed by any of your staff at all or various locations within your portfolio. Always get feedback from your staff regarding the use and effectiveness of the new tools and equipment purchased. Remember your staff should always feel you have their backs and their best interests at heart. If there are issues with the equipment or tools in terms of function and use, follow up with the training co-ordinator, and if necessary your supplier, to have your concerns addressed.

When it is time to write performance evaluation for your staff, this is also a good time to contact the training co-ordinator. Meet with the trainer and get his or her perspective on the staff being evaluated. At this point you are gathering information and do not have to show the co-ordinator what you have written. You will want to know if the staff being reviewed has/have completed all the recommended training. You can also discuss any new training you are considering for this staff. Do not confirm any dates with the training co-ordinator, because the staff being reviewed may request some training of their own. Therefore, book all new training after you have discussed the performance review with the staff being reviewed. Since the co-ordinator tends to be busy, make notes regarding the staff in question as the co-ordinator/facilitator speaks to you. You can even have the co-ordinator/facilitator type the information as you both speak. That way you do not have to wait for his or her notes in order to complete your performance evaluation. If you have to make the notes yourself, you can later confirm your discussion in an e-mail and ask for any clarification. Follow up with a call, or physically go to the facilitator's department/office. Show a sense of urgency and you will get things done based on your time. As soon as the performance review is approved for discussion with the staff being reviewed and you have met with that staff, arrange all training in writing with the trainer. Be sure to copy your area manager or regional manager and human resources department. The sooner the training date(s) is/are arranged, the better for all. Training done without delay helps staff to grow in their role, as they will get more time to put into practice what they have learned.

I. Human Resources (HR)

Your interaction with HR will be on a case-by-case, needs-analysis basis. You will interact with HR according to individual staffing needs within your portfolio. Attending to staffing issues and concerns can eat up your time and leave you very little energy to get anything else done. When you are at the buildings, you can connect with and understand your staff to find out what they want or are not doing. All the actions are carried out at the buildings, so that is where you should be. When you have a strong awareness of what is happening at each of your buildings, then HR is better poised to assist you.

i.   Note to File

To save yourself time and energy, make it your aim to take exceptional notes regarding staffing concerns. These notes will speak in defense of you, both in an HR meeting and if you need to go to court. Your Note to File and notes to self are writings you make about any discussion or conversation with staff regarding concerns or issues. Your Note to File and notes to self are your regular "bank deposits" to HR. Be the king or queen of detailed note taking. Let this be known of you. To compile the best notes, do the following things:

1. Make them as the events are happening.
2. Include the date, time and location.
3. Include who was present.

Read your notes back to the staff to confirm that you have captured the essence of the conversation or discussion. You can also have them sign and date the notes. That way you miss nothing. It is also important that you make side notes to yourself, such as the following:

*   what the participants were wearing, including any uniform
*   if participants were wearing earrings, and if so the colour
*   where participants were sitting and in what position
*   whether participants smiled, laughed, cried or sneezed when you were having the discussion
*   your reaction to any of these things/behaviours

No, you are not being creepy by making these side notes! Following are some reasons these side notes are important. When you pull out your notes in a meeting that you may have been summoned to attend by HR, the staff in question may sometimes deny or add to what you said in the meeting you had with them. They may be convincing. *It is only your notes that will speak for you.* I have had to use my side notes sometimes to counter the claims of some staff who were "truth challenged." If you can recall that many details, it will silence them, which it did for me in the cases of those truth-challenged staff. In the one such case the staff apologized in tears and even asked for forgiveness. If it's not possible to make your notes immediately, write them later in the day or as an early morning project when you get to the office. The longer you take to make your notes, the more likely you are to lose valuable details. As an excellent property manager, you should remember these comments that were shared with me by a legal professional:

1. It is not who is right or wrong, but what you can prove. What she explained to me was, even when you are the person in the right, others will go to great lengths and try to poke holes into your version of the truth and skew it in their favour.
2. The one with the best notes wins.

That is why I personally believe in making notes to self. It helps big-time! An excellent property manager never distorts the truth. When you speak the truth, the details will come to you effortlessly. Your staff and colleagues will respect you for your integrity. Formalize the truth into notes and file these notes away, because things look better on paper and the practice shows consistency. Once you put it on paper, bank it with HR and yourself. How to do it? You can and must find the time to put information on paper by doing the following things:

- Spend five minutes writing notes in your vehicle before you leave the property.
- Jot down as many points as you can. Use names and not pronouns like *they*, *them*, *he* or *she*. The notes are facts and not your opinion.
- Include any unrelated event(s) that happened that day. Did it snow or rain? Was it hot?

These little things can help to stimulate your memory and bring back more of the details. Before long, your memory will be well trained and your note-taking skills will be second nature. In addition, you will earn the reputation of being detailed among your staff and colleagues. Proofread your notes and send them off to HR to add to the relevant employee's file. Be sure to copy your area manager on the e-mail so he or she is in the loop as to what is happening at the buildings in your portfolio regarding staff.

Now that your notes have been banked with HR, you may depending on the circumstances, have to write a discipline notice or a confirmation of the meeting addressed to the staff. If a letter is needed, summarize your Note to File by pulling and building only on the main facts. You do not need your side notes for this letter. Side notes are just for you. After you have written the letter, send the draft to HR or your area manager. If that is your company policy, they may want to review the letter and add to or amend it as they see fit. Once the letter is finalized and approved for delivery to the staff, print it out and arrange to meet with the staff. It is always good to have someone present with you, not just for support but also as a witness. The staff receiving the letter may request to have someone else, either his or her spouse or a colleague, present. Personally, I do not see anything wrong with granting that request. That is why you need someone there to support you. Both approaches show transparency. If your company is unionized, a union representative may be present.

If you are being accompanied by HR or another property manager, discuss with that individual how you will proceed when you meet with the staff. Also go over what you will do if the staff gets upset or is defensive. If no support person will be with you when you meet with the staff, that is ok. You can rehearse aloud with yourself before you meet with the staff. You need to hear yourself in action. Delivering a letter to any staff with no witness requires you to be alert, to be observant and to take even more detailed notes, including body language from the time you make eye contact to the time the meeting ends and the staff leaves. Did the person laugh disrespectfully? In one such meeting, the staff took the letter from me in anger and tore it into pieces. The staff had a grimace of anger on his face. Through clenched teeth and with a mean face, the staff then shouted at me, "How dare you Simone!" I included a description of his behaviour and his exact words in the notes accompanying the letter to be placed in the employee's file. The staff later denied the behaviour vehemently. This staff was later pulled from my portfolio for other reasons. Interestingly, the new property manager to whom this staff was now reporting gave the staff a disciplinary letter. Would you believe the staff did the exact same thing to the new manager as he'd done to me? It was reported that the staff tore up the letter and thumped the table with his fist. The previous notes I had written and banked showed that exact behaviour. The new property manager thanked me for the notes I had submitted. Now the staff had exhibited what looked like a pattern. Based on what he was written up for, along with his destructive violent behaviour, his employment was terminated.

Your Note to File helps not only you but also your colleagues, and by extension the company. When staff are transferred from your portfolio or when you change portfolios, what history do you or the new property managers have to work with? If no one made notes, your doing so will set the trend, because that is what an excellent property manager does. Invest the time in making notes and then banking them. The interest they accumulate will give you or someone else peace of mind.

ii. When Your Staff Complains about You

Sometimes your staff will go to HR and complain about you. If you are asked to attend a meeting with HR, always ask what or whom the meeting is about. All you need is the name of the staff member. Once you are given the name of the staff, always, *always* print out and take with you all your Notes to File, your notes to self and any letters you have written to that staff. Treat this meeting with HR with the utmost importance. Protect your image by being prepared and professional. This is your court date. If you know ahead of time when the meeting will be, resolve to dress in your power suit that day. You never know where the notes from this meeting will end up. Treat this as a "you are going to court" day to defend yourself, defend your image and protect what you stand for. Be human and professional. Be firm but fair. Draw on your notes. In this setting, use all your side notes and speak with confidence. These side notes are your protective shields and de-icer. They will silence and put to pieces any who are "truth challenged." You walk in with details and you leave unconquered, with your self-respect and integrity intact. Let no one push you around. You send that message in your grooming, how you conduct yourself and the notes you take with you. Since you never know when you are going to need those notes, make it a habit of writing them and banking them. The interest your banked Notes to File generates can save your job and your reputation.

iii. When a Staff Person Gets Terminated

At some point in your role as a property manager, you may have to terminate a staff. Never do a dismissal alone. Always take someone with you. You should always be accompanied by an HR personnel, your boss or one of your more experienced property manager colleagues. When that time comes for you to terminate a staff member, follow your company's dismissal policy as best as you can. Once the decision has been made to end the employment relationship, it is essential that you plan a proper and dignifying dismissal. You may not have control over how the employee reacts when he or she is told the news. However, you can influence to a degree how the employee responds by the way you conduct yourself.

In the book *Letting People Go*, the author Matt Shlosberg states, "Every termination is a test of your leadership skill." Therefore, what did you do as the property manager to try to prevent this dismissal? According to Shlosberg, "Letting People go can be implemented in either Hitler's or Gandhi's way and it's up to every leader to determine the strategy he or she will follow. Most companies don't associate themselves with either strategy, but, surprisingly, most terminations look like Hitler's deeds, even if such approach was not planned." Shlosberg relates the firing of a middle manager in a Fortune 500 firm who simply became the scapegoat for a multimillion-dollar disaster. As a result of an integrity problem that occurred outside of this person's control, the firm was about to lose a contract that was worth hundreds of millions of dollars. In order to save this contract and keep the key customer, the company announced that the problem occurred because of this middle manager's ignorance and terminated him immediately. This manager was a hot commodity. He started getting calls from employers, but no one wanted to hire him once they found out about his adventure at the previous firm. One such firm ran a background check and confirmed that he had been fired for an integrity violation. He eventually found a job, but his reputation will take many more years to restore. So what went wrong here? His firm knew that there was no violation on his part. To them, it was about money. They did not think they acted in a Hitler-like way. After all, their actions restored a multimillion-dollar contract, although it was done in Machiavellian way. But they destroyed this human being. Gandhi would probably have done things differently. He would have thanked the employee for his continued contributions and paid him a reasonable severance. He would then personally have gone out of his way to help this individual find a job.

When an employment relationship ends, it can be devastatingly painful. That is because something has died. The pain associated with a job loss is similar to the pain of losing someone to death. Regardless of how someone loses the job or is terminated, respect the staff's dignity. Be human while being professional. These qualities should be displayed by both you and the person(s) accompanying you. However, the onus is on you the property manager. Why? The next time you meet that person could be in court, or under some other circumstance. What is the last image you want this staff to have of you? What are the last words you wish this person to hear from you? Even though you might not care at this point, still strive to be respectful. The situation is already unpleasant for the terminated staff, so protect his or her sore dignity. Never forget that people's paths have a funny way of crossing again. The next time this person's eyes meet yours, where will it be and what will he or she remember? Will it be in court? Will it be at another place of employment? Will it be in a social setting? Will it be in healthcare, with you being the patient and the former staff being the healthcare provider? Treat people well and always be fair with them. That way if and when your path cross again, there will be mutual respect between you.

Get to know your staff and give feedback before, during and after you see things going wrong. Utilize the training co-ordinator and meet with your staff individually after each staff meeting. Arrange further training with the relevant departments and follow up with the departments and staff after and sometimes during the training. When you know that you honestly did not cunningly chart or craft a path for a staff member's termination, when you know that you honestly did all that you could for that staff and you have honest documents to support your actions, your conscience will be clear. You can continue your career with peace of mind. You can look people in the eye without shame or regret. You will look at them with respect.

External Contractors and Trades Persons

To the company, contractors are like friends of the family. They are constantly changing. You will need their support for your very growth and existence in the field of property management. Contractors are human beings just like your staff; hence, you should treat them with respect. You will be close to some, and some will drop in only for the big events, tendering for major projects. It has been said that people will come into your life for a reason, for a season or for a lifetime. Similarly, contractors will come into your life as a property manager for a reason, for a season or for the lifetime of your career in property management. You are going to change contractors and add contractors as the needs of your portfolio and your career in property management changes.

Most likely, various contractors will already be in place as part of the resources available for you to function in your role as a property manager. From the pool of contractors that you have access to, you will have to decide which ones to choose. But how do you go about choosing the best from the various names on your company's recommended trades list? You can narrow down your selection using a variety of methods such as the following:

1. Asking your area manager (AM) or regional manager (RM) what his or her preferences are.
2. Asking fellow colleagues whom they use and whom you should avoid.
3. Reviewing invoices that come to you for signing. Obviously, these would be for work that was completed prior to you joining the company.
4. Asking your staff at each location. Getting the input of your staff is probably the best approach. This is because your staff are the firsthand supervisors of the company for the contractors or trades people. Your staff will know the following things about the contractors that you may not yet know:

    a. Who completes the job properly.
    b. Who delivers nothing but poor workmanship.
    c. Who works messily and has to be babysat.
    d. Who drags out the job and takes longer than the usual time.
    e. Who considers the tenants and the building's operation.

A. Choosing and Assessing Contractors

When choosing or assessing contractors, consider some of these qualities:

- flexibility with regard to time
- trustworthiness
- attention to detail—excellent workmanship and high quality of work produced
- competitive pricing
- safety-consciousness
- honesty in quoting
- supplying quality material
- fair billing or pricing
- sensitivity to tenants' concerns and the concerns of the company
- speed to complete work in required time
- dependability
- organization, carrying out work in a systematic way that reduces or eliminates the impact on tenants and building operation
- the ability to work within city or municipal bylaws
- the ability to work clean and respect the curb appeal of the property (Your staff should not have to babysit the contractor or clean up after him or her)
- the ability to take on the workload and complete the job properly
- the ability to respond well to criticism or feedback
- pleasant personality
- being service-oriented or instead money-oriented

B. Get to Know Your Contractors

The work done by your contractors should give you peace of mind and great confidence. They should respect you and understand your personal standard and brand. This can only happen if they know you. Find the time to meet with and get to know the contractors you eventually choose. Do not get too familiar with them, simply because familiarity breeds contempt. Let politeness and professionalism be the order of the day. This gives you room to offer strong feedback if and when it is needed. The contractor's finished product and work will be a representation of you and your personal brand. Contractors are also part of your team. Treat them with respect and learn to connect with them. Thank them personally when they go above and beyond the call of duty to do work for you. If you do this, they will remember it and feel inclined to do more for you. Go on-site and see them in action. Meet with your contractors to discuss certain quotes and upcoming projects. Some of these projects could be for capital expenditure work or repairs or upgrades inside occupied apartments that may be tied up in a legal process at the Landlord and Tenant Board (LTB) or with a bylaw officer. Do not leave these projects up to your staff. Does that mean you should meet with contractors for every quote? No! However, the more you meet with them, the better you will understand their pricing method and structure. This is also how you learn the business, which will grow your confidence and comfort level. When you meet with a contractor about any project, find out the following from the contractor:

1. How long will the repairs or project take?
2. How will the project affect the tenants or the building's operation? Disruptions may include noise, dust, restricted access or restricted use of certain areas or amenities.
3. Do they have the equipment and manpower to complete the job?
4. Does the job require special permit and who will obtain such permit?

Walk the areas with the contractors and take notes. If you disagree with any of their suggestions, do so respectfully. Be open-minded and listen to suggestions. Remain tactful and be firm about what you want and what you do not want. Stick to company policy and procedures. Make sure safety is always, always emphasized and practised. When you understand the scope of work, you will know where the money is going and what you should pay for once the invoices are submitted for payment. Remember too that the scope of work can change and throw a curveball into your budget. You should also ask about the worst-case scenario for any project. Unforeseen situations can blow your budget. Having a deeper understanding of the scope of work will put you in a better position to request adequate funds to finance similar projects in the future at other locations.

C. Obtaining Quotations (Quotes)

It is normal for companies to request that more than one quote be submitted for a job. When requesting quotes for major projects, it is always best to physically go on-site at the location where the work will be done and for which the quote is needed. Choose the contractors you will use based on the type or category of work to be done. When I started out in property management, I used to meet individually with contractors about the same type of work. This was only wasting my time. I realized if I typed and e-mailed the scope of work to the selected contractors based on the category of work to be done and met everyone at the same time at the same location, I would be saving valuable energy and time. This approach also worked in my favour, and not just for timing; the contractors all knew who they were up against, so each one had to put his or her best foot forward. They also tried to give the best price and submitted quotes early. The best thing was the wiggle room with regard to price. The contractors would let me know that if I had concerns about the price, I should talk to them and they would work with me.

When you meet with the contractors on-site, it is very important that you get the building managers involved during the meeting. Sometimes your building managers can give you ideas, since they tend to see things from an operational and tenant-focused standpoint. If you have no idea of what the scope of work should be or how to word the scope of work, still meet with the contractors and tell them in your own words what you want the finished job to be or to look like. The contractors will translate your ideas into their jargon or terms. The presence of your building managers will also serve you well in that they can help to communicate your ideas to the contractors and clarify your thoughts.

This was something I learned that carried over from my work in the hotel industry. Whenever I met with prospective guests about their event planning, I took my executive chef with me. All such meetings were planned around his schedule. It was great teamwork, as we would share ideas aloud to clarify and confirm, and also to ensure that the unspoken needs of the guests were met. In property management, this approach builds respect with the staff, fosters buy-in and results in a sense of contribution from inception to completion with the team leader at the site level. When your staff who contributed ideas walk the property once the work is completed, they do so with a great sense of accomplishment and ownership.

Evaluating quotations

Make sure you establish a deadline for when you want to receive all the quotes from the contractors. You do not want to be waiting too long for quotes. Remember you want to complete your project on time. The last thing you want is for contractors to hold you up. Once you have collected all the quotes, you need to carefully review what each contractor has submitted. Below are some suggestions on how to select the quote that is most suitable for your project(s):

1. Compare apples to apples, meaning that the contractors must provide a quote for the exact same work. To ensure consistency, it is best to send the scope/specifications to all the contractors involved in the bid/submission. This document should cover the following:
   a. materials to be used. You want to make sure the materials are specific to the type of work you want done. If you are using tiles make sure the size, colour, type and or model number of the tiles are clearly stated
   b. the area to which the work is to be done. Make sure the contractors specify the area including size of where the work will be done
   c. any permit that will be needed including the cost and who will obtain the permit, either you or the contractor
   d. a time line for completing the project if the contractor is awarded the job (Knowing how long the contractor will take to complete the job will give you an idea of how to schedule the work to minimize its impact on tenants and building operation.)
   e. a summary of how the work will be done, which will tell you how tenants will be impacted
   f. any details specific to the company or property
   g. whether cleanup of the site is included or is an additional charge
   Be careful of the wording. Some contractors will mention supply and installation in the quote, but what about any removal? Is that included? Let the contractors specify. Or if they do mention that they will remove any material, will there be an additional cost for doing so? For example, there could be an additional charge for the removal of asbestos tiles.
2. Will the contractor do all the work, or will you have to call in subtrades? For example, with the installation of a handicap-accessible door, will the contractor supply and install the door operator *plus* add the power supply? Or do you need your electrician to submit a quote to do the wiring to operate the handicap door?

3. Focus on quality. Even though you want the best price, ensure the work will not be a shortcut and will meet any necessary code.
4. Determine whether or not the quote meets your budget.

In addition to the above make sure you clearly state before hand the penalty for poor workmanship including incomplete work. Make sure you are very clear on procedures regarding any changes to the scope or specification of the work. You should clearly state that the contractor must discuss any unforeseen aspect of the work with you first, before he or she can move forward. In my experience, depending on the cost of the unforeseen work and who your contractors are, they may not charge you for the extra work. This could be based on the volume of business you give them or on their professional liking for you. On the other hand, the work that is now discovered which was not originally in the scope of work, may be in your bracket of authority to approve. However, if the new addition to the scope of work is above your dollar bracket of authority, you must get the approval from your AM. A quotation is a binding agreement. Therefore, review it carefully before you sign and award the job to the contractor that meets your standard. If the project is a major project, it never hurts to get the opinion of your AM.

D. Competing for the Time and Attention of Contractors

Do not forget that your colleagues have access to the same contractors you use. Whenever there is crunch time for projects, an emergency or a quick pop-up, your contractors must choose who gets their time: either you, your colleagues or another company. Ask yourself what sets you apart from the others and puts you in a position to be chosen over them. These are some of the things that can set you apart and maintain your image of an excellent property manager:

A. Your efforts to forge a meaningful professional relationship with your contractors. Make sure they understand the work culture of each location, the needs of the property, the tenant base at each location, and the standards of the company. Do follow-ups on major projects from beginning to end. This helps you to keep the lines of communication open. Regular communication ensures that contractors stick to the scope of work and lets you know if there should be an adjustment made to the scope of work based on unforeseen work.

B. Actions that show you care about your contractors. If you hear that one of your contractors is sick, has had a death in the family or has a new addition to the family, give him or her a call or send an e-mail pertaining to the situation. Depending on the professional relationship you have with the contractor, send a greeting card personally signed by you and your staff from each property within your portfolio. Even if your company sends flowers, you should add your own personal but professional touch. These gestures tend to hit the correct nerve and will cause you to stand out as being caring, compassionate and sensitive to the emotional situation the contractor is experiencing. Keep it professional by letting the card speak for itself. There is no need to pry. I sent an e-mail to one contractor who had lost a loved one and to another contractor who had just had a baby born. Both contractors were moved by the very simple gesture of compassion. I sent another contractor who was hospitalized for an extended time a card signed by all the staff in my portfolio. I personally purchased the card and had all my staff sign it. Somehow the card made its way to the contractor without me having gotten a chance to sign it. Nonetheless, the contractor called to express his gratitude, stating that he knew the card came from me because all my staff had signed it. That card led to a professional bond with the contractor even though I had not had the chance to sign it. The gesture touched the correct nerve.

C. Inviting a contractor or a key representative from his or her company to one of your staff meetings, either an individual property meeting or a combined staff meeting. This way your staff can ask questions or relate ongoing concerns and determine how they can collaboratively resolve them.

D. Talking to your colleagues about the urgent nature of the work that needs to be done in your portfolio. Hopefully they will understand and allow the contractor to work on your project. If you know your colleagues are going to say no regardless of the fact, approach your AM or RM so he or she can make the decision for the contractor.

E. When Contractors Cross the Line

Your contractors can help to enhance or destroy the relationship between you and your tenants. When contractors are asked to do work in a rented and occupied apartment, their main purpose should be to complete the required work in the allotted time on the Notice of Entry and not cause undue upset to the tenant. Once your contractors are scheduled to perform work in the apartment of a difficult tenant, meet with or speak directly to the contractor about the tenant before the work is started and after the work is completed. You should provide only basic information to the contractor about the tenant that will not violate privacy laws. Basic information could include but is not limited to the following:

- That the repair is based on a court order, or on an application the tenant has made to the LTB. (In such a case, send your very best trades person.)
- That the contractor is not to have any conversation with the tenant. Whoever does the repair should just go in, complete the job, clean up and leave the apartment. Where possible, take pictures of the completed job.
- That nothing inside the apartment that is not related to the repair is to be used or touched.
- That all Notices of Entry must be respected and the entry door to the apartment must be locked when the contractor leaves the work apartment.

The above pointers may look very simple. Because they are matters of common sense, everyone should know them, but people, including contractors and trades people, sometimes need a reminder. As a tenant, I have had my own personal headache experience with contractors when requested repairs were being completed in my apartment. After arriving home from work one evening, I realized my bathroom door was opened. I'd locked the door before I'd left in the morning because it was not part of the work area. When I looked around the bathroom, I saw evidence that the contractor had used my toilet. How did I know? Sadly, the contractor / trades person had diarrhea, and I had to clean up the remnants. I could also see pieces of dried-up plaster on the floor and around the base of the toilet. There is no scale that could accurately measure how *furious* I was. On another occasion, the contractor had used my microwave, leaving the microwave door open and a dish towel close by. I groaned in disbelief and anger. There was also another incident where the contractor had watched my TV. When I returned home, the television was on a station I never watch.

If you have concerns about jobs your contractors have performed, take pictures of the areas of concern, send the pictures to the contractor and/or meet with the contractor physically at the job-site to discuss the concerns and how they should be addressed. Do not be afraid to put payment of invoices on hold until incomplete or substandard work is completed according to the standard of the company. In some cases, you will have to take drastic steps for incomplete or substandard work that cannot be brought to a finish by the original contractor. If your contractor cannot complete the scope of work originally agreed upon, he or she should be informed in writing either through a letter or an e-mail (be sure to copy your AM/RM) that he or she has left you with no choice but to get a second contractor to complete the job and to deduct the cost from what you would have originally agreed to pay.

When your contractor consistently behaves or performs below standard, it is time to part ways. A contractor's inability to deliver should be documented with letters and pictures, which then should be presented to your AM/RM. As you get comfortable in the role of property manager and grow with the company, at some point you will have to make the decision to hire and/or fire contractors. Whatever you decide, always discuss your concerns with your AM/RM. You must also comply with your company's administrative procedure for hiring or firing a contractor. In your role as property manager, you will come to appreciate that having good contractors is just as important as having good staff. Contractors are a representation of you and the company. Therefore, ensure they comply with your company standards and policies.

Government Organizations and Regulatory Bodies

Love them or hate them, you cannot do without government organizations and regulatory bodies. Hence, you must learn to put up with them by complying with their requirements. They are organizations or regulatory bodies at the federal, provincial or municipal level that enforce certain guidelines and systems for the safety and well-being of all. They can make your job seem like a never-ending battle. On the other hand, once you co-operate, comply and keep your buildings consistently in compliance, you will develop a respected reputation with them—but this won't grant you immunity from their visits. Most times when you are contacted by one of these organizations or regulatory bodies, it is because of unresolved or allegedly unresolved complaints. You could also be contacted for a random inspection or investigation carried out by one or more of these organizations or regulatory bodies. Let your staff know that when any of these representatives show up at the properties, your staff should notify you immediately. As an excellent property manager, you should also feel free to contact any of these organizations or regulatory bodies for clarification and assistance when necessary to perform your duties to the fullest extent. Each location and the tenant base within your portfolio will determine the degree of involvement or interaction you have with any of these organizations. Some of these organizations are as follows:

A.   Landlord and Tenant Board (court)
B.   the fire department
C.   the police department
D.   Technical Standards and Safety Authority (TSSA)
E.   city inspectors / bylaw officers
F.   the Workplace Safety and Insurance Board (WSIB)

A. Landlord and Tenant Court

In Ontario, the court of justice for landlords and tenants is called the Landlord and Tenant Board (LTB). This court falls under the Social Justice Tribunals Ontario (SJTO). Whatever dispute or unresolved matter there is between you and your tenants will most likely end up at the LTB (or the court system in your region designated for such purpose). An appearance at the Tribunal happens because either you or your tenant believes or knows that your rights under the Residential Tenancies

Act (RTA) have been violated and the matter must be resolved. You cannot tell by looking at any of your tenants and know which of them will take you to the Tribunal, or if you will take any of them to the Tribunal, to settle any dispute. For that reason, make sure you and your staff do your due diligence by upholding the RTA. If you stick to what the RTA says, you *may* have to make fewer trips to the Tribunal. You can avoid problems by doing the following things:

- Making sure you and your staff maintain the rental units and the buildings in a good state of repair. This must also be done in a timely manner.
- Listening to and acting on complaints brought to you by your tenants. Investigate where necessary with urgency.
- Listening to your staff and acting on complaints about the building and the tenants they bring to your attention.

Make a practice of keeping accurate records to confirm that you have complied with the RTA. Hence, when it is time to go to the Tribunal, whether you made the application or the tenant made the application, most of your leg work or groundwork will have already been completed. The only preparation you should have to do is organizing the facts and taking the time to get there. This level of input by you and your staff toward this aspect of your work builds respect and a professional bond with your legal department.

Share stories about victories at the Tribunal with your staff. You should also review the steps that made the victories possible. This will boost your staff's self-esteem and self-confidence. Your individual staff members will also be able to see how their contributions fit into the big picture. They will be inclined to perform their duties with a greater sense of purpose and pride. If you are not successful at the Tribunal, still review the ruling or outcome with your staff. This would be like a postmortem. The review will let everyone see what areas they can improve on and how to prevent a reoccurrence. Sometimes, regardless of how well you prepare, your tenants will outsmart you and get their way. Your greatest challenge will be not in dealing with the tenant who won but in dealing with your staff. Your staff members will have to live with the tenant at the building and endure the taste of defeat every time they see the tenant and make eye contact with him or her. If that happens, let your staff know this is part of the job and they can move on by improving. Improvement is part of the growth process. In addition, victories can be disguised as defeats. Sometimes it is in the best interests of the property and by extension the company to settle instead of pursuing a matter. You cannot lose sight of the goals that the property must achieve.

If you must complete any legal forms, *always go to the Web site of the LTB*. This allows you always to use the most up-to-date forms. You should make it a habit of going on their Web site and getting familiar or comfortable with its features. View the section for landlords as well as the section for tenants. Learn how you can use the legal process to solve problems you are experiencing with your tenants. If you are in Ontario, some forms you might use are listed in the next section. If you are in another region, search out what tools or forms are available to you. Also learn the options your tenants have if you fail to uphold any aspect of the RTA or whatever law is in effect in your region. An excellent property manager will endeavour to understand how the system works. This understanding makes you better prepared and allows you to be proactive in your approach. It also makes for better communication with the legal department of your company.

i.   Some Legal Forms to Assist You in the Process

If you are in Ontario, following is a list of some of the forms you may use to assist you. Visit the Web site, http://www.sjto.gov.on.ca/ltb/forms/, to see the full list of forms along with their instructions. If you are outside the jurisdiction of Ontario, know and understand the forms or procedures in place *within your own jurisdiction* and use them accordingly.

Notices of termination for landlords

N4: Notice to End a Tenancy Early for Non-payment of Rent
N5: Notice to End your Tenancy for Interfering with Others, Damage or Overcrowding
N6: Notice to End your Tenancy for Illegal Acts or Misrepresenting Income in a Rent-Geared-to-Income Rental Unit
N7: Notice to End your Tenancy for Causing Serious Problems in the Rental Unit or Residential Complex
N8: Notice to End your Tenancy at the End of the Term
N11: Agreement to End the Tenancy
N12: Notice to End your Tenancy Because the Landlord, a Purchaser or a Family Member Requires the Rental Unit
N13: Notice to End your Tenancy Because the Landlord Wants to Demolish the Rental Unit, Repair it or Convert it to Another Use

Notices of rent increase for landlords

N1: Notice of Rent Increase
N2: Notice of Rent Increase (Unit Partially Exempt)
N3: Notice to Increase the Rent and/or Charges for Care Services and Meals
N10: Agreement to Increase the Rent Above the Guideline

Application forms for landlords

L1: Application to Evict a Tenant for Non-payment of Rent and to Collect Rent the Tenant Owes
L2: Application to End a Tenancy and Evict a Tenant
L3: Application to End a Tenancy – Tenant Gave Notice or Agreed to Terminate the Tenancy
L4-: Application to End a Tenancy – Tenant Failed to Meet Conditions of a Settlement or Order
L5: Application for an Above Guideline Increase
L6: Application for Review of a Provincial Work Order
L8: Application Because the Tenant Changed the Locks
L9: Application to Collect Rent the Tenant Owes
A1: Application about Whether the Act Applies

A2: Application about a Sublet or an Assignment

A4: Application to Vary the Amount of a Rent Reduction

Other forms for landlords

Affidavit

Bulk Application Information Sheet

Certificate of Service

Fee Waiver Request

Information from your Landlord about Utility Costs

Information from your Landlord about Utility Costs (One or More Utilities are no Longer Provided in the Residential Complex)

Information to Prospective Tenant about Suite Meters or Meters

L1/L9: Information Update as of the Hearing Day Form

Landlord's Motion to Set Aside an Order to Void – Form S3

Landlord's Notice to a New Tenant about an Order Prohibiting a Rent Increase

Landlord's Notice to Terminate Obligations to Supply Electricity

N14: Landlord's Notice to the Spouse of the Tenant who Vacated the Rental Unit

Payment Agreement

Request for Accommodation or French-Language Services

Request for Hearing Recording

Request for the Board to Issue a Summons

Request to Amend an Order

Request to be a Litigation Guardian: Mental Incapacity

Request to Extend or Shorten Time

Request to Re-open an Application

Request to Reschedule a Hearing

Request to Review an Order

Schedule of Parties

Summons (Lawyers and Paralegals Only)

Source: © Queen's Printer for Ontario, 2015. Reproduced with permission.

B. Fire Department

The fire department can be your best friend or worst enemy. Resolve to be their best friend. The choice is yours. The fire department is there to help your buildings before and during a fire-related emergency. Build a strong, solid and professional relationship with the fire department. Their desire is to help you bring and keep your buildings up to code. Think about it: the firefighters who show up at your buildings put their own lives at risk to save the lives of your tenants and their occupants, as well as your property. That is a tremendous sacrifice. Show your appreciation and your willingness to work with the fire department by keeping your buildings up to code and your staff properly trained and respectful. This is how you become the fire department's best friend. As an excellent hands-on property manager, get to understand the fire code and fire system at each of your buildings. You do this by first forming an appreciative and working relationship with your company's life safety specialist (LSS) or its equivalent. That is to say if the services of the Life Safety Specialist is outsourced or contracted through the fire equipment company. Get involved and actively participate in a few monthly building fire inspections. Once you know what to look for, you can always ensure these things are in place when you visit your buildings. Your staff will also sense your keen interest and know that they cannot cut corners. If you do not care about fire safety or ensure your buildings are up to code, you will see another side of the fire department. You will feel as though you are on fire from the pressure to comply. That is one fire they will not put out until you bring your buildings up to code.

Should your staff call to inform you that a fire prevention officer (FPO) is on-site, first call your life safety specialist and then make your way to the property. You should be more willing to do this in your first year with the company. During your first year with the company, demonstrate a sponge-like attitude by soaking up as much information as possible. This thirst for knowledge and the desire to put your knowledge to use will take you far and give you a greater understanding of your duties. Treat the visit of the FPO as important and urgent. Your staff should never feel alone when the FPO visits. Your presence also sends a strong message to both your staff and the FPO that you care and you are involved in the operation of the building. Being physically present on the property gives you the opportunity to personally meet the FPO and start the job of building a progressive professional relationship. Your presence during the visit of the FPO helps to prevent your staff from volunteering unnecessary information. Sometimes circumstances will prevent you from going to meet the FPO while he or she is at your building. If that is the case, inform your staff to take his or her business card. They can even text you a closeup picture of the business card. When you get a chance, call the FPO and introduce yourself. If there is no answer, send an e-mail stating you understand that the FPO was at your building and asking how you can be of assistance.

I did not quite understand the role of the FPO until one day when my staff at one of the locations called to let me know that a FPO was at that building to do a random inspection. Based on my experience working in the hotel industry, I always made it my point of duty to meet with any uniformed government personnel when they showed up on the property to conduct any inspection. Since I was new on the job as property manager, I felt I had to make my way to the building to meet the FPO and learn more about the role of these dreaded officials. Thankfully, I was not far away from the building and got there before the inspection was started. I introduced myself and exchanged business cards. I saw the vehicle with the city logo, and the FPO was in full uniform. I knew for sure he was from the fire department. The inspector told me he was there for a random inspection. He said the building had not undergone an inspection in quite a while. Therefore, he wanted to see all the utility rooms, some apartments (only for tenants who were home) and other areas of the building, and check the logbooks, including old logbooks, on the property. Interestingly, I had walked that same building a few weeks before with the LSS.

As I walked the building with the FPO, I started to connect the dots. I got a better understanding of life safety and learned of its seriousness. Tenants who were home allowed the FPO to check their smoke alarms/detectors and door closures to confirm that these items were working. Some of those tenants who had removed the installed smoke alarms/detectors were ordered to immediately put them back and were warned not to interfere with them ever again. Those tenants were also told the consequences, including fines, of removing such an important safety device. I also observed the elevator recall in phase 1 and 11 operation. The inspection was thorough and methodical. The FPO explained why he was inspecting certain areas as the inspection progressed. I was thankful to the FPO for allowing me to be in on the inspection from start to finish. I felt even more pleased that I had recently walked the building with the LSS. The visit from the FPO reinforced what I had learned and sparked a greater appreciation for fire safety and sense of purpose given the urgency in complying with the fire code. At the end of the inspection, I was told that the building had very minor infractions. These got addressed within two days. From that point onward as I did my own building inspections, I tried to see the buildings through the eyes of the FPO and LSS. Deficiencies that I pointed out to my staff got addressed with urgency. Where the staff needed training, training was given, and opportunities were given to ensure the trained staff were putting their knowledge to use.

As my portfolio grew from city to city, I still made it a priority to participate in any FPO inspections at my buildings. I always obtained the contact information for the FPO who visited any of my buildings. If I did not understand any infraction, I contacted the FPO via e-mail for clarification. I copied the LSS on such e-mails. All infractions were dealt with in a timely manner. As an excellent property manager, learn to build relationships with your FPOs by complying with urgency. The importance of building a working relationship is that it leads to a partnership-type relationship. Because I built that relationship, if an FPO showed up at any of my buildings unexpectedly, sometimes the FPO would call my cell from the building he was visiting to conduct an inspection. Make no mistake: this was not a casual friendship. Behind their smiles, FPOs are firm about what they do. It was a professional working relationship or partnership to the point where I was sometimes notified ahead of time that an inspection was scheduled and I should clear my calendar to be present. This approach worked very well, because I could arrange for my key staff to be present, as well as the LSS, who can answer questions and explain things much better than I could. During such inspections, as deficiencies were pointed out (the FPO always finds something), I would be calling or e-mailing contractors about what had to be done. By the time the inspection was completed, half or most of the items were already scheduled with contractors for completion. Items that can be done by the staff were noted on the spot during the inspection, and a time line was given for when such deficiencies would be rectified.

Since you are notified of some infractions by way of typed document, it will sometimes take a few days for the fire department to formally serve or send you a copy depending on the severity of the infraction. If you are told you will be getting a report/order/infraction, try to correct the deficiencies that were pointed out to you before you get the official report. Hence, by the time you get the infraction, work to correct such deficiencies is already completed or almost completed. Bear in mind that there are apps available that will allow the fire prevention officer to document the inspection on electronic devices. This new method is faster allowing the FPO to send you the infraction notice via e-mail before he or she leaves your property. Regardless of how notice of the infraction is given to you, demonstrating urgency to correct the deficiencies shows you value life and the work the FPOs do. Then FPOs will like to work with you as a property manager. You will stand out as different in a good way. Why is this? Some FPOs have related to me that it is a pleasure when they come across property managers who are willing to work with them. Sometimes when they show up at buildings to conduct inspections, some owners say they do not speak English, or there are no staff to give them access to the building. It can be frustrating when they encounter such situations. Another scenario an FPO related to me is the case of infractions being written but the apartment company doing nothing to correct the problems, and the FPO has to constantly follow up to ensure infractions are corrected. Therefore, your willingness to work with the fire department builds respect and a progressive professional working relationship, which benefits you in the long run.

If and when the FPOs show up at your buildings or call you about a concern at any of your buildings, do not sigh and say to yourself, *What do they want now?* Welcome their visits, even if the FPO is new. A new FPO may have sharper eyes and catch things others may have missed. Never underestimate what you can learn from any new FPO. Of course, some will want to show you how tough they can be. Always comply and seek to reach the human part of the person. As tough as they are, they all have a heart. You can reach their hearts if you demonstrate a genuine willingness to comply.

At one location, a contractor installed a fire separation door to an apartment. Sadly, the door was not properly installed and a tenant called the fire department regarding the improper installation of the door. The FPO who was sent to assess the door was new and extremely firm, with no smile, just all authority. The door was eventually replaced, but no adjustments could be made to the door, such as installing a mail slot. Because the door manufacturer did not build the door with the mail slot or give instructions on how to install the slot, any attempt to install a mail slot would be deemed a compromise to the integrity of the fire rating of the door. I was warned not to tamper with the door and told of the consequences by the fire department if it were tampered with. I assured the new FPO that I had established a professional working relationship with the fire department and I intended to keep it that way. Hence, there was no need for me to tamper with the door. The new FPO said he would be checking the door periodically. In my annoyance, I told the FPO he was free to check the door at midnight. This person was getting on my nerves.

A few weeks after that tense conversation, I had a fire at one of the properties in the same city and same region to which that new FPO was assigned. As with any fire, I made my way to the property. After speaking with my staff, I met with the fire department, police, and ambulance attendants. Whom did I see at the fire location? Yes, that new FPO. We shook hands, I spoke to the platoon leader, who commended the staff for doing a great job. Unattended cooking was the cause of the fire. All fire equipment functioned well. The fire was contained to the affected apartment. After that fire, as the months and years progressed, there were many more fires, more than ten. Yes, that is correct. It could be more but not less. All of these were due to unattended cooking or vandalism in the stairwell. Again, the FPO and I would meet up and gradually the tension vanished like it had never existed. As sad as it was, the upside to these fires were that I had no choice but to work with the fire department. I visited the fire department and got to know some of the staff. When a new building was purchased and added to my portfolio, I invited the new FPO to the open house, and the FPO showed up. We now had a progressive professional working relationship. I learned a great deal from that new FPO. That relationship resulted in community-related activities between the properties and the fire department.

If you go to the Web site of the fire departments in the cities where you have your buildings or properties, you will see they are community-friendly. That is right. The fire department wants to help you. Make use of the fire department's willingness to involve and work with the community. See how you can partner with the fire department. You can plan a visit with your team and get a tour of the station, taking pictures with the fire trucks. You can also do something different by volunteering one of your properties as a site for the fire department to conduct training. The fact that you volunteer your property for training does not mean you should fall behind on the upkeep of your property and expect favouritism from the fire department. *That will not work.* If you are consistently on top of your game, you will have nothing to worry about and will actually volunteer your property with pride. You now set a benchmark for the other properties within your portfolio and by extension within the company. If there is a fire prevention week, partner with your local fire department and see how best you can educate your tenants. This is also a good time to remind your tenants to purchase contents insurance or renters insurance for their apartments, if they have not done so already. Remember the fire department can be your best friend or your worst enemy. An excellent property manager will make the choice to make the fire department his or her best friend by keeping properties up to code and exhibiting a willing attitude to work with the fire department.

C. Police Department

The police can be a tremendous resource to your property. Their job is to serve and protect. However, when you become of service to the police or partner with them in the fight against crime, this can greatly enhance your relationship with them and produce win–win results. The police will show up at your buildings for various incidents or circumstances when called by you, your tenants or your staff, or when the fire monitoring company signals the fire department to go to your property. When the visit of the police directly involves the property, they will normally contact your building staff or you if further information is required.

You can utilize the services of the police department for non-emergency situations such as gangs forming in your buildings, or if you suspect drug trafficking taking place on your property. Most city police Web sites have information or tips on how to deal with certain crime or crime-related activities in your buildings such as graffiti, domestic violence and gangs. Call and arrange to meet with the police station/precinct that serves each of your properties where you are having problems. In fact, don't even wait for a problem to arise; go meet the police and introduce yourself. Your meeting puts a face to your name, your voice, your buildings and by extension your company. Your meeting also shows you are serious about eradicating any form of crime-related activity taking place on your property.

I have visited acquaintances at other apartment buildings where cameras are on every floor and was told the installed cameras are connected to and monitored by the closest police station. While such a setup may work for certain companies, I have found that giving the police direct access to the property works even better. At one of my very challenging locations, I was visited by the police. The timing of their visit was perfect, because I was present at the building and I personally wanted to meet with them. They related some concerns based on complaints they were receiving. I was just as concerned as they were. During our meeting, I asked the police officers if they would come to the property in civilian clothes. They flatly said no. They explained that they did not wish to hide who they are. They wanted their presence to be felt and to echo throughout the property. Their uniform, they said, was the best, in that it sends a strong message to the perpetrators that the police are around, acts as a deterrent and shows they are vigilant about potential crime and have a good relationship with management. With that in mind, I asked if I could give them access keys to the buildings. Since they were at the building, it saved me a trip to the station. They were very grateful for the keys, stating it was something they'd wanted from a long time. The keys gave access to the lobby and garage. That way they could come and go as they wished. They were then given a tour of the common areas, including the underground garage, where a lot of the "action" tended to happen.

When I was given two other buildings with similar issues, I did not wait for the police to come to me. This time I went to them. I related the problems I was experiencing at the new location and gave them lobby and garage keys for the location. Not long after that meeting, the staff called one night to tell me that the building had been put on "lockdown." I was familiar with fire drills. But, lockdown? What was that? Because this was earlier on in my career as a property manager, at that time, I had no idea what lockdown meant. This is not a joke. Did it mean the building had no hydro because of some major internal electrical problem? I had to ask the staff to explain. They told me that a man was seen walking the hallways with a gun, looking to shoot a tenant. Because the gunman did not know which apartment the tenant lived in, he was knocking on different doors with the gun displayed in his hand. Hence, the police were called in. The staff stated that the building was surrounded by police, and they were all told by the police to stay inside. They said no one could get in or go out and I should not even try to venture onto the property. The next thing I knew, the police called me on my cell. They wanted information to assist in their investigation, so I had to go to the office that night to provide the police with the information they needed.

Interaction with the police became a normal part of my job. If I went on-site to any of the properties and saw the police, when appropriate I would always introduce myself and ask if they were being assisted. To further strengthen my relationship with the police, I extended them an invitation via e-mail to tenant events. At one location, the police accepted the invitation to a tenant appreciation barbecue event. Their interaction with the tenants and the children was very heartwarming. Some of the police helped to serve food to the tenants, while other officers gave children, and parents of toddlers, stickers to wear on their clothes. All the kids thought it was cool to have the police present. Some children sat in the police vehicles and spoke candidly to the police. The presence of the police and their interaction with the tenants and children was amazing and pleasing to watch. It also demonstrated that the building had a good working relationship with the police department and the staff. If I had rented a bouncy castle, the kids would not have had so much fun.

i. Crime-free Multihousing Prevention Program

Interestingly, there are crime-prevention training programs for building owners and/or property managers that are taught by police officers in various locations across Canada and the United States of America. The aim of such programs is to keep illegal activities common to rental properties off those properties. It was during the research for *I Am an Excellent Property Manager* that I learned about the crime-free program that is being practised here in Canada and the United States, the latter being where the program got started. I had achieved tremendous success at the aforementioned location that I had managed regarding crime-related activities. However, had I known about this program when I started out in property management, it would have made my job less stressful at some of the rougher and more challenging communities I'd managed at some point. The practice of the Crime -free Multihousing Prevention Program has been thoroughly examined by Regina University, Regina, Canada, to determine its viability in the United States, Canada and more specifically the city of Regina. As a property manager, if you have challenging locations, this crime-prevention program is worth exploring. Even if you do not have any property that is classified or labelled as "rough" or "challenging," I recommend you still enroll in the program for the following simple reasons:

1. You need to know, understand and be alert to the factors that can cause your properties to slip from excellent/good to bad, thus chasing tenants away.
2. Your portfolio can change or shuffle.
3. Your company may purchase additional buildings.
4. You may move on to other companies that have "rough" or "challenging" buildings.

The following are excerpts from the Ottawa Police Crime-free Program.

What the Program is all about
- Multi-faceted approach to crime prevention geared specifically for the rental community.
- Partnership between police, landlords and residents.
- Copyright program (Mesa Police) that utilizes a three-phase certification process.
- Comprehensive screening process for new residents and renewed leases.
- Benefits to all partners involved.

Benefits for Landlords:
- More stable and satisfied resident base – extended lease term.
- Lower maintenance and repair costs – improved property values.
- Improved personal safety for owners and managers.
- Appreciation for dedication to Community involvement – appreciative neighbours, improved communication.

Benefits for Residents:
- Safer and more pleasant place to live – want a longer-term residency.
- Community environment – neighbours actually speak to each other.

- Identify with owners and managers who care and make a difference.
- Develop a sense of personal pride & ownership.

Benefits for Police:
- Reduced calls for service.
- Better use of police resources.
- Better communication –– exchange of information.
- Cooperation and better relationship with owners, managers and residents for the purposes of crime prevention, detection and enforcement.

Source:
https://www.ottawapolice.ca/en/safety-and-crime-prevention/Crime-Free-MultiHousing.asp, 2017. Reproduced with the permission of Ottawa Police Service, 2017.

D. Technical Standards and Safety Authority (TSSA)

The TSSA promotes and enforces public safety. TSSA has delivered public safety services on behalf of the Government of Ontario in four key sectors, as follows:

- Boilers and pressure vessels, and operating engineers
- Elevating devices, amusement devices and ski lifts
- Fuels; and
- Upholstered and stuffed articles.

Source: Reproduced with the permission of TSSA, 2017.

If ever you are contacted by TSSA, it usually means you are not in compliance with some safety requirements at one of your buildings. Their visit could also be for the purpose of conducting a random inspection. To better understand how the TSSA works, visit their Web site. You can also sign up or subscribe to receive TSSA newsletters, get the latest information on what is happening to improve safety and determine how your buildings measure up. The newsletter will also let you know who has violated the standards of safety and the repercussions of those violations. Being safety-conscious and understanding the potential risks involved in any area of your buildings (structure, equipment/ device or amenities) is the best way to practise safety as an excellent property manager.

Risk-informed decision making (RIDM)

The most tangible way to understand safety is in terms of risk. The International Standard Organization defines *safety* as a "freedom from risk." So, how do we define *risk*?

It is best described as:

- the probability or frequency that a regulated technology, product, device or infrastructure could lead to harm of the public (noted as the cause); and
- combined with the severity of that harm (noted as the Effect).

Risk is about predicting the future and evidence – obtaining the right information – increases the certainty of prediction.

It essentially works like this: TSSA gathers data related to incidents and non-compliance, examines trends or patterns, then makes risk-informed decisions to manage future public safety matters. In such a quantifiable way, TSSA seeks to prevent incidents through an understanding of their occurrence and effectively controlling that risk."

Source: Reproduced with the permission of TSSA, 2017.

An excellent property manager will always be safety-conscious. When you are, you will see and inspect things differently. Your inspection should even be more meticulous, especially with people whom you have contracted to maintain certain technical aspects of the buildings. Contractors like your elevator or escalator technicians should be monitored to ensure they are doing the job they are paid to do and meeting all the required standards. Therefore, if the elevator or escalator logbooks for any of your buildings are not up-to-date, this is a serious matter that should be given urgent attention. Failure to maintain the logbooks is an indication you are paying for maintenance services you are not receiving. Not having up-to-date logbooks for your elevators or escalator can lead to fines leveraged against the elevator company servicing your elevators or escalator. Poorly maintained logbooks also leave the company open to potential fines and lawsuits. Remember to inspect what you expect. When people are aware that you check to confirm that they are doing their work, they are usually more careful.

If TSSA shows up because there are defects to any of the technical devices at any of your buildings, always listen to what their concerns are. Ask them to explain the nature of their concerns to you as best as they can. If the concern is in an area where you have limited knowledge, be sure to take the inspector's name and contact information and follow up with him or her. If the concern is with the elevator or escalator, contact your elevator company first, as well as your elevator consultant. The consultant will advocate for the company's interest and can break down for you exactly what the issues are so you can understand the nature of the violation. Should you have any accident or injury on the property relating to any technical device, follow the TSSA's reporting procedure with urgency. Depending on the accident or injury, TSSA may have to visit the site and conduct their own investigation. Once clearance is given to address the cause of the accident or injury, treat this with priority and bring the device back into compliance. No matter the organization that is designated to enforce safety within your region for your properties, always demonstrate compliance. This builds respect for you and the company. Also form a habit of maintaining proper records to show you have complied.

E. City Inspectors

City inspectors will show up when tenants call them with concerns. In most cases your tenants will call the inspectors before they notify the building staff that they have a problem inside their apartments. Note also that the reasons for tenants' complaining to the city are not limited to the tenant's apartment. Tenants will also call the city about your amenities and any present or perceived defects in the common area. That is why it is important to do regular building inspections and follow up to ensure concerns are addressed with urgency. Regardless of what is brought to your attention by any bylaw officer, listen carefully and conduct your own investigation, documenting thoroughly as you go along. If the complaint is regarding an apartment, a rule of thumb is to check the tenant's file to see if the reported problem has a history and how the matter was addressed. Depending on your tenant base, your interaction with the city can be about any of the following complaints:

- swimming pool or hot tub (may be seasonal if outdoor, or year-round if indoor)
- heating (especially in the cold season)
- air conditioning (if included in the rent)
- general repairs—in-suite and common area
- noise
- pests
- capture of wild or nuisance animals
- care of pets, or animals attacking other tenants
- parking
- landscaping and snow removal
- capex projects

Despite your very best efforts, some tenants will feel the need to report you as a way of trying to control you. Do not take their complaints personally. You never know what the tenant's previous tenancy involved or what he or she had to endure. The person may have had reasons not to trust his or her previous landlord and will view you in the same light, until you can prove yourself. If the tenant is trying to beat the system, your organized approach to things will expose his or her ill intent. Do not try to be tough with the inspector; just comply. Compliance is not weakness. I learned through a course in negotiation skills that you can be uncomfortable and still be effective and efficient. After you comply, then you can complain.

Each municipality and each inspector is different. Therefore, get to know each of the inspectors. From experience, I have found that if you develop a professional relationship by demonstrating your willingness to comply, the inspectors will work with you by allowing you to correct the infraction within a certain time, instead of first writing an order. If you fail to do the repair in the specified time, then your company will be given an order. An order from the city does not look good on you the property manager or by extension the company. If the concern that is brought to your attention by the city requires a contractor, call the contractor yourself. Show active involvement by explaining to the contractor what is required and any time-sensitive date for the repair. Regardless of how large or small the order or repair is, always inform your area manager (AM) or regional manager (RM) and let him or her know what you are doing to correct the concern. Sometimes, depending on what needs to be addressed, you and your AM or RM will have to work together. Be sure to provide updates to your AM as you go along until the infraction is corrected and the matter is considered closed.

I had a case where I was contacted by a city inspector about mould after he visited an apartment within my portfolio. This was an inspector I had worked with many times in the past and had developed an excellent rapport with over the years. The inspector said the area inside the apartment looked mouldy or like mildew and required testing. The inspector said that he had asked the tenant if she had reported the matter either to me or my staff. (Based on the condition of the apartment, the inspector determined that the mould had not developed overnight.) The tenant told the inspector no. The inspector said he told the tenant that he would contact me the property manager about removing the mould. According to the inspector, he also related to the tenant that he had worked with me and my staff multiple times and knew for sure that once anything was brought to my attention, it was normally addressed. The inspector stated that he had noted the problem as a matter of protocol and would follow up with me in a few days. That statement was profound. For that I worked assiduously to address the problem within the time frame that the inspector and I had agreed on. Proof, along with the invoice and some pictures, that the work was completed was later sent off to the inspector within the agreed-upon time frame. An order was not written and the case was considered closed.

Some tenants will try to use the system to their advantage. That is why it is very important for you to act fast when you are contacted by the city or any other enforcement organization. You should also show evidence of your compliance and, in some cases, write the tenant a letter and copy the inspector who was assigned to the case as evidence when the investigation is completed. The inspector will sometimes send you a letter or e-mail stating that he or she conducted an investigation and found no cause for further action and has now deemed the case closed. You can print that e-mail and place it in the tenant's file so others can refer to it for future use. Tenants have a way of trying the same old trick if the property manager is reassigned to another location or moves on to another company. If you do not practise the art of creating a paper trail, these tenants will slip through the cracks.

I had a case where there was a huge leak one night inside an apartment and the staff had to go in to Shop-Vac the carpet. The staff also made arrangements with a contractor to have the carpet professionally shampooed later in the morning. The tenant related to the staff that she wanted to sleep and asked if the shampooing could be done not in the morning but the following day. As agreed, a Notice of Entry was served to have the carpet shampooed on the day the tenant had requested. The tenant was also asked to remove all furniture and personal items out of the affected area. When the contractor showed up the following day to shampoo the carpet, the area was not prepared, so the contractor went away. When the staff called me to report what had happened, I told the staff to document everything in a report, which he did. He was also instructed to serve a mandatory

Notice of Entry to have the carpet shampooed the following day. This tenant was a "drama tenant," capable of anything and everything.

The next thing I knew, a city inspector called me stating the tenant was concerned about mould and that nothing had been done about the wet carpet since the leak. The inspector stated the date of the leak and said by now something should have been done to address the wet carpet. Immediately I forwarded a copy of the notice that had been served to the tenant, including notes the staff had written indicating that the tenant said she wanted to sleep. The notes also indicated that the contractor had shown up to do the carpet but, because the work area had not been prepared by the tenant, the contractor left. The mandatory notice that was served to the tenant indicating that she had to comply was also sent to the inspector. This time the tenant complied and the carpet was shampooed. No order was written, so the inspector sent an e-mail confirming the case was closed. All e-mails from the inspector relating to the matter were printed and placed in the tenant's file.

The following month the tenant did not pay her rent, citing the apartment was not fit for living and saying she wanted a rent abatement. *Really? For what? Absolutely not!* I thought. In addition to the N4 that was served to the tenant for not paying her rent, I wrote the tenant a letter and quoted the findings of the city inspector. The letter also stated that any claim for accommodation should be made through the tenant's apartment insurance, which fact was clearly stated in the lease that she had signed. Because all reasonable attempts to address the carpet had been made in a timely manner, this tenant was denied a rent abatement. The letter mentioned that her failure to pay the rent would result in further legal actions, including eviction. Later she paid the rent in full.

Some inspectors will try to use their authority to intimidate you. Remember—once presented with an issue on your property, you must first listen and then comply. If you feel the need to defend yourself, do so respectfully. If you are in the wrong, apologize and work fervently to correct the infraction. Depending on the inspector who shows up, you may be given time to correct the infraction instead of first receiving a formal written infraction. If you need more time, do not be afraid to ask for more time. If you feel the need to complain, you can do so afterward. Never forget that everyone reports to someone. I remember being contacted by an inspector about an issue that should not have been an issue. The tenant was complaining about an outside light being too bright. The light in question had been like that for years but had suddenly become an issue to the tenant simply because the tenant could not have his way. The inspector who was assigned to the case was the egotistical type and was not afraid to demonstrate that ego. The manner in which the inspector spoke down to me was horrendous. That did not sit well with me. I informed the inspector that I would comply by making an adjustment to the lighting. I also called the contractor on the spot while the inspector was still present and arranged for the work to be done the following day. After the call to the contractor, I stated to the inspector that I was not pleased with the manner in which he spoke to me and said that I would be contacting his supervisor. I then mentioned the good rapport I had with the other inspectors (I did not mention any names) and said I intended to keep things that way. The matter of respect was a two-way street, I said. For someone with the office that he held, I was expecting nothing less. I looked forward to continuing to work with the inspector in the future, I said, but not if he continued to speak to me in the manner he had earlier.

I later contacted the inspector's supervisor and copied the inspector on the e-mail. From that time onward, all interactions with that particular inspector were more tolerable.

Another scenario was when I had to repair the entrance at one of the properties. I called the city and requested repairs to the street at the entrance of my property on the city's side. I was told that would be my responsibility. I could not accept that prospect because the repair in question was on the road that belonged to the city, not on the property I was managing. When it snowed, it was the city who cleared that area. Therefore, why should I have to repair it? I thanked the person I spoke with and told her I would be contacting city council. I sent a picture of the area that needed repair to the city council and copied the person I had spoken with earlier. In the e-mail, I stated that I'd been told to repair the damage to a city street. I further stated that the damaged street was not part of the property I was managing. Since it was on the city's side, it was also quite possible that a permit would have to be obtained if I had to do the repair. There was no way the property I was managing should have to do the city's work when I was paying property taxes. I further mentioned that I would be delighted to have a favourable response by the end of the day. About an hour later, the person I had spoken to earlier replied to the e-mail (she was copied on the e-mail) confirming that the repair would be done before 3:00 p.m. that day. At the end of the business day, I received another e-mail confirming the repair had been completed. I had my staff at the location verify that the repairs were completed and thankfully there were completed. When the city approaches you about an issue, it is because they want you to address the issue. Whenever you approach the city regarding an issue on their property that is affecting your interest, be respectful and persistent until you get the matter addressed.

The same inspector who'd dealt with the wet carpet contacted me again about the possible removal of some trees at one of my other properties. Someone from the neighbouring property had called the city to complain about the trees. Interestingly, at the time of the call, I was reviewing the landscaping budget and awaiting a second quote about the trees in question. I had dealt with this inspector several times over the years but had never met the inspector in person. So, I related I could meet him on the property the same day. I was finally able to put a face to the name. I agreed to remove the trees so peace could be maintained with the neighbouring property. I even thanked the inspector for the call and related that I was awaiting a second quote, adding that removing the trees would not be an issue. I am not sure what I'd said, but the inspector looked happily surprised and then asked me if I needed his help with anything on the property. Other than the trees, everything else was ok, I said. I thanked the inspector for the offer of assistance. I was also pleased to hear the offer of assistance extended. When an inspector can say that to you, it speaks volume about your ability and reputation to deliver, as well as the rapport you have developed with the inspector.

i. Parking

To achieve proper organization of parking on your property, you will need to request parking enforcement for those who violate the property's parking rules. Your property can only be approved for parking if it has the recommended signage posted at strategic spots throughout the property. If you are not aware or sure of how to proceed, contact the parking department at your municipal office and request their assistance. They may walk you through the process over the telephone. While that is good, I find that if you make an appointment to meet them on the property where you would like the enforcement, this works to your advantage. This approach allows them to walk the property with you and point out critical signage locations. You can ask all the questions you and your staff wish to ask. Some of these signs include but are not limited to the following:

- Tenant Parking Only
- Staff Parking Only
- Contractors Only
- Visitor Parking
- Fire / Emergency Access Routes
- Wheelchair by Permit Only
- Paid Parking
- No Parking

Try your best to implement parking enforcement. Initially it can be a pain to get everything done. Keep at it and the rewards will exceed any effort you put forth. Once enforcement is granted, it allows the city bylaw officers who attend to parking matters to enter your property and ticket vehicles that are in violation of the posted signs. The city benefits from the tickets that are issued for any violation. However, your benefits are far greater. Consider the following:

1. Parking enforcement protects the parking spot of the rightful registered user. Therefore, no tenant or visitor can park in the spot of another tenant. If anyone should do so, he or she can be ticketed.

2. It helps to control parking on the property. Visitors or guests from your competition are prohibited from parking on your property. If they do park on your property, they will be ticketed. I had a location where the tenants and guests of the competition had a good time parking on my property because I did not have parking enforcement. That did not last long. Once the parking enforcement authorization was approved, those violators were ticketed. And they never returned, because word got around. That was marvelous!

3. It forces tenants to pay for parking instead of getting a ticket, thus increasing your parking revenue, which is the ultimate goal.

Can you use private parking companies to do the enforcement? Absolutely you can! The disadvantage I find with these companies is that they are very slow to act. When they are called about a violation, by the time they get to the property, if they get there at all, the driver and the vehicle have left the property. The tenants become aware of this and the whole thing looks like a joke. From my experience, once you have a private company enforcing parking on your property, the city will not get involved. You cannot have both; you can only have either/or. When you have private parking enforcement, the city, say the matter is complicated, and stays away.

Authorized enforcement works best when you conduct your own internal parking audits. The parking audit, if done properly, will show which tenants are paying and which tenants are not paying for parking. The audit also shows what parking spots you have available. Remember that property where, after the annual in-suite or apartment inspection, a plan was carefully drafted to get rid of the gangs? Well, part of that plan also included parking control. That control was achieved by implementing enforcement by the city, as outlined above.

As soon as the enforcement was approved, a notice was sent to all the tenants informing them of the approved enforcement. In the notice, tenants were asked to complete a two-week date-sensitive form providing the following information: their apartment number, parking spot numbers, vehicle makes and models, and plate information. The collected information was matched against the rent roll, and later a proper parking log was developed. New parking stickers were issued to tenants who'd submitted their completed audit forms. Stickers were colour-coded for underground parking, outdoor parking, and parking on the different properties in the community or complex. A final notice was later sent as a reminder, asking all tenants to ensure they had valid plate stickers. All inoperable vehicles should be removed, tenants were told; otherwise, they would be ticketed and towed off the property.

What transpired as a result of that notice was alarming. It was uncovered that several tenants were not paying for parking and immediately had to do so, at the new price. The tenants who started paying for parking reported other tenants who they knew were not paying for parking. At the end of the audit, all the parking spots were accounted for. Tenants who violated the parking rules and the posted signs were ticketed. Finally, there was order, tight control and, best of all, increased revenue from parking. All superintendents and building managers were added to the parking enforcement forms.

Note well that some cities may require you to send an updated enforcement form every year. That way they are aware of those on your staff who are authorized to call and enforce parking rules on the property. Whenever you have new staff, they should be added to the form after they have hurdled the probationary period. Adding these new staff to the list helps to keep the parking control consistent and in place regardless of which staff are on duty or not.

F. Workplace Safety and Insurance Board (WSIB)

The following is an excerpt from the Web site of WSIB:

> The Workplace Safety and Insurance Board is an independent trust agency that administers compensation and no-fault insurance for Ontario workplaces.
>
> (4) The employer shall give a copy of the notice to the worker at the time the notice is given to the Board. 1997, c. 16, Sched. A, s. 21.
>
> **When to report an injury or illness to the WSIB**

As required by the Workplace Safety and Insurance Act, you must report a workplace injury or illness to the WSIB within 3 days after learning of your worker's injury or illness, if the injured worker:

- requires treatment from a health professional (beyond first aid), or
- is absent from work (e.g. if the worker has to leave work for any reason pertaining to the injury or illness), or
- earns less than regular pay (e.g. working fewer hours or being paid less per hour)

You must also report a workplace injury or illness, if the injured worker:

- does not receive health care, and requires modified work due to the injury or illness, and
- has been doing modified work at regular pay for more than 7 days

In this case, the reporting obligation begins on the 8th day of modified work.

Note: Modified work is any change in a regular job while a worker recovers from an injury or illness, such as being assigned different duties.

Even in cases where the injured worker agrees to do modified work at regular pay, you must report the injury or illness to the WSIB, if the modified work continues beyond 7 days.

Reporting rights and responsibilities

If a worker informs you about a workplace injury or illness, you are obligated to investigate it. If the injured worker only needed first aid and did not require any further health care, you are not required to report it to the WSIB. However, the law requires that you keep a record of all first aid details.

Note: A worker qualified to handle a workplace first aid station can give first aid. When a company doctor or nurse gives only first aid, it is not considered health care, since it did not require their professional skills.

If more serious treatment is required, transport the worker to the appropriate medical facility. Depending on the severity of the injury or illness, you may need to assign someone to accompany the injured worker or call an ambulance. *You must pay the costs for transporting the worker.*

Continue to pay the worker's full day's wages on the day of the accident. If the worker has lost wages and the claim is allowed, WSIB loss of earnings benefits start the working day after the injury or illness occurs.

If the worker receives only *modified work* at full pay following the injury, you are not required to report the injury until the 8th day following the accident. You must report workplace injuries or illnesses that go past 7 days of modified work. You must keep a record of the incident and what happens during the time your worker recovers.

You must report all cases where a worker suffers a *needlestick injury*, unless you have a surveillance protocol in place. A surveillance protocol is a formal procedure a health care institution follows to test and monitor a person exposed to an infectious disease to see if the person develops that disease.

Note: It is against the law to discourage a worker from reporting a workplace injury or illness. If you do, you could face a financial penalty as well as prosecution.

Source: http://www.wsib.on.ca. Reproduced with permission from WSIB, October 2017.

Given the importance of reporting work-related injuries of staff, as a property manager it is very important that you know when your staff volunteer to work on their days off or volunteer to work overtime. This is not something you should find out after the fact. It must be approved before. After an injury occurs, the next question to ask is, "Was this a work-related injury?" Even this can be a grey area. Why? Given the nature of the work of the site staff, not all overtime will be reported ahead of time. For example, when an emergency occurs on a property, it is natural for staff who live on the property who might be on their day off to go and assist with the emergency. On the other hand, dealing with emergencies would most likely have been covered during interviews for the job and by any subsequent job description, as well as training.

If some site staff live on the property, the next question to ask is, "Where is the workplace?" Steps to Justice defines *workplace* by posing and answering the question below:

I wasn't at work when I got hurt. Could this still be a work injury?

Answer
You're "at work" if:

- you're doing something that helps or benefits your employer
- you're in a place that your employer controls or supervises

Examples of being "at work" include:

- being in a parking lot or common areas, or on an access road that your employer controls or supervises
- driving to a work site if your workday starts when you get in your car
- going to and from work if your employer provides the transportation, for example, this could apply to migrant farm workers or miners working in remote areas
- going away from your work site to get something you need for work, such as supplies or tools

You could also be "at work" if:

- you're working at home and that's where you do your work
- you're doing some work at home because your employer asked you to

Source: https://stepstojustice.ca/common-question-plus/employment-and-work/i-wasnt-work-when-i-got-hurt-could-still-be-work-injury. Reproduced with permission from CLEO (Community Legal Education Ontario / Éducation juridique communautaire Ontario), October 2017.

Whatever the organization is called in your region for reporting work-related injuries, be sure to comply with their reporting procedures and those of your company. In doing so, you must conduct your own investigations. The investigations can also be conducted by a member of your company's joint health and safety committee if you have such a committee. It is also very important that you work with your AM and HR department, or the individual who acts in that capacity, who will most likely complete the relevant forms for submission to WSIB or the relevant organization for reporting work-related injuries.

19

The Financial Statement

A. The Numbers Capture a Picture and Tell a Story

I completed a short photography course so I would be able to take professional-looking pictures for any staging or redesigning jobs I did. I learned in the photography course that pictures we take are made up of little dots called pixels. In one of the classes, the instructor told me to zoom in on a picture I had taken with the digital camera so I could observe the dots in their different colours and shades that helped to form the image that was captured by the camera. Similarly, as a property manager, every decision you or your staff make is like a dot or pixel that helps to form the financial picture of that property. In this case, the accounting department becomes the camera capturing the dollar amount of every decision you and/or your staff focus on and make.

So, what is the financial picture of your property or properties? This picture comes in the form of the financial statement, which is a report prepared by the accounting department showing revenue generated and how you have utilized the funds allocated to you for each of the properties within your portfolio. In other words, it shows the images that you and your staff, who have become the photographers, have captured. Your company may review this report monthly, quarterly, semiannually or annually. Regardless of how often the review of the financial statement is done, you need to be able to explain in a nutshell, during your financial review meeting, your rationale for spending or overspending the funds. Chances are you will remember how some of the major expenses came about. However, the trick is when you have had many small expenditures of the same kind or of different kinds that eventually add up. Since a long pencil is better than a short memory, it is prudent for you to make your notes when you sign off on invoices for payments from your repair and maintenance (R&M) budget, whether that approval or signing off is done weekly, biweekly or monthly.

When you take a picture, you will not always capture every image. Some images will be more in focus, whereas others will simply fade into the background. However, when you stand back and look at the whole picture, it can be a beauty, a masterpiece. That is how you want your properties to look, financially well maintained, while keeping expenses down and producing impressive revenues. So, how do you, or how can, you stay in focus financially?

1. You stay in focus financially by studying all the principles detailed in the previous chapters. You cannot focus on the principles from one chapter alone, because all the chapters build on each other and make references to each other.

2. When you understand the principles in the chapters, this increases your financial peripheral vision, in other words, your analytical skills. Therefore, while you are focusing on the main image of profit, you can see what is happening at the sides and check your blind spots in the process. It is these analytical skills, and your understanding of the repercussions of your decisions or lack thereof, that will help you not to lose sight of the important things such as increasing revenue and keeping expenses down.

B. Dissecting the Financial Statement

Move-ins or new rentals, in addition to collecting rent on occupied apartments plus any rent increase, and rent charged for certain amenities will impact your revenue for the good. If you cannot rent the apartments that is called vacancy loss. For tenants who are unable to pay their rent and leave or end up being evicted, their unpaid rent is your credit loss. Keep this at the back of your mind - vacancy loss and credit loss will eat away at your revenue like termites. That is why it is very important for you and your staff to rent the apartments and collect the rents.

Your expenses will arise from actions that take place either behind the apartment door (most times called "in-suite") or outside the apartment door (most times called common areas and grounds). Move-outs or turnovers, as well as the day-to-day operation of the property with the maintenance of the occupied apartments, will affect your expenses. Depending on your tenant base or tenant type and the amenities you offer at your properties, revenue and expenses may be categorized in different ways.

Following are some types of revenue:

- Potential apartment rent
- Parking space rental
  - o   Residential
  - o   Non-residential
- Laundry (if not in-suite and you have a common laundry room shared by all tenants)
- Locker room rental
- Other rentals
  - o   Air-conditioning fee (if hydro is included in the rent and tenants must supply their own AC and pay extra for hydro usage)
  - o   Late fees (NSF)
  - o   Party/social room
  - o   Vending machines
  - o   Roof top lease (for antennas and cell tower equipment, or advertising banners/signs)
- Suite rental (if your suite is signed up with Airbnb or listed on some hotel search engine site)

Subtract from the revenue any vacancy loss due to unrented apartments or credit loss stemming from your tenants' inability to pay their rent.

Following are some types of expenses:

- Insurance
- Advertising
- Property management fees (if you used the services of a management company or your staff payroll)
- Property taxes (set by the local municipal government)
- Utilities
  - Water
  - Hydro (even if tenants pay their own hydro, you still need hydro for the common area)
  - Heating fuel
- Repair and maintenance
  - In-suite
    - Appliances
      - Air conditioner (applicable if AC is provided by the property and included in the rent)
      - Dishwasher
      - Refrigerator
      - Stove
      - Microwave
      - Washer and dryer combo (where applicable in some apartments)
    - Bathroom
      - Bathtub
      - Faucet
      - Fittings such as towel bars, tissue holder, shower curtain rod
      - Medicine cabinet
      - Tub surround
      - Vanity
      - Toilet
    - Cabinets, doors and doorframes, baseboards, cupboards
    - Cleaning – to prepare for move-ins or address emergencies
    - Electrical
      - Light fixtures including bulbs
      - Electrical or receptacle covers
      - Repairs from external contractors
    - Flooring
      - Carpet
      - Plank (LVP/LVT)
      - Ceramic tile
      - Vinyl composition tile (VCT)

- Painting
- Pest control
- Plastering
- Plumbing
- Other or miscellaneous expenses
- Common area
  - Appliances
    - AC in amenity rooms such as laundry room, cinema room or social room and game room
    - Dishwasher (social room)
    - Refrigerator (social room)
    - Stove (social room)
    - Microwave (social room)
  - Bathroom (social room or laundry room)
    - Faucet
    - Fittings such as tissue holder, dispensers
    - Vanity
    - Toilet
  - Cabinets, doors and frames, baseboards, cupboards in social room
  - Cleaning
    - Cleaning supplies
    - Contract cleaning
  - Electrical
    - Lights fixtures including bulbs
    - Electrical or receptacle covers
    - Repairs from external contractors
  - Equipment
    - Compactors
    - Boilers
    - Elevator and or escalator
    - Fire systems
      - Sprinkler system
  - Fire monitoring
  - Flooring
    - Carpet
    - Ceramic
    - Plank (LVP/LVT)
    - Vinyl composition tile (VCT)
  - Garbage and waste disposal
  - Painting
  - Pest control
  - Plastering
  - Plumbing

- Security and/or security systems and equipment
  o Grounds/landscaping
    - Garage
      - Cleaning
      - Door
    - Ice melts
    - Lawn maintenance
    - Lawn sprinkler system
    - Snow removal
    - Snow removal equipment such as snow blower etc.

C. Net Operating Income (NOI)

When all is said and done, the total operating revenue, less vacancy loss, credit loss and less the total operating expenses, will be your net operating income (NOI), provided the number is positive. This excludes non-operating expenses such as mortgages, depreciation and capital expenditure. If the number falls on the negative side, meaning your expenses exceeded your revenue, you have a net operating loss (NOL). Given the fact that you are managing an income-producing property, the last thing you want is a loss. Your job as the property manager is to make sure there is more revenue coming in than expenses being paid out. This helps to give you an impressive NOI. Therefore, ask yourself, What are some things my team and I did to achieve those numbers? If you have an NOL, ask, What are some things the team and I can do different and better that will help the numbers for my properties to trend in the right direction? It is always good to meet with your staff and include them in the process and make it a team-building project. If you have prepared or you are preparing for an internal financial review, and your numbers are on the positive side, this is the time to celebrate your achievement with your staff and come up with new tactics for the next financial year. At a convenient time before your financial review meeting, be sure to share your ideas with your area manager (AM). Your AM may have some ideas that could build on what you already have. Below are some strategies you could implement:

i. Strategies to Increase Revenue

Your pricing structure for any of the following things can greatly affect your revenue:

Apartment rent

- Serve the maximum guideline you are allowed for your N1 or notice of rent increase for apartments, parking, storage lockers, etc.
- Realistically push the rent on turnover to obtain maximum rent by way of rent mapping the apartments based on the following:
  o view
  o location
  o accessibility

- o   size
- o   unique layout
- o   upgrades done in the apartment

Short stay suite rental

Investigate how to and if you can obtain an Airbnb account as well as advertise the guest suite on hotel booking sites. That way, when your guest suite is not in use for company reasons, you can increase occupancy thus increasing your revenue. The rental could be for a few days to a few weeks. Be sure to clearly state in the advertisement that the suite is self-contained and what guests can pretty much expect to get for their money. You want to ensure your site staff are not tied up doing suite related work, when they should be focusing on core building operation duties. Your company should decide ahead of time, if the same lease or tenancy agreement will be used, or a special contract will be drafted for this purpose.

Storage rooms/lockers

Most times the rent will depend on the size of the locker. Check out the price of lockers at self-storage companies and you will see that the prices are not all the same even if the lockers are the same size. I have seen where some companies, in addition to charging more for larger lockers, will charge more for the amenities they offer with the storage, such as surveillance camera, safety locks, accessibility and convenience of the lockers. Rethink the way you price the storage you have on your property. This could impact your revenue favourably.

a.   If you have a storage room or lockers in the hallway on each floor, those spaces can be rented at a premium because of their convenience and easy accessibility.

b.   If you have any storage at the basement level, the rent for the storage spaces on B1/P1 can be a little higher than the rent charged for storage on B2/P2 given the accessibility to the first floor.

c.   Locker rooms closest to the elevators can be priced as premium too. Make sure floors inside the locker rooms and the floors leading to them are clean and that lighting is excellent in your storage rooms. Storage rooms should be inviting, as this helps to project a sense of safety and spaciousness.

Parking

You could also rent map your parking. This pricing concept for parking is not new. Observe carefully the parking fees for hospitals. Parking facilities that are on the hospital's property will boldly tell you they offer premium parking, meaning you will pay more. Parking facilities farther away from the hospital will charge lower parking fees. Also consider event parking. The closer you are to the venue, the higher the parking fee will be. Even municipal parking will charge you more if the parking locations are closer to high-demand areas or to main facilities and attractions. Below are some strategies you could implement:

a. Location
   Parking spots on your first parking level should be charged a premium price, more than those on the lower levels. Indoor/covered parking should be higher in rent than outdoor parking.

b. Accessibility
   Parking spots that are closer to the entrance of the building from the garage, or closer to exits, should also be charged premium rates.

c. Convenience
   Any convenience such as an electric outlet for cars that require charging should be priced at a higher rate rent regardless of where it is located for the simple fact that the car is utilizing the hydro/electricity.

d. Bundling
   You can bundle the parking cost if a tenant has two vehicles. Normally each vehicle must park in its designated area as indicated on the building parking sticker. By using a special parking sticker, you can offer flexi-park at an additional price. This flexi-park will allow any of the two vehicles to park in either spot. Oftentimes when a tenant is given a parking violation ticket for parking in the incorrect spot, the vehicle owner will sometimes say something to the effect of "I parked in my girlfriend's [or wife's, or boyfriend's, or husband's] spot, and she [or he] parked in mine." However, if you have a flexi-park system, you can eliminate this confusion. I remember booking a flight online and was informed that I could choose my own seat if I paid an extra fee. Otherwise, a seat would be assigned to me.

e. Bike rack rentals

f. Event parking
   There are now apps available that you can sign up any temporary available parking spots for short term parking. Why not use one of your contractor parking spots as a trial. A word of caution is to use only one spot at all times. Since you never know when an emergency will occur at the property, you want to ensure parking is always available for your contractor if and when they show up for any emergency.

Party room

If you have notice holders on each floor and inside the elevator(s), place a nice flyer advertising the party or social room in the notice holders. Give your tenants reasons to use the social room. You should advertise close to major holidays. Advertising serves as a reminder to tenants that you have a social room that is available for them to use.

Vending machines

Are vending machines owned by your company, or does the company rent the space out? Rent map the placement or location of these vending machines too. Nope, it's not crazy. It is a matter of location, location, location!

    a. If you rent the spots, you can charge more if the owner wants the vending machine placed in a high-traffic area such as in the laundry room, in the cinema room or outside the cinema room or lobby.

    b. Don't forget that these machines use electricity to operate and your site staff provide a unique service by cleaning off these machines daily, regardless of where they are located.

    c. In addition, who calls the vending machine company to replenish the supply or service the machine when there is a problem? Your staff! Hence, you also provide a bit of administration service.

Now do you see the picture of premium rental cost? I hope you do.

Methods to support and monitor your strategies/plans

You must conduct your regular market survey of the competition. It will give you an idea of what the market is able to bear in terms of rent and other amenities. Do not be afraid to test the market. You can test the market by adding even an extra $5 to parking, storage etc. Remember these low amounts add up over 12 months and impact your NOI. As an excellent property manager, be sure to monitor what you have implemented by doing the following:

- Maintain proper and tight parking control by conducting annual parking audits and increasing parking rental on turnover, based on residential and non-residential parking in the area. Conduct random checks when you go to the buildings. Do not forget that tenants can also list their parking spot(s) on parking apps as **available** and rent those spots out during special events. If your property is close to any attractions or office buildings, your parking garage or parking lot should be closely monitored. Why is this so? During special events, there is always a demand for parking. In addition, if the tenant leaves for work in the days, it is easy for them to rent their spot out so that it is occupied while they are away at work. Please ensure your lease or tenancy agreement have clear rules about subletting or the illegal use of the garage or parking lot. Be sure your parking enforcement forms are up-to-date and all your staff at the property are listed to call the bylaw officer or applicable authority for ticketing illegally parked vehicles on your property.

- Ensure your staff are doing the following:

    o Doing their door knocking and ensuring tenants are paying their rent on time.

- o Renting apartments. You will also have to be vigilant in marketing your apartments to ensure you have heads and beds in those apartments.
  - o If you fail in any of these aspects, it will be like termites eating away at your revenue.

- Keep the property clean, including inside the building, and do landscaping to attract and retain tenants. This can be accomplished by conducting regular building inspections and acting on the findings, as well as implementing and enforcing a time constraint cleaning checklist or cleaning routine.

- Ensure work orders submitted by tenants to address maintenance issues inside their apartments are completed by your staff in a timely manner.

- Reposition the building by doing capital improvement upgrades.

- How do you measure up to the competition? What is the condition of your apartments when compared to the competition? Are you doing major upgrades inside apartments on turnover? Why not consider adding extra appliances such as washer and dryer combo inside some apartments? Upgrades should also include Smart Wi-Fi plugs as well as light switches that can synch to electronic devices. Upgrading is the new trend and will continue to be. You can add more to the rent when apartments become vacant and they have more than the average appliances.

- When you are going to do several substantial capital upgrades, consider applying for an AGI (above guideline increase) to change your tenant base and increase your rent roll.

- Hold tenant appreciation events. These tell tenants they belong somewhere, that they have a home. It helps with tenant retention and draws others who are friends or relatives of existing tenants to the property as new tenants.

- Treat your staff well by appreciating their skill and loyalty to you and the company. If you do this, they will go above and beyond the call of duty to make things happen by doing things and not even charging you.

ii. Strategies to Minimize Expenses

Here are some other practical steps you can take to keep your building expenses down:

- Install motion detector lights in chute rooms and common area laundry rooms. That way, lights do not have to be left on constantly. They should automatically come on when the door opens or motion is detected inside.

- Do not hand over absolute power of the building operation to your staff so they can order as they wish, call contractors as they wish and otherwise do as they wish. Empower them by doing the following:

  - setting brackets of authority on certain decisions
  - consistently training them by having them accompany you the property manager on various inspections (This helps your staff to align with your thought process)
  - conducting regular staff meetings and setting measurable and achievable goals

- Train staff and have them do some of the smaller repairs instead of calling contractors.

- Do partial repairs on renovations where possible inside turnover apartments. Some apartments are so nicely maintained that when the tenant moves out, all you have to do is clean it before the next tenant moves in. You may inspect another apartment and see that the walls need painting but that the ceiling is ok. Some apartments may need just a single coat of paint. This could be purely based on your type of tenant; some may want to see or smell some evidence of fresh paint.

- Practising preventative maintenance will help to minimize damages to certain equipment such as fire equipment.

- Hire staff who have a teachable attitude and train them to your standard.

- Treat any pest reported or observed swiftly and aggressively. Fast acting helps to contain and eradicate pests.

- Scrutinize invoices before you pay them to determine if you must pay in full, pay in part or pay nothing at all.

- Scrutinize quotes properly to ensure you are getting value for money.

- Keep your accounts receivable (AR) down by giving tenants different options for making payments. Set targets for the properties and ensure staff are working to collect the outstanding rent.

- Ensure building/site staff do not order more supplies than necessary.

- Select good tenants and inform them of the need to care for the rental unit during their tenancy. This is training your new tenants and setting the expectations from the beginning. This will reduce the maintenance cost during their tenancy and the turnover cost when they move out.

- Evict disruptive tenants. This will help you to retain the good tenants, which spells less turnover cost. The other advantage is that your staff will be happy and it will help with staff retention.

- Since new staff tend to go through a learning curve, which can sometimes be costly, keep your staff happy by listening to them, supporting them, rewarding them where necessary with commendations and providing them with tools needed to carry out their jobs. This will reduce staff turnover and build staff morale.

D. Explaining the Numbers

Some software systems are capable of allowing you to make a comparison of the current financial period, measuring it against the exact time the previous year. By doing that comparison, you will have a good measuring stick to analyze your financial performance for growth, stagnation or regression. Wherever you fall short, you need to understand some of the factors that contributed to your results, especially if those factors threw a curveball into your budget and lowered your NOI or, worse, resulted in a net operating loss (NOL). Some of these factors could stem from any of the following:

Weather

1. If you have a harsh winter and you have buildings with dated, drafty and faulty windows or balcony doors, this may cause heat to escape. Therefore, your tenants may compensate for the low heat or heat interruption by using their ovens or space heaters to warm their apartments. If hydro is included in the rent, you are most likely to pay for the hydro that is going out the windows. No one wins when you have these kinds of windows. This may explain any increase in your hydro bill. This is a time to tactfully push for new windows. Or the scenario could be that you have installed new windows and you are now reaping the benefits of newly installed windows. Therefore, your hydro bill could be lower than the previous year. A spike in hydro does not have to be from faulty windows. It could be that you unknowingly have a marijuana/pot grow operation or just a bad winter. You may review *Marijuana/Cannabis Grow Operation* which was discussed in details under the chapter titled Emergencies.

2. Bad weather can also cause freezing pipes, thus affecting the operation of the building. Freezing pipes can result in major flooding, forcing you to do major restoration work such as drywall repair, plastering and painting, as well as address damages to flooring. There is a possibility that the restoration expenses may have to be absorbed by your building's R&M budget, if there is no emergency contingency account.

3. Thawing ice from many snowfalls can result in leaks or flooding.

4. Damaged fire equipment can lead to false alarm fees if your staff fail to perform routine drum drips, which can cause major damage to the sprinkler system.

Staffing

In our chapter on *Staffing*, we had stated that most of your time as a property manager will be spent on staff related concerns. We also stated that your budget will revolve around your staff and how they execute their duties. Your staff or the lack thereof can drive a huge hole in your budget based on the following:

1. Staff may be unable to rent out apartments, thus increasing your vacancy loss.

2. New staff have a learning curve, and some learning curves will be steeper than others. Staff who are lazy and lack confidence tend to call external contractors for most or all repairs. Address this matter with your staff and get the necessary training for them to improve.

3. Aggressive and harsh staff behaviour toward tenants can drive tenants away. I inherited a superintendent who was so harsh and unreasonable that no one could have a civil conversation with him. Vacancy at his location was very high. When he was placed at another location within my portfolio, his behaviour was the same, maybe even worse. Many tenants vacated, and my office line became a hotline for multiple complaints regarding that staff member.

4. Staff with domestic issues can disrupt the peace of the other tenants and chase them away. Your tenants will report such instances to you. If you fail to act, it will hurt you financially. Get the staff member the required help first. If that fails, where legally necessary you must part ways with the staff.

5. Site staff sometimes profit from tenants by collecting rent monies and fees, pocketing them and not recording or reporting these transactions.

6. Employees sometimes steal building supplies.

7. Some staff are lazy and unwilling to work and are just there for the benefit of the "free apartment." Make sure you document these instances. Don't let up on these staff members.

8. Sometimes you may lack staff and be forced to use security or external contract workers.

Unwise selection of tenants

Your failure to select proper tenants can adversely affect your budget in the following ways:

1. Some tenants will trash the unit on turnover, to the degree that you wonder if it is a war zone. When some tenants vacated an apartment in a location I had before the tenant base

changed, you could not tell what colour the carpet was and would be led to believe the stove was a grease collector.

2. Tenants with poor housekeeping abilities sometimes have offensive smell emitting from their apartments that disturbs other tenants and chase them away.

3. Some students tend to wreck their apartments before they leave. Sometimes they leave the apartment full of personal items and you must foot the bill either to store them for a while or dispose of these items.

Emergency

An emergency of any kind can wreck your budget. An emergency can stem from human error or be a natural disaster. Put together an emergency response plan to minimize the impact of the emergency. Preventative maintenance can help to prevent certain emergencies.

Uncontrolled pests of any kind

Review the consequences of not treating pests.

Other areas to analyze are the move-outs/turnovers and move-ins or rentals. Remember move-out will affect your expenses and move-in will impact your revenue. What if your comparative report shows you have more move-outs or turnover this year than the previous year? What are the causes for the move-outs/turnovers? Answers to the questions below can provide you with greater insight:

1. Is the rate of move-out/turnover consistent with the season or time of year? Buildings tend to have fewer move-outs in the fall and winter. What if you are seeing an unusual spike in the turnover at that time of the year? Investigate the cause.
2. Is the move-out pest-related?
3. Where are vacating tenants moving to?
   a. Is it the competition?
   b. What does the competition have that you do not have?
4. Is your tenant base mostly students from nearby colleges/universities? Your turnover cycle might be a little busier at the end of each semester/term, especially toward the end of the traditional school year.
5. Do you have extensive renovations going on in the building or on the property, such as underground parking garage restoration or balcony replacement/upgrade, and tenants are not able to deal with the excessive prolonged noise?
6. Is the new rent stemming from an AGI too high for your tenant base?
7. Are tenants unhappy because of rude or incompetent staff?
8. Are tenants unhappy because of disruptive tenants and their occupants, or multiple car break-ins?

Move-in will impact your revenue. If your apartments are filling up as fast as the tenants vacate, that can be good, as long as the new tenants stay to the end of the lease/tenancy agreement or stay beyond the term of the lease. Even though you want more revenue, you must be careful not to be too aggressive with increasing the rent, as this could lead to major vacancies. Did you have a higher vacancy loss this year or the previous year? If you are not renting fast enough, you should be asking what is causing the vacancy loss. Some questions or factors to consider and investigate to determine the cause of excessive vacancies are as follows:

A. How are you marketing your apartments? Do you need to change your approach?
B. Is the rent too high above market value?
C. Is your product dated and not in keeping with industry trends or inconsistent with the competition's product?
D. Do you have challenging staff or incompetent staff with no sales skills?
E. Does the season have anything to do with the loss?
F. Does the building have pests?
G. Is there a lack of staff?

Your careful analysis of these factors will allow you to meditate on the financial picture and on the story, you want your properties to tell. If for any reason you end up with a net operating loss, understand what created the loss. This will put you in a better position to come up with strategies to bounce back from the loss before the next financial statement.

20

Professional and Personal Development

A. Continuous Learning

Every year many residential property managers look to engage in some form of capital improvement project at the properties they manage. These improvements enhance the value of the properties in the portfolio. If the purpose of capital improvement projects is to extend the useful life of an asset, then property managers must look for ways to improve and expand their knowledge through continuous professional development. In an online article titled, "The Difference Between Personal and Professional Development," the author Rachel Matthews, of Bray Leino Learning, states the following:

Professional development involves developing yourself in your role to entirely understand the job you do and how you can improve. It involves enhancing the necessary skills to carry out your role as effectively as possible and is something that will continue throughout your working life.

With changes to our working lives happening every day, be it economical change, amendments in legislation or even the advance of technology, it is important to develop your skillset to remain effective in your career.

Effective professional development involves ensuring your knowledge and understanding of your area of expertise for your career is always at the highest possible level. It is the acquisition of skills and knowledge for career advancement, but it also includes an element of personal development.

Source: https://brayleinolearning.co.uk/blog/2014/october/09/what-is-the-difference-between-personal-and-professional-development/, October 9, 2014. Reproduced with permission from Bray Leino Learning, January 26, 2018.

Hence, if you are aspiring to become an excellent residential property manager, professional development is not an option; it is a necessity. Remember what you learned earlier, that you are the healthy heart that keeps the staff, or "blood," pumping. View professional development as an exercise that keeps you, the heart, healthy. Another way to view professional development is to liken it to the oil that keeps the engine moving. Improving who you are as a residential property manager helps you to function more efficiently in your career. It is what helps to make you an excellent property manager. Some of the benefits of professional development are as follows:

- It keeps you up-to-date with what is new and relevant in your industry or chosen profession.
- It helps you to improve any weakness or skill set.
- It helps you to learn a new skill.
- It enables you to learn new and improved methods for doing things.
- It helps you to maintain competency, which is similar to improving the useful life of an asset.
- It builds your credentials or allows you to maintain a designation.
- It causes you to build on what you have and helps you begin to stand out because your improved performance becomes noticeable.
- It helps to refine your skills and gives you increased confidence.
- It helps in your overall growth.
- It helps you to recognize challenges as opportunities.
- It is self-fulfilling.

B. Examples of Professional Development Courses

Make it your aim to engage in some form of continuous learning or professional development each year. You can do this in a variety of ways, such as the following:

- Taking short courses, in class or online
- Attending workshops
- Attending conferences
- Participating in in-house training
- Taking seminars
- Taking extended courses as in a degree program or for a specific designation
- Participating in coaching and mentoring programs. If you cannot afford a mentoring program, find a mentor. Model the good you see in others.
- Connecting with a professional membership association
- Joining a committee at work (health and safety or emergency or disaster preparedness)

C. Where to Find Professional Development Courses

Where can you go and what kinds of professional development can you engage in? That depends on where you are and how far you want to advance in property management. Whether you are sure or unsure of where you can find courses for professional development, the following are some ideas you may wish to consider:

- Go on the Internet and research "professional development." The results will give you a broad idea of what is available in your geographic location, such as what colleges or universities are offering.

- Attend a leadership and team-building course.
- Take a customer service course.
- Enroll in a negotiation course.
- Improve your public speaking skills. Toastmasters, a global public speaking club, is a great place to start. It's fun and inexpensive. There is always a club close to you. Visit their Web site at www.toastmasters.org to learn more.
- Join an industry-related association or increase your knowledge through courses offered by reputable institutions geared specifically toward property management, either commercial or residential. Consider the following:
  - Buildings Owners and Managers Association (BOMA) International. Visit the Web site at www.boma.org to learn more about BOMA International, or www.bomacanada.ca to learn more about BOMA Canada.
  - Building Owners and Managers Institute (BOMI). An independent institution, BOMI offers courses specifically geared toward property management, with their primary focus being on commercial property management. Bear in mind that some residential apartment buildings include a commercial component. Visit the BOMI Web site and see what they have to offer that may be of interest to you: www.bomi.org.
- University of Toronto has great leadership courses and offers a Leadership Essentials Certificate. Visit the Web site at www.utoronto.ca to learn more.

We live in a constantly changing world. Everything gets updated—vehicles, home appliances and other fixtures and fittings. Think also of the electronic gadgets and mobile devices around you, such as cellphones and GPS devices. New streets get built. One-way streets become two-way streets and vice versa. If you do not update your GPS or buy a new one, how will you have accurate directions to get you from point A to your desired or intended destination? Many devices we use are now part of our daily lives. They get updated every year or sometimes within a few months. When you turn on these devices, they will alert you that updates are available. If you fail to do the updates, the device will not operate at its optimum. Now, put yourself in place of those devices and you will see that if you are not updating or improving your knowledge, you cannot operate at optimum capacity in your chosen career. How do you expect to get from one career point to the next if you do not update your skills? You are bound to get lost and be left behind. Hence, if you are aspiring to become an excellent residential property manager, professional development is not an option; it is a necessity.

D. Personal Development and Self-development

Personal development and self-development can take place only through your awareness. It happens when you are consciously incompetent, which means you know that there is a weakness in more than one area of your life that you need to improve. These areas could include but are not limited to your health, finances, emotions, relationships, dress and grooming. Personal development is about you the person, not necessarily your profession. It is about reaching your fullest potential and becoming a better version of yourself. This was confirmed by Tyler Leslie, in the April 14, 2016, *Success Magazine* article titled "3 Ways Self-Improvement Can Change Your Life." Here are three specific ways that focusing on self-improvement can change your life:

1. **It presents you with new opportunities.**
   Growth in yourself eventually leads you to new opportunities, opportunities that don't come about *until* you grow into the person who is ready for them. All you have to do is focus on self-improvement—start by reading personal development articles, books, blogs—and implement the things you learn into your own life.

2. **It increases your self-esteem to new levels.**
   Self-confidence is ultimately the starting point to following your dreams—you have to believe in yourself and your dreams enough to go after them. As you grow, you're building up that mindset, that belief.

   When I picked up my very first personal development book—*Think and Grow Rich* by Napoleon Hill—that's when my self-esteem started rising, when I really started to believe in myself and my goals. Reading success books was what pushed me to grow, to change, the motivation behind my goals.

3. **It can help you become a better version of yourself.**
   Becoming a better version of yourself is the main goal of self-improvement—to improve in your job, your business, your relationships. Whatever area of your life you're working on, that's part of growing as a person. You have to constantly look at what you can improve and have the awareness to know what needs to be done to do it.

   The most effective way of finding out how to get better is to ask the people around you to make a list of what you're best at and where you could make improvements. Take the list of improvements and work on them one by one."

   Source: http://www.success.com/blog/3-ways-self-improvement-can-change-your-life, July 9, 2017. Reproduced with permission from *Success Magazine*.

Personal development is part of maintaining your image. Never forget to engage in personal development. To learn more about personal improvement and self-improvement, you can read books or listen to audio books that will encourage and inspire you to grow personally, professionally and emotionally, as well as financially. Following is a list of some books that focus on personal development:

- *Think and Grow Rich*, by Napoleon Hill. This book helps you to think your way positively out of every problem by having a definite purpose and a definite plan. Visualize the outcome and work/act persistently to achieve that which you have visualized. This book teaches you to embrace and learn something from every defeat or failure and then to move on.

- *Success Through Positive Mental Attitude*, by Napoleon Hill and W. Clement Stone, teaches you to have a hopeful mental state and outlook amid any circumstances.

- *The 21 Irrefutable Laws of Leadership*, by John C. Maxwell, gives a clear description of what leadership is and explains how you can lead your team effortlessly and with joy. I recommend reading all of John Maxwell's books on leadership.

- *The Richest Man in Babylon*, by George Samuel Clason, teaches the basic principles of how to save some of your earnings and how to invest what you save.

- *Rich Dad Poor Dad*, by Robert Kiyosaki and Sharon Lechter, teaches that financial success comes from improving your financial knowledge.

- *Success Magazine* zooms in on people who are successful and explains the processes they used along the journey, including how they hurdled obstacles to achieve their success. The audio version is great because it allows you to listen as you travel in your vehicle.

These books increase your awareness and allow you to look deep within yourself. They help you to readjust the way you think and your outlook on every aspect of your life. If you enrich the lives of others by adding value to them, you enrich your own life. You should expect the best for yourself. From your enriched mind, you begin to visualize the new or improved you with a balanced mindset, and then you practise what you've learned. Once the results are favourable, you keep doing more of it.

Personal development or self-improvement can also be about learning a hobby, such as the following:

- joining a gym and making full use of the membership
- painting or drawing
- baking and cake decorating
- vacation cooking
- winemaking
- playing the piano or another musical instrument
- hiking
- biking
- mountain biking
- playing golf
- playing tennis
- swimming
- kayaking
- professional photography
- ballroom dancing
- knitting
- sewing
- jewelry making
- horseback riding
- creative writing

Make a list of the hobbies you want to learn. You can learn a hobby by yourself, with a friend or as a family. Do whatever makes you happy. Whomever you can draw some inspiration from can accompany you. Once you have achieved any personal or professional improvement goals, celebrate these achievements, small or large, with yourself first. No, it's not crazy; you are just absorbing the moment and embracing your journey for all it is worth. Take time to look back and commend yourself for sticking to your goal, knowing that when you wanted to quit, you did not quit. Your true self would not allow you to quit. Once you have celebrated with yourself, then you can expand the celebration to include those closest to you.

i. Saving Your Money

a. Save with Your Company

Does your company have a pension plan that you must make contributions to out of each pay cheque? Does your company match your contributions? If they do, great! Then max out that contribution. If the minimum contribution is $15 and the maximum is $50, make the sacrifice and contribute the maximum of $50. Let us say you are paid biweekly; this is what your contributions will look like for the year:

- Minimum contribution
  $15 × 26 pay cheques = $390 from you and $390 from your company. Your total savings for the year will be $780.
    <u>Or</u>
- Maximum contribution
  $50 × 26 pay cheques = $1,300 from you and $1,300 from your company, for a total savings of $2,600.

Which one is better? You decide. Never leave money on the table.

b. Save with Your Bank

To develop a more disciplined approach toward your personal savings, set up a standing order with your bank where your pay gets deposited. This arrangement tells the bank to take from each pay cheque deposited to your account a predetermined amount and to put that amount into another account. That account can be an investment account or whatever you choose. Regardless of the account(s) you choose, make sure you have some of what you have saved in the form of liquid (cash) that is readily available to you for use, if you need it. Because the money comes out before you see it, you are forced to live on whatever is left. In the book *Richest Man in Babylon*, the author encourages readers to save 10 percent of their earnings. Let that be 10 percent of the gross. This would be like paying yourself first. Hence, that amount must be taken out first, before living expenses. As the author said, you will not miss it. I found this to be very true. If you are given a pay increase, I personally recommend adding that increase to what you are already putting into that special account. If you cannot add all the pay increase, try to add some of it, even if it is $5 extra from each pay cheque. Another method some financial experts recommend is paying or contributing to God (Jehovah) or a charity first. Charitable contributions help to reduce the amount you pay in taxes at the end of the year. Make sure you get a tax receipt. After charity you can pay yourself and then live off of whatever is left.

A word of caution is, do not flaunt what you have saved. Doing so is an invitation to those around you; they will know that you have money to give away or lend. I was once advised by a very successful businessman to lend to friends or family only what I could afford to lose. Meaning, if you do not get back the money, how will it affect you? How comfortable would you be stepping away from that amount? I also learned you should get comfortable telling others "no." When you lend to friends and family, this is how your money tends to come back to you:

1. You get back the money in bits. You may never get the money back in one lump sum.
2. You are not repaid on time. There tends to be something more important than the date the person promised to return the money.
3. You may never get back the money. Then you will have to deal with the loss and the damaged or strained relationship.
4. You may get part back but never the full amount.
5. If you get the money back, you will not get it with interest regardless of how long it took for the person to pay you back.

That is why you lend *only what you can afford to lose*. If you do not get the money back, then no big deal, just carry on.

Savings alone will not bring you financial stability, success or freedom. What saving does is provide a springboard for investment. Savings is also a type of safety net that gives you peace of mind should you have to deal with any unexpected crisis or turbulence. Some people also call their savings a safety cushion. The difference between a net and cushion is that a net will sustain a harder fall, whereas a cushion is more for resting. A cushion cannot sustain a fall. When is a safety cushion needed? Sometimes you may need a financial cushion to rest, probably after an illness, family emergency or disaster. You will need a safety cushion to get you through any processing period if you have applied for certain insurance. From personal experience, sometimes that processing period can be anywhere from two weeks to two or more months. Make sure you set aside funds that will carry you through however long or short the processing period is. Not having to worry about money or bills while sick or when dealing with an emergency helps you to focus on recovery. A safety net, on the other hand, allows you to spring back to your feet or rest longer from your illness. When you have this safety net, you do not have to run to anyone in a panic for help to survive. What you have set aside in savings helps to keep your dignity and pride intact while you weather your unexpected crisis, storm or unexpected turbulence in private, without fear or worry.

Some people may say saving is a waste of time. Everyone is entitled to their own opinion, and you are entitled to protect your own dignity. If you find yourself in a situation where you are at the mercy of friends and family and they help you out financially, that is great. However, some may feel the need to use the fact that they had to come to your aid financially as a license to talk down to you or treat you less than. If that has ever happened to you, or if you have witnessed it happening to someone you know, you will understand the bitter taste it leaves and the heavy embarrassment it causes. Remember you never know when an emergency will happen. However, when you have savings set aside, from a financial standpoint, it makes dealing with such crises or turbulences less stressful or overwhelming.

So, is saving your money a criterion to become a property manager? Absolutely not! However, your personal savings helps you to weather unexpected personal and financial storms or emergencies with your dignity intact, thus assisting you in maintaining your image and function efficiently as an excellent property manager.

c. *Discipline Yourself to Save*

Some people write down what they've spent after they have spent money. That approach is no good and will get you nowhere. Start with a personal budget. Most cellular phones have apps and spreadsheets that will allow you to set up a personal budget. This budgeting exercise helps you to see how you will spend your income *before* you get the pay cheques. Be determined to follow the budget as closely as you can and do not deviate. Do not try to work things out in your head; put it on paper or on your phone in the spreadsheet. You need to literally see it. The beauty of these spreadsheets and apps is that they have built-in formulas, or you can input the formula if there is none. The formulas will allow you to see instant results and calculate as you make additions or changes.

Budget according to how you are paid. If you get paid weekly, then do a budget for each week in the month, such as week 1, week 2, week 3 and week 4. This is because you have different expenses each week and you need to see where your money is going. If you get paid biweekly, you should set the budget for each pay cheque or deposit to your account. When you see where your money is going, you will become more disciplined. Budget how much money you are putting into savings. Do not fall into the habit of spending first, then saving whatever is left. You should do the reverse. You pay yourself first. This was one of the options mentioned earlier. The other option was, first you set aside money for God (Jehovah). If you are not religious, choose a reputable charity. Just make sure you get a tax receipt. Then you should set aside money for savings. Whatever is left over, goes toward bills or living expenses. Learn to figure out a way to let that work. Cut back on nonessentials. You know what those nonessentials are. At first it will be uncomfortable to do this, but you will get used to being uncomfortable. Make this your way of life. It works.

Savings alone will not make you financially successful. Speak with a reputable financial advisor about how to invest what you have saved. Even if you do not agree with the advisors, you can learn something from them. You can find a financial advisor at your bank or any reputable investment company. Do not be quick to get into any get-rich networks and throw away your hard-earned money. Find a mentor and make it your aim to increase your financial intelligence and apply what you have learned. If you do not have a mentor, observe and study the habits of others who are successful and who have achieved their success in a legal way. Whatever you are doing, try to increase your knowledge to do it in a better and smarter, not harder, way.

When you have reached your fullest potential, you have balance in all areas of your life. The process of reaching your fullest potential is a journey and not a destination. Embrace each stage of your career and keep moving forward. Like with a moving bicycle, maintaining that balance requires continuous pedaling or effort. That is something you owe to yourself. Self-improvement is an investment in yourself that you should always be willing to make. You cannot lose.

Conclusion

In the preceding chapters, we learned that residential property management is indeed complex and multifaceted, and requires an integrated management approach. As a mentor and a guide, I have provided you with real-life cases and examples demonstrating how being in the middle of the action is the only way you can become hands-on and remain hands-on. Excellence is not a title but a progressive work ethic that manifests itself in results stemming from decisions made. We have also established the ripple effects your decisions will cause, showing how one decision affects the other. Excellence can only be achieved by staying focused and increasing your awareness. As an excellent residential property manager, be determined to do the following things:

1. Know and understand your professional DNA and be willing to change it. Get to know yourself first, then create and maintain a professional image of yourself.
2. Have a routine, set professional goals and pursue them tenaciously.
3. Understand your tenant base.
4. Physically inspect your buildings. This will help you to know your buildings inside and out and help to form part of your emergency preparation.
5. Understand the market, and do not be afraid to test the market.
6. Know your company lease or tenancy agreement, which may also include any rules and regulations or addendums.
7. Know, understand and work within any local laws relating to tenants and landlords. Make sure you are aware of any changes in the laws, and adapt to them. During the preparation of this publication, I learned there were amendments to the RTA, the implantation of a Standard Lease for Ontario and the new Cannabis Act that had to be reflected herein.
8. Learn to satisfy the needs of your tenants by resolving complaints swiftly and showing your appreciation for them. Remember tenants must also be respectful to you and your staff.
9. Build and maintain a respectful and progressive relationship with the departments you work with. Learn to work as a team with other departments. Working with some of these departments also helps to form part of your emergency preparation.
10. Be hands-on by getting involved. If you are not involved, you are an absentee manager, which makes you mediocre or average.
11. Know your staff and which building or location will bring out the best in them. Meet with your staff regularly and work as a team. Breaking bread with your staff will help to break down and remove any tension. Understand your staff so you can build, lead and motivate them with emotional intelligence. Don't forget to document, document and document.
12. Build a good relationship with your external contractors. Ensure their work meets your company standards.

13. Build a progressive working relationship with the pertinent government organizations and regulatory bodies, and keep buildings in compliance. Remember—even if it is uncomfortable, you can still be effective.
14. Keep up with trends in the industry.
15. Celebrate the accomplishments, large or small.
16. Understand the numbers and the story they tell. Plan and create the financial picture you want taken and the story you want told of your properties. Set the scene and let that be your guide.
17. Find a mentor. If you cannot find one, learn something from everyone around you by looking for the good in them.
18. Take care of yourself by adding to your knowledge through continuous learning. Remember things around us are constantly updating and upgrading. Updates help us to operate at the optimum level.
19. Save your money and invest it wisely. While not a criterion to become a property manager, personal savings helps you to weather unexpected personal and financial storms with your dignity intact, thus assisting you in maintaining your image and functioning efficiently as an excellent property manager.

Please, get involved and be hands-on. This cannot be overemphasized. The action is at the properties, not in your office. See your challenging properties not as a lost cause; see them as opportunities for growth to make a positive impact on the financial statement. Keep a copy of *I Am an Excellent Property Manager* in your office and on your person while at the properties, either print or e-format. Like with your GPS, be sure to refer to it from time to time. If you need to go places, you must have your GPS with you. Also, learn from your mistakes and move on by taking the GPS approach and getting back on track, as long as your GPS is updated. Your ability to rise above the challenges and turn your properties around for the better is what will make you an excellent residential property manager.

Index

Glossary or Use of Terms

AGI — Above guideline increase, a percentage amount the landlord wishes to add to the rent of occupied units that is beyond the limit/guideline set by the province/government. Before the landlord can add this extra amount to the rent, the landlord must apply to the Landlord and Tenant Board (LTB) stating, within limits, the reasons for the increase. The increase is usually to offset capital expense, such as major repairs, renovations or upgrades the landlord has done to the property.

AM — Area manager, the branch or regional manager who oversees the duties and responsibilities of all property managers and other department heads.

Apartment — Used interchangeably with *unit*.

Block treatment — Associated with pest treatments. In addition to treating the apartment that is affected by the pest, you inspect and/or treat where possible the apartments that are located to the left, to the right, above and below the infested apartment.

BM — Building manager, the individual(s) responsible for the day-to-day function and operation of the property. The BM reports directly to the property manager. BMs rent apartments, collect rent, do repairs and maintenance, clean, order supplies and sometimes submit invoices for payment. They also submit confirmation of delivery note/slips for materials received at the building or for services rendered by external contractors. They help to supervise the work of some contractors. Depending on the size and setup of the building or community, some BMs may have a team consisting of cleaning staff, maintenance staff, including rental agents doing some form of reporting to them. They usually live at the building. Depending on the size of the building, you can have a single building manager or a team building manager.

Building cleanout — Treating all the apartments in the building at once over a set time, in hopes of eliminating pest(s).

Building inspection	Sometimes called a property inspection, this is usually conducted on a regular basis, which can be monthly or as stipulated by your company. Building inspections help to comply with health and safety rules by spotting potential safety hazards so they can be corrected. Building Inspections are also a form of preventative and corrective maintenance, helping to preserve the useful life of the property. The property manager usually does the inspection. The inspection results are recorded either on a hard copy form or electronically on some mobile device.
Building walk-through	A brief inspection done by the building or site staff to check for anything out of the ordinary in building systems. This is normally done daily at the start and sometimes at the end of a shift or workday.
Cannabis	Used interchangeably with marijuana. Other names given or used depends on geographic location or culture. Some of these names are but not limited to: ganja, pot, weed, dope or vegetable matter. For the purpose of this publication, only the names cannabis or marijuana will be used.
Capex	Capital expenditure, such as major repairs, renovations or upgrades done to extend the useful life of an asset.
Common area	There are two types of common areas, internal, such as utility rooms accessible only by staff and contractors, and external, which are used by the general tenant population of the building and include the lobby, hallway, stairwell, garage, laundry and other amenities.
Community	Two or more buildings at a location that share the same staff and sometimes the same rental office. Though there are multiple buildings, they operate as one. The buildings may be on the same property/land or separated by street(s), road(s) or alley(s).
Dumpster shopping	Sometimes called dumpster diving. Refers to the action of individuals who make it a habit of searching or rummaging through the garbage either on a property or elsewhere in hopes of finding things they consider to be of value that they can take back to their apartment.
Floor	Sometimes used interchangeably with *hallway*.
Grounds	This includes landscaping which covers, outdoor lighting, outdoor signage, lawn, garden and or flora. It also involves the seasonal maintenance of roadways, parking lots, pathways, walkways, sidewalks that are on or part of the property.

LTB	Landlord and Tenant Board, the court in Ontario that resolves disputes between residential landlords and residential tenants.
NOI	Net operating income, total revenue less total operating expenses.
Notice of Entry	A document from the landlord indicating when entry will be made to the rental unit. The Notice of Entry should be given at least 24 hours (or as stipulated by your regional laws) in advance of the date and time of entry. The notice must state the reason for the entry. The Ontario RTA states that entry must be made between 8:00 a.m. and 8:00 p.m. The days are not stated, but because tenants are entitled to a reasonable enjoyment of the rental unit, it is recommended that you give the tenant a four-hour window of the time of entry.
PM	Property manager, the individual in charge of the property, including the physical building and its systems, grounds, tenants, staff and contractors. Also in charge of marketing, renting apartments, collecting rents and evicting tenants by applying applicable regional or local laws where necessary to achieve results. Building managers, superintendents, cleaners, leasing agents and project managers report to the property manager. The property manager reports to the area manager. This chain of command will vary according to each company.
Portfolio	A group of properties/buildings that are allocated to you the property manager for care and oversight. These properties can be in one or more cities, spanning different geographic locations.
Property	Sometimes used interchangeably with *building*.
Rent mapping	Setting the price or rent or amenities based on several factors such as view, location, accessibility, size, unique layout and upgrades done in the apartment or amenities.
Reposition	To alter through major renovation or makeover, which includes some updating or modernizing. Repositioning is done to enhance the image of the overall property or apartments in the market.
Riser	A column of apartments ending with the same number, e.g. 105, 205, 305, 405, 505 and so on. This would be called the "05" riser. If the numbers ended in 9, it would be called the "09" riser. If the numbers ended in 12, it would be the "12th" riser—and so on—meaning all the apartments along that particular line. Sometimes the word *riser* is used to identify plumbing pipes or air ducts. When this happens, the numbering can change because these features share

certain aspects, especially when you get to the top or bottom floor, where the layout of some apartments may differ because the risers overlap.

R&M   Repair and maintenance. It usually refers to the budget that is used to up-keep the property, which covers the daily operating expense to take care of matters related to normal wear and tear of the property. These repairs can take place in the common areas, grounds, in occupied apartments or in apartments that are repaired on turnover.

RTA   Residential Tenancies Act, the laws that protect tenants and landlords.

Shutdown   This usually refers to temporary disruption in building service to facilitate repairs for certain areas such as plumbing, electrical, elevator, air conditioning or heating. When there is a shutdown, there is no or limited access to one or more of these services.

Super   Superintendent, who assists the building manager(s) in the day-to-day operation of the property. A super usually lives at the building. Depending on the size of the building, you may have a single superintendent or a team of two superintendents.

Tenancy agreement   As of April 30, 2018, a standard lease for Ontario came into effect. Most individual landlords and apartment management companies in Ontario, are now required by law to use the standard lease also call Residential Tenancy Agreement. Tenancy agreement is used interchangeably with *lease*.

Tenant base   Sometimes called "tenant type," this is the demographics of your tenants: age range, income and nationality; whether they are mostly students, seniors, professionals or retired professionals; whether they have children and, if so, the ages of the children; whether they have pets; and how they treat the building and their apartments.

Turnover unit   Apartments/units that are in the process of vacating or moving out. Or these are vacant apartments being renovated or repositioned for the next tenants to move in.

Utility room   These rooms are restricted only to staff and some contractors. Also referred to as internal common areas. They may include any mechanical rooms such as the electrical room, sprinkler room, boiler room, sump pump room, elevator room, housekeeping and janitorial supplies room, storage room, maintenance workshop or generator room.

Bibliography

Canadian Centre for Occupational Health and Safety (CCOHS). "Hotel Housekeeping." November 1, 2016. https://ccohs.ca/oshanswers/occup_workplace/hotel_housekeeping.html.

Centeno, Antonio. "How the Car You Drive Impacts Your Image: Vehicles Reflect a Man's Style, Backed by Science." Real Men Real Style. https://www.realmenrealstyle.com/car-affects-image/. Accessed April 24, 2017.

CLEO (Community Legal Education Ontario / Éducation juridique communautaire Ontario). "I wasn't at work when I was hurt. Could this still be a work injury?" https://stepstojustice.ca/common-question-plus/employment-and-work/i-wasnt-work-when-i-got-hurt-could-still-be-work-injury.

Financial Samurai. "A Pricing Strategy to Maximize Rental Income and Minimize Turnover." September 6, 2017. https://www.financialsamurai.com/a-pricing-strategy-to-maximize-rental-income-and-minimize-turnover/.

Foster, Bradley. *Ten Steps to Successful Goal Setting*. May 7, 2013. https://www.huffingtonpost.com/bradley-foster/how-to-set-goals_b_3226083.html. Accessed November 6, 2017.

Health Canada
https://www.canada.ca/en/health-canada/topics/cannabis-for-medical-purposes.html

Landlord and Tenant Board.
http://www.sjto.gov.on.ca/ltb/forms/.

Lawrence, William E., Eberle, D. J., & Asturias, S, "Emergency Response Plan Model for Apartment Buildings." San Diego County Apartment Association, Greystar Multi-Family Services. Unified San Diego County Emergency Services Organization, Office of Disaster Preparedness.

Llopis, Glenn. "6 Ways Successful Teams Are Built to Last." *Forbes*. October 2012. http://www.forbes.com/sites/glennllopis/2012/10/01/6-ways-successful-teams-are-built-to-last/#bbdad6268dd5.

Matthews, Rachel. "The Difference Between Personal and Professional Development." October 9, 2014. Bray Leino Learning. https://brayleinolearning.co.uk/blog/2014/october/09/what-is-the-difference-between-personal-and-professional-development/. Accessed January 26, 2018.

Maxwell, John C. *Effective Teams*.

———. *The 21 Irrefutable Laws of Leadership*. Nashville: Thomas Nelson: 2007.

Moore, Terry. "A Wealth Building Strategy to Be Proud Of. Part 2 of 4, Repositioning — Massive Upgrades Grow Equity and Serve Upscale Residents." http://aciapartments.com/2015/05/11/repositioning-apartments-wealth-building-strategy-proud-part-2-4-4/. Accessed February 9, 2017.

Ontario Ministry of the Attorney General. February 22, 2017. https://www.attorneygeneral.jus.gov.on.ca/english/family/pgt/estatesadmin.html.

Ontario Remediation Services. "Cleaning Up a Loved One." http://www.ontarioremediation.ca/2015/11/cleaning-up-a-loved-one/. Accessed July 12, 2017.

Ottawa Police Services. "Crime-free Multihousing." https://www.ottawapolice.ca/en/safety-and-crime-prevention/Crime-Free-MultiHousing.asp.

Residential Tenancies Act, 2006, c. 17. http://www.mah.gov.on.ca/Page137.aspx.

Senik, Simon. "Circle of Safety in the Marines" (YouTube video). Accessed March 7, 2017.

Sewell, Gerald F. *Emotional Intelligence and the Army Leadership Requirements Model*. December 2009.

Shlosberg, Matt. *Letting People Go: The People-Centered Approach to Firing and Laying Off Employees*.

Telgian. "Fire. Safety. Security. Fire Sprinkler Dry Pipe Systems—Weekly Maintenance." November 30, 2016. www.telgian.com. TSSA. https://www.tssa.org/en/index.aspx. Accessed September 19, 2017

Resource Section

Consultant

- Simon Sinek
  Learn your why – http://bit.ly/LearnYourWhy.
  Get daily notes to inspire – http://bit.ly/NotesToInspire
  Follow Simon on Instagram – http://bit.ly/simonsaysinspire
  Follow Simon on Twitter – http://bit.ly/SimonSinekTweet
  Listen to Simon's podcast – http://bit.ly/SWWpodcast
  Get the books – http://bit.ly/SimonSinekBooks
- Terry Moore, CCIM
  SVP/Principal
  ACI Apartments
  Author of *Building Legacy Wealth*

Equipment

- KJA, elevator and escalator consulting engineers, Toronto, Canada
  https://www.kja.com
- Telgian, a worldwide provider of comprehensive fire, security, life safety consulting and engineering/design services
  www.telgian.com

Grooming

- Hyundai Canada
  www.hyundaicanada.com
- Real Men Real Style
  www.realmenrealstyle.com
- Naturalizer Shoes
  www.naturalizer.ca

Outside entities

- Canadian Centre for Occupation Health and Safety (CCOHS)
  www.ccohs.ca

- CLEO (Community Legal Education Ontario / Éducation juridique communautaire Ontario)
  www.cleo.on.ca
  http://stepstojustice.ca/
  http://yourlegalrights.on.ca/
- Landlord and Tenant Board (LTB), Ontario, Canada
  http://www.sjto.gov.on.ca/ltb/
- Ministry of Labour, Ontario, Canada
  www.labour.gov.on.ca
- Ontario Ministry of the Attorney General
  www.attorneygeneral.jus.gov.on.ca
- Ottawa Police Services
  www.ottawapolice.ca
- TSSA
  www.tssa.org
- West Allis Fire Department, Wisconsin, USA
  https://westallis.net/departments-divisions/fire-department/
- Workplace Safety and Insurance Board (WSIB)
  www.wsib.on.ca

Restoration

- Ontario Remediation Services
  24-hour emergency service
  1-866-945-9995
  info@ontarioremediation.ca

Pest control

- Apex Control Inc.
  www.apexpcservices.com
- Rat Lab Exterminators
  www.ratlabexterminators.com

Professional development

- Buildings Owners and Managers Association (BOMA) International
  www.boma.org
- BOMA Canada
  www.bomacanada.ca
- BOMI
  www.bomi.org
- Bray Leino Learning
  https://www.brayleino.co.uk

- Toastmasters
  www.toastmasters.org

Insurance

- Square One Insurance
  www.squareoneinsurance.com

Other

- Mercedes-Benz Superdome
  Smoothie King Center
  Champions Square
  PO Box 52439
  New Orleans, LA 70152
- Access to Cannabis for Medical Purposes Regulations (ACMPR)
- Health Canada
  www.canada.ca/en/health-canada
- San Diego County Apartment Association
  http://www.sdcaa.com
- Department of Canadian Heritage
  www.canada.ca/en/canadian-heritage

About the Author

Simone Grant is a Jamaican Canadian author. She earned her Bachelor of Arts degree in hospitality management with honours on a scholarship from Huston-Tillotson University, formerly Huston-Tillotson College, Austin, Texas, USA. Simone was the recipient of another scholarship that allowed her to pursue her Master's Degree in tourism and travel management, with a concentration in destination management, at New York University, in New York, New York, USA. Simone has experience working as a teacher in Jamaica and a tutor in the United States. Also, she has worked in the hotel industry in various capacities.

After immigrating to Canada, Simone made the decision to go into residential property management, which she found to be very fulfilling and rewarding. Simone's portfolio included managing nine high-rise multifamily residential apartment buildings, totaling over 900 units that spanned three cities in southern and southwestern Ontario. On account of her portfolio change or shuffle, over a period of six years, Simone has worked with a total of 24 different high-rise multifamily residential apartment buildings, ranging from 6 to 26 floors. This figure does not include buildings that were temporarily added to her portfolio when she covered for colleagues when they went on vacation.

Simone has written several multifamily due diligence reports. She is a firm believer in continuous learning. She has completed a public speaking course and has a certificate in dealing with difficult people. Simone is also a certified UltimateStager and Redesigner. She is currently pursuing a certificate in leadership essentials at the University of Toronto. Simone enjoys baking and decorating cakes, as well as writing inspirational poems.

Like a mentor, Simone draws upon her wealth of professional experiences from her different careers in education, hospitality and property management to relate how she navigated challenges and their possible or eventual outcomes. By reading *I Am an Excellent Property Manager*, your awareness of high-rise multifamily residential property management will increase and you will learn ideas for how to build on the foundation in all areas of high-rise multifamily residential property management. If you have a theoretical understanding of residential property management but lack the experience, this book will give you clarity on how to put the theory into practice.

Without being intrusive, *I Am an Excellent Property Manager* builds awareness on how to get involved at the departmental level to learn what your staff learn and to do what your staff do. Taking this hands-on approach to management will allow you to get involved and lead by example. *I Am an*

Excellent Property Manager looks at high-rise multifamily residential property management from a practical standpoint so you will have a better understanding of the various aspects of the job and how each decision impacts the bottom line. It will help you to visualize as you make decisions (while checking for blind spots) and see the end results reflect favourably on the financial statements.

Made in the USA
Monee, IL
19 May 2021